FAMILY THERAPY IN SCHIZOPHRENIA

THE GUILFORD FAMILY THERAPY SERIES
Alan S. Gurman, Editor

AESTHETICS OF CHANGE
Bradford P. Keeney

FAMILY THERAPY IN SCHIZOPHRENIA
William R. McFarlane, Editor

MASTERING RESISTANCE: A PRACTICAL GUIDE TO FAMILY THERAPY
Carol M. Anderson and Susan Stewart

FAMILY THERAPY AND FAMILY MEDICINE:
TOWARD THE PRIMARY CARE OF FAMILIES
William J. Doherty and Macaran A. Baird

ETHNICITY AND FAMILY THERAPY
Monica McGoldrick, John K. Pearce, and Joseph Giordano, Editors

PATTERNS OF BRIEF FAMILY THERAPY: AN ECOSYSTEMIC APPROACH
Steve de Shazer

THE FAMILY THERAPY OF DRUG ABUSE AND ADDICTION
M. Duncan Stanton, Thomas C. Todd, and Associates

FROM PSYCHE TO SYSTEM: THE EVOLVING THERAPY OF CARL WHITAKER
John R. Neill and David P. Kniskern, Editors

NORMAL FAMILY PROCESSES
Froma Walsh, Editor

HELPING COUPLES CHANGE: A SOCIAL LEARNING APPROACH
TO MARITAL THERAPY
Richard B. Stuart

FAMILY THERAPY IN SCHIZOPHRENIA

EDITED BY

WILLIAM R. McFARLANE

*College of Physicians and Surgeons of Columbia University
and
New York State Psychiatric Institute*

Foreword and Afterword by C. Christian Beels

THE GUILFORD PRESS
New York   London

To the memory of Albert Scheflen, whose humanity and profound understanding of the workings of complex systems permanently enlarged the perspective of all his students. His thought and work have pointed the way to a truly systemic paradigm for schizophrenia.

© 1983 The Guilford Press
A Division of Guilford Publications, Inc.
200 Park Avenue South, New York, N.Y. 10003

Printed in the United States of America

Library of Congress Cataloging in Publication Data
Main entry under title:

Family therapy in schizophrenia.

(The Guilford family therapy series)
"This volume is in part a proceedings from a conference entitled 'Schizophrenia: new approaches to the family,' sponsored by the Fellowship in Public Psychiatry, Department of Psychiatry, College of Physicians and Surgeons of Columbia University, April 2 and 3, 1981, in New York City"—Acknowledgments.
   1. Schizophrenia—Congresses.   2. Mentally ill—Family relationships—Congresses.   3. Family psychotherapy—Congresses.   I. McFarlane, William R.
II. Series.   [DNLM: 1. Family therapy.   2. Schizophrenia—Therapy.   WM 203 F198]
RC514.F34   1983   616.89'8206   82-11742
ISBN 0-89862-042-2

CONTRIBUTORS

Carol M. Anderson, PhD, Department of Psychiatry, University of Pittsburgh, Western Psychiatric Institute and Clinic, Pittsburgh, Pennsylvania

Nancy Atwood, MSSS, Trinity Mental Health Center, Framingham, Massachusetts

C. Christian Beels, MD, MS, Department of Psychiatry, College of Physicians and Surgeons of Columbia University, and New York State Psychiatric Institute, New York, New York

Ruth Berkowitz, PhD, MRC Social Psychiatry Unit, Institute of Psychiatry, London, England

William T. Carpenter, Jr., MD, Maryland Psychiatric Research Center and Department of Psychiatry, University of Maryland, Baltimore, Maryland

Lawrence Dyche, ACSW, Morrisania Neighborhood Family Care Center, Mental Health Services, Bronx, New York

Ian R. H. Falloon, MB, MRCPsych, Department of Psychiatry, University of Southern California School of Medicine, Los Angeles, California

Michael J. Goldstein, PhD, Department of Psychology, University of California, Los Angeles, Los Angeles, California

Steven J. Goldstein, PhD, Morrisania Neighborhood Family Care Center, Mental Health Services, Bronx, New York

Agnes B. Hatfield, PhD, Institute for Child Study/Department of Human Development, College of Education, University of Maryland, College Park, Maryland

Douglas W. Heinrichs, MD, Maryland Psychiatric Research Center and Department of Psychiatry, University of Maryland, Baltimore, Maryland

Hal S. Kopeikin, MA, Department of Psychology, University of California, Los Angeles, Los Angeles, California

Liz Kuipers, MSc, MRC Social Psychiatry Unit, Institute of Psychiatry, London, England

Julian P. Leff, MD, MRCP, FRCPsych, MRC Social Psychiatry Unit, Institute of Psychiatry, London, England

Robert P. Liberman, MD, Department of Psychiatry, UCLA School of Medicine, and Rehabilitation Medicine Service, Brentwood Veterans Administration Medical Center, Los Angeles, California

Cloé Madanes, Licenciada, Family Therapy Institute of Washington, D.C., Chevy Chase, Maryland, and Department of Psychiatry, University of Maryland, Baltimore, Maryland

Valerie Marshall, MA, Department of Psychology, University of California, Los Angeles, Los Angeles, California

William R. McFarlane, MD, Department of Psychiatry, College of Physicians and Surgeons of Columbia University, and New York State Psychiatric Institute, New York, New York

Lyman C. Wynne, MD, PhD, Department of Psychiatry, University of Rochester Medical Center, Rochester, New York

ACKNOWLEDGMENTS

I extend special appreciation to C. Christian Beels, whose support, advice and constructive criticism have been invaluable during the entire process of preparing this volume. Grateful thanks also go to Henry Harbin, Monica McGoldrick, Stephen Cole, and Kenneth Terkelsen, for their help and encouragement in the conference from which this book arose and in the early phases of its editing. Finally, I am deeply indebted to the contributors, whose efforts have far surpassed the initial expectations.

This volume is made up in part of proceedings from a conference entitled "Schizophrenia: New Approaches to the Family," sponsored by the Fellowship in Public Psychiatry, Department of Psychiatry, College of Physicians and Surgeons of Columbia University, April 2–3, 1981, in New York City.

William R. McFarlane

FOREWORD

These days there is less and less money and time to spend on the treatment of the severely ill psychiatric patient. Both the government and the psychiatric profession seem to have found other interests. This is a special pity because we may just be beginning to understand how to carry out that treatment. It is a grim irony that the deinstitutionalization movement of the 1950s and 1960s, which all but emptied the state hospitals, ran out of government money just when it was beginning to see some of the consequences of the experiment. In particular, we were beginning to get some answers to the question: If not in the state hospitals, then where and how should these people live?

The families of schizophrenic patients are being hit especially hard by that irony, since they have had to bear the burden of responsibility for the patient's care, either because the patient is living with them, or because they have to find housing and treatment for the patient in the nonsystem of posthospital care. This book began with a conference of experts who have continued to try to find ways of easing the burden of those families. As the reader will see, that effort recently has begun to yield more usable fruit.

This book enlarges the reports of that conference and makes the implementation and evaluation of the methods more explicit. Several people who were not at the conference have contributed chapters and interviews, so that a complete spectrum of approaches toward families and patients is presented. Clinicians and administrators will be able to compare their own settings and cases with those described here. Epidemiologists and evaluators will also find new ideas in the various kinds of family treatment discussed.

Evaluators will note especially that the literature on the family therapy of schizophrenia is no longer what it was a generation ago: brilliant case reports which no one but the original experts could replicate. We now have:

1. Specificity of diagnosis.
2. Clear descriptions of phases and treatments.

3. Large enough series for statistical analysis.
4. Specific outcome criteria.
5. Follow-up of more than 2 years.
6. Treatment by regular therapists which can be replicated by others.

It is clear from this perspective that schizophrenia is an illness with different courses and different phases within those courses. A treatment appropriate at one time may not be at another. The distinction between the first or second episode, later episodes or a later course of unremitting dependency, can begin to be made. The practitioner is faced with a number of choices, and in the last chapter William McFarlane and I propose some hypotheses about how one might be guided in making those choices.

This book is part of a larger movement in the history of our understanding of schizophrenia. Earlier, the partisans of theoreticians, from Freud and Jung to Sullivan, Fromm-Reichmann, Bateson, Lidz, and Scheff in later times, tried to capture the etiology and treatment of schizophrenia for their faction in the debate on the nature of human nature. Now, with increasing experience, we begin to embrace the complexity of this condition, and the more we learn the less it seems necessary, or even wise, to have a unitary theoretical model. Such monolithic models, in psychiatry, are the torches we light to keep up our courage in the dark, until epidemiology and experiment bring the light of day to the varied features of the terrain. I have some further thoughts about that process in the Afterword.

In the meantime, waiting for more light, therapists are confronted by families and patients who need help getting through the years of struggle which accompany this illness. They will find here detailed descriptions of, and solid evidence for, the programs that families need in order to survive, and to overcome.

C. Christian Beels

CONTENTS

INTRODUCTION

William R. McFarlane

Throughout the course of the preparation of this book, I have pondered the question of why it has taken so long for a volume on this topic to appear. After all, family therapy was born almost 30 years ago, out of the attempt to understand schizophrenia, the archchallenge of psychiatric theories. Since then, both as a body of theory and an increasingly effective approach to the entire gamut of disorders of the mind and problems of living, the field has made remarkable strides. Family therapy is practiced everywhere and on almost everything. Outcome studies (Gurman & Kniskern, 1978) provide powerful arguments that, for marital problems and nonpsychotic disorders of children, the treatment of the family is the treatment of choice, almost regardless of the "school" or method adhered to.

Yet, during the 25 years that family therapy has been developing, there has been, until very recently, a nearly linear decline in interest in the family treatment of schizophrenia. Reports of treatment techniques and even research studies have dwindled in the family literature, while most family therapists have become increasingly reluctant to treat the families of schizophrenic patients. Services that are oriented toward the schizophrenic often do no more work with the family than was done before family therapy arrived on the scene. Drug therapy is still the mainstay in dealing with schizophrenic psychoses, while research on this baffling condition has become almost completely oriented toward its biological aspects. A cursory survey leaves one with the impression that—to stretch a metaphor—family therapy has abandoned its mother.

Explanations for that abandonment and for the late arrival of this volume seem closely related. That is, conventional family therapy with schizophrenics has not provided enough in the way of results to warrant either a book or its continued use. This is a sore point for many family therapists, who from the beginning have emphasized problem solving and outcome as the proper measures, not just of a therapy, but of the theory

WILLIAM R. McFARLANE. Department of Psychiatry, College of Physicians and Surgeons of Columbia University, and New York State Psychiatric Institute, New York, New York.

upon which it is based. Thus, poor results strongly suggest, with respect to schizophrenia, not only that there is something wrong with the therapy, but that the theory is in error at some basic level. For family therapists generally it has not been sufficient simply to argue that the process of therapy justifies itself, either because it is intensely fascinating or formidably difficult, or because it is in conformity with a well-respected theory.

The approaches presented here are all—with the single exception of multiple family therapy—very recent additions to the field of family therapy, having been devised after 1975. They differ radically from approaches used in the past in two critical ways: (1) They seem to have major therapeutic effects on the schizophrenic process, beyond those achievable with drug therapy; and (2) they all—with the exception of the systemic variety—start from a major expansion of family systems theory that includes extrafamily factors. Thus, this book may have taken so long in coming because it is only these new approaches that seem to satisfy the field's insistence on definable results as the only justification of a therapy and as the ultimate confirmation of a theory.

In order that readers may appreciate these new family therapies for schizophrenia more fully, it seems important to review briefly the historical and intellectual background from which they have arisen. Much of their value lies in the ways in which they differ theoretically from the early family therapies. That is because the contextual, metacommunicational aspects of these approaches—arising from a new perspective—are essential to their success, perhaps more than the particular techniques employed. The core of that point of view is this: Most of these therapies assume that there is a biological contribution to the etiology of schizophrenia and therefore see family work as a complementary aspect of a comprehensive treatment package, not as the "cure" for the fundamental "disease." As may be seen later, such an outlook has major effects on the design, results, and acceptability of family therapies based on it.

In general, family theory and therapy were radical departures from psychoanalytic thinking. From hindsight, however, the family viewpoint on schizophrenia seems much more an extension of the analytic perspective than a substantial rejection of it, because both theories placed culpability for the condition on parenting practices. From Freud's analysis of the Wolf-Man forward, the cause of schizophrenia was placed somewhere in the relationship of the preschizophrenic child and his or her parents, and its later internalization. One can readily trace this perspective through Mahler's theory of symbiosis, to Fromm-Reichmann's "schizophrenogenic mother," to Laing's theory of mystification. It is ironic that Freud actually seems to have believed, with Kraepelin, that schizophrenia is probably a neurological disorder at its root, and that the Wolf-Man, upon which the later psychoanalytic perspective on schizophrenia was based, may well have been an atypical manic–depressive. Regardless, by 1950, almost everyone believed that the family drives the schizophrenic crazy.

There are many everyday clinical realities that make this bias plausible. Especially in the context of long-term hospitalization—before deinstitutionalization—it was common to observe symptomatic collapse during or shortly after family visits. Similarly, it seemed that patients recovered somewhat in the hospital (even without drugs), were sent home to their families, and almost always relapsed and returned; the families must have done "something" in the interim to provoke the patients' regression. Most patients at one time or another will blame their parents for everything that is wrong with them, and thereby confirm a clinician's suspicions. During visiting hours, for those who choose to watch, remarkably dysfunctional family interactions can be observed, with confusion, double messaging, stormy emotional exchanges, even outright violence. Many parents will display quite erratic behavior toward the patients and sometimes with each other, suggesting an underlying ambivalence. The same is readily concluded from some families' attempts to close ranks and abandon the patients, leaving them for the institution to repair and reengage in the larger community. With the advent of drugs, a family's lack of conviction in assuring that the patient continues to take them is more "evidence" that family members need the patient to be ill for their own stability.

From these basic observations, a number of family researchers elaborated a set of hypotheses that attempted to make symptomatology intelligible by relating it to family interactional or dynamic processes. Lidz, in 16 families, found that half of the parents had "skewed" marriages, while the other half had "schismatic" marriages. In addition, one of the parents in the skewed couples evidenced gross psychopathology, often including poorly disguised psychotic thinking. Bateson, Jackson, and their colleagues at the Mental Research Institute, although they did not actually observe families, concluded that the families of schizophrenics engaged in double binding. These constructs have proved to be invaluable for understanding all sorts of dysfunctional interaction and symptoms, but for that very reason their specificity to schizophrenia is questionable. Nevertheless, Jackson went on to develop fascinating techniques involving therapeutic double binds, which he utilized with individual patients. It is upon his work that the systemic approach of the Milan group, described in Chapter 10, is based.

Bowen hospitalized whole families of schizophrenic patients and studied them in some detail. From that experience he developed his three-generational hypothesis, which in gross outline ascribed schizophrenia to the amplification of "immaturity" and lack of differentiation over three succeeding generations, so that the schizophrenic was claimed to represent the least mature and least differentiated state possible, as was his or her family. Reiss, to his great credit, decided to study families using a controlled experimental design. His findings (Reiss, 1975) were far more complex than any of the preceding theories would have predicted. The parents of schizophrenic patients indeed seemed to have difficulties in solving problems and keeping on track while attempting to perform semistructured cognitive tasks. However, not *all* of them did, and the differences between them and parents of character-disordered patients were not large. Mishler and Waxler (1975), continuing to make things less clear, published a volume of several studies that, while more rigorous, presented quite a confusing picture of what was supposedly a monolithic concept—the "schizophrenic family." Based on that research, about all one could say with any certainty was that many schizophrenics' parents seemed to have conflicted marriages and to do poorly with structured tasks in a laboratory setting, particularly when it involved joint decision making.

Wynne (1981) and Singer (Singer, Wynne, & Toohey, 1978) did some of the most careful research on families of schizophrenics. They set out to explain the structure of schizophrenic thought by relating its formal characteristics to patterns of communication habitually used by other family members. They developed their instruments for measuring "communication deviance" (CD) to such a high degree that they could blindly describe the patient's subtype (i.e., paranoid, hebephrenic, etc.) on the basis of the style and structure of the parents' communication with each other (while trying to reach a consensus about what a Rorschach card looked like). In large samples, they showed that this characteristic of the parents was *relatively*, but not *absolutely*, ubiquitous in and unique to schizophrenia. They did not ascribe a causal explanation to their findings, instead seeing CD as a contributing factor or perhaps an intervening variable. They specifically *in*cluded one possibility—that CD may represent the subclinical manifestation of a common, underlying genetic and/or neurophysiological deficit. Several other studies have confirmed the association of CD and schizophrenia, although Hirsch and Leff (1975) found a significant overlap of CD between schizophrenic and nonpsychotic patients' relatives, implying that, though present, the association is not so specific. Regardless, the growing implication was that if parents of schizophrenics are unusual, they are unusual in ways that are similar to the ways in which the patients are unusual, and not in ways that require the attribution of unconscious exploitation, à la Laing. It was Wynne's and Reiss's findings that began to suggest that the families of schizophrenics might need help, rather than blame and family therapy, although what that help should be was anything but clear. Also, it was implicit in their work that the family's role in the etiology of schizophrenia might turn out to be a singularly complicated matter, not easily subsumed under any of the "grand theories," as Beels has called them. By the end of the 1960s, just when family therapy began to be popular as a treatment for schizophrenia, the research literature was beginning to cast doubt on simple theory of family causation, upon which must of that therapy was based.[1]

About 1970, this corner of the field began to be affected in complex ways by at least three separate but increasingly interrelated phenomena. For one, the deinstitutionalization movement began to have observable effects on the daily lives and the overall course of illness of schizophrenic patients. For present purposes, one of the major outcomes was that more and more patients were spending more and more time at home with either their parents or their spouses. Thus, after having been judged to be responsible for their offspring's illness by one segment of the psychiatric community (family theorists and psychoanalysts), the parents, especially, were being asked to assume total responsibility for the care of the patients by another segment (community psychiatrists). One might assume that general confusion in such families could follow from such an odd set of contextual messages, and in many clinicians' experiences, it seemed to do just that.

The second phenomenon was that many young professionals began to take family therapy seriously and were attempting to learn and apply the techniques being espoused by the founders of the field. Psychiatrists, especially, began to treat many families of schizophrenic patients. The experience proved to be an increasingly unhappy one for all concerned. As one founder (Murray Bowen) finally stated out loud, the families in his practice did not seem to be amenable to change, and the patients just went right on having psychotic episodes. One looked in vain for a criterion by which the process might appear even vaguely useful.

For some of the younger family practitioners, however, the process was not a total loss. They got a much more comprehensive sense of what having a schizophrenic in the family was all about, and that sense was upsetting to those who had taken the founders' words at face value. They saw that relatives were utterly confounded and perplexed by this recurring catastrophe; that they were besieged by guilt that rippled endlessly through the family in complex elaborations; that they seemed to be forever trying to understand and repair the "damage"; and that they were, after a variable period, simply exhausted by it all. At that point many families seemed to become grossly demoralized, and some turned on or abandoned the patients—events that led straight into relapse and rehospitalization. Some therapists began to sense that the subtly accusatory metamessage of family therapy was exaggerating this downward spiral, not stopping it. As experience increased, it also became obvious that these families were remarkably alone, socially and intellectually; no one seemed either to understand, or to be able to and/or interested in helping, *them*. Further, the families seemed to vary considerably: Some were disturbed, to be sure, but some were not, as far as one could tell. These observations did not fit well with existing family theories of schizophrenia, which seemed to have told only about half the story.

These realities *did* fit with the third phenomenon. That was the fact that while family therapy did not seem to work, in any basic or reliable sense, drugs did, and not just by "tranquilizing" patients. The phenothiazines provided an all but unassailable argument that some very crucial part of the problem was biological. This general awareness arose at about the same time that the results of several genetic studies were showing that between 10 and 40% of the cases could be explained as being partly the result of hereditary—and not interactional—transmission. The question began to arise: Could at least some of those dysfunctional family processes that seemed to very influential be the *result* of schizophrenia, rather than a cause?

At least in the literature, 1975 was the end of the original impetus and the beginning of the process that has brought this book into being. In essence, the younger generation stated that the Emperor was wearing no clothes. Massie and Beels (1972) had already asserted that family therapy, in its usual forms, did not help schizophrenics or their families enough to warrant its continuation. Likewise, Jacob (1975) and Goldstein and Rodnick (1975) reviewed the family interactional research and concluded that, except for CD, and possibly a factor called "expressed emotion" (EE) in England, there was nothing that would satisfy even the most rudimentary of criteria for a concept of a "schizophrenic family." Reiss (1976) stated what the necessary criteria would be, and why nothing so far had met them. A consensus arose that what was really required was longitudinal, prospective research that would seek to document that processes existed in families *before* any member was clearly schizophrenic, and that these occurred *only* in those families. In fact, it was about then that Goldstein, Rodnick, and their colleagues at UCLA undertook just such a study. Recent reports have shed some interesting light, but also seem to confirm Wynne's earlier conviction that it is all a very complicated, multidetermined, issue. In the UCLA project, it is beginning to appear that when, and only when, CD and EE coexist in a family, schizophrenia is likely to follow (Doane, West, Goldstein, Rodnick, & Jones, 1981). Neither of these factors alone are specific to schizophrenia, but are associated with other syndromes—especially, for CD, the borderline variety—as well. All that can be asserted with any confidence is that neither CD nor EE meets (or is likely to meet) Reiss's criteria. Thus, their relationship to schizophrenia is apt to be contributory at most, rather than etiological, while EE is probably more influential over the course rather than the onset of the illness.

Before proceeding to the therapies described within these covers, it seems advisable to underline what was wrong with the original theories, not so much as a critique as a contrast with the theoretical underpinnings of most of these new approaches. The error and its present correction are a common theme in the history of science. Consider Newton, reflecting on the apple that struck his head. His great discovery was not just that the earth was attracting the apple, but that the apple was also attracting the earth. The fact that the apple fell was the final result of an interaction between forces exerted by earth *and* apple. Similarly, Heisenburg made history not just by noticing that it was difficult to determine the speed and the location of an electron simultaneously, but by realizing that it was the actual process of observation that made it theoretically impossible: The observer inevitably interacted with the observed, in unpredictable ways. Again, Darwin could have stated that the environment produced morpho- logical changes in finches' beaks, but he did not; rather, he went the crucial step beyond, and asserted that minute changes in the finches' beaks altered the finches' interaction with the environment, which subsequently altered the beaks even further. In all these conceptual advances, one sees the primacy of circular, interactive causality over linear causality.

While family theorists have attempted to use systemic and circular reasoning from the very beginning, it is precisely with respect to schizo- phrenia that the application did not go far enough. In all the historical examples cited, the crucial element is the attribution of influential, dynamic characteristics to *both* of the interacting subsystems: The apple has a gravitational field, the observer is influencing the experiment, and beaks must first change before being influenced by the environment. To return to the present topic, one might add that some inherent, constitutional char- acteristics of the schizophrenic may be strongly affecting the family, as well as vice versa. From a particular perspective, that is the truly circular, systemic formulation of the problem. (Actually, if one adds time as a variable, the true pattern is a spiral or helix; i.e., "helical" processes might be the preferable term.) And that is what makes the new therapies concept- ually quite distinct from their forebears. (Any implication that this para- digmatic shift ranks in significance with those of Newton, Heisenburg, and Darwin is unintended.)

Some readers will doubtless find the emphasis on this point to be beating the proverbial dead horse. After all, the evidence for a biological component to schizophrenia seems, at this juncture in history, over- whelming. Wyatt, Cutler, DeLisi, Jeste, Kleinman, Luchins, Potkin, and Weinberger (1982) have recently reviewed the literature and tentatively described five subtypes of schizophrenia, each of which is apparently either biochemically or anatomically distinct from the others; thus, as Bleuler has taught for years, there is no *one* schizophrenia. One report from Sweden, by Sedvall and Wode-Helgrodt (1980), is especially pertinent: They found that cerebrospinal fluid metabolites of dopamine and serotonin were well outside the normal range in those who had relatives with schizophrenia, regardless of whether they themselves had schizophrenic symptoms. Those without schizophrenic relatives had normal metabolities, again regardless of whether they were themselves symptomatic. One implication is that one can have abnormal genes and neurotransmitter metabolism and be free from schizophrenia, or can be schizophrenic without the (usual) genetic or neurochemical background. Thus, the picture becomes even more complex: There are probably many forms of biogenic schizophrenia, yet perhaps not everyone with the constitutional disorder will be clinically ill. With this as one's starting point, a theoretical explanation for schizophrenia, now still well beyond the grasp of therapists and clinicians, nevertheless seems likely to include very complex and heterogeneous kinds of helical interactions between diverse biological and constitutional factors in the patient and diverse and often idiosyncratic factors in the social environment, especially in the family. Further, these helical processes of positive feedback almost surely continue beyond the point of the first episode, with illness affecting family affecting illness, and so on.

While the present discussion can in no way do justice to this enormous topic, it should suggest that a single-minded, family-etiological theory of schizophrenia is now out of the question, although an occasional tortured effort is made to try to rescue the idea (Dell, 1980). What must take its place is a more formidable undertaking—a multiple-level theory of schizophrenia, much as has been suggested by Albert Scheflen (1981). While the final edition of such a theory does not yet exist, the contributors to this volume have isolated a few of the crucial and seemingly reliable passages from it and have gone on to design therapies that specifically include many levels and as much information as is available about them.

From this new perspective, the development of schizophrenia is primarily the outcome of accidents of fate and essentially normal human reactions and adaptations on the part of the family. To construct a speculative hypothesis that fits with well-known biological and interpersonal factors, interacting in deviation-amplifying ways, one does not need to impute severe parental psychopathology, let alone unconscious exploitative motivation. This is not to say that these latter variables do *not* occur in some families with schizophrenic members—only that such "deeper" problems are *additive*, but not essential, factors in etiology and course. When present, they probably magnify morbidity and resistance to many forms of treatment. In other words, the early observations of severe enmeshment, double binding, pseudomutuality, and so forth, probably are relevant and accurate in many cases, but not to all of those families, and not as primary causes.

Further, the assertion of a homeostatic function for the illness as the explanation for these dysfunctional processes can easily be argued the other way around: "Homeostasis" may be the result of having a highly disturbed and relatively unchanging offspring. Another systems principle—

equifinality—may be more applicable: One can arrive at a final state—the enmeshed, overwhelmed–overwhelming family—via several routes, not all of them involving "schizophrenic family" processes.

One could also argue that a reasonable test of the family-etiological hypothesis would be to offer a large number of families a supportive, educational, and explicitly nonblaming treatment package that includes specific training in coping skills, such as how to reduce stimulation, set clear limits, and handle unsettling life events. Surely if all, or even most, families were dependent on the patients' insanity for their stability, such an approach would be roundly rejected, while relapse would ensue as a defensive maneuver to ward off real change. The experience of the contributors to this volume constitutes a relatively comprehensive test of the old theory. The evidence suggests, in short, that it is wrong. The great majority of families accept and use these "linear" interventions in gratifying ways, while relapse dramatically decreases. For purposes of comparison, Table 1 summarizes the outcome of these treatments as things presently stand.

While one must be cautious in interpreting data from studies in progress, these results suggest that one must first give the family of the schizophrenic the benefit of the doubt and offer its members directive, specific, empathic help (even if that is based on a nonmedical model, as is Cloé Madanes's approach) before family therapy of the conventional sort. (Beels and I elaborate on the implications of this assertion in Chapter 15.) For families that resist all this direct assistance, the systemic approach outlined in Chapter 10 appears presently to be an ideal alternative. That is, paradoxical methods that avoid struggling with the family may produce more useful change in this "resistive" family subgroup.

TABLE 1. *Outcome of Combined Family and Drug Treatment*

Project	Exposure (months) to Therapy	Risk	n	Relapse rate Family therapy	Individual therapy
Anderson	12	12	57	2/28 (7%)	10/29 (34%)
Falloon	9	9	36	1/18 (6%)	8/18 (44%)
Goldstein[a]	1.5	6	49	0/25 (0%)	4/24 (17%)
Leff	9	9	24	1/12 (8%)	6/12 (50%)
				[4/83 (5%)]	[28/83 (34%)]

Note. Families in Goldstein's study were presumably mixed high- and low-EE; the others involved only high-EE families.
[a]"Moderate-dose" patients only.

The "test" therapy is, as may be apparent, a composite of the new family approaches described in Parts II and III. They arise from a theoretical foundation very different from that of their predecessors. They share with one another the assumption of reciprocal interactions between certain identifiable family variables and a relatively specific deficit in the schizophrenic member. The function of these therapies (with the partial exception of the systemic variety) is to enlist the family as an adjunct therapist, whose job it is to compensate in focused ways for the difficulties of the patient. The aim is the rehabilitation of the patient and the relief of the family, not the reversal of a "schizophrenic family" dysfunction. Concern about cure is beside the point and is generally agreed to be beyond the reach of family or any other currently available therapy. The long-range goals are to achieve, first, as low a frequency of relapse as possible, and, second, as high a level of social and occupational functioning as is attainable. While the family is seen as being quite powerful enough to negate these goals entirely, it is also taken as a given that it is precisely the family's power that is necessary and mobilizable to achieve them. In fact, the family is assumed to be the only social influence that has the requisite leverage.

To succeed in these efforts, the therapist using these new methods must build a solid alliance with all members of the family, especially the parents, since they control the crucial variables. The relatives become part of the total treatment team, which is composed of the therapist(s), psychiatrist, occupational therapist, and social skills trainer. The therapist who feels that he or she is working against the family to protect or rescue the patient is—by definition—in serious trouble, since the essential therpeutic alliance is clearly absent. Blaming the family is explicitly countertherapeutic, even if such blame is unexpressed. The patient–therapist alliance is also important, but is not as central as in other family treatments. To make the contrast more vivid: While the old paradigm saw the task as making the family normal, the new may require the emergence of somewhat abnormal family processes, such as keeping emotion at a low level, artificially simplifying communication, and establishing age-inappropriate parental control over the patient. While such interventions may seem distasteful to some family therapists, the results suggest the wisdom of their design. Even systemic family therapy may have as its goal setting the stage for these types of interventions. While the favorable outcome of these therapies may implicitly provide support for a multilevel, reciprocally interactive theory of etiology and course in schizophrenia, their ultimate distinction and value lie in their pragmatic concern with achieving better lives for patients and their families.

There are two aspects of the present treatment of schizophrenia that make these approaches especially important: the distressing realities of deinstitutionalization on the one hand, and of drug therapy on the other.

For the patient under 40, deinstitutionalization is all too real. In the nearly ubiquitous absence of structured community residences, the caring agent has become the family of origin. For instance, in fiscal year 1980–1981, 51% of all dischargees (with stays less than 3 months, 80% of those released) from New York state hospitals were sent to live with family members. There has been a steady *decrease* over the past 6 years in the number of patients discharged to alternative residences. At this writing, the federal government is further reducing funds for community services and Social Security disability payments for chronic patients. There is no indication that the trend toward the family's becoming the patient's de facto caretaker will be reversed. Schizophrenia may be in the process of evolving a new kind of natural history: The afflicted live at home, doing very little, taking medication erratically, periodically overwhelming and/or being overwhelmed by family members, decompensating, and reentering the hospital for very short stays. It is by interrupting this grim cycle that these approaches will have their greatest effect. Most of these therapies seem to relieve families' suffering, confusion, hopelessness, and sense of being alone with the problem. They offer what Agnes Hatfield, in Chapter 2, has stated that families of schizophrenics *say* they need. Here, the public health implications of these methods—if they continue to be effective and gain wide use—may be very significant. They seem to have arrived not a minute too soon.

The other possible role for the new family interventions relates to recent developments in drug therapy for schizophrenia. Two aspects have become increasingly problematic—tardive dyskinesia and the exacerbation of deficit, or negative, symptoms (the reine syndrome). The former needs little comment beyond saying that any means for the reduction of total lifetime dosage that does not lead to relapse will appreciably lower the risk for irreversible side effects. The deficit syndrome is only beginning to be investigated, but Heinrichs and Carpenter, in Chapter 12, have suggested that neuroleptics may lower some patients' motivation and energy levels below those accompanying the illness itself. For patients in frequent contact with their families, these approaches may be one of the keys to reducing medication levels, especially for male "good prognosis" patients, who Kopeikin, Marshall, and Goldstein, in Chapter 3, find do as well with family therapy alone. If so, the combined approach of family intervention and carefully monitored low-dosage (or even intermittent) drug therapy could turn out to be a more effective and safer alternative.

To summarize, the case seems strong that the future treatment of schizophrenia should involve family members, because (1) these therapies seem to be effective in preventing frequent relapse and in promoting more productive lives for the patients; (2) they may hold the key to safely reducing drug dosage; (3) families have become the functional replacement for the ward staff of the old state hospital; and (4) families cannot be expected to do the job alone.

It is my hope that the reader, having studied the succeeding chapters, will be moved to begin the exciting and challenging task of putting these new therapies to work in everyday clinical practice. They are eminently practical, in spite of their origins as research projects. It is now only by being used by large numbers of practitioners that their real worth can be judged. The unmet needs of schizophrenic patients and their families have recently become so great that there should be ample opportunity to test out these approaches, not only for their effectiveness, but for their relevance and acceptability to all concerned. The evidence to date suggests that the clinicians who use these therapies will be amply rewarded for their effort by seeing that something useful *can* come out of family intervention in this most difficult of disorders. In the final analysis, family therapists may well owe the families of schizophrenics a good trial of these methods, if only to compensate for the errors of the past.

NOTE

[1]Readers unsatisfied with this superficial survey of the early family research are urged to read Wynne's (1981) and Liem's (1980) comprehensive reviews of this area, as well as Hoffman's (1981) excellent summary of the prominent family therapists of that period.

REFERENCES

Dell, P. Researching family theories of schizophrenia: An exercise in epistemological confu-
    sion. In D. Bagarozzi, A. Jurich, & R. Jackson (Eds.), *New perspectives in marriage
    and family therapy.* New York: Human Sciences Press, 1980.
Doane, J. A., West, K. L., Goldstein, M. J., Rodnick, E. H., & Jones, J. E. Parental communi-
    cation deviance and affective style. *Archives of General Psychiatry*, 1981, *38*, 679–685.
Goldstein, M. J., & Rodnick, E. H. The family's contribution to the etiology of schizophrenia:
    Current status. *Schizophrenia Bulletin*, 1975, *14*, 48–63.
Gurman, A. S., & Kniskern, D. P. Research on marital and family therapy. In S. L. Garfield &
    A. E. Bergin (Eds.), *Handbook of psychotherapy and behavior change.* New York:
    Wiley, 1978.
Hirsch, S. R., & Leff, J. P. *Abnormalities in parents of schizophrenics.* London: Oxford
    University Press, 1975.
Hoffman, L. *Foundations of family therapy.* New York: Basic Books, 1981.
Jacob, T. Family interaction in disturbed and normal families: A methodological and sub-
    stantive review. *Psychological Bulletin*, 1975, *18*, 35–65.
Liem, J. H. Family studies of schizophrenia: An update and commentary. *Schizophrenia
    Bulletin*, 1980, *6*, 429–455.
Massie, H. N., & Beels, C. C. The outcome of the family treatment of schizophrenia. *Schizo-
    phrenia Bulletin*, 1972, No. 6, 24–37.

Mishler, E. G., & Waxler, N. E. (Eds.). *Family processes and schizophrenia.* New York: Jason Aronson, 1975.

Reiss, D. Individual thinking and family interaction, II. In E. G. Mishler & N. E. Waxler (Eds.), *Family processes and schizophrenia.* New York: Jason Aronson, 1975.

Reiss, D. The family and schizophrenia. *American Journal of Psychiatry*, 1976, *133*, 181–185.

Scheflen, A. *Levels of schizophrenia.* New York: Brunner/Mazel, 1981.

Sedvall, G. C., & Wode-Helgrodt, B. Aberrant monoamine metabolite levels in CSF and family history of schizophrenia. *Archives of General Psychiatry*, 1980, *37*, 1113–1116.

Singer, M. T., Wynne, L. C., & Toohey, M. L. Communication disorders and the families of schizophrenics. In L. C. Wynne, R. L. Cromwell, & S. Matthysse (Eds.), *The nature of schizophrenia.* New York: Wiley, 1978.

Wyatt, R. J., Cutler, N. R., DeLisi, L. E., Jeste, D. V., Kleinman, J. E., Luchins, D. J., Potkin, S. G., & Weinberger, D. R. Biochemical and morphological factors in schizophrenia. In L. Grinspoon (Ed.), *American Psychiatric Association annual review.* Washington, D.C.: American Psychiatric Association, 1982.

Wynne, L. C. Current concepts in family relationships of schizophrenics. *Journal of Nervous and Mental Disease*, 1981, *169*, 82–89.

I
FROM LONG EXPERIENCE:
THE VIEW FROM OPPOSITE SIDES
OF THE ROOM

1

THOUGHTS ON FAMILY THERAPY AND SCHIZOPHRENIA: INTERVIEWS WITH CHRISTIAN F. MIDELFORT AND CARL A. WHITAKER

The family therapies for schizophrenia described in Parts II, III, and IV of this book are almost all very recent additions to the clinical repertoire, some having been initially reported as late as 1980. One can distinguish them, in a rough sort of way, as examples of two seemingly opposing constructs: the medical model and communications theory. While the therapies are new, neither of these constructs is particularly novel. Nothing seems to illustrate the longevity of this dialectic better than the work of Christian F. Midelfort and Carl A. Whitaker, whose interviews on the subject of family therapy and schizophrenia are presented here.

It should be emphasized that the fundamental and most compelling reason for asking these most senior of family therapists to describe their nearly lifelong interest in treating families of schizophrenic patients is that they have probably accumulated more experience in, and devoted more thought to, that type of work than have any other living family therapists. Both men began working with schizophrenics before family therapy had even been "invented." In fact, Midelfort could be considered the first family therapist of schizophrenia, and has seen over 3000 families with a psychotic member. And they are both still doing clinical work, some 40 years after they began. Thus, their work stands as a kind of monument to their persistence, their creativity, and, ultimately, their humane commitment to schizophrenic patients and their families. They are both pioneers, in that distinctly American tradition of using intuition as a guide in uncharted territory and of not waiting for the cartographers to complete their work before setting out. They have been influenced very little, as far as one can tell, by the major family and schizophrenia theorists of the 1950s and 1960s. They are family therapists, first and foremost—"garage mechanics," as Whitaker puts it—and not epistemologists or researchers.

In that pragmatism, they find good company with the architects of the therapies described in this volume. From their experience, they have gained a unique, valuable, and very long-term set of insights into the families of schizophrenics; while the two men differ on some points, they share an emphasis on the tremendous difficulties the families face, their need for empathy and sensitive guidance, and their capacities for growth and restitution. Therapists and clinicians all have a great deal to learn from them.

The other reason for presenting their views here is that, in their different orientations, they embody the same tension that still characterizes the field as a whole. That is, Midelfort is a representative of the medical model, with its emphasis on the biological and sociocultural aspects of schizophrenia; Whitaker shares much with the best parts of the communications school, with its emphasis on family enmeshment. That tension, though it can be seen as confusing, seems equally to be a source of strength from which to build a more comprehensive therapy. The fact that these two veterans deeply respect each other's work can be seen as a stimulus for their professional descendants to continue working toward finding the common ground behind the seeming contradictions.

Midelfort was interviewed by C. Christian Beels on December 1, 1981, at the Family Institute of Westchester, with the assistance of Monica McGoldrick and the Institute's faculty. Whitaker was interviewed by William R. McFarlane on February 1, 1982, at the Philadelphia Child Guidance Center. The transcripts have been edited by the respective interviewers.

CHRISTIAN F. MIDELFORT

C. CHRISTIAN BEELS: I'm looking forward to this very much, Dr. Midelfort. I have been fascinated by your therapy program ever since you described it at the last AFTA [American Family Therapy Association] meeting. I will try not to get too much in your way as you describe your follow-up study of treatment of families with schizophrenia, over how many years?

CHRISTIAN F. MIDELFORT: Twenty-five to thirty years.

CCB: That's really an extraordinary experiment. The other thing is, you did it all yourself. You were the therapist, so that this is, for all of those patients, an extraordinarily economical and focused therapy.

CFM: Yes.

CCB: Do you want to tell us about the setting that you work in and what goes on?

CFM: Yes, I work in a Lutheran hospital, General Hospital, and a clinic that is attached to it called the Gundersen Clinic. All are Norwegian-connected. I deal with people from Iowa, from Minnesota, and Wisconsin —both from the villages, the cities, and from the rural areas. I've been interested in the context—its ethnic, religious, occupational, residential (or geographic) aspects—for at least thirty years. I've collected much information about the relationship between these four variables and different types of mental illness, including schizophrenia and the depressions. The fact that I happen to be a Norwegian and Lutheran, I think, is of primary importance in this setting. They come to the Gundersen Clinic because my father-in-law, who started the Clinic in 1891, was from Norway and trained there, as was my father, who started another clinic north of there in Eau Claire. The natural thing for all Norwegians is to come there. The percentage of Norwegians is roughly fifteen percent in LaCrosse, twenty percent in Eau Claire, and in the rural areas about eighty percent. Wisconsin, Minnesota, and Iowa are very unique to me, because you have ethnic groups alongside of each other. For example, on the ridge will be a Norwegian Lutheran community, and in the valley may be an Irish Catholic community, and in another area a little farther away a Bohemian Catholic community, and so forth. So that you have a chance to see the acculturation process between these groups and also to study them in more or less pure culture, so to speak. I've been interested in the cultural aspects of family life. . . .

CCB: So this is mainly a Norwegian group, but it's also a farming group.

CFM: In the LaCrosse area. I've also been working in Chicago, mainly at Lutheran General Hospital—run by the American Lutheran Church, another fundamentally Norwegian group—to compare the family life in Chicago with that in LaCrosse and the rural area around Eau Claire. There are tremendous differences in the treatment of schizophrenia. If you wanted to supply an environment that would guarantee the patient wouldn't get better, you couldn't do better than to go to Chicago.

CCB: But the sample you're going to be talking about is, mainly, a sample of farming people.

CFM: Well, they are from villages; they are retired farmers, from the city of LaCrosse and other smaller places around, yes.

CCB: So, that's their culture. And one of the things we want to get into is how that is a much better context for the treatment of schizophrenia than the city.

CFM: Right.

CCB: Maybe it would help, though, if we'd start with a description of your experiment. You decided at an early point to compare three different kinds of therapy.

CFM: I learned about subcoma insulin therapy from Tom Rennie when I was at Payne Whitney. He had had the same background as I had had, beginning at Peter Bent Brigham, in internal medicine, with Henry Christian, and then with Adolph Meyer in Baltimore. Therefore it was congenial for us to think in terms of a medical model and not just to *play* doctor but to *be* doctor, in contrast to what the average psychiatrist is. . . . Rennie and I and others have felt that internal medicine, neurology, psychiatry— and I have added theology—are of primary importance in being a family therapist. I've taught theology as it relates to psychotherapy at our seminary for twenty five years. . . .

CCB: So one of the things you did was to integrate the medical approach and the theological approach.

CFM: I was fortunate at LaCrosse Lutheran Hospital inasmuch as my father-in-law had always insisted, since 1905, that the families of old people and children should be allowed to stay with their patients overnight or throughout the twenty-four hours. So, when I came back there, . . . I had the family live in the hospital, General Hospital, around the clock with the patient. Whatever occupational and recreational therapy [that was done] was done by the family. They were in a ward with other types of patients so as to not get an accumulation of psychiatric complaints that is so harmful to people with schizophrenia, as in a typical psychiatric institution.

CCB: It occurs to me that there's also a similarity between that—the family living in—and the farmhouse. This is a type of family that's accustomed to living together and working together.

CFM: Yes, that's true. When the family comes in and lives with the patient (even though the family has something to do with the illness, which, I thought, would make it rather difficult to have the family stay with the patient), the therapeutic possibilities are much greater than with either individual therapy or being outside the hospital. There is an intensity in two to three weeks of relationship with the therapist that has a lasting influence on the patient, especially with good follow-up and continuity of care.

CCB: You mentioned that there's something about this therapy that made it possible to not just play doctor but to really be doctor. I was wondering, were you talking about the insulin therapy?

CFM: My father was a surgeon and a general practitioner from 1893 to 1938. I went rounds with him and he always examined the patient with the family present. I learned how to sit with the family and be comfortable with them. . . . I had this feeling [in my later work] that if the family could be gotten together, all of the nonverbal aspects that are so important in culture and religion could be brought to bear as assets as well as liabilities.

CCB: But what did insulin therapy have to do with all of that?

CFM: Insulin therapy is still open for grabs as to what's going on. Insulin is essential to the metabolism of the brain, as is glucose, and when the blood level of sugar goes down, the brain doesn't function normally; it's a life-threatening experience. This may have something to do with the chemistry at the synapse, that makes it possible to return to the older primary processes that are established in the brain through former relationships that are lasting and primary. I don't know. I did not use full-coma insulin at any time. In any case these people, these Norwegian people, look upon mental illness as something that can be cured physically. The people accept this as a normal way of treating mental illness.

CCB: If the Norwegian family didn't have a medical model for treating mental illness, what would they think it was?

CFM: Well, they would think it is a sign of weakness; they would think it was a sign that people hadn't behaved properly—were sinful or unclean, or "worthy only of condemnation," to quote Luther. They would say that it's best to hush it up, not talk about it. We don't talk about our weaknesses. We can handle it best by not saying anything.

CCB: So by staging this sort of medical treatment, you allow them to talk about it.

CFM: You enter at the level where people are. I wouldn't start with a Unitarian at that level.

CCB: What would you do with a Unitarian?

CFM: It would have to be at a social level, with lots of words, lots of talking. Norwegians don't talk much, so you have to observe the facial expression, tone of voice, and gestures, to hear what's going on.

CCB: What actually happens during an insulin coma? How is the family involved?

CFM: They sit there and watch, first of all, to see when the reaction is too marked. . . . It is rather dramatic, because there's an infusion, sweating, and hunger. The family feels something is being done that's worth doing.

CCB: And they're involved in it? They monitor the process?

CFM: They are the nurses, and they're much better than the average nurse, much more accurate, much more attentive.

CCB: And what's the role of the doctor in all of that?

CFM: First of all, I'm a doctor, and as such, I represent the institution of the hospital and the Gundersen Clinic. My authority is based on that. At the same time, I'm one with them. I speak Norwegian with them; I understand their farming problems, religious preoccupations, their economic difficulties, and their history. History is of tremendous importance because that's where the real value system is. That is what keeps these people going.

CCB: You ask them about their history as the treatment goes on?

CFM: Oh, yes. What they believe, and how they celebrate. If I'm lucky, they'll cook a Norwegian meal, bring it in, and we'll share it together.

CCB: In the hospital?

CFM: In the hospital, or in the clinic.

CCB: So this treatment which begins with sort of a subcoma insulin experience then goes on with more interviews?

CFM: They're in the hospital two to three weeks, and by that time the majority of hallucinations and delusions have disappeared. They disappear rather quickly.

CCB: And you're getting the history of the family.

CFM: We're talking about what the needs are. I establish a history of the disruptions in structure, speaking of the brain. Are they in relationship to the supernatural? Or to one's mythology? Are they in relationship to the social relationships, to the ethnic background? Has there been a cutoff in relationship to one's siblings, or is there lack of understanding or distortion of understanding of what this means? And what part does the physical play in this? This is the most neglected part, the physical part. So, I'm very grateful for the ten years I had of internal medicine.

CCB: So, you have three or four different areas that you can look to for a solution?

CFM: The entire structure of the system, with the religious at the top, and the mythological, and then the ethnic, then the social, then the psychological, then the physical.

CCB: How does the religious come into it?

CFM: Well, I always ask them, "What church do you belong to? Where do you come from? What about your grandparents? Did they belong to any church? Have they changed churches? What does faith mean to you? Do you go to church? Does it help you? Or, what are your reactions or feelings about it when you go and don't go?" So I get to know where the family sits in its religious life.

CCB: And there's a minister involved, also?

CFM: At times, the minister comes in, and the teacher comes in if that's essential in treatment of a child in the family. I'm very much interested in theology and know a little about it, the various denominations. This is of tremendous importance for the majority of people that I see.

CCB: You have, in some of the things that you've written, some marvelous stories about the ways some of these therapies go. I was wondering, do you have a story that would give us an idea of how the religious side of it comes in?

CFM: Yes, perhaps I can introduce you to a Lutheran pastor's wife, since that dumps you right in the middle of religion. She had abdominal pains; they did a posterior culdoscopy to see if there was anything wrong, and blew in air to look around inside the pelvic area, during which she was conscious. Nothing was found. She felt as though her abdomen was going to explode and splatter over the wall. At that moment she saw God in the far corners of the room, and she said, "I give myself into Your hands." Then she became very calm and accepting. For about three or four days everything went very well. Then there was a return of her symptoms, some of which were abdominal pains. She felt that God had intended that she should have a better sexual life than she had been experiencing. So she had sex relations and went across the street naked to the church to take Communion afterwards. Her husband realized at that point that there was something wrong. So the husband and his wife were admitted to the hospital.

CCB: That was the first psychosis?

CFM: Yes. She thought that God was using her voice to express what He wanted. "This isn't my voice, this is His voice. And I'm going to die." Where did that idea come from? "It came from two years ago when I was sitting in a church and I saw you [CFM] across the church listening to an organ concert. I had the idea that my husband and you should get together to help people. So now God is saying through my voice that I am to die, so that my husband and you will get together to help people." So her husband and I agreed that she should have a chance to test this. So we said a prayer together. She laid down in bed. Death started crawling up from her toes, which is the way the devil comes into the body, as well as death in tradition. . . . It came as far as about midthigh and stopped. She sat up in bed and she said, "I misjudged God." And she really believed that she had. Before she went home a week later—she was in only a week—her daughter, age ten, came in and stayed with her overnight. The patient tucked her into the cot, and it was just like being at home. She made a point of this.

What she liked about me was that I respected her intellect. This is very common in schizophrenic people that I've known. The intellect becomes of tremendous importance. She had been a very bright student at the University of Minnesota, with honors. She was not Norwegian. Her father was Polish, ex-Catholic; her mother was German and Lutheran. Her father had always made fun of religion. And she'd married this Norwegian Lutheran pastor whose family just adored him. He was so busy with the church that he resented having to take a day off every two weeks to go shopping with her, to buy the groceries. That was the amount of time that she spent with him, he was so busy. . . . Well, I [have] followed her for roughly twenty years. She's been through a cancer of the breast operation, her husband has had a stroke, and she's maintained her health. So there's an example of how I took her intellect and her religious beliefs seriously, gave her a chance to find out what this experience meant. I was lucky to think that way instead of trying to change it—I let her change it.

CCB: Right. "Instead of trying to change it." You see some therapists as working to try to change that sort of system.

CFM: I feel comfortable with it. I remember Esther Richards as saying that "The thing that bothers me about patients with schizophrenia is that I have a chill that goes up and down my spine. There's something odd and peculiar." When I see a family of the patient with schizophrenia, I'm very comfortable. They don't seem too odd and peculiar to me at all.

CCB: And you work to make them comfortable.

CFM: Yes, I join them, so to speak—in a kind of dual role, as a member of the family and as also the authority.

CCB: We ought to spend just a moment talking about the comparison group that you used so that we understand it. You stopped doing subcoma insulin.

CFM: In 1955. I stopped because other methods became available, and I wanted to compare them. From between 1946 and 1955 I saw eighty-eight families that had patients having subcoma insulin. From then on I used the phenothiazines, without insulin. Some were in the hospital and some outside. Of the thirty-seven with insulin that I've been able to follow, seventy-five percent have remained well. Of those fifty patients who had the therapy without insulin, who were treated in the outpatient and the hospital both, forty-six percent have maintained their health.

CCB: So it's not quite so good without insulin.

CFM: No. In the individual therapy group, in which I just saw the patient, eighteen percent have remained in reasonably good health.

CCB: That's a big difference. You're the therapist in each case, right?

CFM: I'm the only therapist.

CCB: How did you assign the patients to individual or family therapy?

CFM: Depending on how florid the symptoms were, there'd be a question of hospitalization.

CCB: If hospitalization, then family therapy?

CFM: And family therapy in the outpatient aftercare as well.

CCB: If not hospitalization, then individual therapy?

CFM: If they were not in the hospital, they may have had either family therapy or not. Among the individual therapy patients, there were some eighty [out of] a total of one hundred sixty-seven families that I've been able to follow these years.

CCB: If there is a selection bias, it sounds like it's in the direction of the easier cases getting the individual therapy.

CFM: That's correct. The most sick people get into the hospital.

CCB: And get a family treatment?

CFM: Yes.

CCB: So the lower recovery rate in the individual therapy cases is even more striking.

CFM: I think so. I've become convinced that individual therapy, in my hands, is not a very effective way of treating schizophrenia. And I didn't see much improvement either at Payne Whitney or at Phipps Clinic. It was the same sort of chronic, deadly atmosphere.

CCB: I think some of them might agree with you if they really had to.

CFM: If you could catch them on a dark night.

CCB: There's a view of this illness in this population which is really very negative, without your very strong recasting of it.

CFM: Yes, especially by the medical profession, and especially by psychiatrists. The worst group of people to deal with in this regard are the psychiatrists.

CCB: How so?

CFM: Most of them have psychoanalytic leanings, and they don't want to change, that's all.

CCB: Even in Wisconsin?

CFM: Oh, yes, it's penetrated into the wilderness. I think it's very helpful not to be preoccupied with psychoanalysis if one is interested in family therapy.

CCB: I would agree. Now there's another aspect of all this. That is, that there's a side of the context of the community that I'd like to talk about. You have some suggestions that you make to them, as they go from the hospital back to where they're going to live, and it's possible for them to carry out those suggestions. Could you say a little about that?

CFM: With the family taking part in the interviews, we plan very carefully what the activities of the patient shall be. I want to say something about the context. The farm—the church and the farm go together in the Norwegian community—is sacred space, as is the land. That land is part of the personality of the family, or even part of the structure of the brain of the members of the family. The church, then, is an extension, but fully a part, of the way the brain functions. So when you're dealing with a relationship, you're dealing not only with a person's brain in relationship to the body and to the immediate members of the family, but to the land, to the geography, to the church, and to the community. There are limits set beyond which one shouldn't go, although this is breaking down. It's remarkable how the Norwegians—say they came over in 1860—are still living on the farm, in the third generation, as they were in 1860.

CCB: When you say "sacred space," though, you mean that there are marked-out activities that belong in certain. . . .

CFM: Well, I think that the relationship with the supernatural, as understood by Norwegian-American farmers, includes the concept of the sacredness of the land itself, and of the occupation of farming.

CCB: Could you tell us a little about that?

CFM: You see, the Lutheran religion is a pessimistic one, in the main, although when you talk to Lutherans they won't admit it. Farmers are pessimistic; they expect bad crops and bad weather, and they usually get it. They don't expect to succeed, and often they don't. But they have this church that is based on failure and the next world, so the whole thing holds together as one system. The supernatural becomes of tremendous importance as a stimulus to keep on, in the face of disaster. . . . As you look at probate records, only about ten percent of the Yankees [in Minnesota and Wisconsin] have left their farms to their descendants. Eighty percent of the Norwegians have left their farms to their descendants. So there's a feel that the land is sacred.

CCB: In the sense of something enduring, connected to something beyond the individual.

CFM: The supernatural.

CCB: That sounds like a geographic treatment for both depression and schizophrenia.

CFM: That's a very important part of treatment.

CCB: Now, when you send people home to that environment, how do you make use of that, in terms of what you recommend that they do with the patient who's had a psychiatric decompensation?

CFM: The women, of course, are concerned with the church, and with the home, and with the chickens and the pigs and the calves. They get back into all of that gradually. And when a woman in the house gets sick, some of her daughters will come home to help. . . . They sit in on the family interviews. And they help the patient to do what is reasonable and to act in a reasonable fashion, until there is a recovery sufficient for the mother to be on her own.

CCB: After the hospitalization, there's something for those sisters to do. To help with things, and so forth. What about the men?

CFM: The men are busy on the farm. They get back into that—if they can, if it's permitted. The men are encouraged to talk about their farming problems and to find solutions. I become, then, the one that mobilizes their assets in handling farming problems. Of course, men are older when they get depressions, and sometimes are living in villages where they don't belong. You can't get them on a farm again.

CCB: You get them back on the farm in some way?

CFM: Yes.

CCB: If you have a man who breaks down in town, do you find him a farm to go and work on?

CFM: Sometimes. If they have moved to town, then they go back on the children's farm to help out, to talk about farming problems, and to find solutions. And there are conglomerates, now, of three or four farms that have amalgamated, and they get a part-time job.

CCB: With some kind of sheltered work understanding? That is they don't have to work as hard as everybody else?

CFM: They get back into the whole production. Of course, sixty percent or so are women, in these patients with schizophrenia.

CCB: And what about the child-rearing side of the rehabilitation?

CFM: Children are of particular importance in the treatment of the paranoid aspect of schizophrenia. Or paranoid reaction, for that matter. The patient is an expert at child rearing. A schizophrenic patient understands children very well. And the therapist will go to the patient through the child, and vice versa; then this tends to build up this person's role as mother or father. The place where many rehabilitations take place is the role of parent to child or child to parent.

CCB: But it's something you start in the hospital. You mentioned the woman tucking the child into bed.

CFM: They stay overnight and take part, play a game with the child, talk to the child with the other spouse present.

CCB: So there's some sort of a nonverbal re-creation of the relationship?

CFM: The relevant fifty percent of what I do is nonverbal. It has to do with the right side of the brain, so to speak.

CCB: The course of schizophrenia is said to be much better in developing countries, as compared to the industrial countries and particularly the cities of industrial countries. And I think you're casting some light on why that should be so.

CFM: I feel comfortable when I talk with the people from Zaire or Tanzania or Kenya or Uganda, which I do at the World Council of Churches, because they're doing the same thing I'm doing; only it's the village that treats the patient. And the family is not the genetic family; it's anyone who is socially involved with the family. All of them are involved in therapy. The results are that the typical schizophrenic illness does recur in less than ten percent. In contrast, across the Mediterranean, over eighty percent of them in Europe are back in hospitals. I often have felt that I have much in common with the Africans, not only because they're so smart and they're so realistic, but they're doing the same thing.

CCB: What is it about the village that makes so much of a difference? Is it the same kind of integration of the spiritual and the physical?

CFM: Yes, just try to live in a small Midwestern village and not go to church. . . .

CCB: Here we are, walking around in our very unsacred space. And I guess that's part of the problem, you would say, right? We have no sacred space at all. I agree with you that the problem in treating schizophrenia is to create a village within this very threatening society. Have you seen anybody who's been very successful at it, in Chicago, for example? Do you know of any way in which this kind of thing can be approached in the urban environment?

CFM: Well, in Norway at Ulabel Hospital they have a family treatment center in the hospital, where the family lives with the patient. That was started about fifteen years ago.

CCB: So one approach is to take the family as the nucleus that is not totally shattered by the city and to work with that.

CFM: Encourage them to come, early. And not to be afraid.

CCB: And after the hospital?

CFM: After the hospital they have mental health clinics all over the town, where people are assigned. And usually they go. And they do it for the funniest reasons.

CCB: What's that?

CFM: The community expects them to do it.

CCB: How is that?

CFM: It's the strangest thing. Here's a woman in her eighties that sits up straight at the table and takes a walk every day. She's related to my brother's wife. "Why do you do that," she's asked. She says, "The community expects it." They think in terms of the community. They accept this, going to a mental health center. In Chicago, they don't accept anything, as far as I can see.

CCB: Well, you introduced an idea which I think is quite important. You say, how can we get the community to expect that psychotic people will go to this place which is down the street, which is well known as the place that psychotic people go to—and their families. Right? That sounds like a problem of public education, to some extent. Something that we believe in, in this country, right?

CFM: Theoretically.

CARL A. WHITAKER

WILLIAM R. MCFARLANE: I'm interested to know how you got interested in working with families of schizophrenics.

CARL A. WHITAKER: It's a crazy business, really, but I suspect that it started in Syracuse in '38. I did an OB-GYN residency in New York and then went back to Syracuse to practice where I had been to medical school. I decided to go to work in a psychiatric hospital for a year and fell head over heels in love with schizophrenia, right off.

Looking back on it from this perspective, it seems fairly clear to me that, when I left my isolated farm in the Adirondacks at thirteen as a freshman in high school and moved to Syracuse, I entered a four-year period of schizophrenia. I think I was probably simple, so that I didn't have enough delusion formation to make trouble for myself or the rest of the world. I was just plain isolated. I think I did a self-cure. When I went to college after four years of high school isolation, I found two guys in my high school class, one the most popular, the other the smartest, and made us into a trio. For three years we had lunch two, three times a week together, and I think they socialized me. I just got myself a couple of cotherapists and learned how to live in the social world. So I think my devotion to schizophrenia has come out of my having been one. That's gradually been amplified as I've become more and more convinced that we're all schizophrenic in the middle of the night when we're sound asleep, and wake up in the morning and make believe nothing happened.

If you aren't willing to treat a schizophrenic, I think you don't become a psychotherapist; you become some kind of social game player. If you aren't willing to get into the craziness of people you don't really stay a psychotherapist, just like if you don't play with your kids you aren't really a mother, just an imitation, a nurse.

WRM: Where did you go from there?

CAW: Well, once I had discovered this, I never did go over to the OB hospital. I decided I had to go to child psychiatry to find out how people got crazy. I went to Louisville where I was lucky enough to get into a setting like the old Child Guidance Clinic. I spent a year in the playroom, with children. I took extensive notes and became very enamored of the kind of craziness that children are so wonderful at. Then I spent the next three years in a delinquent institution doing psychotherapy with kids. Then Malone and Warkentin and I began in '44 or '45 to take on schizophrenics intensively. Two of us would see the patient. I think the reason I've maintained my fascination and absorption with schizophrenics is because it was cotherapy. I think the individual treating schizophrenics usually burns out, he can't tolerate that much invasion, that much breast feeding for very long. For a fair number of years—five, six, eight, something like that—John Warkentin and I or Tom Malone and I and at one point the three of us would work at it, two of us as cotherapists, and then, when we wrote it up, the third one would do the commentary. By 1959 we were pretty well convinced that the individual treatment of schizophrenics was a transference cure. They go back home and go crazy again.

WRM: Like after the hospital.

CAW: Yes. Even though we had made tremendous progress, we thought, and had gotten out of the psychosis through the depression up through a lot of neurotic defenses and into fairly adequate social living. So we moved into families in a kind of gradual transition. Then when I moved up to Madison in '64, I decided, sort of administratively, that I would do nothing except families—that I would see no more individuals at all. . . .

WRM: So how did you approach it initially? What was your idea about what you were going to do?

CAW: Well, the idea was to try to help the families resolve this craziness in their midst, which they sequestered into a kind of state hospital of their own. Looking back on it now, I'm more and more convinced that the problem was how to get the mother over her phobia of craziness.

WRM: A phobia of her own craziness?

CAW: Yes.

WRM: Not the patient's craziness?

CAW: No. No. Of her own.

WRM: And that was what you were working on then?

CAW: Well, that's what we gradually come around to. Our work with schizophrenics has been, I guess like Fritz's [Midelfort], much more clinical. I'm not really much interested in the research components. I'm glad to be a garage mechanic. I'm not interested in studying the components of the metal that go into the car.

WRM: Well, that may be a great advantage. I'd be interested in expanding on this idea—a concept of what you tend to run across when you see families with schizophrenics.

CAW: Well, what I start out trying to do is to get rid of the red light that's like an aura around the schizophrenic. I try to turn my back on the schizophrenic, and try to activate and expose the craziness that I think of as equal in all the other members. For example, everybody in one family I have seen for four years is crazy except mother. She promised herself and her sister when she was thirteen that, since all of her family was crazy, she would never be crazy, so father and three sibs have all had crazy episodes.

WRM: But not her?

CAW: To protect mother from her phobia—which she is very clear about and which she says very clearly—I tried to expose the craziness in the rest of the family during the first interview, because I think that's the time when you're most apt to get access to it as a purely intellectual kind of investigation.

WRM: Is that something that would qualify as your family theory of schizophrenia? Is there something specific about a fear of the craziness of the identified patient that keeps everybody else in some rigid position?

CAW: Not the craziness of the identified patient. Craziness as such. The mother and father get a divorce around the time of the mother's pregnancy with the kid, and then when the kid is born the father, if he doesn't have access to his father and mother and she doesn't have access to her father and mother (they're dead, or unavailable for one reason or another), is apt to go out and get an attachment to a secretary, or to some money or to some other thing. Mother and son get into this bind in which the kid says, "I'll be the crazy half, the infantile half of an individual, and you can be the adult half." So they set up a two-person individual. Then that goes underground and then reemerges in adolescence, at which point the mother's in a panic. So the therapy has to invoke a process of getting mother over her phobia, getting father and mother reattached to making a pair. Then the kid will automatically find himself because he isn't symbiotically locked into this "crazy part, you're the sane part" combination with mother. The problem first is how to disconnect mother so that she can have some kind of security in and of herself.

WRM: That's not that different [from] family work with a lot of different kinds of problems.

CAW: Oh no, I don't see it as any different.

WRM: A little more extreme in degree?

CAW: I don't know. It's certainly more invasive of the therapist. In a funny kind of way, if you're going to make it, then you are into the position of becoming the new lock-in with the patient. You have to help [the son] mature by protecting him from his mother and allowing his Christ-like competence to be directed toward himself, rather than toward mother–father and the rest of the world. But I don't think it's qualitatively any different. I think it's another example of the parentified child.

WRM: Or triangulation?

CAW: Sure, sure.

WRM: So that's key. You would not see the family of the schizophrenic as being particularly different than, say, those with anorexia or a severe behavior disorder?

CAW: Or psychosomatic. I think psychosomatics are frequently much more difficult. I think that the problem that the schizophrenic poses for the therapist is unique because it's an interpersonal family dedicated to chaos. Like Jay Haley says, they can't get any closer. If you get them either any closer or any farther apart it's helpful, but they have a specified distance and enmeshment with each other that's profound. If you get down close enough, you've got to face the probability that the same thing is true of the schizophrenic that is true of ulcer or epilepsy or asthma or a lot of other things. That is, the dynamics of the individual may have a biological substrate that makes the weakest link. In this type of family, it seems to me that the weakest link would then be interpersonal rather than biological.

WRM: Well, they're related, of course.

CAW: Sure.

WRM: The biological problem of schizophrenics results in their inability to track what is going on, socially.

CAW: Sure, sure. Their receptivity is no different than that of an infant. An infant can pick up these kinds of signals just like the schizophrenic can.

WRM: That raises an interesting question. Have you seen any families of schizophrenics who were not locked into this kind of pattern, in other words, more normal?

CAW: Well, that's the thing that I was implying. That you can have schizophrenia in a normal family because of the situational horror that happens.

WRM: Because of the ramifications of the illness and what it does to the family?

CAW: No, no. Because of the ramifications of their life set. Take this family, for example, with all four grandparents unavailable. You have, then, a dependency relationship between father and mother that's very profound. During the pregnancy father retreats because he's lost his wife in this other affair she's having, and then if she has such immaturity from her previous growth experience that she gets isolated by this and can't get her husband back, or if he's got such an inadequate background that he isn't going to come back, then all of a sudden she's stuck with this kind of marriage to the intrauterine individual.

WRM: And she stays stuck?

CAW: And she stays there, or they set it up that way.

WRM: Symbiotically merged?

CAW: Sure. Unless she hasn't had such an inadequate background, or unless she's lucky and breaks out of that bind. For instance, if she finds another husband or if she finds a big sister whom she had lost contact with. I assume that a tremendous number of us had the base material for schizophrenia, like I did, and are broken out of it by the circumstances of life. . . .

WRM: Why do you call it a "normal" family? And what's a "normal," as opposed to an "abnormal," family?

CAW: In a normal family the mother and father are not pathological.

WRM: According to what? What does that mean, the mother is not pathological?

CAW: Not neurotic, not isolated, not psychotic.

WRM: Are you suggesting that she becomes like this, needing the son, when father leaves?

CAW: Yes, but I don't think of that as being intrapsychic, that's interpersonal. The implication is not that she has intrapsychic problems. I think of marriage as a normal interpersonal bilateral dependency, not a pathological one.

WRM: That's really very consistent with a lot of the research being done on social support. Families of schizophrenics, in fact, don't seem to have anybody out there to back them up. Who would you *not* want to treat if they came with a crazy son or daughter?

CAW: Oh, I wouldn't care how they came. I wouldn't care whether it was mother or father or kids, I want the whole gang.

WRM: So that would be one requirement?

CAW: Oh, yes.

WRM: Everybody has to participate?

CAW: I'm pretty insistent about that. Of course, once you get under way, that doesn't always carry over. Like with one family, we started out with all five kids; mother, father, psychotic daughter, and one of the other kids came into the hospital for three weeks in the beginning.

WRM: And they lived there?

CAW: They lived in the hospital for a couple of weeks. I usually like to do it that way and then discharge the patient first and the other members later. During that first psychosis I treated all of them. By the time they came back, which was six or seven years later, with the other son, who was now psychotic also, there were no sibs left at home except him. Mother and father had an empty nest, and he came back to the nest.

WRM: He'd been out?

CAW: Oh, yes. He'd been driving a transcontinental truck for four or five years. I don't know what the signals were, but they were very clear. Mother's newfound independence was scaring the dickens out of this kid.

WRM: Let's talk about what you do. How do you start?

CAW: By taking a massive history. First, dragging the most outside person, the father ordinarily, into relating with me, and then the other kids and then mother and then finally the patient.

WRM: The patient comes last.

CAW: Oh, yes. I try hard to keep from seducing the patient into my family.

WRM: How do you frame the therapy? Your goal is growth, differentiation. How do you tell them what you want to do? Or do you?

CAW: I don't ever tell them. I just ask them what they want, or how I can help. With this family, the one Dave Keith and I videotaped right through, we diagnosed it early as an abnormally normal family. You don't have to help if you have normality.

WRM: Can you explain that? It's an interesting idea.

CAW: We didn't try to explain it; we just said they were too normal to be enjoying each other.

WRM: What did they say?

CAW: They just bought it, like you buy any kind of paradox.

WRM: It sounds like a tall order in a way, because a lot of families I've seen come and say, "We want this kid patched up. Do something quick; do it now; do it completely; and don't blame us for the trouble." That's the underlying request. I assume that's happened to you too.

CAW: Yes. And I just say, "Don't bother me, I'm not interested; find somebody else." They have to go through the telephone struggle. I do all my own telephone calls, and the first telephone call I assume is a front in the game.

WRM: Is that when you begin to move with the father?

CAW: I just maneuver whoever calls into calling back. I think of the project really as a project of parenting or, if you want another metaphor, of being a coach to a baseball team, with the mother and father as the pitcher and catcher and the kids as the infield, and the grandparents as the outfield. Well, I'm not going to coach the team if everybody isn't there. And I'm not going to play any of the parts; I'm not going to play first base, or pitch a game. I'm the coach and they're the ones who have to play. If they don't want to win, that's all right with me. If they don't want me to coach, all they have to do is mention it.

WRM: So you've won the first round and you start in working with the family. What happens then? Could you describe working around the issue of the craziness?

CAW: Well, I just get the story. You know, "What do you want?" including the final story from the psychotic. The story from the father and the kids is "How does the family operate? what kind of family is this?", like you would describe the Green Bay Packers or the Philadelphia Phillies. I push to get the sense of the whole. Then with the psychotic, I ask how I can help him [or her] tolerate this kind of family, this craziness. "Do you think your being the Christ is really going to solve their problem? Do you think mother and father ought to stay together, even though they hate each other's guts and each one wishes the other one dead?" Then, once we've set up this process of my knowing something, I back off and declare my inpotence and force them to lead, and as they lead I try to help them become more crazy, to be part of my own craziness.

WRM: Do you challenge the kid to leave the parents to their own devices?

CAW: I don't challenge [the psychotic]. I'm very clear in my own head about not wanting to set up an inquiry. I share my fantasies, but I put out *my* orientation rather than trying to push them into putting out theirs.

I started with this battle for structure; you could well say it's a battle for my I-position, à la Bowen. Then the next war—which may go on forever—is the battle for them to take their I-position. Now, I'm glad to be their foster mother, but I'm not about to be an adoptive parent and I'm not about to be a biological parent. I'm very clear that they're welcome to live their life out there any way they like. It's almost like a psychoanalytic position, which is kind of an embarrassing thing to say, because I've never been analyzed and I'm not an analyst. But the concept is that I'm in there to help them with their struggle, not to take it over, not to be a part of their group.

WRM: Well, with some families that must be a very good thing to do. But my experience has been that they'll let you in for a while, but if you try to be more active, they'll spit you out at the first moment. Then you feel tremendously defeated, disqualified. . . . You want to quit.

CAW: I think most people do. And I think the central reason why I haven't, aside from my own teenage craziness, is the cotherapy thing. I wouldn't treat a schizophrenic family alone, and I don't think anybody else should. I think it's like a single-parent family, it's insane.

WRM: That helps you stay out, *and* with?

CAW: That's right. I have all sorts of freedom to join. I'm pretty good at it, having grown up on a big dairy farm where the problem of feeding and caring for was part of my infant development. But the problem of getting out is technical, deliberate, and learned very slowly. I think it's the big struggle. I think you have to have a system to treat a system. An individual is not a system, [but] a subsystem of a family.

WRM: And a vulnerable one.

CAW: Oh, God! As soon as you care, you're vulnerable.

WRM: I think what you're describing is the experience of an empathy going toward the family but not always coming back.

CAW: But that empathy is like the empathy for children. The parenting project is just like raising children. In the beginning, you're life-and-death important to them. As time goes on, you need to be very clear that you're going to be less and less important. But you're going to get your throat cut endlessly. The difference between family therapy and raising children is that you may start out with an infantile family and fifty minutes later they may be eighteen years old. You've got to face the dependency and the empty nest in the same hour, or within a matter of a very few hours; and that takes having a mate. The reason I tolerate our empty nest, now that our six kids have gone, is because I have my wife. And I think it's the same thing with psychotherapy.

WRM: That sounds like an absolute.

CAW: It sure is. I wouldn't think of doing it alone.

WRM: I'm still thinking of the middle phase of this process. You've written a lot about the absurd, the use of paradox. Sometimes we give a paradox to the schizophrenic[s], and they either don't get it or it blows so many circuits that they're back in the hospital. That doesn't sound like that's been your experience.

CAW: A lot of mine, I think, make a difference because they're not on purpose; it's not artificial. It comes out of my free associating. The middle phase of therapy, to me, is the time when I'm trying to be crazier than the patient. If you assume that this mother–child combination is that she's always sane because of her phobia and he's always crazy, then when I get into the transference set and replace mother, I do a flip. I become the crazy one and he becomes the sane one.

WRM: What does she do?

CAW: In the middle of all this, when she and I have it well locked in, when she's clear that this craziness that the whole family and I are into is for fun, then she sees that it's like any other silliness. It's not uniquely weird.

WRM: We'd better back up because we must have missed something there. How did you get there with her?

CAW: You get there with her by seducing the whole group into assuming everybody is crazy.

WRM: You just talk about that a lot?

CAW: Yes. Then you move into it. This father I was telling you about that had such a homicidal rage against his mother-in-law: He and I opened that up between us. I stood him up the third session because I had something more important to do during that hour, and he went into a kind of mini-horror state in which he looked like he was going to kill me in the next minute. So we struggled with that one for the next three or four interviews, how frightening it was to me and how frightening it must have been to his wife. God knows how frightening it must have been to his son.

WRM: You pick something up around this theme and then go with it with different people in the family?

CAW: Yes. I assume they're all equally crazy and that the others are just concealing it. The mother's crazy, too. She's just phobic about it. And I move into it by activating my own craziness.

WRM: Does anybody ever say, "Cut it out"?

CAW: You mean patients?

WRM: Any member of the family.

CAW: Oh, sure

WRM: That doesn't stop you?

CAW: No. They're not that important to me. The example that I like is the one in which they had a psychotic who thought he was Christ. I was trying to do this initial history taking and it was dead. All of a sudden it occurred to me that the problem was that he hadn't been baptized right. The father would be John the Baptist, the mother would be the Virgin Mary, and the three sisters Martha, Mary, and Mary Magdalene. "Which one would like to be Mary Magdalene?" "Oh, I'd love to be Mary Magdalene," at which point the psychotic got up and came over and said, "Hey, look, cut it out. I'm not really Christ. That's not fair." You take the other end of the interactional system. You're crazier than [the patient] is and then [the patient] has to be the normal one. Once you've exposed that in the family, their orientation is very different.

WRM: I want to track this process. After you make mother less phobic and less attached, what do you do then?

CAW: Well, what's happened in this family is that first the father confessed his craziness of some years back. Then the oldest daughter, who was a freshman in college, had a psychotic episode, went out of college, came home, was quite paranoid, but didn't bring it to the interviews. Then the younger son began to share his grandiosity. So, the only one that's left is mother.

WRM: Like a wagon train that surrounds.

CAW: Yes. The son has now left the family, finished college, gone out to the West where he's looking for a job and apparently is in fairly good shape. And we (Dave Keith and I) essentially, I guess, talked crazy all the way through.

WRM: Stayed behind the family, in a sense?

CAW: Oh yes.

WRM: While they moved?

CAW: We made them the psychiatric nurses to us. Mother raves, "There he goes, he's gone to sleep again, why in hell don't you stay awake when we're here. We're paying good money." "I don't know." And this goes on every third, fourth, or fifth interview.

WRM: What happens to father? Does he get divorced from his outside connections?

CAW: Sure. Those are only there because he hasn't been able to find a way to reattach to mother.

WRM: You really think that happens? In other words, that there is some shift in the basic relationship pattern in the family?

CAW: Yes. I don't think it's the kind that you'd like to see; they don't become a "normal" family in the usual sense. These two have a very carefully regulated relationship. But it's more and more clear that they're enjoying it.

WRM: So what's the time course of all this? It sounds like it goes on a very long time. Years, not months.

CAW: There's a lot of variation, depending on how much they want out of it and on how much is process schizophrenia and how much is reactive.

WRM: You see a difference?

CAW: Sure.

WRM: Qualitatively or quantitatively?

CAW: I think it's quantitative, depending upon how disorganized the family is.

WRM: I'd like to pursue that a little bit, because that might relate to outcome. With somebody who's more "process," you would accept their hanging around the house?

CAW: I assume that they would.

WRM: You'd be looking for something else to be happening, like more fluid, interesting relationships?

CAW: Sure.

WRM: Or [the patient] not being as involved in some way?

CAW: I think there comes a point in working with the seriously disturbed families of schizophrenics or psychosomatics where you're not really the therapist any more. You are a member of the extended family. You're like the grand[parents]: They come to visit from time to time; you enjoy them when they're there; and yet they know they're free to go.

WRM: You're saying that you stay out, but I would suspect that many of the family members would experience you as being there with them at certain points.

CAW: Oh. You're misunderstanding me. I maintain my right to be a separate person, but during that interview I'm up to my ass.

WRM: With them.

CAW: Sure.

WRM: And they experience that.

CAW: Sure.

WRM: My sense is that families who see Selvini[-Palazzoli] do not experience that.

CAW: I think that's true. It may be that with greater power they [the Milan group] can do this [cure schizophrenia], but time will tell.

WRM: That's a fundamental difference. You're there, available when needed in a sense, with the option to get out.

CAW: We use a tremendous amount of humor.

WRM: Yes, it sounds like it. You tease them about their craziness?

CAW: Yes.

WRM: Must be a lot of fun after a while. Do they go with it?

CAW: Oh, yes. They're sometimes very mystified, but then we share with each other how ridiculous it is to have people who don't understand. We're just trying to be reasonable about the world. It's the world that's crazy.

WRM: Do you think working with these families has changed anything in you?

CAW: It seems to me as though it's made me much more free to be loving with people. It has allowed me access and use of, an integration of, my sadism. I suppose I have had six years of therapy, individual and couples and family, and I would assume that this work has filled in the interstices. I'm very, very apt to be free with my own pathology.

WRM: I wonder if it is a similar process with the families. They must not be so ashamed and sensitive and reactive to craziness after you've met with them. Must be nice for yourself, as well.

CAW: Yes.

WRM: That might be useful for a lot of young therapists to know.

CAW: I think the freedom to share your free associations or fantasies, your disgust with [the patient and family], your anger with them, and the freedom to tease them gives them the freedom to tease each other and to be more flip.

WRM: Do you have any idea of what the relationship of your work is to the degree to which any of those patients have relapsed, spent miserable years in hospitals, and so on? You said you don't care so much about outcome. But what is the outcome of not caring about outcome, as far as you can tell?

CAW: I think I always care for the people. I think that's forever. I see no possible way of not always staying locked in to families you've seen, for me at least. It's like being the extended family; you know, they're always mine.

There's no way I can ever, or would ever, expect to be disconnected. A lot of the outcomes are very difficult to handle.

WRM: Why?

CAW: I don't think the success is all that happy. Some of my individual schizophrenics kill themselves. With lots of families I see, it feels to me as though I've not changed their world in the way I'd like to. Some of them are great. Take one that Dave and I have been working with where the son was schizophrenic. As that became pretty ridiculous and no one was taking him seriously, father finally got into his alcoholism, mother got into her right to be an individual, and younger sister got over her grandiosity and seductiveness.

WRM: So a lot happened?

CAW: Oh, yes, a lot happened. I think a lot always happens in a family. The question of whether the patient gets over his [or her] schizophrenia is a difficult thing to say, and I don't know how to answer that.

WRM: Actually, in a lot of the work being done today, they [therapists] say, "Well, they're not going to get over it, but let's see what we can possibly do to make it better."

CAW: The family gets better, and I think many times the psychotic maintains himself [or herself]. It's not always true, and I don't know what the difference is, or why the difference.

WRM: Do you have any interest in finding that out? That might be good to know.

CAW: Oh yes, sure. The whole process of follow-up is fascinating. That's, of course, where Fritz [Midelfort] is so wonderful.

WRM: His outcome is pretty interesting, and rather impressive by anybody's standards, but he's not invested nearly what you have, from what I can see.

CAW: Well, I think he's probably seen very many more families. Of course he's in the middle of it. I don't know. I see a lot of other kinds of patients than schizophrenics.

WRM: Thanks a lot.

CAW: Thanks for asking.

2

WHAT FAMILIES WANT OF FAMILY THERAPISTS

Agnes B. Hatfield

Only in the last decade has serious attention been paid to the role that families play in the care and rehabilitation of mentally ill family members. Families were once thought to have a noxious influence on a patient; thus it was deemed best to limit contact. Large, remote state hospitals served this purpose well. Little change in this attitude occurred until the massive deinstitutionalization movement began a couple of decades ago and it became apparent that there was no way society would provide for the many needs of a patient in the community without the family. Families, in fact, became the principal care givers, and more positive attitudes toward the family began appearing in the literature. For example, Evans, Bullard, and Solomon (1961) reported that, contrary to the popular belief that families abandon their mentally ill relatives, even after long separation, families maintain involvement with them; and not only do they maintain interest, but, according to Freeman and Simmons (1963), they are the key influence on the patients' ability to function and to remain out of the hospital.

Uzoka (1979), writing about families in general, says that recent empirical investigations show more mutually supportive relationships between kin than once thought. Family members usually turn to families before using available social agencies. Uzoka feels that clinical workers have advanced a distorted version of the nuclear family as the norm and have inadvertently weakened the bonds between members. Further, he says that "labeling relationships as dysfunctional simply because they do not fit the practitioner's model is far from infrequent. True desire for mutually gratifying contact is labeled as dependency and repression or suppression of desire for such contact is equated with psychologically adaptive behavior" (p. 1102). For most people, continues Uzoka, the most important persons in their lives are those flawed but very real people with whom they have

AGNES B. HATFIELD. Institute for Child Study/Department of Human Development, College of Education, University of Maryland, College Park, Maryland.

strong ties—their families. If this is true for most families, it seems especially true for families that find themselves in the crisis of mental illness.

When the President's Commission on Mental Health made its recent comprehensive study of problems in this country, it showed a refreshing respect for the family. The *Task Panel Reports* to the Commission (1978) assigned a significant role to the family in the care and support of the mentally ill. It was stated that "people are usually better off when care is provided in settings that are near families and friends, and supportive networks" (Vol. 1, p. 12) and that "whenever possible, people should live at home and receive outpatient treatment in the community" (Vol. 1, p. 16). The *Task Panel Report on Community Support Systems* noted that professionals, until recently, had little awareness of the nature and function of natural support systems in clinical practice. The natural care-giving networks occur outside the formal care-giving institutions and are invisible to the human service structures. The *Report* recommends identifying these natural helping networks and establishing links with them (*Task Panel Reports*, Vol. 2).

Recognition of families as a valuable asset in the care of mentally ill persons was not accompanied by an equal concern for the inordinate burden such a responsibility might entail. Only very recently are counselors and therapists beginning to ask such basic questions as the following: How well are families able to manage care giving on a 24-hour basis that was once done by a staff on three 8-hour shifts? Do families as well as professionals suffer from burnout? In what ways are the rest of the family at risk if appropriate help is not forthcoming? And, finally, what is the most appropriate form of help for these families?

HOW FAMILIES ARE AFFECTED

It has long been known that a severe or chronic physical illness can have a devastating effect on the family's capacity to cope. Research supports findings of strained family relationships and feelings of futility and entrapment; heavy emotional stress when a person's prognosis is uncertain, illness episodic, or disfigurement great; and depleted energies when sleep is interrupted and respite unavailable (Debuskey, 1970; Travis, 1976). Debuskey (1970) studied family reactions to such diseases as leukemia, heart disease, and cystic fibrosis and found that families suffered from shock, guilt, fear, and confusion. Recently researchers and therapists have begun to ask questions about the well-being of families of the mentally ill; their answers suggest that their sense of devastation could be no less.

In 1974, Kreisman and Joy undertook an extensive review of the literature and concluded that the burden experienced by families caring for the mentally ill had been poorly assessed and that as a consequence the mental health community was not meeting the needs of these families. Lamb (1979) asserted that the burden was indeed very great: "For the parents whose mentally ill child has been discharged from the hospital and come home, there has been more than a discernible impact; there has been a major upheaval in their lives and the lives of all family members" (p. 35). In an interview study, Kreisman, Simmons, and Joy (1979) found families of deinstitutionalized persons significantly less happy than a comparison group. The difference was marked enough that they thought these families were "at risk" for symptomatology or role impairment. The burden of care was only part of the explanation. Just the knowledge of the patient's impairment brought on anger, frustration, and hopelessness.

Doll (1976) used a sentence completion test to tap the subjective burden of the care giver in the family. His findings confirmed those reported above—that families are placed in an emotionally demanding and untenable situation. In fact, he noted, "Much of the time the feelings of helplessness, permanent entrapment came across as a *leitmotif* throughout an overall protocol." Families expressed fear that "this could go on forever." The amount of burden related consistently to the psychiatric condition of the patient. Thompson, Doll, and Lefton (1977) found that the burden was especially heavy when a single adult was coping alone with no one else to share the responsibility. Those who had another adult to support them experienced less disruption and less financial burden. In their concluding statements, the authors suggest that there are forces that are "pervasively, silently, corroding the stability of these families"; by neglecting these silent forces, they warn, the success of the whole community-centered mental health care experiment is threatened.

Hatfield (1978) surveyed 89 members of a self-help group in which 57% of the families had a relative living at home. Many of the patients were reported to be displaying psychiatric disturbances of considerable severity —suspiciousness, auditory hallucinations, nonsensical speech, and unpredictable mood change. Over a third of the patients had threatened suicide, and four had succeeded. Families lived in a state of high tension, constantly on guard. Irregular sleeping patterns and disturbed eating behavior were problems. Families were frustrated because they were unable to motivate their relative to better grooming and personal hygiene, sensible handling of money, and compliance with medication. The effect on the family was highly detrimental: Severe marital tensions developed, families felt they neglected their own children, and social life dwindled.

Holden and Lewine (1979) expanded upon Hatfield's study, seeking greater quantitative and qualitative data and a larger group of subjects. Their findings were consistent with those of the earlier study. They found that families were severely stressed, experiencing aggravated health problems and a loss of leisure time and social contacts. They experienced a sense of frustration at the lack of practical information and coping strategies and the inability of professionals to direct them to community resources. Community living often failed because there was a lack of outreach support and little help was available in times of crisis.

Are some families more at risk than others? Hatfield (1981) did an in-depth study of 30 families over a period of 30 months to identify factors relating to success in coping. For those rated high in coping effectiveness, there was a clear differentiation between the way they felt initially and their present capacity to accept their fate and move forward. Whereas their initial reaction was characterized as "shock," "grief," "guilt," "bewilder-ment," or "helplessness," they now had come to some kind of acceptance. Some felt they could almost pinpoint the time at which they came to resign themselves to dealing with a severe long-term condition. They began to pride themselves on their ability to survive. Those low on coping had not cleared that hurdle. Those most effective were older; were better educated; and had mentally ill relatives who were older (average age = 31.8 years), were deemed more ill, and had been ill for a greater length of time (average length = 11.7 years). Those coping less well had more functional but more disturbing relatives, who were younger (average age = 22.9 years) and who had been ill a shorter time (average length = 7.9 years). Good copers were involved in more activities outside the home and had more social supports.

The studies reported above agree that mental illness is experienced as devastating. Few studies have been reported regarding the needs for support and service as the potential consumers themselves see the need. Families in Hatfield's study (1979) stated the following needs as paramount:

- Understanding symptoms (57%)
- Specific suggestions for coping with patient's behavior (55%)
- Relating to people with similar experiences (44%)
- Substitute care, for family respite (30%)
- Having patient change place of living (27%)
- More understanding from relatives and friends (18%)
- Relief from financial distress (18%)
- Therapy for self (12%)

The same study revealed that families most frequently sought friends, relatives, and individual therapy (in that order) for support and help. Friends (84%) and relatives (73%) significantly outweighed therapy (55%) in their perceived value to the care giver. Group and family therapy rated about the same. In a comparison of a small number of persons identified as highly effective with persons low in effectiveness, the latter had rated therapy more highly than had their more successful counterparts (Hatfield, 1981).

Holden and Lewine (1979) assessed family satisfaction with the kinds of assistance they had received. Families reported that their involvement with professionals left them feeling guilty and defensive. Others felt that they had been left out of treatment plans or ignored by the professionals. They criticized professionals for inability to communicate and to provide families with basic information about mental illness and its everyday management. They felt unsupported by professionals throughout the illness and very much abandoned as the patients reentered the community. The majority of families (74%) reported dissatisfaction with mental health services; however, in spite of this dissatisfaction, they continued to seek help from professionals.

Families clearly need help. But therapists need to know much more precisely what it is that they are seeking and what is, indeed, helpful. Families are consumers; they purchase services. Their needs and their satisfactions will ultimately determine what will be used. The study to be reported here was planned to further an understanding of what families need to help them deal effectively with mental illness.

THE STUDY

A questionnaire was sent to 400 families of mentally ill persons to determine (1) what kinds of help they sought from professionals; (2) what kinds of help they got; (3) how they rated the personal and professional qualities of professionals; and (4) to what extent they were able to make informed choices of service. Respondents were directed to answer the questions in terms of their most recent experience with a therapist. Respondents were members of self-help organizations for families of the mentally ill in California, Missouri, Colorado, Maryland, Pennsylvania, Kentucky, Mississippi, Georgia, and Wisconsin.

A total of 198 (50%) of the questionnaires were returned; 152 (77%) of respondents indicated in the affirmative that they had received or were presently receiving counseling. After incomplete and erroneously completed responses were eliminated, 138 responses were used in the study.

DEMOGRAPHIC CHARACTERISTICS OF RESPONDENTS AND PATIENTS

The respondents were largely female and mothers, married and in their 50s (Table 1). The fact that such a large percentage of respondents were mothers did not come as a surprise. Other studies (Hatfield, 1979; Holden

TABLE 1. *Characteristics of Respondents* ($n = 138$)

Characteristic	Category	Number	Percentage
Sex	Male	29	21.0
	Female	109	79.0
Marital status	Married	90	65.2
	Divorced	17	12.3
	Widowed	19	13.8
	Other	12	8.6
Age[a]	Below 40 years	17	12.3
	40–49 years	23	16.7
	50–59 years	58	42.0
	60–69 years	34	24.6
	Over 69 years	6	4.3
Relationship to patient	Mother	95	68.8
	Father	22	15.9
	Sibling	9	6.5
	Spouse	8	5.8
	Other	4	2.9
Education	Graduate degree	43	32.1
	Baccalaureate	37	27.7
	High school and college	53	39.5
	Junior high school	1	7

[a]Median age of respondents = 54.0 years.

& Lewine, 1979; Kreisman *et al.*, 1979) also reported mothers as the primary respondents and presumably as the more involved parents in the care of ill persons. They tended to be well educated, with well over half having baccalaureate or graduate degrees.

Respondents characterized the mentally ill persons with whom they were dealing as primarily schizophrenic, largely male, and in their 20s and 30s (Table 2). The largest percentage had been ill from 6 to 10 years; however, length of illness varied widely, with over 20% having been ill over 15 years. The largest percentage (44.1%) were living with families, with another 22.1% living in their own apartments (probably under family supervision, since only 15.4% had professionally supervised housing). Although educational level was fairly high, nearly half with some college or a degree, over 60% were presently neither in training nor at work.

NATURE OF THE SERVICE USED

In order to receive help in coping with mental illness in the family, respondents indicated that they had most recently received help from male psychiatrists, estimated to be younger than themselves and in private practice (Table 3). Respondents were most often seen with spouses or the patients or both together; only a fourth were seen alone. It appears that these therapists are usually practicing some form of family therapy.

Respondents were asked to rate the therapists in terms of 11 personal and professional characteristics considered important to successful outcome. Table 4 summarizes these ratings. The care givers in these families saw therapists as strongest in their capacity to listen, in their respect for family expertise, and in their appreciation for the difficulties faced by families. Therapists were most often rated poor in apprising the family of what is going on, in lack of sympathy for the family's suffering, and in their

TABLE 2. *Characteristics of Patients* ($n = 138$)

Characteristics	Category	Number	Percentage
Sex	Male	86	62.3
	Female	52	37.7
Age	Below 20 years	19	13.7
	20–29 years	65	47.1
	30–39 years	38	27.5
	40–49 years	7	5.1
	Over 49 years	9	6.5
Diagnosis	Schizophrenia	117	84.8
	Manic–depressive illness	7	5.1
	Other	16	10.1
Length of illness[a]	0–2 years	22	16.7
	3–5 years	21	15.9
	6–10 years	36	27.1
	11–15 years	26	19.0
	Over 15 years	28	20.3
Education[a]	College degree	27	19.7
	Some college	37	27.0
	High school diploma	47	34.3
	Below high school	26	18.9
Residence[a]	Family	60	44.1
	Own apartment	30	22.1
	Supervised housing	21	15.4
	Hospital	21	15.4
	Other	4	2.9
Day involvement[a]	Work	25	18.2
	Training	19	13.8
	Both	7	5.1
	Neither	85	61.8

[a] $n < 138$ due to missing data.

TABLE 3. *Characteristics of Professional Service Utilized by Respondents*

Characteristic	Category	Number	Percentage
Sex	Male	97	81.9
	Female	25	18.1
Professional identity	Psychiatrist	92	66.7
	Social worker	24	17.4
	Psychologist	16	11.6
	Other	5	4.3
Estimated age	Below 30	7	5.7
	30–39 years	41	33.9
	40–49 years	35	29.0
	50–59 years	31	25.6
	Over 59	7	5.7
Who attends	Self	34	25.2
	Self/spouse	20	14.8
	Self/spouse/patient	44	32.6
	Self/patient	24	17.7
	Other	13	9.6
Use of cotherapist	Yes	38	30.4
	No	87	69.6
Location of therapist	Private practice	63	46.0
	Community mental health center	31	22.6
	Hospital	17	12.3
	Other	26	19.0

Note. *n*s vary due to missing data.

use of time in a meaningful way. Overall, therapists were rated relatively high on personal and professional qualities.

WHAT FAMILIES WANT FROM THERAPY AND WHAT THEY GET

The questionnaire listed 21 goals for therapy. Respondents were asked to go through the list and check those that comprised their objectives in seeking therapy in their present or most recent use of service. They were then asked to go through the same list of goals again and indicate the degree to which these goals were addressed by checking "none," "some," or "a great deal." For purposes of presentation, the 21 items have been arranged into categories of related concerns and presented in the next set of tables.

It was presumed that many families would be seeking help in understanding mental illness and in learning ways to cope with difficult behavior.

Table 5 presents this group of concerns. Family priorities were high for knowing appropriate expectations, learning to motivate the patients, and understanding the illness. Of less importance were dealing with such difficult behaviors as substance abuse and poor hygiene. There was, however, no significant relationship found between what a respondent wanted (or did not want) in therapy and what was achieved.

Coping with psychiatric symptoms and management of medication were important to somewhat fewer families (Table 6). Understanding of medications and their side effects was most often wanted in this group of goals. Again, there was no significant relationship between families' priorities and what was seen as the focus of therapy.

Four of the therapy goals in the questionnaire seemed related in that they would in some way improve the quality of the care givers life. In Table 7, it is shown that reduction of anxiety was an overwhelming need of these families ($n = 92$). Many fewer ($n = 65$) saw guilt as a problem, and even fewer were seeking ways to gain time for personal life. No significant relationship was found between goals of therapy and what respondents felt was achieved in therapy.

Somewhat fewer families were seeking help in changing attitudes and behaviors of other family members (Table 8). There were no significant

TABLE 4. *Personal and Professional Characteristics of Therapists*

Therapist characteristic	Poor		Adequate		Good	
	n	(%)	n	(%)	n	(%)
Provides clear, reliable information	25	(18.8)	47	(35.3)	61	(45.9)
Listens attentively/hears accurately	22	(16.8)	27	(20.6)	82	(62.6)
Encourages family to set goals	34	(27.0)	29	(23.0)	63	(50.0)
Respects families' expertise	25	(19.5)	30	(23.4)	73	(57.0)
Appreciates difficulties faced by families	27	(20.1)	36	(26.9)	7.	(53.0)
Is sympathetic to family suffering	36	(28.1)	33	(25.8)	59	(46.1)
Provides realistic hope and reassurance	29	(22.1)	49	(37.4)	53	(40.5)
Sets pace comfortable to family	26	(21.5)	40	(33.1)	55	(45.5)
Uses time in meaningful way	33	(26.2)	34	(27.0)	59	(46.8)
Apprises family of what is going on	45	(35.4)	33	(26.0)	49	(38.6)
Regards family as ally in treatment of patient	27	(21.1)	38	(29.7)	63	(49.2)

Note. ns vary due to missing data.

TABLE 5. *Understanding Mental Illness and Coping with Behavior*

Goals of therapy	Degree achieved (%)			
	None	Some	Great deal	χ^2
Learning about nature of mental illness				
Goal of families $(n = 81)$	14.8	60.5	24.7	2.26
Not a goal $(n = 28)$	25.0	60.7	14.3	
Knowing appropriate expectations of patients				
Goal of families $(n = 88)$	21.6	55.7	22.7	2.04
Not a goal $(n = 24)$	33.3	54.2	12.5	
Learning to handle threats of violence				
Goal of families $(n = 51)$	37.3	43.1	19.6	1.35
Not a goal $(n = 24)$	45.8	29.2	25.0	
Reduction of nonproductive arguments				
Goal of families $(n = 60)$	26.7	51.7	21.7	3.43
Not a goal $(n = 34)$	44.1	44.1	11.8	
Learning to motivate patients to do more				
Goal of families $(n = 86)$	44.2	38.4	17.4	1.14
Not a goal $(n = 25)$	56.0	32.0	12.0	
Getting better hygiene with patients				
Goal of families $(n = 47)$	63.8	27.7	8.5	1.05
Not a goal $(n = 26)$	53.8	30.8	15.4	
Help in control of substance abuse				
Goal of families $(n = 40)$	45.0	40.0	15.0	.87
Not a goal $(n = 19)$	57.9	31.6	10.5	

Note. ns vary due to missing data. No χ^2s significant at .05 level.

relationships between what families sought and what they got in this group of objectives.

Families' needs for linkage with other services in the community were relatively high (Table 9). Many hoped for assistance during times of crisis ($n = 80$); however, no significant relationships between goals and achievement of goals were found for either of the items in this table.

In summary, it can be stated that for none of the 21 goals for therapy was there a significant relationship between what these care givers said they wanted to accomplish and what they saw as having been accomplished. Whether something was or was not a goal for the respondent, it had the same likelihood of being a focus of therapy.

TABLE 6. *Coping with Psychiatric Symptoms and Medication*

Goals of therapy	Degree achieved (%)			χ^2
	None	Some	Great deal	
Understanding medications and their use				
Goal of families $(n = 76)$	27.6	43.4	28.9	.94
Not a goal $(n = 26)$	30.8	50.0	19.2	
Learning side effects of medication				
Goal of families $(n = 72)$	38.9	38.9	22.2	1.39
Not a goal $(n = 28)$	28.6	39.3	32.1	
Achieving compliance with medication				
Goal of families $(n = 53)$	34.0	39.6	26.4	.96
Not a goal $(n = 28)$	42.9	39.3	17.9	
Learning to respond to such psychiatric symptoms as hearing voices, talking to self, and paranoia				
Goal of families $(n = 62)$	37.1	51.6	11.3	.70
Not a goal $(n = 26)$	42.3	42.3	15.4	

Note. ns vary due to missing data. No χ^2s significant at .05 level.

TABLE 7. *Getting Supportive Help For Care Givers*

Goals of therapy	Degree achieved (%)			χ^2
	None	Some	Great deal	
Help in acceptance of the illness				
Goal of families $(n = 74)$	2.6	55.4	23.0	2.84
Not a goal $(n = 25)$	8.0	72.0	20.0	
Alleviation of guilt and blame				
Goal of families $(n = 65)$	15.4	46.2	38.5	.48
Not a goal $(n = 29)$	17.2	51.7	31.0	
Reduction of anxiety about patients				
Goal of families $(n = 92)$	25.0	55.4	19.6	2.92
Not a goal $(n = 24)$	29.2	37.5	33.3	
Gaining time for personal life				
Goal of families $(n = 45)$	24.4	53.3	22.2	.01
Not a goal $(n = 33)$	24.2	54.5	21.2	

Note. ns vary due to missing data. No χ^2s significant at .05 level.

TABLE 8. *Improving Family Relationships*

Goals of therapy	Degree achieved (%)			χ^2
	None	Some	Great deal	
Gain order and control over household				
Goal of families ($n = 60$)	31.7	43.3	25.0	1.63
Not a goal ($n = 24$)	45.9	37.5	16.7	
Reduce friction over patients' behavior				
Goal of families ($n = 69$)	33.3	46.4	20.3	.63
Not a goal ($n = 27$)	40.7	44.4	14.8	
Get acceptance of patients by siblings and/or spouses				
Goal of families ($n = 51$)	45.1	37.3	17.6	.76
Not a goal ($n = 26$)	42.3	46.2	11.5	
Get family members to share responsibility for ill persons				
Goal of families ($n = 38$)	50.0	39.5	10.5	2.25
Not a goal ($n = 31$)	64.5	22.6	12.9	

Note. ns vary due to missing data. No χ^2s significant at .05 level.

A review of all tables reveals that the five most important goals for these families were the following:

1. Reduction of anxiety about the patients ($n = 92$)
2. Understanding appropriate expectations of patients ($n = 88$)
3. Learning to motivate patients to do more ($n = 86$)

TABLE 9. *Linkage with Community Services*

Goals of therapy	Degree achieved (%)			χ^2
	None	Some	Great deal	
Assistance during crises				
Goal of families ($n = 80$)	23.7	37.5	38.7	3.83
Not a goal ($n = 25$)	44.0	28.0	28.0	
Locating resources for pateints—housing, treatment, income maintenance, etc.				
Goal of families ($n = 74$)	41.9	37.8	20.3	1.86
Not a goal ($n = 25$)	56.0	24.0	20.0	

Note. ns vary due to missing data. No χ^2s significant at .05 level.

4. Learning about the nature of mental illness ($n = 81$)
5. Assistance during times of crisis ($n = 80$)

Reduction of anxiety might presumably occur if families were better pre-pared to understand how the illness was affecting their relatives' capacities to move forward in life and if the families knew how to help them. These families needed information and skills—essentially, education—and they needed practical help during times of crisis. Therapists need to be better prepared to respond to these needs.

How well informed were these families when they selected their particular therapist or counselor? Respondents were asked if they had had prior information about their therapists before engaging them. A total of 37% said they had had no information; however, very few who had information were able to report anything very substantial. The common responses were these: "I was told it would help my son," "They said it would help me cope," or "It was *assumed* it would help me and the patient." Many families said that their therapists were chosen during times of crisis when they had little time to make inquiries; others had little choice because of financial reasons.

IMPLICATIONS FOR TREATMENT

Dropping out of treatment is a predictable outcome when clients feel that their needs are not addressed. Graziano and Fink (1973) reviewed a number of studies and reported that the rate of client dropout in general is very high, reported variously between 40 and 84%, and that dropout is the result of lack of congruence between what clients see as their needs and the perceived focus of therapy. Therapists, they noted, often attributed drop-out to lack of motivation. Borghi (1968) did home interviews with clients who terminated treatment early and again found lack of common goals a factor. Clients' primary goals were for advice, information, and suggestions. Therapists saw them as having unreal expectations. Heine and Trosman's study (1960) further supports the hypothesis that high dropout rate occurs when clients and therapists have expectations that are not compatible.

Although the issue of dropout was not specifically raised in the present study of families of the psychiatrically disabled, it is a likely phenomenon, given the low congruence between family need and professional response. Responses to open-ended questions in that study certainly indicated considerable movement from one therapist to another. A few of their comments should be noted:

> The person was only one among many professionals in connection with my daughter's illness. A few of them were very good; many were atrociously badly trained and insensitive.

> My last experience [with a professional] was excellent only because of miserable, unhelpful experiences which taught me [whom to choose].

> We came across so many people who not only do not know their jobs but give you such a run-around it is enough to drive parents crazy. That's why Dr. _____ is such a professional in his practice.

> The sad reality is, I have been to approximately 33 psychiatrists in about 15 years and profited from their services in assessing how not to treat people, mentally ill or otherwise.

With a high dropout rate of clients comes a waste of money, continued anger and frustration, and a diminished respect for the mental health community.

One way that distance between clients and professionals can be reduced, of course, is for clients to alter their goals to match those of their therapists. Dewar (1978) assigns the term "professional client" to consumers who take on their therapists' definitions of the problem and assume a relationship dependent upon and controlled by the therapists. Clients find it difficult to challenge persons thought to have knowledge, authority, and expertise. Dewar alerts therapists to possible unfortunate outcomes if this passive, subordinate posture carries over into life outside the clinic and detracts from clients' ability to be effectual family members or friends. This could be especially true when the clients are heads of households in which mentally ill persons live and in which a strong, assertive, authoritative style may be necessary in order to cope successfully.

Thus counselors are led to the conclusion that they consider restructuring their concept of a good therapeutic relationship. Coyne and Widiger (1978) favor a mutually participatory model in which responsibility for therapeutic decisions are shared and in which final judgments as to outcome are left to those who are served. Lazare, Cohen, Jacobsen, Williams, Mignone, and Zisook (1972) have conceptualized a "customer approach" to patienthood, in which the patients' requests are the starting point and initial interviews serve as a negotiating process between clients and therapists. These writers report a strong resistance to using a customer approach on the part of clinicians, who may feel that clients cannot formulate their own needs and that therefore it is irresponsible to ask clients what they want; it is tantamount to turning over authority for treatment to the clients. Probably even more of a deterrent, note Lazare *et al.*, is that clinicians are afraid that Pandora's box will be opened and clients will make a host of demands that cannot be met. Nevertheless, they believe, the customer approach has the potential for better client satisfaction and staff morale.

It is the contention of this chapter that a new approach to working with families of the mentally ill, and thus new curricula and different training, are needed. Before appropriate curricula, can be developed however, a better knowledge base needs to be created. Therapists need to know more about families.

IMPLICATIONS FOR RESEARCH AND TRAINING

What is reliably known about families and mentally ill persons—what are they up against, how do the problems present themselves, and how do they cope? Stierlin (1974) presents a synthesis of family theory as a basis for understanding families of schizophrenics. He enthusiastically supports family theory and thinks it may represent a paradigmatic shift in the way therapists think about people. However, as one reviews his chapter and notes his perceptions of families only in terms of their wide variety of deficits, one wonders how families will respond to seeing themselves from Stierlin's viewpoint; how likely it is that good therapeutic relationships can be developed; and how probable it is that families will receive what they need to cope successfully.

Since Stierlin incorporates into his work the theories of the major family therapists, one can see how families of schizophrenics have been viewed over the last couple of decades. These families have "family bonds which are restrictive, impoverished, and stereotyped" and their relationships are characterized by "pseudomutuality" and "pseudohostility." Their "exchanges are tediously monotonous and predictable" and their "roles appeared unduly rigid and fixed." The mother is an "overadequate, self-sacrificing martyr"; "the father, the underadequate irresponsible squanderer." They seem to treat boys more like girls and girls more like boys and therefore appear to have "homosexual leanings." He further reports that "one member's 'sickness' is instrumental to the other member's survival," and that they "mystify their offspring and invalidate them." It might occur to the reader that the language quoted here tends to mystify and invalidate the very families therapists intend to help. Furthermore, no evidence is offered to support any of the contentions made.

What are evident here are the limitations that accrue when observations are made in the artificial social context of the clinic or office. There the therapist controls the situation, manipulates the participants, and places restraints on the options for response. There is little attention to representativeness. In the natural setting of the community, persons create their own social worlds, but in the clinic and laboratory, conditions are created to fulfill a therapist's particular theoretical point of view. It is time to seek new directions for research and training. The following ideas may be worthy of consideration as precursors to new theories and new approaches to families.

PARTICIPANT OBSERVATION

As an alternative to the clinic and laboratory, studies of families should be done *in situ*. Notes Baumrind (1980), "Only under conditions where individuals are observed in characteristic contexts and where naturally occurring constraints are at work on the selection and construction of these contexts can enduring personality and behavioral traits be measured" (p. 651). Researchers, then, need to utilize the technique of participant observation, which involves direct, structured observations in the naturalistic setting of the home. The validity of such findings can be high if variables are embedded in a theoretical framework (Kerlinger, 1973). Of course, there are difficulties with the approach that would have to be overcome. There must be a willingness of subjects to be observed, and there is concern that the observer's presence might alter the situation. Kerlinger says there is evidence to show that observers have little impact after the initial adjustment. More important are the skills observers bring to bear, their objectivity, and, more important, their capacity to make useful inferences from what they see. Technical means for the successful application of observational techniques have advanced appreciably in the last 10 to 20 years.

COPING AND ADAPTATION AS A THEORETICAL FRAMEWORK

Most of the studies reported on the study of family coping lack a theoretical framework that could assist researchers in formulating questions and interpreting findings. The theory of coping and adaptation has been found useful in studying families facing a variety of painful and difficult circumstances (Mechanic, 1974; Parad & Caplan, 1965; Rapoport, 1965; White, 1974). It seems appropriate for studying families of the mentally ill, who are facing highly taxing situations that are similar to the impact of other catastrophic events, such as life-threatening illnesses, mental retardation, and other handicapping conditions. The theory of coping and adaptation has recently appeared in the literature of the mentally ill (Hatfield, 1981; Marcus, 1977).

"Coping" is the problem-solving effort made by individuals when the demands they face are highly relevant to their welfare and tax their adaptive capacities (White, 1974). It is an attempt to deal with a fairly drastic change in life that defies familiar ways of behaving, requires the production of new behavior, and gives rise to uncomfortable affect such as anxiety, guilt, and despair (Rapoport, 1974). Success in adaptation depends on the severity of external demands and a person's resources for dealing with them. Mechanic (1974) contrasts this way of viewing persons with that of ego psychologists and psychodynamically oriented researchers, who view humans as reactive and their mode primarily intrapsychic.

Healthy crisis resolution, according to Rapoport (1965), involves cognitive perception of the situation, management of affect, and development of patterns for seeking and using help. Three main factors must be assessed if therapists are to help: (1) situational dimensions (i.e., what is going on in a complex situation); (2) personal dimensions (i.e., the individual's strengths, way of managing affect, and resources for need satisfaction); and (3) dimensions of social support (i.e., either the natural community of family and friends or professional supports).

For those steeped in the tradition that families are pathogenic, a new perspective is hard to accept. Marcus (1979) indicates what is involved in the new viewpoint: (1) The focus is on developing competencies and coping skills; (2) the approach is pragmatic and addresses tangible problems in a realistic way; (3) strategies are adapted to the families' ways of coping; and (4) attitudinal barriers between families and professionals must be removed. These barriers he identifies as judgmentalism toward families' values and customs; failure to recognize ineffective management as the result of responding to unusual situations; and failure to respect families as experts on their own members.

AN EDUCATIONAL APPROACH TO FAMILIES

Somehow families must become prepared to deal with an array of ongoing, highly difficult problems if a modicum of normal family life in the face of mental illness is to be preserved. For this they need knowledge and skills— that is, education. Professionals are not now adequately trained to do the job that must be done. Attention must be given to a new model of service; for that, training institutions must be rethinking curriculum.

First of all is the necessity for clarifying conceptual models. The idea of therapy fits a medical model, and as Guerney, Stollack, and Guerney (1971) note, educational and medical models differ in several ways:

1. *The goal in the educational model is not healing or curing symptoms, but, rather, teaching skills that the recipient can apply in solving present and future problems.* Since the emphasis is on learning how to do something that is transferable to many situations, there is an efficiency in this approach—important in this period of dwindling resources. The em-

phasis in therapy, and in the medical model, is on solving the presenting problem, with no certainty that there will be carryover to other situations.

2. *Educators are up front about what they are doing.* The assumptions and values by which they are guided are overt rather than covert. It has been noted that families in the study described in this chapter felt they were not apprised of what was going on. Therapists using a medical model make an assumption of universal values; thus they do not see the need of making them explicit.

3. *The medical model uses a case orientation and deals with individuals; the educational model results in a program that is suitable for the widest range of students.* Attention to individual students is provided as needed.

4. *The role of assessment is different in the two models.* In the educational model, there is not diagnosis; the assumption is ignorance. The instructor has the knowledge and skill to overcome the deficit. What caused the deficit does not matter.

5. *There is less stigma attached to psychotherapy in an educational model.* Terms such as "pathology," "diagnosis," and "therapy" are resisted. An educational model will have greater public acceptance, little embarrassment, and less resistance.

6. *It is easier to measure outcome in an educational model.* When knowledge is the goal, it can be measured. Much of psychotherapy research has been criticized because it lacks criteria for measurement of outcome. The criteria used all too often for clinical judgments are subjective, and the situations being studied cannot be replicated.

MODELS OF EDUCATIONAL APPROACHES

One of the earlier models of practical help to families was reported by Pasamanick, Scarpetti, and Dinitz (1967), who set up a home care program in which nurses were made available to families on a 24-hour basis. They found themselves much depended upon to provide help in management of difficult behavior, as well as in advising about responses to symptomatology and a host of other problems. They predicted that "when a community mental health center emerges, it is safe to assume that this function of 'educating' families will become a vital and integral part of the worker's role" (p. 75). In a follow-up study of that project (Davis, Dinitz, & Pasamanick, 1974), extensive regression of patients occurred when the support money ended and the comprehensive support program was withdrawn. In spite of these findings, little knowledge of family education is yet provided.

Good models of educational approaches are more abundant from those who work with younger children. The concept and methodology might be adaptable to those that work with older persons. Graziano (1974) stressed the importance of families as cotherapists. He noted the need for a valid body of knowledge as the basis for practical reality-oriented training for parents. This will happen, he felt, only with a strong consumer advocacy movement, for the profession on its own will not develop better programs. A strong consumer movement is now appearing on the horizon, as I note later in this chapter, so this contention of Graziano will soon be tested.

The TEACCH model in North Carolina is a well-developed strategy for working with families of highly disturbed children. Their emphasis, as reported by Marcus, Schopler, Lansing, and Logie (1979), is on developing competencies and coping skills; it is a pragmatic approach in which the clinician adapts strategies to fit a family's style of coping. They operate under the assumption that families are the experts on their children and that clinicians should avoid a judgmental attitude. There must be an awareness of all the demands on a family—economic, social, and emotional.

There are a few educational programs for families of the mentally ill that show much promise. A successful combination of supportive and educational services to families in a multiple family group setting has been reported by Anderson, Hogarty, and Reiss (1980). Their goals were to present information, enhance coping skills, eliminate wrong ideas, and establish networks. The rationales behind their various approaches were well-delineated. The conceptual model appeared to be a blend of educational and medical models. No outcome data for families have yet been published.

Kanter (1980) has developed a behavioral model for aiding families of the mentally ill in which unusually specific coping behavior is outlined. He has drawn upon his long experience in working with patients in day care settings and translated his observations into techniques that can be useful to parents. He advocates that families identify behaviors that are most annoying to them and for which they have the motivation and energy to carry through a consistent approach to the elimination of the undesirable behavior.

Creer (1978) believes that strategies with each family have to be devised individually, since the extent of present knowledge is so limited. Families, she feels, learn a great deal through trial and error; from this, social workers can build up a body of knowledge to pass on to others. Wing (1978) feels that the counselor needs to know as much about the disability as does the family in order to help, but this is rather unrealistic at this time, he notes, for few counselors are appropriately trained.

It is surprising that there has been little useful material written specifically for families to explain mental illness to them, to provide them with practical management skills, and to direct them toward the kinds of community resources that are available. In that respect Clara Park's book, *You*

Are Not Alone (1976), is one of a kind and illustrates what could be done. Writing from the viewpoint of a parent with a disabled child, she is able to convey the experience through the eyes of one who has dealt with a problem and to offer a perspective as to how families might increase their effectiveness. "What are we to do now?," she notes, is not a desperate question but a practical one. Families should ask it daily, for each day is composed of action, and doing one small thing rather than another is what matters. Further, she says, the question should be asked of professionals who serve families, and it should be expected that they learn to find answers.

IMPETUS FOR CHANGE

If real change is to occur for those caring for the psychiatrically disabled in their role as consumers, it will come about because strong cultural forces develop and support the more progressive attitudes within the mental health profession. Or, as Kessen (1979) notes in describing psychology as a conservative discipline, "Psychology follows culture but often at a discreet distance" (p. 819). Professional attitudes toward and perceptions of the feminine role changed dramatically when the feminist movement developed and women refused to accept the definitions of themselves created by a male-dominated culture and reflected in the psychiatric literature. Homosexuality provides another example; "pathology" changed to "sexual preference" when gays took to the streets.

Even closer to the issue of mental illness is the shift in thinking about autism. Autism was first identified by psychiatric professionals; thus it was defined as a psychiatric illness, and little progress was made in correcting it. Ritvo (1976) credits Fenichel with advocating a break with the deep-rooted official doctrine that psychotherapy is the prescription of choice for autism, and he credits Rimland with intensive efforts to get rid of the "noxious parent" label. The National Society for Autistic Children has taken the position that autism should not be defined as an emotional disorder and that a good educational environment is the most effective treatment. A great deal depends on who has the power to define the problem.

It should not come as a surprise to the mental health community, then, that consumer advocacy groups of families of mentally ill persons are springing up all over the country. What is unusual is the rapidity with which the movement has spread—indicative, it appears, of a deep discontent now finding long overdue expression. With its beginnings only 3 or 4 years ago, the movement has grown to 150 groups with an involvement of over 6000 persons (at a conservative estimate). In September 1979, about 100 of such groups came together to form the National Alliance for the Mentally Ill.

Herbert Pardes, director of the Institute for Mental Health and guest speaker at that meeting, noted that the Alliance was formed in an ideal time—a time in which there is much impetus for change; he predicted that this would indeed be viewed as a new force on the mental health scene (*Advocacy for Persons with Chronic Mental Illness*, 1980). Lamb and Oliphant (1979) anticipate that the mental health profession will be increasingly affected by the new consumer advocacy movement. It may appear threatening, given the accelerated pace at which theories, actions, expertise, and priorities of professionals and efficiency of service delivery are being questioned. Such questioning will empower formerly helpless care givers and lead to a useful redefinition of problems.

Through the National Alliance for the Mentally Ill, advocacy and consumer education will come together as a powerful force for change, for consumer education can arm individuals with the knowledge and the self-confidence needed to make choices that can increase individual satisfaction, marketplace efficiency, and the public good. Consumer education can make a difference between marketplace exploitation and fair competition, and, according to Willett (1977), is an agent of change on the model of the civil rights and women's movements. It is a means of insuring that laws are obeyed and policies enforced.

In the general marketplace, various means are used to inform potential consumers of the merits and availability of a product and to do some periodic accounting. Progressive organizations continually monitor the market for indications of a need to modify the product. Mental health providers have sought little consumer information, have monitored the market infrequently, and therefore have lagged in new service development (Hornstra, Lubin, Lewis, & Willis, 1972). A vigorous consumer movement should eventually change much of that.

It might occur to one to ask why there has been such a lag in vocal consumerism in the field of mental health service. Gartner (1979) explains that in using the services of the "doing good profession," it has been thought unnecessary to take a stance of "buyer beware." Discussion of fees has been considered taboo; therefore, price comparisons are impossible. Furthermore, there are often no real alternatives; in most places there is a virtual monopoly in the provision of mental health services.

Mental health providers have helping people as their goal; therefore, there has been little demand for accountability. Enlightened consumers must come to recognize that service providers have political interests that are masked by their "caring role." Behind these masks are services, their systems, techniques, and technologies, writes McKnight (1977) in a recent issue of *Social Policy*. They are businesses in need of markets; an economy seeking new growth potential; professionals in need of an income. Further, he says that the masks of love and care obscure the critical political issues of modernized societies: the necessity to manufacture needs to meet the needs of professionals.

These facts are not necessarily bad, as long as they are recognized for what they are and consumers are able to deal with professionals on an equal footing. Consumers must retain for themselves a right to help define the problems and an expectation that professionals cease their mystification of problems by using language incomprehensible to the average citizen. That professionals have their legitimate needs is granted; this points to McKnight's recommendation that there be research effort toward understanding the legitimate, specific needs of professionals.

With the growth of the consumer movement, families of mentally ill persons will see themselves as "customers" who as a matter of personal rights and good economics will insist on knowing the nature of the service they are purchasing, evidence as to its effectiveness, and projected costs, so they can take their business where it best suits them. Gerald Klerman, former chief of the Alcohol, Drug Abuse, and Mental Health Administration, addressing the annual meeting of the American Psychological Association in 1979, predicted that with the growth of the consumer movement, there will be a climate that demands more than custom as a justification for reimbursement. Good intentions and testimonials of experts are not enough, he said; "only evidence as to outcome will suffice in the rigorous climate of consumerism and mental health insurance coverage" (*APA Monitor*, 1979).

Consumer groups may further their cause by insisting that professional organizations live up to their own statements of ethical principles. Historically, ethical codes were developed by professional organizations to protect professionals from regulation by outside agencies. In doing so, they made a commitment to promote the welfare of their patients and assure their rights (Hare-Mustin, Marecek, Kaplan, & Liss-Levinson, 1979). Ethical principles of the American Psychological Association, they point out, require that clients be provided with sufficient information to make informed choices regarding (1) procedures, goals, and possible side effects of therapy; (2) the qualifications, policies, and practices of therapists; and (3) available sources of help other than therapy. There was little evidence from the 138 families in the study reported earlier in this chapter that much attention is given to these ethical principles.

Further support for the need for consumers to get involved comes from Miller, Brodsky, and Bleechmore (1976) as they state; "Those whose business is service to the public must be prepared to answer to the public. Any operation or even entire profession, acting for long without external scrutiny tends to develop expedient idiosyncratic procedures of possible detriment to the public" (p. 277). Hare-Mustin *et al.* (1979) recommend that training foster an image of clients as powerful, responsible adults and inculcate in professionals a sense of responsibility for clients' rights and dignity.

Will the psychiatric community pay any attention to these admonitions to heed the consumer? Beels (1978) answers this question by predicting that it is politically inevitable that it do so. The politics and economics of psychiatry are such that it cannot ignore either the government's requirement for community boards, the disillusionment of former clients, or recent press activity. "The public," he notes "simply does not trust us to run things anymore" (p. 519).

SUMMARY AND CONCLUSIONS

New treatment modalities for persons with mental illness have brought the family into the picture as the primary care-giving institution. Families, in turn, are turning to mental health professionals for assistance in becoming more effective care givers for their disturbed relatives and in coping with the many problems that develop. Professionals are not now prepared to provide families with appropriate help, as is evidenced by the findings of little congruence between what families want from therapy and what they get. This calls for a new look at training and at the theory and research upon which training is based. This is a propitious time for change. Many of the articles cited in this chapter indicate considerable restlessness within the professions, and there is a strong voice outside the professions in the rapidly developing consumer movement that is beginning to articulate its desires for new directions.

REFERENCES

Advocacy for persons with chronic mental illness: Building a nationwide network. Proceedings of a National Conference. The Wisconsin Center, Madison, Wis.: National Alliance for the Mentally Ill, 1980.

APA Monitor. Klerman challenges professions to prove therapy works. December 1979, p. 1.

Anderson, C., Hogarty, G., & Reiss, D. Family treatment of adult schizophrenic patients: A research-based psychoeducational approach. *Schizophrenia Bulletin*, 1980, 6, 490–505.

Baumrind, D. New directions in socialization research. *American Psychologist*, 35, 639–651, 1980.

Beels, C. C. Social networks, the family, and the schizophrenic patient. *Schizophrenia Bulletin*, 1978, 4, 512–520.

Borghi, J. H. Premature psychotherapy and patient–therapist relationship. *American Journal of Psychotherapy*, 1968, 22, 460–473.

Coyne, J. C., & Widiger, T. A. Towards a participatory model of psychotherapy. *Professional Psychology*, 1978 9, 700–710.

Creer, C. Social work with patients and their families. In J. Wing (Ed.), *Schizophrenia: Toward a new synthesis.* New York: Grune & Stratton, 1978.

Davis, A., Dinitz, S., & Pasamanick, B. *Schizophrenia in the new custodial community.* Columbus: Ohio State University Press, 1974.

Debuskey, M. (Ed.). *The chronically ill child and his family.* Springfield, Ill.: Charles C Thomas, 1970.

Dewar, T. R. The professionalization of the client. *Social Policy,* 1978, *8,* 4–9.

Doll, W. Family coping with the mentally ill: An unanticipated problem of deinstitutionalization. *Hospital and Community Psychiatry,* 1976, *27,* 183–185.

Evans, A., Bullard, D., & Solomon, M. The family as a potential resource in the rehabilitation of the chronic schizophrenic patient: A study of 60 patients and their families. *American Journal of Psychology,* 1961, *117,* 1075–1083.

Freeman, H., & Simmons, O. *The mental patient comes home.* New York: Wiley, 1963.

Gartner, A. Consumers in the service society. In A. Gartner, C. Greer, & F. Reissman (Eds.), *Consumer education in the human services.* New York: Pergamon Press, 1979.

Graziano, A. *Child without tomorrow.* New York: Pergamon Press, 1974.

Graziano, A. M., & Fink, R. S. Second-order effects in mental health treatment. *Journal of Consulting and Clinical Psychology,* 1973, *40,* 356–364.

Guerney, B., Stollack, G., & Guerney, L. The practicing psychologist as educator: An alternative to the medical practitioner model. *Professional Psychology,* 1971, *3,* 276–282.

Hare-Mustin, R., Marecek, J., Kaplan, A., & Liss-Levinson, N. Rights of clients, responsibilities of therapists. *American Psychologist,* 1979, *34,* 3–16.

Hatfield, A. Psychological costs of schizophrenia to the family. *Social Work,* 1978, *23,* 355–359.

Hatfield, A. Help-seeking behavior in families of schizophrenics. *American Journal of Community Psychology,* 1979, *7,* 563–569.

Hatfield, A. Coping effectiveness in families of the mentally ill: An exploratory study. *Journal of Psychiatric Treatment and Evaluation,* 1981, *3,* 11–19.

Heine, R., & Trosman, H. Initial expectations of the doctor–patient interaction as a factor in continuance in psychotherapy. *Psychiatry,* 1960, *23,* 275–278.

Holden, D., & Lewine, R. *Families of schizophrenic individuals: An evaluation of mental health professionals, resources, and the effects of schizophrenia.* Chicago: Illinois State Psychiatric Institute, 1979.

Hornstra, R., Lubin, B., Lewis, R., & Willis, B. Worlds apart: Patients and professionals. *Archives of General Psychiatry,* 1972, *27,* 872–883.

Kanter, J. *Coping strategies for families of the mentally ill.* Paper presented at Threshold: Alliance for the Mentally Ill, Bethesda, Md., November 10, 1980.

Kerlinger, F. *Foundations of behavioral research* (22nd ed.). New York: Holt, Rinehart & Winston, 1973.

Kessen, W. The American child and other cultural inventions. *American Psychologist,* 1979, *34,* 815–820.

Kreisman, D., & Joy, V. Family response to the illness of a relative: A review of the literature. *Schizophrenia Bulletin,* 1974, *10,* 34–57.

Kreisman, D., Simmons, S., & Joy, V. *Deinstitutionalization and the family's well-being.* New York: New York State Psychiatric Institute, 1979.

Lamb, H. Empathy and advice: Counseling families of the mentally ill. *Behavioral Medicine,* 1979, *6*(9), 35–38.

Lamb, H., & Oliphant, E. Schizophrenia through the eyes of families. *Hospital and Community Psychiatry,* 1978, *29*(12), 805–806.

Lazare, A., Cohen, F., Jacobsen, A., Williams, M., Mignone, R., & Zisook, S. The walk-in patient as a "customer": A key dimension in evaluation and treatment. *American Journal of Orthopsychiatry*, 1972, *42*, 872–883.

Marcus, L. Patterns of coping families of psychotic children. *American Journal of Orthopsychiatry*, 1977, *47*, 388–398.

Marcus, L., Schopler, E., Lansing, M., & Logie, C. *Collaborating with parents of autistic children to enhance coping strategies.* Paper presented at the 56th annual meeting of the American Orthopsychiatric Association, Washington, D.C., 1979.

McKnight, J. The professional service business. *Social Policy*, 1977, *8*, 110–116.

Mechanic, D. Social structure and personal adaptation: Some neglected dimensions. In G. Coelho, D. Hamburg, & J. Adams (Eds.), *Coping and adaptation.* New York: Basic Books, 1974.

Miller, H., Brodsky, S., & Bleechmore, J. F. Patients' rights: Who's wrong? The changing role of the mental health professional. *Professional Psychiatry*, 1976, *7*, 274–276.

Parad, H., & Caplan, G. A framework for studying families in crisis. In H. Parad (Ed.), *Crisis intervention: Selected readings.* New York: Family Services Association of America, 1965.

Park, C. C., with L. N. Shapiro, *You are not alone.* Boston: Little, Brown, 1976.

Pasamanick, B., Scarpetti, F., & Dinitz, S. *Schizophrenics in the community.* New York: Appleton-Century-Crofts, 1967.

Rapoport, L. The state of crisis: Some theoretical considerations. In H. Parad (Ed.), *Crisis intervention: Selected readings.* New York: Family Services Association of America, 1965.

Ritvo, E. Primary responsibility: With whom should it rest? In E. Ritvo (Ed.), *Autism: Diagnosis, current research, and management.* New York: Spectrum, 1976.

Stierlin, H. Family theory: An introduction. In A. Burton (Ed.), *Operational theories of personality.* New York: Brunner/Mazel, 1974.

Task Panel Reports (2 vols.). Reports submitted to the President's Commission on Mental Health. Washington, D.C.: U.S. Government Printing Office, 1978.

Thompson, E., Doll, W., & Lefton, M. *Some affective dimensions of familial coping with the mentally ill.* Paper presented at the 54th annual meeting of the American Orthopsychiatric Association, New York, April 13–17, 1977.

Travis, G. *Chronic illness in children: Its impact on child and family.* Stanford, Calif.: Standford University Press, 1976.

Uzoka, A. The myth of the nuclear family: Historical background and clinical implications. *American Psychologist*, 1979, *34*, 1095–1106.

White, R. Strategies of adaptation: An attempt at systematic description. In G. Coelho, D. Hamburg, & J. Adams (Eds.), *Coping and adaptation.* New York: Basic Books, 1974.

Willett, S. Consumer education or advocacy—or both? *Social Policy*, 1977, *8*, 2–8.

Wing, J. The management of schizophrenia. In J. Wing (Ed.), *Schizophrenia: Towards a new synthesis.* New York: Grune & Stratton, 1978.

II
THE PSYCHOEDUCATIONAL APPROACHES

3

STAGES AND IMPACT OF CRISIS-ORIENTED FAMILY THERAPY IN THE AFTERCARE OF ACUTE SCHIZOPHRENIA

Hal S. Kopeikin
Valerie Marshall
Michael J. Goldstein

Aftercare is critically important in the contemporary treatment of acute schizophrenia. Hospitalization has been traditionally utilized in managing this disorder, and the hospital continues to be the initial setting for intervention. However, current practices afford inpatient care a limited role: Patients are hospitalized only until their most florid and debilitating symptoms subside, usually in 1 to 3 weeks. Discharged as soon as a partial restitution is achieved, they typically return to the community in a moderately symptomatic and fragilely integrated state. Outpatient aftercare services are then provided, commonly consisting of both psychosocial and pharmacological treatments. Aftercare is intended to protect the patient from clinical regression during reentry into the community, and to facilitate the gradual process of recovery. Thus, aftercare currently assumes the major role in rehabilitating acute schizophrenics.

This chapter describes the results of a controlled clinical trial with an experimental aftercare program. The program comprised 6 weeks of outpatient psychological and pharmacological treatment. It was conducted immediately after the patients—predominantly young first-admission schizophrenics—were discharged from a brief period of inpatient care in a community mental health center. First we describe the treatments, explaining their rationale and content. A discussion of research results

HAL S. KOPEIKIN, VALERIE MARSHALL, and MICHAEL J. GOLDSTEIN. Department of Psychology, University of California, Los Angeles, Los Angeles, California.

69

follows, emphasizing the outcome of treatment and how it may be optimized for particular patients.

OVERVIEW OF THE AFTERCARE PROGRAM

The aftercare program was developed through the collaboration of UCLA and the Ventura County Mental Health Center in Ventura, California. The purpose of our collaboration was to design, implement, and evaluate a state-of-the-art aftercare treatment for acute schizophrenia. Research and clinical experience guided formulation of the program.

The need for improving aftercare was disturbingly clear. Approximately one out of every two schizophrenics deteriorates to the point of rehospitalization within half a year of discharge from inpatient care (Taube, 1974); this national statistic was comparable to the 6-month relapse rate of 42% in Ventura County (Evans, Goldstein, & Rodnick, 1973). Existing aftercare services were unable to prevent a series of relapses and short, incomplete recompensations—a pattern that largely precludes social and personal reintegration.

Additional statistics collected in Ventura County revealed that the highest risk of relapse occurred during the 6 weeks following discharge. During this period, 31% of schizophrenic patients require rehospitalization (Evans, Rodnick, Goldstein, & Judd, 1972). It was therefore concluded that aftercare should begin immediately upon release from inpatient treatment, last at least 6 weeks, and deal directly with the stressors definable within this high-risk period.

The events that transpire in the 6 weeks after hospitalization prompted the development of a crisis-oriented family therapy. The return of residually symptomatic schizophrenics to relatives ultimately responsible for their care poses serious adjustment problems for both. Coping with these problems is exceedingly important, since family environment has been found to be a potent influence on the course of schizophrenia (Brown, Birley, & Wing, 1972; Vaughn & Leff, 1976). Hence, a brief problem-focused therapy was designed to help patients and their families cope with stresses of the hospital-to-home transition.

Medication was also included in the aftercare program, since pharmacological support has been found to offer significant protection against short-term regression (Hogarty, Goldberg, & Schooler, 1975; Hogarty & Ulrich, 1977; Schooler, Levine, Severe, Brauzer, DiMascio, Klerman, & Tuason, 1980). It was expected that combining the crisis-oriented family therapy with drug treatment would yield greater returns than either could individually.

CRISIS-ORIENTED FAMILY THERAPY

Crisis-oriented family therapy was designed to support acute schizophrenics and their families during the difficult period of social reimmersion. Typically leaving the hospital in a state of partial remission, patients are especially vulnerable to the inevitable tensions of returning to a family recently disrupted by a psychotic breakdown. Other family members are also under considerable duress and may find it hard to support the patient. First they have had to cope with the decompensation of a relative and often suffer guilt over provoking it; now, they must bear the responsibility of caring for a residually symptomatic schizophrenic. The potential for conflict is high, as is the patient's vulnerability to it.

Crisis-oriented family therapy attempts to manage the potentially disruptive events of this period effectively and to minimize stress for the patient. During the high-risk postdischarge period, the patient and family members meet with a therapist, in six weekly sessions, for shared problem solving. The sessions primarily concentrate on current circumstances that participants identify as particularly stressful to the patient. Treatment is directed toward identifying problematic situations, avoiding them when possible, and assuaging the destructive impact of them when they occur. Thus, the therapy is brief, concrete, and problem-focused.

Although the topics addressed in therapy vary considerably, dictated by the particular needs of each family, two foci are initially appropriate in the majority of cases. The first is that of unrealistic expectations about the length of recovery. Usually expectations are overly positive: The patient or relatives may believe that work and school should be resumed almost immediately. Such expectations translate into demands exceeding the patient's functional capacity, jeopardizing stability, and leading the patient and relatives to anger and hopelessness when failure is encountered. Occasionally, there is unwarranted pessimism about the patient's long-term prospects, leading to despair and resignation. In both cases, the therapist must help in setting modest short-term expectations while bolstering hope for the long term.

Patients and relatives are informed from the start that full recovery often takes 6 months to a year, and that premature pressure on patients can be gravely counterproductive. Frequently, this theme requires reiteration over the course of treatment. To minimize discouragement, the therapist can highlight progress from week to week, however slight it may be. The concept of the "internal yardstick" suggested by Anderson, Meisel, and Houpt (1975) can be helpful in sensitizing patients and families to small increments of progress.

The need to correct unrealistic expectations is illustrated in the case of Mark. This patient's parents found it very difficult to accept the fact that Mark slept for much of the day and, when awake, stayed close to home. The therapist had to remind the parents and the patient repeatedly that this was normal and necessary for a fragile and medicated schizophrenic in the early phases of recovery.

MRS. S: Mark still sleeps the whole day. He never goes out and he's always tired.

THERAPIST: Well, very often after hospitalization like this, people tend to sleep an awful lot. It's important for them to be calm and quiet and take good care of themselves. So his sleeping is a good sign. How do you feel about it, Mark?

MARK: I'm just not ready to go out. I get too nervous.

THERAPIST: You feel you need more time to just relax.

MRS. S: But I think it's important for him to see people again.

MARK: Well, I went to day treatment this week. I saw people then.

THERAPIST: So you went to day treatment. That's really a positive step! Last week you didn't want to go anywhere.

A second topic in therapy is each participant's experience of the events leading up to and during the schizophrenic decompensation. We have found that therapists rarely inquire about the subjective reactions of patients and their families to these events. Hence, important feelings are neglected, while the breakdown is often perceived as shameful. Discussion of the schizophrenic episode desensitizes family members to the behavioral manifestations of florid psychosis, allowing them to acknowledge odd behavior exhibited by the patient. Open conversation also permits the treatment participants to validate their perceptions of specific symptomatology, helping them recognize the signs of an incipient breakdown should future regressions occur. Of primary importance, though, are the feelings of empathy and relief for both patients and relatives that grow from sharing what had been confusing, frightening, and commonly alienating experiences. These points are illustrated by the case of Steve, who described an intensely emotional experience that he had previously been too ashamed and confused to discuss.

STEVE: I was waiting in the airport to go to Vietnam and I couldn't stand it. I started shaking and I couldn't breathe and I couldn't think.

THERAPIST: That sounds so frightening. You must have been in a panic. That happens some times when people are really afraid.

STEVE: Yeah, um . . . (crying) . . . Well, I saw this Oriental girl and I . . .

um . . . couldn't stop thinking about her and I went to the bathroom and I wouldn't come out. I started to masturbate and I just kept getting more and more frightened. They [the military police] came to get me and I wouldn't leave (*still crying*). This is so hard for me to say. I don't want to talk about it any more.

THERAPIST: I know it must be so hard. But there are times when it's important for you to talk about it. When terrifying things happen, sometimes we do things that we wouldn't ordinarily do. Going to Vietnam is a very frightening thing.

MOTHER: It's all right, Steve. You have to let it out.

STEVE: I didn't want to tell you.

MOTHER: It's okay. I'm glad you told me. I never knew what you went through (*crying*).

As this dialogue shows, discussion can help the family appreciate the full impact of stress on the patient and often fosters a more empathetic, supportive set.

Exploration of the psychotic break also serves to prepare the family for the remainder of treatment. Relatives often gain awareness of how severe the patient's disturbance really is, an awareness that can be utilized in setting more realistic expectations regarding the course of recovery. Beyond recognizing that the patient really does need help, family members often realize the importance of their role in assisting the patient. Sometimes family members are maintaining the patient's psychotic behavior, and this must be understood before it can be corrected. The case of Mary is instructive. At the time of her decompensation, Mary came to believe she was a werewolf. Although this belief was abandoned during her hospitalization, it had begun to recur when she returned home. Mary's mother disclosed that she used to bring home books on the subject, at Mary's request. She also stated that Mary recently asked her to visit the library and bring home another book on werewolves. The therapist responded by gently exploring the subject, supporting the mother's desire to please her daughter, but agreeing that the request might be harmful. He then invited Mary and her mother to consider what other types of books were interesting but did not run the risk of upsetting Mary.

Perhaps most significantly, exploration of the psychosis usually reveals connections between stressful events and decompensation. Directing attention to stressors that precipitated the breakdown, the therapist explains that stress may trigger psychotic episodes. Parenthetically, when a family member is part of a precipitating event, it is imperative that the event and not the relative be labeled the stressor, thus avoiding unnecessary blame and guilt. In discussing the potential for stress to exacerbate schizophrenia, the value of preventing and adequately coping with stress is introduced. Finally, the therapist briefly explains the treatment rationale of improving stress management to promote recovery and avert regressions. The family is also informed that the remainder of therapy will be devoted to identifying, preventing, and coping with situations stressful for the patient.

After the preliminary work of (1) suggesting realistic recovery expectations, (2) exploring the psychosis, and (3) explicating the rationale for stress control, crisis-oriented family therapy turns to managing the patient's stress. A four-objective treatment model guides the conduct of sessions. Briefly, the objectives involve (1) identifying the two or three current, most hazardous stressors threatening the patient; (2) developing strategies to prevent stress and cope with it; (3) having families implement the strategies, evaluate them, and refine them; (4) engaging in anticipatory planning to prevent and cope with future stresses. These objectives are pursued sequentially, with the latter activities dependent on those previously accomplished.

We found that the number of sessions devoted to each objective varied from case to case, with an average of 1.5 sessions per objective. In retrospect, six sessions were clearly not enough for some patients. For these reasons, we describe the progression of therapeutic activities instead of offering a session-by-session account of treatment.

Objective 1: Identifying Stressors
The initial objective of identifying situations stressful to the patient is pursued in three steps. First, each participant is asked to list current circumstances that subject the patient to stress. Second, these stressors are briefly discussed, leading to agreement on the two or three most threatening to the patient's stability. Finally, the most threatening stressors are explored in detail, yielding specific and concrete descriptions of each stressor. These two or three stressors subsequently become the focus of therapy.

The identification of stressors often begins with considering whether problems that precipitated the schizophrenic episode are still creating difficulty. Precipitating stressors are first explored because of their apparent capacity for disruption. They may also serve as vivid examples of the kind of situations therapy participants are expected to identify. After determining whether precipitating factors remain problematic, each participant is encouraged to identify other situations that threaten the patient now or in the immediate future. Patients and their relatives commonly respond by mentioning broad and general problems: Pervasive patient–relative conflict, job or school concerns, drug abuse, and religious cult involvement exemplify the sorts of stressors frequently noted.

The next step is discussing each stressor, with the purpose of determining which pose the greatest risk of disrupting the patient's stability. The discussion is initiated with an explanation that each problem will be briefly explored to assess its potential disruptiveness. When examining stressors, the probability both of occurrence and potential destructiveness merits consideration. After each stressor has been discussed, the therapist asks participants to reach a consensus on which two or three are most hazardous for the patient. Therapists must occasionally take an active role in helping families reach a consensus, especially in cases were cooperation or communication is poor and the readiness for conflict is great. We believe that agreement on the most threatening stressors is an important foundation for the subsequent work of shared problem solving.

The final task is obtaining specific, detailed descriptions of the selected stressors. Initial formulations of problems tend to be quite global. Subsequent treatment activities require more precise, concrete descriptions. Explaining this, the therapist requests detailed accounts of the two or three stressors. All family members are encouraged to share in elaborating on the stressors, redefining general problems into scenarios that detail potentially disruptive stress events. Before moving on, the following information about a stress event is gathered when possible: Who is involved? What, where, when, and how does the situation occur? Frequently, patients and relatives are quick to criticize and blame one another during these discussions. This can be exceedingly destructive and must be avoided. Often, family members need assistance in learning to express requests and opinions without criticism and blaming, as the case of Tim demonstrates.

MRS. T: One major problem is that Tim never cleans up his room. It looks like a pigsty and he lives just like a pig. I can't stand it. He is just (*interrupted*).

THERAPIST: You sound very upset about this. I'm sure it must be very difficult for you.

MRS. T: Yes, it is. The rest of the house is just beautiful and he just goes around destroying (*interrupted*).

THERAPIST: I can understand how frustrating that is to you. I have children of my own. What I found very helpful, though, is when I tell them what I would like them to do, I'm not too hard on them. Sometimes it's easier for them to hear and understand that way. Would you try saying it that way to Tim, without criticizing, telling him specifically what you would appreciate?

MRS. T: You mean, like, "Tim, I would really like you to clean up your room"?

THERAPIST: Right, but be even more specific about what you want him to do.

MRS. T: Tim, I would really like you to pick up your clothes and make your bed. I don't think it will work, though; I've tried before.

THERAPIST: Well, it's important to try again. This time both of you try, okay?

Such training in communication skills can assist the family members in making requests of one another without provoking conflict. Discussion of interpersonal stressors is often an appropriate time to develop these skills.

Finally, the therapist should conclude the exploration of each stressor by checking to ensure that the final account is understood and acceptable to all involved.

Objective 2: Developing Stress Prevention and Coping Strategies

Devising plans to prevent and cope with stressful events is the second objective in treatment. Prevention strategies are plans designed to avoid the patient's exposure to stressful situations. Coping strategies aim at minimizing the destructive impact when prevention fails and stress is engendered. Both prevention and coping strategies are developed for each of the stress events identified previously.

Prevention strategies are intended to protect the patient from hazardous levels of stress by avoiding exposure to noxious events. These plans may prescribe action for the patient, the relatives, or both. Some prevention plans have the patient prepare for or avoid specific activities (e.g., the patient is instructed to find out about a movie before attending it to avoid terrifying or bloody scenes). Similarly, prevention plans may mandate certain action from a relative (as when a family member is to cease asking the patient about returning to work) or from more than one family member (as when parents are asked to avoid arguments in the patient's presence). In other instances, stress prevention may require all family members to avoid certain provocative issues (e.g., esoteric religious beliefs) when dealing with the patient.

Prevention strategies often address conflict between the patient and a family member. Plans may call for reducing contact between conflict-prone parties; others restrict specific sorts of contact, including particular conversations or interaction in certain problematic situations (e.g., when the father is rushing off to work); still others focus on defusing interpersonal tension at it begins and preventing escalation into destructive interchanges.

Residual schizophrenic symptoms and family reactions to them comprise a common source of conflict. Hallucinations, delusions, social withdrawal, excessive sleeping, and other symptoms are typical at this point in recovery. Relatives often react critically to the symptoms, and this frequently leads to more generalized interpersonal tension. Since symptoms are largely beyond the patient's control, stress prevention strategies must concentrate on the interpersonal consequences rather than on the symptoms. Prevention plans generally help the family deal with schizophrenic behavior in a manner less challenging to the patient. The following conversation illustrates this point.

MOTHER: We don't understand why Cindy won't go to the movies with us. We want to go, but can't if she won't come.

CINDY: I don't see why you can't go without me.

THERAPIST (*to the parents*): You could try going to a movie on your own. You've been through a lot as well, and you could probably use some time of your own.

FATHER: But what about Cindy? Is it safe to leave her? I don't know.

THERAPIST: How do you feel about that, Cindy?

CINDY: I'll be all right if they go. It's no big deal.

MOTHER: But how will we know if you want to go?

CINDY: Just ask me, okay?

MOTHER: Well, sometimes you change your mind at the last minute.

CINDY: You can just go without me then. Just don't worry.

FATHER: I can't help worrying.

THERAPIST: What would make it easier for you to go without worrying?

FATHER: Well . . . maybe she could have a friend over.

THERAPIST: How do you feel about that, Cindy? Any other suggestions?

CINDY: Yeah, that's okay. Or they could just call me and ask how I'm doing.

THERAPIST: How does that sound to you?

MOTHER: Fine

FATHER: Okay.

THERAPIST: Good. Let's review the plan to be sure we all have it straight (*proceeds to do so*).

Coping plans become important when strategies for prevention fail and the patient encounters stress-producing circumstances. Sometimes coping plans involve the relatives. They may be called upon to terminate stressful interactions, to engage a mediator to resolve a dispute peacefully, to intervene in arguments between the patient and another, or to offer the patient emotional support in the aftermath of a disturbing experience. However, coping plans that can be utilized by the patient are especially emphasized, for they provide the schizophrenic with badly needed means of self-protection. Recognizing when and how to terminate stressful interactions, seeking a mediator and/or emotional support, and engaging in poststress cathartic activities (e.g., exercise, diversionary pursuits such as painting, venting feelings in a safe environment) can help the patient respond to stress adaptively rather than through psychotic regression.

Prevention and coping strategies are developed for each of the stress events identified previously (see "Objective 1"). One at a time the events are considered, first from the standpoint of prevention, next from a coping perspective. Strategies are generated by formulating a few alternative plans, clarifying what each entails (who does what to whom, and when); exploring the strengths and weaknesses of each; improving the plans in light of the exploration; and being certain that final strategies are understood and accepted by those destined to carry them out.

Therapists must generally take an active role in the initial work of this objective. A careful, comprehensible explanation of prevention and coping strategies is required at the start, since these ideas are alien to most treatment participants. Even with a good explanation, most families need substantial guidance in the beginning. The therapist may select a stress event, suggest the first prevention and coping plans, and lead participants in exploring and improving them. It is also the therapist's responsibility to ensure that the strategies are understood and acceptable to those who will ultimately enact them. The patient and relatives can be encouraged to take increasing initiative and responsibility as plans are developed for successive stress events. As they emulate the therapist's actions, the participants ideally learn to formulate prevention and coping strategies without professional assistance.

Objective 3: Implementing and Evaluating Stress Control Strategies
Implementing, evaluating, and improving the stress prevention and coping strategies is the third therapy objective. Participants are instructed to implement the strategies as soon as circumstances permit. Shortcomings of the plans are frequently revealed as the family attempts to follow them. Failure to implement the strategies may also be found. In this phase of treatment, obstacles to successful stress prevention and coping are identified and overcome.

When patients and relatives employ the stress control strategies, they often encounter difficulties. To assure continued effort, therapists may reinforce the attempts with praise and underscore any benefits that were reaped. The next step is obtaining a description of the attempt so the strategies can be made more effective. Sometimes a minor adjustment or elaboration is all a plan requires. Other times, strategies may need substantial modification or even replacement. The nature and extent of alteration depends on how successful the original strategy was and what would be necessary to correct its insufficiencies. The process of refining a strategy is basically the same as creating one (see "Objective 2"), with the exception that development revolves around aspects of the strategy that require modification.

Otherwise sound stress prevention or coping strategies can fail if the person carrying them out lacks requisite psychosocial skills. Problems of skill deficits are most likely with the patient, a schizophrenic in the early stages of restitution. When plans require an awareness of one's impact on others, assertiveness, or the recognition of emotions (to name but a few) the patient may find them unmanageable. Significant others may also be unable to implement strategies, especially when the plans call for inhibiting criticism and anger or for empathizing with the patient. Rarely will treatment participants recognize what is awry in these situations, so the therapist must be particularly alert for skill limitations. When crucial skills are absent, a strategy that does not demand them may be developed. Alternatively, necessary skills can sometimes be developed through instruction, modeling, coaching, and practice within the treatment sessions. Whether to switch to a less demanding strategy or to develop specific skills depends on the relative expediency of the two possibilities, their relative chances for success, and secondary benefits that may result from skill acquisition.

Failure to implement a stress prevention or coping plan is another common problem. This may occur for a number of reasons, and determining the basis for noncompliance is usually the first step in eliminating it. Individuals who fail to enact a strategy may not understand what is expected of them, in which case a careful explanation is in order. They may find some aspect of the strategy unacceptable; either their objection must be worked through by discussion, or the plan must be altered. Sometimes cues for enactment are not recognized, and a detailed examination of when to implement the strategy is required. Finally, motivation for utilizing the plan may be insufficient. This calls for reducing the "costs" of implementation by amending the plan and/or reemphasizing the importance of protecting the patient from stress. It should be remembered that family members often feel badly about these failures, so therapists must handle implementation problems with tact and sensitivity. The experiences of Jon M and his father show how plans may misfire and subsequently may be corrected.

THERAPIST: How did things go last week?
JON: Not so good. You know we decided that whenever things got bad at home I could take the car and go see Bill? But last week Dad never let me use it.
MR. M: Well, I had things to do!
JON: You didn't follow the deal!
THERAPIST: It sounds like there were some problems. What went wrong?
MR. M: I need my car to go to work. I can't just give it to him whenever he wants it.
THERAPIST: That does sound like a problem. Jon, is there any other way to get to Bill's house?
JON: No.
THERAPIST: Well, let's explore this. How did you get there in the past?
JON: Um . . . I used to take the bus, sometimes.
THERAPIST: That sounds like a great idea.
JON: Yeah, I guess so.
THERAPIST: Where's the bus stop?
JON: Four blocks away.
THERAPIST (to Mr. M): Could you drive him to it?
JON: Oh, I can just walk.

MR. M (*to Jon*): I'll drive you when I can.
THERAPIST: Okay, so the plan is . . . (*repeats*). Is that all right?

Objective 4: Anticipatory Planning
The fourth treatment objective, anticipatory planning, prepares the patient
for taxing events likely to transpire in the months following therapy.
Anticipatory planning includes identifying potentially disruptive upcoming
events and devising stress prevention and coping strategies for managing
them. This final stage in treatment consists of repeating the first two
objectives, only this time with future stressors rather than current ones.

As patients recover, they may resume employment, education, dating,
or other social contacts; grow progressively independent, perhaps move to
their own apartments; and generally assume increasing responsibilities.
Sometimes they regress and suffer acute symptoms, and may even be
rehospitalized. Anticipatory planning is conducted to help prepare the
patient for the challenges ahead by recognizing potential problems and
devising plans to control them. The actual format of this preparatory work
is essentially the same as for the first two objectives. First, stressors are
identified and analyzed into stress events. Second, stress prevention and
coping strategies are devised.

The distinguishing aspect of anticipatory planning is its concentration
on future instead of current stressors. A particularly important potential
crisis situation is exacerbation of the schizophrenia. This generally warrants
attention, since effective prevention and coping plans may prevent minor
regressions from becoming complete decompensations. A more subtle
feature of anticipatory work is the added importance of the patient's
participation and comprehension. Prior efforts to control patient stress
may often have afforded relatives major roles in prevention and coping
plans. In the future, the patient will probably bear more responsibility for
managing stress. Hence the patient's understanding, willingness, and ability
to enact the stress control strategies is especially critical in effective anticipatory planning.

GENERAL COMMENTS

The four objectives of crisis-oriented family therapy are pursued sequentially, with each step building upon previous ones. At times, however,
stressful situations that demand attention are revealed in a later session.
These instances are handled by returning to earlier objectives—identifying
stress events and developing prevention and coping strategies to deal with
them. Despite the clear structure of this treatment model, therapists use
clinical judgment in adapting it as necessary. And although we present the

treatment model's unique features, nonspecific factors of psychosocial treatment (e.g., therapist warmth, empathy, respect, and positive expectations) are also undoubtedly important.

This form of treatment is concrete, problem-focused, and relatively simple conceptually. Because of these characteristics, the therapeutic model is especially appropriate for assisting acute schizophrenics in the initial stages of recovery. Of the patients we studied, half were able to complete the objectives meaningfully in six sessions of therapy. Those who could not would probably have benefited from more extended treatment.

Although it is a family intervention, our treatment approach is somewhat patient-centered. It aspires to reduce the patient's stress and calls upon the family's assistance. We believe this is appropriate in view of the patient's vulnerability at the time of intervention. This vulnerability also accounts for the concentration on current and near-term difficulties. The narrow focus of crisis-oriented family therapy seems justified because, as is shortly to be discussed, it yields substantial short-term effectiveness. Nevertheless, the circumscribed focus probably also accounts for a more modest long-term impact. We therefore recommend this treatment for the purpose for which it was designed (i.e., for application in the high-risk posthospital period). After that, additional treatment to improve family relations, promote vocational rehabilitation, or foster long-term adaptation in other ways may prove worthwhile.

MEDICATION

The 6-week aftercare program included pharmacological treatment. Medication has repeatedly been found helpful to schizophrenics in the early phases of recovery, as noted previously. However, noncompliance with drug regimes is exceedingly common among outpatient schizophrenics (Evans et al., 1973) and obviously limits the effectiveness of treatment. The noncompliance problem in this program was solved by utilizing depot injections of fluphenazine enanthate (Prolixin). These injections can be given biweekly, eliminating the need for patients to remember their medication daily.

All patients received phenothiazine injections upon discharge from the hospital, 2 weeks later, and again in another 2 weeks. Prophylactic antiparkinsonian drugs were also provided, consisting of 2 mg of benzotropine mesylate with each intramuscular injection of Prolixin, and 5 mg of trihexyphenidyl daily during aftercare.

Two dosages of medication were contrasted in our studies of the aftercare program. A moderate dose (1 ml) was compared with a minimal, dubiously therapeutic "low" dose (.25 ml). Patients were randomly assigned to either the moderate or low dosage and received their assigned dose throughout the 6 weeks of aftercare. The only exceptions were patients who relapsed and required additional drugs.

METHOD FOR INVESTIGATING THE AFTERCARE PROGRAM

RESEARCH DESIGN

Effects of treatment were assessed by randomly assigning patients to one of four treatment conditions: moderate dose with family therapy, moderate dose without family therapy, low dose with family therapy, or low dose without family therapy. This 2×2 factorial design made it possible to measure separate effects of medication dose and crisis-oriented family therapy, in addition to their combined or interactive effects.

PATIENT SELECTION

All consecutive inpatient admissions to the Ventura Mental Health Center were screened for inclusion in the study. Patients with more than one prior admission were eliminated. The remainder were independently interviewed by a project psychiatrist and psychologist who, using a 5-point scale (Mosher, Pollin, & Stabenau, 1971), rated the probability that each patient was schizophrenic. Patients who passed these initial screenings were observed for 2 or 3 days, then rated on the New Haven Schizophrenia Index (Astrachan, Harrow, Adler, Brauer, Schwartz, & Tucker, 1972). Since those scoring 4 or higher are very likely to receive clinical diagnoses of schizophrenia (see Astrachan *et al.*), patients meeting this criterion were accepted into the aftercare program.

Of the 103 patients thus selected, 69% were first admissions and the rest had had a single prior admission during the same year. The were young (mean age = 23.26 years, $SD = 4.21$) and predominantly White (79% Caucasian, 14% Hispanic, 7% Black). Forty percent had not graduated from high school; 35% had, and an additional 25% had attended college. Twenty-three percent were married, 15% were divorced, and the remaining 62% were single; slightly over half (54%) were male. Before beginning aftercare, the patients were briefly hospitalized (mean = 14.24 days, $SD = 5.97$). The informed consent of each patient and a relative was required for participation in the aftercare program.

PREMORBID ADUSTMENT AND TREATMENT ASSIGNMENT

Previous research indicates that psychosocial competence before the onset of schizophrenia relates to the course of recovery and response to treatment (e.g., Evans *et al.*, 1972, 1973). Peer relations, leadership, dating and sexual experience, and involvement in organizations and recreational activities during late adolescence (16–20 years) were assessed with the UCLA Social Attainment Scale (Goldstein, 1978) as an estimate of pre-morbid adjustments. Patients were classified as having "good" or "poor" premorbid adjustments, using a median split. Since females generally have higher scores on this measure than males do, different cutting scores were employed in classifying the sexes: Good premorbids were males scoring above 18 or females above 22, and those with lower scores were classified as poor premorbids.

Patients were stratified by premorbid status and randomly assigned to the four treatment conditions. This guaranteed equal proportions of good and poor premorbid patients in each condition.

TREATMENT COMPLIANCE

Of the 103 patients consenting to participate in aftercare, 96 (92%) actually underwent treatment. The eight who did not were spread across the treatment conditions: two in moderate-dose/therapy, three in low-dose/therapy, three in low-dose/no-therapy. Three of these patients left Ventura County immediately when released from the hospital. The other five rejected compliance with the treatment assigned them.

ASSESSMENT PROCEDURES

Treatment outcome was measured upon conclusion of the 6-week aftercare program, at a 6-month follow-up, and at a long-term follow-up covering the 3rd through 6th year after treatment. Since details of these assessments are reported elsewhere, we merely summarize the procedures and refer the reader to original sources for more comprehensive information.

At the conclusion of aftercare and at the 6-month follow-up, systematic behavioral ratings were made by a psychologist blind to the treatment assignments. Overall and Gorham's (1962) Brief Psychiatric Rating Scale (BPRS) was employed to measure the severity of residual symptoms. The BPRS taps 16 symptoms, which, when factor-analyzed, yielded four symptom factors: Hostility–Suspiciousness, Anxiety–Depression, Withdrawal, and Schizophrenic Thought. Overall psychopathology was measured by summing the ratings on all 16 symptoms. Overall psychosocial functioning was assessed with Endicott, Spitzer, Fleiss, and Cohen's (1976) Global Assessment Scale (GAS). "Relapses," defined as regressions serious enough to necessitate emergency intervention, were also tabulated. A thorough description of these procedures is reported by Goldstein, Rodnick, Evans, May, and Steinberg (1978).

The long-term follow-up took advantage of extensive computer records maintained by Ventura County as part of a program evaluation system. Every contact between a patient and any Ventura County mental health facility was recorded, listing the date, patient, facility, and type of service provided. These records made it possible to track our patients' usage of outpatient services (medication appointments, psychotherapy sessions, use of day treatment facilities) and crisis interventions (dispatch of a mobile medical emergency team, hospital admissions, days of inpatient treatment). Although detailed information about symptomatology was not available, the utilization of treatments afforded a meaningful measure of long-term clinical course.

Three years of treatment records had accumulated when the long-term follow-up was undertaken. There was an average of 20 months between the conclusion of aftercare and the initiation of treatment recording (this is an average interval, because all patients did not receive aftercare concurrently). Thus, the follow-up began an average of almost 3 years subsequent to aftercare and examined treatment utilization over the next 3 years. The methods of this investigation have been presented in depth by Goldstein and Kopeikin (1981).

Additional data were collected on patients assigned to crisis-oriented family therapy. Therapists rated their patients' degree of success on each of the four treatment objectives explicated earlier in this chapter. They also made BPRS ratings of patient symptomatology during therapy sessions. Audiotape recordings of the sessions were available for 21 of the 52 therapy cases, providing additional information about the behavior of patients and family members during treatment. These measures made it possible to identify behavior associated with success and failure on the four treatment objectives.

EFFECTS OF AFTERCARE

Detailed analyses of treatment effects have been published by Goldstein *et al.* (1978) and Goldstein and Kopeikin (1981). We review the major results of these outcome studies here before presenting heretofore unpublished findings about the process of crisis-oriented family therapy.

RELAPSE

The percentage of patients relapsing by the end of aftercare (6 weeks) and the short-term follow-up (6 months) have been calculated by Goldstein *et al.* (1978) and appear in Figure 1. "Relapses" were defined as regressions serious enough to require immediate emergency intervention, and usually rehospitalization.

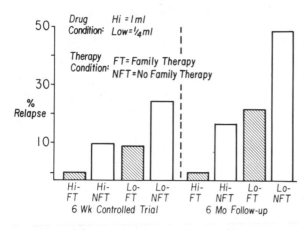

FIGURE 1. *Relapse rate within each treatment condition at the end of the 6-week controlled trial and at the time of the 6-month follow-up contact.*

The aftercare condition combining crisis-oriented family therapy with a moderate dose of medication completely prevented relapse. Not one of the 25 patients in this treatment group relapsed over the 6-month period. In contrast, 24% of the low-dose/no-therapy group relapsed during aftercare, and by 6 months 48% had relapsed. The two treatment groups differed significantly at both points in time, $p < .05$ and $.01$ at 6 weeks and 6 months, respectively. It therefore appears that crisis-oriented family therapy with adequate medication is quite effective in averting short-term psychotic regressions.

Both crisis-oriented family therapy and the moderate dose seem to contribute to patients' stability. This is illustrated by the intermediate relapse rates for patients treated with family therapy or the moderate dose, but not both (i.e., the low-dose/therapy and moderate-dose/no-therapy conditions). Judging from the rates displayed in Figure 1, adequate medication and crisis-oriented family therapy have additive effects, offering maximum protection against relapse when the two are combined.

Medication level was most consequential for patients with poor premorbid adjustments. By 6 months, poor premorbids had a relapse rate of 48% (10 out of 21) on the low dose versus 10% (2 out of 21) on the moderate dose, $p < .05$. Poor premorbids are apparently prone to regress during or shortly after treatment unless they receive adequate medication. This finding is reminiscent of Goldstein's observation (1970) that poor premorbids are highly responsive to inpatient pharmacotherapy.

Crisis-oriented family therapy was particularly important for females with good premorbid adjustments. By 6 months, good premorbid females had only one relapse (6%) in the therapy conditions, as compared with six (46%) in the no-therapy groups, $p < .05$. In contrast, good premorbid males rarely regressed, regardless of aftercare treatments (i.e., they had a total of only one relapse in all four treatment groups). Therapy thus seems especially helpful in preventing the short-term regression of good premorbid females.

In sum, crisis-oriented family therapy combined with a moderate dose entirely prevented relapse over the short term. Both the psychosocial and pharmacological treatments seemed to contribute protection against regression. Adequate medication was particularly important for patients with poor premorbid adjustments, whereas good premorbid females appeared especially sensitive to the family therapy. When employed together, the two interventions were sufficient to prevent relapse for all patients.

SYMPTOMATOLOGY

Ideally, aftercare not only prevents regression but also improves psychosocial functioning. Patients who do not relapse yet remain highly symptomatic are partial treatment successes, at best. To determine the effects of aftercare on symptomatology, Goldstein *et al.* (1978) analyzed BPRS ratings collected at the conclusion of treatment and at the 6-month follow-up.

By the conclusion of aftercare, crisis-oriented family therapy had significantly reduced symptomatic severity. Therapy patients exhibited less overall psychopathology, $p < .01$; Withdrawal, $p < .02$; and Anxiety–Depression, $p < .05$; there was also a trend toward less Schizophrenic Thought, $p < .09$. Interestingly, these effects were unrelated to medication level. It was the psychosocial component of aftercare that reduced observable psychopathology.

At 6 months, patients in all four treatment conditions were far less symptomatic. One difference among the aftercare conditions was found: The moderate-dose/therapy group was significantly less withdrawn than the rest, $p < .05$. Although therapy produced immediate reductions in Withdrawal, this benefit was only sustained when patients also received the moderate dose during aftercare. Once again, the moderate-dose/therapy combination was superior to the other treatment conditions.

Although medication level had no simple effect on symptomatic severity, a dose × sex interaction was discovered. Males showed more extreme symptomatology on the moderate dose than on the low dose, while the reverse was true for females. This pattern was found at 6 weeks and 6 months on overall psychopathology and on Anxiety–Depression, $.001 < p < .05$. The interaction was equally evident among therapy and no-therapy groups, and for good and poor premorbid patients. Hence, it is a robust finding. The moderate dose reduced symptomatology in females, but exacerbated the severity of symptoms among males.

Summarizing these results, crisis-oriented family therapy decreases symptomatic severity by the conclusion of aftercare. When therapy is combined with a moderate dose of medication, the reduction in Withdrawal is sustained over a 6-month period. Comparing the low and moderate doses, females are less symptomatic on the higher dose while males are less so on the lower dose, and these effects persist months beyond the conclusion of treatment.

LONG-TERM EFFECTS

Beginning approximately 3 years after treatment, Goldstein and Kopeikin (1981) studied patients for a 3-year period. Utilization of Ventura County mental health services was examined as a measure of long-term clinical course. Records of treatment use were available for 58% of the original aftercare cohort, and these patients constituted the follow-up sample. The other 42% did not receive assistance from Ventura agencies; no other information about them was available, and their fates remain undetermined. They may have left Ventura, possibly obtaining help elsewhere, or may have recovered sufficiently to preclude the need for further assistance.

The patients who continued receiving treatment in Ventura (i.e., the follow-up sample) were disproportionately those with poor premorbid adjustments. Among the original aftercare patients, 68% of the poor premorbids and 49% of the good premorbids utilized mental health services during the 3- to 6-year period. Poor premorbids therefore were overrepresented in the long-term follow-up. Otherwise stated, poor premorbids seem more inclined to require treatment years after their initial schizophrenic episodes.

Medication dosage, crisis-oriented family therapy, and their interaction with premorbid adjustment were unrelated to whether or not treatments were utilized in the 3rd through 6th year. This meant that each of the four treatment conditions were equally represented in the follow-up sample, and that the tendency of poor premorbids to seek additional treatment was uneffected by the aftercare interventions.

Medication appointments, in which the patient met with a psychiatrist to obtain neuroleptic drugs, were significantly related to the dose level provided during aftercare. Patients originally assigned to the moderate dose had significantly more medication contacts over the long term, $p < .03$. This effect was actually limited to the poor premorbid patients: Poor premorbids made more medication visits if assigned the moderate dose (mean moderate dose = 29.9, low dose = 11.1; $p < .02$), whereas no relationship between aftercare dose and subsequent medication was found with good premorbids, $p > .5$. Thus, the sensitivity of poor premorbid patients to aftercare drug level, observed in the short-term results, remained evident years later.

The number of group and individual psychotherapy appointments was also related to aftercare treatment. Neither dose nor crisis-oriented family therapy alone influenced subsequent psychotherapy utilization, but there was a significant interaction of the two interventions: The moderate-dose/therapy condition led to fewer sessions over the 3- to 6-year period (mean moderate-dose/therapy treatment = 7.8 sessions, other aftercare conditions = 29.4, $p < .01$). As Goldstein and Kopeikin have suggested, the sustained reduction of social withdrawal found at 6 months for patients previously treated wtih the moderate dose and family therapy may explain why this aftercare treatment reduces the need for long-term psychotherapeutic support.

Use of day treatment facilities and emergency services was unrelated to aftercare treatment, premorbid adjustment, sex, and the interaction of these factors. The lack of association between aftercare condition and emergency treatment is disappointing, as this implies that medication dose and crisis-oriented family therapy during aftercare do not influence relapse over the long term. On the other hand, emergency services and day treatment were both used fairly rarely. The modal patient (33% of the sample) had no more than a single, one-contact emergency treatment in the 3rd through 6th year after the initial breakdown; among the rest, relapse was infrequent (mean of 3.4 episodes) and abbreviated (mean of 4.45 treatment contacts per episode). Since emergency treatments did not necessarily consist of hospitalization—they included crisis outpatient treatments and inpatient confinements for a few hours of observation—the data are rather encouraging in terms of general clinical course. Day treatment utilization was also quite limited, as 57% of the sample never utilized that service and 20% had only 1 to 34 contacts over the years of follow-up.

In summary, the long-term follow-up revealed that patients with poor premorbid adjustments were particularly likely to continue receiving Ventura County mental health services 3 to 6 years after their initial schizophrenic episode. When aftercare provided the poor premorbids with the moderate dose of medication, as compared with the lower one, they continued receiving more medication over the long term. Good and poor premorbid patients in the moderate-dose/therapy aftercare conditions went on to receive less psychotherapy in the following years. Finally, utilization of emergency services and day treatment facilities was infrequent and unrelated to aftercare treatment.

DETERMINANTS OF EFFECTIVE CRISIS-ORIENTED FAMILY THERAPY

Research reviewed so far shows that crisis-oriented family therapy is substantially beneficial. With its effectiveness established, new questions arise. What aspects of therapy are efficacious? What types of family behavior impede or facilitate successful treatment? And, ultimately, how can therapy be conducted more effectively? The results of three investigations provide some answers to these important questions.

ATTAINMENT OF THE THERAPY OBJECTIVES

The defining feature of crisis-oriented family therapy is a four-objective treatment model. The objectives are intended to minimize patients' stress, thereby fostering stability and progressive recovery. Hence, successful completion of the objectives is theoretically expected to maximize the impact of treatment. King and Goldstein (1979) tested this prediction by dividing therapy patients into two post hoc groups: The 50% who failed to successfully complete more than the first two objectives were designated "nonachievers"; the other 50% who mastered at least the first three objectives were termed "achievers." Since only achievers successfully implemented stress prevention and coping strategies (see "Objective 3"), the achievement distinction captures a meaningful difference. By comparing these groups, it was possible to identify consequences of achieving the objectives, as well as patient characteristics associated with achievement.

Two differences between achievers and nonachievers were found at the 6-month follow-up. Achievers displayed significantly less Schizophrenic Thought, $p < .01$, and better psychosocial functioning (on the GAS), $p < .04$. No other differences were discovered. The absence of other differences is interesting, because mere participation in crisis-oriented family therapy (irrespective of achievement) was previously found to decrease symptomatology and relapses. Apparently, some treatment effects depend on successful completion of most objectives, while others do not.

King and Goldstein also explored pretherapy patient attributes that might be related to subsequent mastery of the objectives. None of the following predicted achievement: form or level of psychopathology; premorbid adjustment; and sex or other demographic variables. Nor was achievement related to the number of relatives participating in therapy or to medication levels. One interaction of factors did influence mastery of the objectives. The interaction involved BPRS Hostility–Suspiciousness, measured before aftercare, and drug level. Relatively hostile patients achieved more objectives on the moderate dose than on the low dose, while the opposite was true for those less hostile. Other than this, achievers and nonachievers seem quite similar prior to treatment.

DOSE–HOSTILITY SYMMETRY

Kopeikin and Goldstein (1980) further explored the interaction of drug and hostility levels (see above) by classifying patients into two categories: patients with "symmetric" dose and hostility levels (i.e., higher dose and higher hostility, or lower dose and lower hostility); and patients with "asymmetric" levels (i.e., higher dose and lower hostility, or vice versa). Using this symmetry distinction, King and Goldstein's interaction meant that patients with symmetric levels were more likely to achieve the objectives than were those with asymmetric levels, $p < .002$.

Why dose–hositility symmetry was related to the achievement of treatment objectives was clarified by examining patients' behavior during therapy. Patient behavior was assessed by therapist BPRS ratings of 16 symptoms. Symmetric levels of drug dosage and hostility led to less uncooperativeness and blunted affect, as well as to slightly more anxiety, during treatment sessions, $p < .01$. These characteristics were further found to facilitate achievement of the objectives, $p < .007$. Thus, symmetric levels made patients more cooperative and emotionally responsive, thereby increasing the chances of achievement.

The association between achievement and 6-month outcome was also clarified. Among therapy patients, symmetric levels of dose and hostility usually led to achievement. When patients with symmetric levels mastered the objectives, they showed less thought disturbance and psychosocial dysfunction at the 6-month follow up. When they did not achieve the higher-level therapy goals, symmetry was unrelated to outcome. It therefore seemed that symmetry influenced the outcome of therapy patients by, and only by, facilitating achievement of the objectives. This interpretation was corroborated by analyses with the no-therapy group. Symmetry could not influence therapeutic achievement in the absence of therapy, so it was no surprise that dose–hostility symmetry and outcome were unrelated for these patients. It thus appears that symmetric levels foster success on more of the therapy objectives; that achievement of the higher-level objectives improves 6-month outcome; and that symmetric levels improve 6-month outcome by fostering the achievement of most therapy objectives.

FAMILY BEHAVIOR IN THERAPY

Marshall and Goldstein (1981) analyzed audiotapes of the therapy sessions with a coding system that rated the areas of content and style of communication among family members. Each treatment participant was rated on each code during two 15-minute samples of treatment. Samples were taken from the second and fifth sessions, enabling detection of changes over the course of treatment. Two sets of analyses were conducted, one examining patient behavior and the other focusing on the communication of relatives. These analyses revealed within-session differences between achievers and nonachievers, and between the relatives of these types. Drug effects on communication in treatment were also noted.

Patient Behavior in Early Sessions

Generating strategies for coping with stress is crucial to achievement of the therapy objectives. Early in treatment, achievers offered more coping strategies than did nonachievers (mean for achievers = 1.64 and for nonachievers = .71; $p < .055$). As this behavior is essential to achievement, the nonachievers' early inability to proffer coping plans impeded successful realization of the therapy model. Patients having difficulty in formulating strategies at the start of treatment probably need extra encouragement and guidance if they are to learn effective stress control skills.

Overall, achievers exhibited more positive communication patterns than did nonachievers. A profile was constructed from the "positive" style and content codes, comprising (1) amount of speaking during the session; (2) number of monologues (i.e., 20 seconds or more of uninterrupted speech); (3) number of remarks to family members conveying warmth, love, or compliments; (4) number of suggestions for dealing with problems or coping with stress. Achievers had significantly higher scores on this profile than nonachievers had (means of 2.71 vs. 1.29, respectively; $p < .02$), which indicates that those who interact constructively in the initial treatment transactions are inclined to attain the treatment objectives. In contrast, no difference was found between achievers and nonachievers on a profile of "negative" communication described below. It was the presence of positive communication, rather than the absence of negative communication, that led patients to accomplish the objectives.

Medication level related to nonacknowledgment (i.e., ignoring family members' remarks) (mean moderate dose = .55, low dose = 1.75; $p < .034$). The moderate dose, in reducing nonacknowledgment, enabled patients to attend and respond more appropriately to what others were saying. There was also an effect of drug level on resistance, but only among nonachievers (mean low-dose nonachievers = 1.0, moderate-dose nonachievers = .17, low-dose achievers = moderate-dose achievers = .14; $p < .05$). The moderate dose suppressed the tendency of nonachievers to ignore therapist suggestions and/or object to treatment. As mentioned above, negative patient behavior did not relate to achievement, so these drug effects did not lead to the mastery of most objectives. However, drug level did have some impact on the attainment of treatment goals, as nonachievers on the moderate dose tended to accomplish at least the first objective, whereas low-dose nonachievers did not (see Table 1).

Patient Behavior in Late Sessions

Near the end of therapy, the communication patterns of achievers and nonachievers were indistinguishable. The early lack of positive behaviors on the part of nonachievers was no longer observed and may have been remedied by treatment participation.

TABLE 1. *Number of Therapeutic Objectives Achieved by Moderate-Dose and Low-Dose Nonachievers*

	Objectives achieved	
Dosage level	0	1 and 2
Moderate dose	4	9
Low dose	8	3

Note. Fisher's exact = .0436.

Three drug effects were noted. The moderate dose decreased "lack of focus" (i.e., abrupt conversational transitions that were vague, confusing, and often autistic) (mean moderate dose = .75, low dose = 2.96; $p < .05$). The moderate dose enabled patients to concentrate on a topic, discussing it without digression. Two other consequences of dose level were found with nonachievers and did not apply to achievers. As in the early sessions, the moderate dose reduced resistance among nonachievers (for nonachievers, mean moderate dose = .17, low dose = 4.49; $p < .05$); it additionally decreased criticism and/or harsh evaluations of family members (for nonachievers, mean moderate dose = .83, low dose = 4.5; $p < .05$). Moderate levels of medication appeared to control the nonachievers' recalcitrance toward their therapist and relatives better than the low dose did. Unfortunately, medication did not reduce the negativity of nonachievers' families (see below).

Relatives' Behavior in Early Sessions

The family members of achievers and nonachievers differed significantly on resistance and intrusiveness (speaking for the patients). Relatives of the nonachievers were more intrusive, $p < .05$, and resistant, $p < .012$. These behaviors interfered with treatment by invalidating the patients and the treatment situations. Resistance and intrusiveness were no longer evident later in therapy, but their initial presence appears to have exerted a lasting, detrimental effect on the therapeutic enterprise.

The families of nonachievers had higher scores than the relatives of achievers did on a negative profile combining resistance, intrusiveness, criticism/hostility, nonacknowledgment, lack of focus, and disagreement, $p < .07$. In contrast, the familial incidence of positive behavior was unrelated to the patients' achievement of objectives. Thus, early negative behavior on the part of relatives led to patient failure on the objectives, while positive behavior was apparently insignificant.

Relatives' Behavior in Late Sessions

Families of achievers and nonachievers did not differ on any codes in the final treatment meetings. The relatives of achievers changed little, while those of nonachievers grew less resistant and intrusive over the course of therapy. By the end, nonachievers' families had improved to the point of resembling the relatives of achievers.

A strange and interesting drug effect was observed in the late-session behavior of relatives. The families of patients receiving the moderate dose offered more "ways of dealing" with problems than did relatives of low-dose patients (mean moderate dose $= .665$, low dose $= .175$; $p < .016$). Since patients on the moderate dose were less prone to nonacknowledgment and lack of focus, perhaps their relatives were more motivated and/or able to cooperate and offer suggestions. The pharmacologically induced improvements in patient behavior may have inspired relatives' confidence in the program, increasing their desire to collaborate, and may also have prevented the patients from disrupting their constructive efforts.

In sum, negative communication by family members in the initial therapy sessions seemed to have a lasting detrimental influence on the *pursuit* of treatment objectives. Positive family behavior, in contrast, was relatively inconsequential to pursuit. Conversely, early positive communication by patients led to the *achievement* of therapy objectives, while negative behavior was relatively unimportant to achievement. By the end of therapy, communication differences between achievers and nonachievers, and between their families, had largely disappeared. As to medication effects, the higher, moderate dose was more effective in reducing disruptive patient behavior (lack of focus and nonacknowledgment) and encouraged family members to collaborate in problem solving.

DISCUSSION

The 6-week program combining a moderate dose of injectable phenothiazine with crisis-oriented family therapy yielded substantial benefits in the aftercare of acute schizophrenia. Although both the moderate dose and family therapy were helpful, they were most effective in combination. When employed together, these interventions completely prevented short-term relapse: None of the 25 patients treated with crisis family therapy and the moderate dose relapsed during aftercare or by the 6-month follow-up. This is rather impressive, considering the 48% relapse rate in the low-dose/no-therapy group and comparable rates previously found in Ventura County and nationwide. The primary aftercare goal of promoting patient stability during the stressful posthospital period of social reimmersion was best accomplished by providing adequate medication in conjunction with crisis-oriented family therapy.

Symptomatology was also reduced by the moderate-dose/therapy combination. It was crisis-oriented family therapy that decreased overall psychopathology, affective disturbance, and withdrawal by the end of aftercare. For therapy patients also assigned the moderate dose, withdrawal continued to subside over the months following aftercare. The combination of family therapy and adequate medication thus led to a progressive reduction in withdrawal that continued after treatment concluded. This reduction in withdrawal may be the reason why moderate-dose/therapy patients required less psychotherapuetic support over the years following aftercare.

Response to the drug and family therapy interventions was determined by premorbid adjustment and sex. Patients with poor premorbid adjustments were highly sensitive to medication level. They relapsed quickly and frequently on the low dose but were stable on the moderate dose. The responsivity of poor premorbid patients to aftercare medication remained evident in the 3rd through 6th year following treatment: Poor premorbid schizophrenics, who obtained substantial help from adequate pharmacological support, were more likely to seek long-term maintainance medication when provided with the higher dose during aftercare. The higher (moderate) dose also reduced symptomatic severity among poor premorbid females, but increased the emotional dysphoria of males. Unfortunately, poor premorbid males may suffer more affective disturbance as a result of the higher doses required to prevent their relapse. Since crisis-oriented family therapy alleviates symptomatology, it may counteract the exacerbation of symptoms produced in poor premorbid males by pharmacological treatment. Hence, crisis-oriented family therapy coupled with adequate medication was the aftercare program most effective for poor premorbid patients.

Females with good premorbid adjustments also responded most favorably to the combination of crisis-oriented family therapy and a moderate dose of medication. Therapy reversed their propensity toward short-term regression and decreased symptomatology. Coupled with therapy, the moderate dose further reduced symptomatic severity and sustained this reduction over the ensuing months. Like poor premorbids, the good premorbid females responded best to the moderate-dose/therapy aftercare treatment.

Good premorbid males were exceptional patients for whom the moderate dose/therapy combination was not the best form of aftercare. Since these patients rarely relapsed, irrespective of treatment, protection against short-term regression was not a major concern. As to symptomatology, crisis-oriented family therapy reduced symptomatic severity whereas the moderate dose increased it. Good premorbid males showed a similar drug response in a previous study, exhibiting better reactions to a placebo than to active medication (Goldstein, 1970). Hence, optimal aftercare for good premorbid males may involve family therapy with minimal or no medication.

The effectiveness of crisis-oriented family therapy was greatest when patients mastered the stress-management skills specified by the four objectives of treatment. Participation in therapy decreased symptomatology and protected against relapse even when the objectives were not fully accomplished. Nevertheless, successful implementation of the stress prevention and coping strategies by patients led to superior psychosocial functioning and less thought disturbance at 6 months. Mastery of the stress control objectives therefore appears to enhance treatment effectiveness.

To maximize therapeutic impact by fostering mastery of the treatment objectives, the research results suggest certain ways of working with patients, relatives, and medication levels. Beginning with patients, the ones who had difficulty offering coping plans had poorer chances of achieving the objectives. Without a patient's active involvement, coping plans simply may not get developed. But even when they are, as the therapist and relatives usually provide plans, the patient may not carry out specified activities for lack of understanding or acceptability. It is thus especially important for therapists to procure active patient participation, ensuring that patients understand the tasks at hand and are encouraged to collaborate. In general, higher levels of patient activity in the early treatment sessions led to better outcomes. Constructive participation fostered the achievement of objectives, and negative communication was rather inconsequential. This would warrant encouraging active patient participation, even at the expense of eliciting more frequent negative behavior.

In contrast, the negative behavior of relatives was associated with subsequent patient failure on the treatment objectives. When relatives were intrusive, were resistant, and generally communicated negatively, the treatment process was disrupted. Such behavior tended to occur in the early sessions of therapy and to dissipate. However, the treatment process never fully recovered. Perhaps if additional sessions were offered, the initial disruption could be overcome. The fact that only 50% of our patients could achieve the objectives in six sessions suggests that more sessions may frequently be appropriate. Still, our impression from the recordings of therapy was that early negative behavior had a persistant detrimental influence on the therapeutic endeavor. Avoiding the disruption of early sessions by instrusive or resistant family members seems critically important. The results further suggest that suppressing some constructive communication by family members in the interest of preventing disruption is justified.

Medication level can also facilitate or impede pursuit of the treatment objectives. When more hostile, suspicious patients received a higher dose, and less aggressive patients were given a lower dose, both were more cooperative and emotionally responsive, and these results led to the mastery of objectives. When drug level can be tailored to facilitate crisis-oriented family therapy, hostility and suspiciousness can be used as a guide for dose assignments. Higher doses also controlled patients' inability to remain focused on a topic and nonacknowledgment of relatives' communication. When these attributes interfere with therapy, a higher dose may prove helpful. Of course, protecting a patient from relapse and minimizing other symptoms will not always permit drug assignments guided by hostility, suspiciousness, lack of focus, and nonacknowledgment. But when possible, such assignments appear to hold significant promise in fostering psychotherapeutic progress, making patients more accessible and even increasing the cooperation of family members.

Viewed from a temporal perspective, the effects of aftercare were greatest immediately during and following treatment, remained substantial at 6 months, and were modest 3 to 6 years later. This trend in part reflects a progressive insensitivity of our research in detecting treatment effects (for an explanation, see Goldstein & Kopeikin, 1981). Nevertheless, the diminution of effects over time is probably a real limitation of the brief, concrete, present-focused aftercare program. Crisis-oriented family therapy and the brief medication regime were devised to support acute schizophrenics in the difficult, high-risk period immediately following hospitalization. The interventions are suited to this aftercare role in their simplicity and format, and, as intended, have a high short-term efficacy. Once aftercare is concluded, our results imply that other forms of psychosocial intervention—possibly addressing family relations, personal issues, and vocational issues—and maintainance medication may be helpful in supporting gradual progress toward a higher level of recovery.

REFERENCES

Anderson, C. M., Meisel, S. S., & Houpt, J. L. Training former patients as task group leaders. *International Journal of Group Psychotherapy*, 1975, *25*, 32–43.
Astrachan, B. M., Harrow, M., Adler, D., Brauer, L., Schwartz, C., & Tucker, G. A checklist for the diagnosis of schizophrenia. *British Journal of Psychiatry*, 1972, *121*, 529–539.
Brown, G. W., Birley, J. L. T., & Wing, J. K. Influence of family life on the course of schizophrenic disorder: A replication. *British Journal of Psychiatry*, 1972, *121*, 241–258.
Endicott, J., Spitzer, R. L., Fleiss, J. F., & Cohen, J. The global assessment procedure for measuring the overall severity psychiatric disturbance. *Archives of General Psychiatry*, 1976, *33*, 766–771.
Evans, J. R., Goldstein, M. J., & Rodnick, E. H. Premorbid adjustment, paranoid diagnosis and remission in acute schizophrenics treated in a community mental health center. *Archives of General Psychiatry*, 1973, *28*, 666–672.

Evans, J. R., Rodnick, E. H., Goldstein, M. J., & Judd, L. L. Premorbid adjustment, phenothiazine treatment, and remission in acute schizophrenics. *Archives of General Psychiatry*, 1972, *27*, 486–490.

Goldstein, M. J. Premorbid adjustment, paranoid status, and patterns of response to phenothiazine in acute schizophrenia. *Schizophrenia Bulletin*, 1970, *3*, 24–37.

Goldstein, M. J. Further data concerning the relationship between premorbid adjustment and paranoid symptomatology. *Schizophrenia Bulletin*, 1978, *4*, 236–243.

Goldstein, M. J., & Kopeikin, H. S. Short- and long-term effects of combining drug and family therapy. In M. J. Goldstein (Ed.), *New directions for mental health services: New developments in intervention with families of schizophrenics* (No. 12). San Francisco: Jossey-Bass, 1981.

Goldstein, M. J., Rodnick, E. H., Evans, J. R., May, P. R. A., & Steinberg, M. R. Drug and family therapy in the aftercare of acute schizophrenics. *Archives of General Psychiatry*, 1978, *35*, 1169–1177.

Hogarty, G. E., Goldberg, S. C., & Schooler, N. R. Drug and sociotherapy in the aftercare of schizophrenia: A review. In M. Greenblat (Ed.), *Drugs in combination with other therapies*. New York: Grune & Stratton, 1975.

Hogarty, G. E., & Ulrich, R. F. Temporal effects of drug and placebo in delaying relapse in schizophrenic outpatients. *Archives of General Psychiatry*, 1977, *34*, 297–301.

King, C. E., & Goldstein, M. J. Therapist ratings of achievement of objectives in psychotherapy with acute schizophrenics. *Schizophrenia Bulletin*, 1979, *5*, 118–129.

Kopeikin, H. S., & Goldstein, M. J. *Symmetry in levels of drug and hostility and crisis-oriented family therapy in the aftercare of acute schizophrenia.* Unpublished master's thesis, University of California at Los Angeles, 1980.

Marshall, V., & Goldstein, M. J. *Crisis-oriented family therapy with acute schizophrenics.* Unpublished master's thesis, University of California at Los Angeles, 1981.

Mosher, L. R., Pollin, W., & Stabenau, J. R. Families with identical twins discordant for schizophrenia: Some relationships between identification thinking styles, psychopathology, and dominance–submissiveness. *British Journal of Psychiatry*, 1971, *118*, 29–42.

Overall, J. E., & Gorham, D. R. The brief psychiatric rating scale. *Psychological Reports*, 1962, *10*, 799–812.

Schooler, N. R., Levine, J., Severe, J. B., Brauzer, B., DiMascio, A., Klerman, G. L., & Tuason, V. B. Prevention of relapse in schizophrenia: An evaluation of fluphenazine decanoate. *Archives of General Psychiatry*, 1980, *37*, 16–24.

Taube, C. A. *Readmissions to inpatient services of state and county mental hospitals 1972* (Statistical Note 110). Rockville, Md.: National Institute of Mental Health, Biometry Branch, 1974.

Vaughn, C. E., & Leff, J. P. The influence of family and social factors on the course of psychiatric illness: A comparison of schizophrenia and depressed neurotic patients. *British Journal of Psychiatry*, 1976, *129*, 125–137.

4

A PSYCHOEDUCATIONAL PROGRAM FOR FAMILIES OF PATIENTS WITH SCHIZOPHRENIA

Carol M. Anderson

The treatment of schizophrenia is one of the major problems confronting the mental health professions today. Despite relatively successful efforts to decrease the length of hospitalizations through community care and the use of psychopharmacological treatments, a pattern of repeated relapse constitutes the course of this illness for most patients. Approximately 80% of patients who are not on medication and 40% of patients who are on medication relapse within a year of the time they are discharged from the hospital (Falloon, Liberman, Simpson, & Talbot, 1978; Hogarty, Schooler, Ulrich, Mussare, Ferro, & Herron, 1979; Hogarty & Ulrich, 1977; Schooler, Levine, Severe, Brauzer, DiMascio, Klerman, & Tuason, 1980).

The reasons for these relapse rates are not altogether clear. Some patients do not appear to stabilize sufficiently during their brief hospitalizations, thus reentering the community in a particularly vulnerable state. Others fail to comply with treatment recommendations for outpatient care. For instance, it has been estimated that as many as 50% of these patients fail to connect with aftercare services or discontinue treatment after one or two visits (Taube, 1974). It is not surprising, therefore, that these patients become caught in the "revolving door" of inpatient psychiatric hospitals and consume the majority of time, effort, and resources of the mental health profession. This chapter describes a model of intervention that attempts to address the problem of providing effective aftercare for patients with schizophrenia by forming cooperative relationships with the patients' families.

The model described here was developed as one part of a larger research project that is investigating the impact of various strategies of

CAROL M. ANDERSON. Department of Psychiatry, University of Pittsburgh, Western Psychiatric Institute and Clinic, Pittsburgh, Pennsylvania.

intervention in the aftercare of patients with schizophrenia (Hogarty, Cornes, & Anderson, 1980). The larger research project measures the families of patients in terms of the concept of "expressed emotion" (EE) developed by Brown, Birley, and Wing (1972). Patients with families high in EE are placed on psychotropic medications and randomly assigned to one of four treatment cells: family therapy, social skills training, family therapy and social skills training, or medication alone. Patients and their families are followed in these treatment modalities for 2 years, with various measures of individual and family functioning taken at periodic intervals. The chapter briefly notes the assumptions and goals of the family program, describes its components and stages, presents some preliminary findings about its effectiveness, and lists some of the insights gleaned from the first 3 years of attempting to apply this model.

ASSUMPTIONS

This treatment program is based on the assumption that whatever the "cause" of schizophrenia, patients with schizophrenia appear to have a "core psychological deficit" that appears to increase their vulnerability to internal and external stimuli (Broen & Storms, 1966; Lang & Buss, 1965; Payne, Mattusek, & George, 1959; Rabin, Doneson, & Jentons, 1979; Shakow, 1962; Silverman, 1972; Tecce & Cole, 1976; Venables, 1964, 1978). This vulnerability to stimulation is probably exacerbated by stimulating environments in the home, workplace, or treatment setting, which have been shown to be correlated with high relapse rates (Brown et al., 1972; Goldberg, Schooler, Hogarty, & Roper, 1977; Hogarty et al., 1979; Linn, Caffey, Klett, Hogarty, & Lamb, 1979; Linn, Klett, & Caffey, 1980; Van Putten & May, 1976; Wing & Brown, 1970). For these reasons, this program attempts to decrease a patient's vulnerability to stimulation through the administration of psychotropic medication, and to decrease the amount of stimulation provided by the patient's family, the primary context within which the patient functions.

The family environment is thought to be particularly important, not only because of the amount of time most patients spend in it, but also because, whether or not families contain schizophrenic members, they provide individuals with the most intense emotional experiences they are apt to encounter in their lives. This normal intensity of family life, combined with the range of emotions and behaviors families are likely to display when members become schizophrenic, is likely to have a negative impact on patients vulnerable to stimulation. For instance, when a patient becomes psychotic, the family usually reports feelings of anxiety, guilt, anger, and sadness (Hatfield, 1978; Kreisman & Joy, 1974). Since these problems traditionally have not been addressed by professionals, it is not surprising that many families have found themselves living with chronic stress, unable to help the patients or themselves. It might be hypothesized that many families eventually respond in one of the two ways Brown and his colleagues have described as components of high EE: They become overinvolved and intrusive, constantly attempting to monitor and protect the patients from themselves or the environment; or they become frustrated, angry, rejecting, and withdrawn from both the patients and the systems that treat them (Brown & Birley, 1968; Brown et al., 1972). Either of these highly stimulating emotional responses would appear both to decrease the family's ability to cope with the patient's behaviors, and to be problematic to a vulnerable patient. In fact, data from these British studies of EE support the idea that family emotional factors relate to the course of the patient's illness. These researchers maintain that families manifesting high EE (principally reflected in emotional overinvolvement and/or criticism) tend to have patient members with relapse rates of over 50% in the first 9 months after hospitalization, as compared to a 13% relapse rate among patients from low-EE households (Brown & Birley, 1968; Brown et al., 1972).

Likewise, the communication patterns of families of schizophrenics would also appear to be problematic to a patient vulnerable to stimulation. Communication patterns in the families of schizophrenic patients differ from those of "normal" families. These families are more likely to display communicatie behaviors that are vague, unclear, amorphous, tangential, or lacking in acknowledgment (Goldstein & Rodnick, 1975; Jacob, 1975; Jones, 1977; Jones, Rodnick, & Goldstein, McPherson, & West, 1977; Singer & Wynne, 1965, 1966). While these communication patterns may be a response to living with disturbed family members, it would seem logical that patients who have difficulty controlling and processing stimuli would be more likely to relapse if they are exposed to, and must cope with, these complicated and confusing family communications.

In summary, then, these two forces (patient vulnerability and family turmoil) are thought to interact to a patient's disadvantage in a spiraling manner: The patient's vulnerability to stimuli causes symptoms that upset the family; this in turn upsets the patient; and so on. Because of this hypothesized relationship between patient vulnerability and family anxiety or behaviors, the present model of family intervention was designed to decrease the intensity of the family environment through a program that provides families with support, information, structure, and specific coping mechanisms for use in dealing effectively with psychotic family members. The program was designed with the hope that a directive approach would increase the predictability and stability of the family environment by increasing families' self-confidence and knowledge about the illness, and thus decreasing family anxiety about the patients and increasing their ability to react helpfully to them. The program has four basic overlapping phases, separated here for the sake of clarity.

PHASE I: CONNECTING WITH THE FAMILY

Based on the assumption that no intervention can succeed unless the family can hear and use it constructively, the first phase of treatment emphasizes the establishment of an alliance with the family. Since *all* of our families begin the program during a serious crisis, and most have had multiple unsuccessful contacts with other hospital and professionals, special attention must be give to a family's needs during this time of extreme distress and to the creation of an atmosphere that will increase the family's receptivity to treatment interventions. Immediately after the patient's admission to the hospital, a clinician sees the family members to debrief them about the crises and elicit both their reactions to the patient's illness and to past attempts to cope with it. Ideally, these discussions communicate to the family that the therapist cares about what they have been through, is not critical about their role with the patient, and genuinely wants to know and learn about their ideas and views of what has been and would be helpful. It is particularly important that these initial sessions attend to the needs of family members as well as to those of the patient. For instance, attempts are made to understand other current stresses experienced by each family member. In so doing, attention is paid to events in the workplace, the extended family, and the family's social network. This assessment not only helps the clinician to understand the problems and resources of family members, but begins to establish the legitimacy of needs other than those of the patient.

Once the family has begun to form a relationship with the therapist, he or she is established as their ombudsman or representative in relationship to the hospital system. Since the inpatient staff members of hospitals are most intensely involved with the patient on a daily basis, they are less likely to see the family's perspective or to attend to the family's needs. In the role of a family representative, the family therapist can balance this skewed perspective and prevent the alienation of families from the treatment team. Thus, the family ombudsman must keep the family informed of ward decisions about the patient, ensure the input of family concerns and needs into treatment planning, and provide the family with structure and concrete help in coping with the illness and the hospitalization. In this way, the family therapist also begins to mobilize the family members' concerns and involvement in constructive attempts to help themselves and the patient. By the end of the hospitalization (which usually comes in less than 3 to 4 weeks), the patient, family, and therapist have agreed upon a treatment contract that roughly specifies the goals, content, length, rules, and methods of the aftercare family program, which will continue for 1 to 2 years after the patient's discharge from the hospital.

Specifically, the treatment contract stresses that the initial focus of aftercare will be solely on keeping the patient out of the hospital. Both patient and family are asked to contribute issues for the agenda that they view as most likely to interfere with this very limited goal. During early treatment sessions, the therapist plays an active role in insuring that these issues and topics are dealt with in such a way that potentially problematic behaviors are controlled or avoided. In establishing the treatment contract, the therapist explicitly states that neither the family nor the patient need feel pressured to discuss issues unless they affect or relate to the patient's survival outside the hospital. In order to reinforce the family members' sense of having continuing control over their lives, the therapist reassures them that no treatment goals or issues unacceptable to the family will be a part of the contract. If the family's goals are unrealistic or unwise, the therapist negotiates with the family to make them more attainable, rather than simply asserting his or her own views. In particular, goals that include rapid emancipation of the patient are discouraged during early phases of treatment. The therapist stresses that such topics will be discussable only after the patient has functioned well in the community for at least 6 months.

Finally, since most patients leave the hospital with their psychoses only partially under control, the therapist provides structure in the sessions by establishing rules for the therapy that prohibit the loss of emotional or physical control by any member. If sessions do become chaotic, the therapist reinforces these rules by stopping the interaction, or even the session, until it can be conducted in a less upsetting manner. Further, he or she encourages the family to institute similar controls at home, stressing that neither the patient nor the family will benefit from an overly permissive environment.

PHASE II: THE SURVIVAL SKILLS WORKSHOP

The survival skills workshop is a day-long educative family session that attempts to provide families with information about schizophrenia and its management, and to enable family members to feel less isolated and less stigmatized about having a relative with this illness. A multiple-family group format is used, involving four to five families new to the program. Every attempt is made to encourage an informal atmosphere in which families can question professionals and interact with one another, including the provision of coffee and lunch.

The workshop is held as early in the treatment process as possible, because it also serves to establish the basic themes of the entire family program. Based on the assumption that people are more anxious about what they do not understand, the workshop attempts to provide as much information as possible about the nature of schizophrenia. Because patients are usually still actively psychotic at this phase of treatment, or at least still unable to concentrate sufficiently to tolerate hours of lecture and discussion, they are not invited to the workshop. The same information is provided to them as requested in smaller doses over time by both the family therapist and the nurse clinician who manages the patient's medication. The workshop focuses on the following categories of information.

INFORMATION ABOUT THE ILLNESS

The most recent data about the phenomenology, onset, treatment, course, and outcome of schizophrenic disorders are presented in clear, understandable language. Theories of etiology ranging from genetic and biochemical to family and cultural are explained. What is known about the prognosis of the illness (including the risk of relapse on and off medication) is also outlined, as are various forms of treatment that have been used in recent years (psychotherapy, pharmacology, megavitamins, hemodialysis, etc.). Every attempt is made to discriminate between the facts and the opinion of the staff about theories of etiology and the proven effectiveness of various treatments.

Because compliance with a medication regime clearly relates to relapse rates, a special point is made to explain the use and impact of psychotropic drugs. Although medication is a crucial part of the program, both the pros and cons of its use are discussed. Mechanisms of action, possible negative side effects, and the use of antiparkinsonian agents are explained so that families and patients can make an informed decision regarding whether or not to comply with a medication regime. The importance of the family's ongoing support for and feedback about the medication is stressed as a critical component of the treatment program.

During this entire process of sharing information, the patient repeatedly is labeled as soneone with a serious illness. Since it has been suggested that labeling causes or at least perpetuates illness, and may fixate patient-type behaviors (Doherty, 1975; Erickson, 1962), this is a controversial step. It is taken because it is believed that labeling has advantages that outweigh its disadvantages. When a family member is behaving in a deeply disturbing way, a view of him or her as ill makes it more likely that the family will be able to continue to provide support during those times when the person is unable to function at full capacity. Furthermore, an illness label decreases the tendency to assign negative and emotional meanings to symptoms. If the family can believe that the patient is neither malingering nor attempting to communicate a malicious message, there is likely to be decreased anger at the patient and at the treatment team.

The primary message given to families during the presentation of the information about schizophrenia is that their schizophrenic members have had and will continue to have the vulnerability to stimulation discussed earlier in this chapter. While they are told explicitly that they probably did not cause this problem, they are also told that, given an awareness of this vulnerability, there are specific things they can do to help.

INFORMATION ABOUT MANAGEMENT OF THE ILLNESS BY THE FAMILY

Families are told that, considering the nature of schizophrenia, the normal responses of both patients and families to the crisis of illness and hospitalization may not be the most helpful ones. For example, most families attempt to support the patients by becoming intensely involved, attempting to make sense out of the nonsensical, and avoiding setting limits on persons they view as sick. For a patient who has trouble responding to stimulation, these seemingly helpful responses can make things worse, since they tend to create more stimulation, rather than to establish more distance and control.

Therefore, following the presentation of general facts and theories about schizophrenia, each family is introduced to a series of concrete principles and techniques for managing the patient. Based on the assumption that families cannot accept staff suggestions unless they genuinely believe that the staff members know how hard it has been to cope with this illness, and that the staff members understand the magnitude of the requests being made, this discussion begins with a description of what families have probably done over the years that has not worked. For instance, it is explained that the staff knows that most families have tried their best to help, to adapt to the patient's strange behaviors, to ignore bizarre rituals, to make sense out of nonsensical communications, or to take on extra chores themselves in order to compensate for what the patients no longer appear able or willing to do. In order to protect the patients, family members have usually curtailed their own activities, both social and occupational. They have attempted to watch the patients to insure that they did not kill themselves or hurt other people. To avoid hospitalization, families have tried to normalize the patients' behaviors and have attempted to coax them to behave according to society's rules. Sometimes, a patient has been maintained in the home only because the entire family has learned to ignore its own needs. Families are told that the staff knows that it is only after serious and prolonged pain and anguish that they have turned to an institution for help. Whatever temporary relief hospitals provide, the staff members recognize that most families wish to avoid hospitalization and the patients' resentment of the hospital *and* their families for admitting them.

Because many families are so isolated that they do not know that their own emotional reactions to the illness and its treatment are experienced universally, the common emotional responses experienced by all families are noted. For instance, the most universal emotional reaction is that of guilt. Most families ask, "What did we do wrong?" and genuinely believe that somehow they have caused the patients' illness. Most families also experience a feeling of stigma, since many behaviors related to this illness are socially embarrassing. To make them feel less alone, examples are given of patient behaviors similar to or worse than the ones with which they have been attempting to cope. For instance, they are told that some patients have accused neighbors or employers of attempting to poison them; others have removed their clothing in public; others simply have lacked social skills, rudely ignoring other people's needs; and some patients have imposed strange rules or unreasonable rituals upon their families. Since most families have tolerated unusual, bizarre, and even humiliating behaviors for years before and after resorting to hospitalization, they are told it is not surprising that they have come to feel hopeless or angry. Those family members who are not angry are often overwhelmed by sadness, feeling that their loved ones never will be the persons they once were or hoped to be. They are painfully aware that the patients' capabilities have diminished and that the hopes and dreams they have had for the future may be lost.

Following the review of what families have been through and what they have felt as a result of these experiences, the workshop staff members stress their respect for the families' ability to have coped so well for so long with so little help from professionals. While emphasizing that there is still a great deal that is not known about this illness and its treatment, the staff members suggest that more is being learned each day; that there is hope for the future; and that, by using what is known to develop management techniques, the staff can help families to have the power to influence the course of the patient's illness.

Specifically, an emphasis on the negative role that stress plays in the course of schizophrenia helps families to see that they can influence the course of the disorder (Brown & Birley, 1968; Brown et al., 1972; Goldberg et al., 1977; Torrey, 1973; Vaughn & Leff, 1976). Reemphasizing the themes of the theoretical presentation, the staff members explain the need to decrease stimulation; stress is explained as central to an eventual decrease in patient vulnerability. The families are told that, for the patients, the illness produces a diminished stress tolerance, including a diminished tolerance for the interpersonal stresses common to family life. Studies of the posthospital adjustment of schizophrenic patients are used to demonstrate that relapse is related to the amount of stimulation in the patients' environment. Families are helped to see the need for decreased stimulation and a more benign, low-key family environment. They are told that conflict, simultaneous multiple interactions, unclear power structures, and diffuse generational or interpersonal boundaries are difficult for patients with schizophrenia to tolerate.

Family members are helped to see that certain instinctive behaviors of families in crisis are less helpful than other behaviors. Generally, these less helpful behaviors can be put into three categories:

1. Increased conflict and criticism between one another and toward the patient.
2. Extreme involvement with the patient, be that involvement positive or negative.
3. Decreased involvement with the family members' own social support network or other potential gratifications beyond the nuclear family.

While these behaviors are described as normal responses of family members to a serious illness of any sort, families are helped to see that they are not useful, given the special vulnerabilities of schizophrenic patients. Specific coping strategies are suggested to substitute for these highly stimulating responses, thus mobilizing a family's strengths, ability to help the patient, and reinvolvement in the patient's life in a potentially constructive way. Essentially, the suggested coping mechanisms relate to three main themes that may be hoped to decrease family frustration, concern, and criticism and to allow the patient the necessary psychological space to diminish the intensity of his or her personal environment. This psychological space is created by stressing the need for (1) decreased expectations, (2) reasonable limits, and (3) involvement of both the patient and the family with extrafamilial contacts.

DECREASED EXPECTATIONS

Temporarily modified or decreased familial expectations of a patient make the family less likely to be surprised or "let down" by the patient's behaviors. To facilitate these more realistic expectations, it is suggested that the family regard the patient as though he or she has a very serious illness that will require a process of recuperation. After initial stabilization and control of the overt psychosis, it is predicted that a period of inactivity, decreased motivation, and excessive sleep usually follows, creating the impression that the patient is now healthy but malingering. It is suggested that this period of diminished functioning is for many patients a phase of the illness; what looks like laziness may be the body's response to a debilitating stress, and therefore may be adaptive. Whether it is adaptive or not, it does not seem to respond to attempts to modify it on the part of either families or professionals. In fact, such attempts only appear to increase stress for all concerned. Families are asked, therefore, to regard it as an inevitable phase of the illness. When families can believe that this apparent laziness merely represents another stage of the illness, they can more easily tolerate behavior that is otherwise extremely irritating.

Emphasizing that this request for tolerance of inactivity is time-limited, the staff asks families to avoid expecting or encouraging the patients to perform. Much like the Muzak heard in department stores and dentists' offices, the families are asked to diminish the highs and lows in their family interaction, to allow distance without rejection, to allow the patients to progress at their own pace. They are encouraged to minimize nagging, rejection, fights, and conflicts, as well as extreme concern, overly positive encouragement, and excessive enthusiasm. This last point is important in that many families respond so positively to minute signs of progress that patients feel more aware of their low level of functioning and more pressured to improve. Families, therefore, are asked to create a temporary attitude of "benign indifference." They are taught to allow the patients to withdraw when they seem to need to do so, and to recognize signals that the patients need time out from interaction or activity.

SETTING LIMITS

The families are instructed not to confuse the need for low stimulation with permissiveness. Unreasonable rituals or strange, irritating behaviors that upset other family members are not helpful to the families or the patients. Because patients are sick does not mean that families must allow them to be obnoxious or must do whatever they ask. Families are helped to understand that reasonable and clear limits help to maintain a low-key environment and are reassuring to patients. Families are asked to set limits clearly and without too much detailed discussion before the tension builds and blowups occur. Particular attention is given to the need to limit psychotic or violent behavior, since these are not only behaviors the world will not tolerate, but also behaviors that are destructive to family life.

The only exception families are asked to make to setting limits in this way has to do with paranoid delusions. It has been our experience in this program that if family members set a limit on a paranoid idea directly, patients often become more agitated and even begin to believe that family members are a part of the plot against them. When patients communicate paranoid ideas, therefore, it is suggested that families respond to patient anxiety rather than to the delusions themselves. For instance, a family member might say, "That doesn't make sense to me, but I can appreciate your anxiety if you believe it."

The need for limits in the amount of time and energy families spend on patients and their problems is also stressed. Families are asked to avoid centering their lives completely around the patients. In acute illnesses, it is necessary for families to focus their attentions and their energies on patients. In any long-term illness (asthma, diabetes, heart disease, or schizophrenia), lief must go on for patients and for those who love them. Patients and their families must learn to live with the illness and to manage it effectively without sacrificing the needs and health of other family members.

For this reason, the need for family members to attend to spouses and/or to other children is emphasized. A chronic illness such as schizophrenia often leads to disproportionate amounts of attention to the patient, often at the expense of the needs of the marriage or the patient's siblings. Siblings in a family frequently complain that their parents side with the patient, while they are always expected to understand and avoid conflict. Each patient and his or her siblings are given problem-solving tools to help diffuse potential conflicts as they erupt; but parents are asked to be sensitive to the needs of all of their offspring, not just to those of the one who is ill. If family members do not learn to take care of one another in this way, the illness will be increasingly debilitating to families, and family members may experience so much stress that they will be unable to offer ongoing support and may even cause additional problems for patients. When family members become debilitated by the patients' illness, they not only have less to give; but patients often feel responsible for their families' pain, thereby experiencing their families as a burden, not a support.

DEVELOPING SUPPORT NETWORKS

Most families with schizophrenic members become increasingly isolated over time. Originally it was thought that those family members with fewer or less available social supports outside the immediate family would have a lower tolerance for stress and deviance within the family (Brown *et al.*, 1972; Vaughn & Leff, 1976). For this reason, these family members may also tend to be more overinvolved and critical, since they have fewer people to substitute for needs that are less likely to be met by an increasingly dysfunctional patient, as well as fewer confidants with whom to discuss the pain they are experiencing in regard to the patient's illness.

For these reasons, family members are taught the importance of maintaining a support system beyond that of the nuclear family. They are encouraged to talk of their difficulties to friends and members of the extended family, and to engage such people in psychological and instrumental support services. Three types of extrafamilial contacts are stressed:

1. Interpersonal supports: the use of others to serve as outlets for discussion of concerns, tensions, and needs, and to give support and reassurance.

2. Social and/or recreational outlets: the use of others to serve to distract, amuse, and stimulate areas of interest that would decrease the totality of the family's investment in the patient and his or her illness.
3. Work and/or service: the use of alternative areas of personal competence, altruism, and ability to contribute to others to maintain a sense of self-esteem.

This directive is one of the most difficult for family members to accept. Many family members consider their own needs unimportant when another family member is in crisis. Therefore, to gain compliance with this goal, an emphasis must be placed on helping each family to consider its own needs for survival as essential, *in order to be able to help the patient* on an ongoing basis. The message is given that if family members deplete themselves, in the long run they are less able to help one another or the patient. While ongoing social and work activities are often impossible during the acute phase of illness, the family is encouraged to see the need for a wider variety of management techniques for the "long haul." Long-term management techniques must include a lifestyle that does not center entirely on the patient or even on the family.

It is also common for patients to become socially isolated and devoid of external activities or support systems over time. The lack of friends and social resources may force a patient to spend an inordinate amount of time at home, thus enhancing the chances of family conflict. It certainly is likely that patients with fewer or less available social supports outside their immediate families are more vulnerable to family intensity and family stress, since they are more involved in and dependent on their families. Gradually, therefore, an attempt is made to decrease the intensity of family relationships by distributing this intensity throughout a larger network.

PHASE III:
REENTRY AND APPLICATION OF WORKSHOP THEMES

Highly structured, low-key individual family sessions are held as soon as the acute phase of the illness has been controlled sufficiently to enable a patient to attend. Once the patient has left the hospital, these sessions occur once every 2 to 3 weeks, and continue for at least a year and maybe two. The interventions of these sessions are based on the themes established in the survival skills workshop; they relate largely to the reinforcement of family boundaries and the gradual resumption of responsibility by the patient.

Three kinds of boundaries are stressed during this treatment phase: The interpersonal boundaries between family members, the generational boundaries between parents and offspring, and the family boundary within the larger social community support system. The first two types of boundaries are reinforced, largely by encouraging families to establish clear expectations, reasonable rules, and effective limit-setting processes. The third type of boundary, that between the family and the community, is diminished by stressing the need for patients and families to develop a support system beyond their nuclear groups.

Over time, each patient is gradually encouraged to assume more responsibility for his or her life and functioning. Initially, the entire treatment focus is on the patient's survival outside the hospital. As signs of life and spontaneity begin to occur in the patient, the sessions gradually emphasize a return to effective work and social functioning. This is initially accomplished by the assignment of small household tasks or tasks that involve a minimal amount of socialization with outsiders. For instance, after hospitalization, patients frequently fail to take responsibility for personal hygiene, much less for chores around the house. Small, structured tasks are assigned, with a slow movement toward larger, more ambitious activities. First tasks for patients may be as limited as showering regularly, brushing their teeth, or taking out the garbage. When compliance is a problem, joint chores (those done with another family member) may be assigned to promote activity and positive familial interaction simultaneously. First tasks for family members tend to involve "backing off" from their involvement with the patients in small ways or setting clear and explicit rules about important issues. For instance, families may be asked to allow patients to cook their own breakfast or to stop checking on what patients are doing in their rooms. Later tasks for both patients and family members may involve independent social activities outside the home. As more ambitious tasks are assigned, families are encouraged to increase their expectations of the patients. Since progress on these issues is exceedingly slow, a great deal of support is given to family members to enable them to tolerate periods of inactivity, amotivation, and apathy.

Of particular importance in this entire treatment phase is the idea of making one change at a time. For example, if a patient has obtained a new job, it is not the time to discontinue medication. If he or she has moved into a new apartment, it is not the time to change jobs. This point must be stressed repeatedly for two reasons. First, patients often become impatient because they are so far behind their peers in accomplishing developmental tasks. When they feel good, therefore, they often try to do everything simultaneously. Second, therapists, particularly young ones, value emancipation so highly that they tend to push for its attainment unrealistically. This is often reinforced by the idea that a family is disturbed and destructive, and that therefore the patient should be helped to "escape" immediately. Most families are not destructive, just anxious. However, even if a family is destructive, the patient must take one step at a time and only when he or she is ready to do so. Both the patient and the family are helped to tolerate slow progress by the repeated use of an "internal yardstick," comparing themselves to where they were 6 months ago, rather than to where others are today (Anderson, Meisel, & Houpt, 1975).

PHASE IV: CONTINUED TREATMENT OR DISENGAGEMENT

Once the goals for effective functioning have been attained (and these goals differ, depending on patient ability, length of illness, and level of family tolerance), the model calls for each family to be presented with two possible options for treatment: (1) more traditional family-oriented treatment to resolve long-term family conflicts or unfinished business; or (2) periodic supportive maintenance sessions of gradually decreasing frequency.

After the crisis has passed, families are offered the opportunity to deal with many dynamic issues that exist in any family. In particular, unfinished mourning for past losses, problems in the emancipation process, or marital issues have been planned as potential foci for these sessions. For families that do not elect this option, it is assumed that some form of ongoing support will be necessary, perhaps in the form of quarterly checkups.

PRELIMINARY FINDINGS AND INSIGHTS

To date, approximately 33 patients and their families have been or are involved in the family portion of this research study. The population tends to be a chronic one, with an average age of 29 years and an average length of illness of about 8½ years. Most of the patients are male and live in parental households, although a few live with spouses and a few are parents themselves. The overall relapse rate of patients in the two family cells (family therapy alone, and family therapy plus social skills training) runs about 16%. The cell combining the two modalities does distinctly better than either cell alone, with no relapses in this group during the first 3 years of the project.

Implementing the program has proven to be simultaneously easier and more difficult than expected, depending on research issues, the phase of treatment, and the particular families involved. Phase I, "Connecting with the Family," has become increasingly difficult to implement for logistical reasons. The need for the research team to screen patients and rate their families before they can be assigned to clinicians has resulted in greater delays as the project evolved and the research team became overcommitted. The net result was that families were often not assigned to the family team until the patient was ready to leave the hospital. It is our clinical impression that the longer the delay before establishing the connection is, the more difficult it is both to form an initial alliance with family members and to deal with them throughout the course of treatment. Apparently, the availability of the clinician during the immediate crisis is quite important. It might prove interesting at the completion of the project to examine whether the results from the first 2 years differ from those obtained during later years as this problem developed.

Phase II, "The Survival Skills Workshop," varies each time it is given but is always exciting. Families repeatedly report that it has an enormous impact on them and that the impact is nearly always positive. There does seem to be some difference in the way families of less chronic patients respond, as compared to those of patients who have been ill for many years. Those families with chronically ill family members are uniformly relieved, enthusiastic, and grateful. Those families of first- or second-break schizophrenics are often a little overwhelmed by what they might be in for. In retrospect, it would probably have been desirable to conduct two separate workshops, each with a slightly different emphasis for these two groups.

Nevertheless, the workshop is the most dramatic component of the program. In one day, skeptical, resistant, and angry families become supportive of and intensely involved with the treatment team. It is unclear why the workshop has the power it does. It may be that the information given is useful in decreasing family anxiety and in creating some cognitive distance from the experience of the illness. It may be that the permission to set limits and the suggestions of how to do so give predictability and structure to the family's life. It may be that talking with other families who have similar experiences decreases isolation and guilt. It may be that a different relationship with professionals is created—one that is demystified, mutual, and free from the element of blame that most families feel is an automatic part of family treatment. Whatever the reason for its impact, the educational workshop seems to provide interesting possibilities for use in the design of programs serving seriously ill populations. It would seem important to study the components of such events to determine why they are effective.

Phase III, "Reentry and Application of Workshop Themes," is longer but less intense than originally planned. Because it was to occur during the time of highest risk, those months immediately after a hospitalization, this phase originally was to involve weekly sessions. Experience proved that weekly sessions stimulated problems for families, patients, and therapists operating in this model. However much therapists emphasized that the immediate goal was simply to keep the patient out of the hospital, the metacommunication of weekly sessions seemed to be that something more should be happening. The sessions themselves seemed to become a source of pressure for all participants, including the therapists. Less frequent sessions resulted in fewer crises and more compliance with treatment goals and tasks.

Nevertheless, the time it takes to accomplish the goals of Phase III—stabilization in the community and reintegration into a social and working world—is far longer than was originally expected. Some patients are able to return to work or school after a few months, but most require 18 months to 2 years to accomplish this process; some patients, while stabilized, are never completely reintegrated into community life. Following our principles of using patients' signals of readiness and making one change at a time, 2 years in the project is probably the most realistic estimate of the amount of time needed for most patients to achieve some level of independent functioning. The most difficult issue for families during this phase has been that of coping with the patient's negative symptoms (amotivation, apathy, excessive sleep) during this extended period. A continued focus on small tasks and small gains helps to maintain morale during these difficult times.

Phase IV, "Continued Treatment or Disengagement," has not really materialized for those few patients and their families that have reached this phase of treatment. The length of time necessary to accomplish the initial goals of effective functioning was greater than anticipated, as explained above, leaving less time in the original contract to work on more subtle or more general issues. In general, the content and tone of family sessions has tended to change over time, becoming both more relaxed and more intense as patients develop tolerance for ambiguity and conflict resolution. Nevertheless, the majority of sessions in the 2nd year of treatment still concentrate on improving the patients' work and social functioning and on improving the family's ability to tolerate the slowness of change. With increasing frequency, general family conflict or marital issues are addressed, but only as they seem to evolve naturally out of the ongoing work of therapy sessions. A few families have completed their contracts and have disengaged themselves from the treatment team. Most, however, maintain contact, at least to check in occasionally.

SUMMARY

This chapter describes an experimental form of family intervention that exists as part of a larger research project on the aftercare of patients with schizophrenia. This program has been in effect for slightly more than 3 years, involving approximately 33 patients and their families. The program attempts to decrease families' anxiety and increase their abilities to cope by providing them with information about the illness and how to manage it. This program and similar ones (Goldstein, 1981) seem to be able to increase the likelihood that severely disturbed patients can be maintained and reintegrated into their communities.

ACKNOWLEDGMENTS

This chapter is in part based on an earlier paper published in *Schizophrenia Bulletin* in 1980 with Gerard Hogarty and Douglas Reiss. I gratefully acknowledge their contributions to the model. This treatment program is part of a larger research project directed by Hogarty and supported in part by Grant No. MH 30750 from the National Institute of Mental Health.

REFERENCES

Anderson, C. M., Hogarty, G. E., & Reiss, D. J. Family treatment of adult schizophrenic patients: A psychoeducational approach. *Schizophrenia Bulletin*, 1980, *6*(3), 490–505.

Anderson, C. M., Meisel, S. S., & Houpt, J. L. Training former patients as task group leaders. *International Journal of Group Psychotherapy*, 1975, 25(1), 32–43.

Broen, W. E., & Storms, L. H. Lawful disorganization: The process underlying a schizophrenic syndrome. *Psychologcal Review*, 1966, *73*, 265–279.

Brown, G. W., & Birley, J. L. T. Crises and life change and the onset of schizophrenia. *Journal of Health and Social Behavior*, 1968, *9*, 203–214.

Brown, G. W., Birley, J. L. T., & Wing, J. H. The influence of family life on the course of schizophrenic disorders: A replication. *British Journal of Psychiatry*, 1972, *121*, 241–258.

Doherty, E. G. Labeling effects in psychiatric hospitalization. *Archives of General Psychiatry*, 1975, *32*, 562–568.

Erickson, K. T. Notes on the sociology of deviance. *Social Problems*, 1962, *9*, 307–314.

Falloon, I. R. H., Liberman, R. P., Simpson, G. M., & Talbot, R. E. *Family therapy with relapsing schizophrenics: A research proposal.* Unpublished manuscript, University of Southern California, 1978.

Goldberg, S. C., Schooler, N. R., Hogarty, G. E., & Roper, M. Prediction of relapse in schizophrenic outpatients treated by drug and social therapy. *Archives of General Psychiatry*, 1977, *34*, 171–184.

Goldstein, M. (Ed.). *New developments in intervention with families of schizophrenics.* San Francisco: Jossey-Bass, 1981.

Goldstein, M., & Rodnick, E. The family's contribution to the etiology of schizophrenia: Current status. *Schizophrenia Bulletin*, 1975, *1*(14), 48–63.

Hatfield, A. B. Psychological costs of schizophrenia to the family. *Social Work*, 1978, *23*(5), 355–359.

Hogarty, G. E., Cornes, C., & Anderson, C. M. *Environmental/personal treatment indicators in the course of schizophrenia.* Grant MH 30750 submitted to the National Institute of Mental Health, 1980.

Hogarty, G. E., Schooler, N. R., Ulrich, R., Mussare, F., Ferro, P., & Herron, E. Fluphenazine and social therapy in the aftercare of schizophrenic patients. *Archives of General Psychiatry*, 1979, *36*, 1283–1294.

Hogarty, G. E., & Ulrich, R. F. Temporal effects of drug and placebo in delaying relapse in schizophrenic outpatients. *Archives of General Psychiatry*, 1977, *34*, 297–301.

Jacob, T. Family interaction in disturbed and normal families: A methodological and substantive review. *Psychological Bulletin*, 1975, *82*, 33–65.

Jones, J. E. Patterns of transactional style deviance in the TATs of parents of schizophrenics. *Family Process*, 1977, *16*, 327–337.

Jones, J. E., Rodnick, E., Goldstein, M., McPherson, S., & West, K. Parental transactional style deviance as a possible indicator of risk for schizophrenia. *Archives of General Psychiatry*, 1977, *34*, 71–74.

Kreisman, D. E., & Joy, V. D. Family response to the mental illness of a relative: A review of the literature. *Schizophrenia Bulletin*, 1974, *1*(10), 34–54.

Lang, P. J., & Buss, A. H. Psychological deficit in schizophrenia: Interference and activation. *Journal of Abnormal Psychology*, 1965, *70*, 77–106.

Linn, M. W., Caffey, E. M., Klett, C. J., Hogarty, G. E., & Lamb, H. R. Day treatment and psychotropic drugs in the aftercare of schizophrenic patients. *Archives of General Psychiatry*, 1979, *36*, 1055–1066.

Linn, M. W., Klett, C. J., & Caffey, E. M. Foster home characteristics and psychiatric patient outcome. *Archives of General Psychiatry*, 1980, *37*, 129–132.

Payne, R. W., Mattussek, P., & George, E. I. An experimental study of schizophrenic thought disorder. *Journal of Mental Science*, 1959, *105*, 624–652.

Rabin, A. I., Doneson, S. L., & Jentons, R. L. Studies of psychological functions in schizophrenia. In L. Bellak (Ed.), *Disorders of the schizophrenic syndrome*. New York: Basic Books, 1979.

Schooler, N. R., Levine, J., Severe, J. B., Brauzer, B., DiMascio, A., Klerman, G. L., & Tuason, V. B. Prevention of relapse in schizophrenia: An evaluation of fluphenazine decanoate. *Archives of General Psychiatry*, 1980, *37*, 16–24.

Shakow, D. Segmental set: A theory of the formal psychological deficit in schizophrenia. *Archives of General Psychiatry*, 1962, *6*, 1–17.

Silverman, J. Stimulus intensity modulation and psychological disease. *Psychopharmacologia*, 1972, *24*, 42–80.

Singer, M. T., & Wynne, L. C. Thought disorder and family relations of schizophrenics. *Archives of General Psychiatry*, 1965, *12*, 187–212.

Singer, M. T., & Wynne, L. C. Communication styles in parents of normals, neurotics, and schizophrenics. *Psychiatric Research Reports*, 1966, *20*, 25–38.

Taube, C. *Readmissions to inpatient services of state and county mental hospitals 1972.* (Statistical Note 110). Rockville, Md.: National Institute of Mental Health, Biometry Branch, 1974.

Tecce, J. J., & Cole, J. O. The distraction–arousal hypothesis, CNV, and schizophrenia. In D. I. Mostofsky (Ed.), *Behavior control and modification of psychological activity*. Englewood Cliffs, N.J.: Prentice-Hall, 1976.

Torrey, E. F. Is schizophrenia universal? An open question. *Schizophrenia Bulletin*, 1973, No. 7, 53–59.

Van Putten, T., & May, P. R. A. Milieu therapy of the schizophrenias. In L. J. West & P. E. Flinn (Eds.), *Treatment of schizophrenia*. New York: Grune & Stratton, 1976.

Vaughn, C. E., & Leff, J. P. The influence of family and social factors on the course of psychiatric illness. *British Journal of Psychiatry*, 1976, *129*, 125–137.

Venables, P. H. Input dysfunction in schizophrenia. In B. A. Maher (Ed.), *Progress in experimental personality research* (Vol. 1). New York: Academic Press, 1964.

Venables, P. H. Cognitive disorder. In J. K. Wing (Ed.), *Schizophrenia: Towards a new synthesis*. New York: Academic Press, 1978.

Wing, J. K., & Brown, G. W. *Institutionalism and schizophrenia*. Cambridge, England: Cambridge University Press, 1970.

5

BEHAVIORAL FAMILY INTERVENTIONS IN THE MANAGEMENT OF CHRONIC SCHIZOPHRENIA

Ian R. H. Falloon
Robert P. Liberman

INTRODUCTION

The behavior therapy approach to family problems is little more than a decade old. However, in that brief time these methods have shown prolific growth, particularly in the alleviation of marital distress and childhood disorders. Applications in the treatment of schizophrenia have been even more recent. This chapter traces the development of our methods from our early, basic efforts to the more sophisticated approaches currently employed.

The behavioral approach to family therapy is often equated with specific behavior change procedures such as operant conditioning or contingency contracting procedures. However, behavior therapy, although based largely upon the principles of social learning theory, is unique in its atheoretical framework. Exponents of the behavioral approach experiment with a broad array of intervention methods, provided they can be empirically validated for effectiveness. The measurement of effectiveness of a clearly operationalized treatment modality upon a person, group, or family system is more basic to the approach than a rigid adherence to learning theory, a specific intervention, or a package of interventions. The uniqueness of every individual and his or her interpersonal environment is stressed.

IAN R. H. FALLOON. Department of Psychiatry, University of Southern California School of Medicine, Los Angeles, California.

ROBERT P. LIBERMAN. Department of Psychiatry, UCLA School of Medicine, and Rehabilitation Medicine Service, Brentwood Veterans Administration Medical Center, Los Angeles, California.

The cornerstone of behavioral family therapy is the behavioral analysis of the family system. This assessment assumes that at any point in time, all members of the household are performing at their best possible level of function, given the specific contingencies that they are experiencing. Coping mechanisms that may appear undesirable to an observer, such as social withdrawal, aggression, intrusiveness, or criticism, represent each person's best efforts in that environment at that particular point in time.

Any attempt to modify family interaction is considered carefully for the consequences (both positive and negative) of that change upon the functioning of all family members. The therapist aims to pinpoint areas where intervention may result in maximal improvements of the social functioning of all members of the family. To accomplish this, a detailed systematic analysis of family behavior is conducted prior to starting family therapy. This behavioral analysis continues throughout the entire treatment phase. It involves three levels of assessment: (1) identifying the specific assets and deficits of individual family members; (2) identifying the assets and deficits of the family group as a whole; and (3) identifying the role that specified "problem" behaviors play in the functioning of the family group. This information is gathered from semistructured interviews with individual family members, observation of family interaction while they are all involved in performing specific problem-solving tasks, and observation of family behavior in conjoint family sessions. Whenever possible, some family assessments are conducted in the home environment.

The behavioral assessment of family behavior can be a lengthy process. The interviewer, like a skillful detective, aims to fit all the pieces together so that he or she can develop a well-operationalized hypothesis of the problem-solving potential of the family members in relation to each specific problem they may encounter. He or she attempts to pinpoint a few critical deficits of their communication and problem-solving behaviors that, if improved, would be expected to facilitate positive changes in family functioning. Once these critical deficits have been identified, a clearly specified intervention procedure is systematically applied over a period of time. In a continuous fashion, changes (both positive and negative) are evaluated and further interventions planned that are based upon the status of the problem—improved, partially improved, or minimally changed.

Within this framework of sequential assessment, intervention, and review, we have developed social approaches that address the varied needs of families with members suffering from schizophrenia in its variegated forms. The first description of behavioral family therapy with schizophrenics was published in 1970, based upon case studies of spousal and parent–adult offspring family units (Liberman, 1970). Subsequent development of behavioral methods has been derived from our clinical observations and supported by the published literature. Each approach to intervention is discussed separately, but all may be applied in the management of any one family.

FAMILY PROBLEMS WITH SCHIZOPHRENIA

Despite the development of community mental health programs and the widespread use of neuroleptic drugs, families continue to serve as the principal caregivers for schizophrenic patients. While the burden of providing emotional, social, and instrumental supports for schizophrenics has always fallen mainly on the patients' relatives, this has become even greater since the deinstitutionalization movement of the past 20 years. Based upon intensive interviews with 80 relatives of schizophrenics, a report titled "Schizophrenia at Home," which summarized the problems described by the relatives, was issued (see Creer, 1978). Problems fell into three major categories: (1) distress caused by the patients' symptomatic and socially impaired behavior; (2) anxiety and "burnout" experienced by the relatives; and (3) disturbances in the relatives' own social network.

From the point of view of relatives, schizophrenic family members living at home display two types of behavior that are distressing and difficult to cope with. Social withdrawal and solitary patterns, on the one hand, and aggressive, bizarre, and disruptive behavior, on the other, are found in varying degrees at different points in time during the course of the illness. Social isolation, to the point of rarely exchanging conversation, is the more common pattern; it generates helpless frustration in relatives whose sustained social support for such patients requires a modicum of responsiveness. Another facet of isolated behavior is the apathy and indolence of the chronic schizophrenic, which galls relatives who view the patient as physically able and do not understand such absence of constructive activity.

Relatives speak of being "constantly on a knife edge," "living on your nerves," or "feeling in constant dread of relapse and flare-ups of symptoms." Guilt, exhaustion, depression, anxiety, and anger are frequent experiences of relatives that, in combination with the patients' deviance, do much to explain the high "expressed emotion" (EE) in families—a factor that has been found to predict relapse (Brown, Birley, & Wing, 1972; Vaughn & Leff, 1976; Vaughn, Snyder, Liberman, Falloon, Freeman, & Jones, 1982). EE, consisting of criticism, hostility, and emotional overinvolvement, is an understandable reaction of concerned family members who are at a loss to know how to help their schizophrenic relatives. Overinvolvement can lead to a family giving up its attachments to the outside community and to

spending inordinate amounts of time at home with the patient. Criticism
and hostility can lead to rejection of the patient and, ultimately, to a breach
of the relationship.

EDUCATIONAL WORKSHOP FOR PATIENTS AND RELATIVES

In 1971, as a response to the needs of family members who were living
with chronic mental patients attending a day hospital, Liberman con-
vened a weekly meeting for patients and their relatives. Meeting for 1½
hours early in the evening for the convenience of working relatives, the
sessions reviewed the nature of mental illness, the effects and side effects of
the various psychoactive drugs, and coping methods that the relatives
could use. Two formats were developed and found to be useful and well
attended: (1) a 4-month sequence that was continuously repeated and that
all new patients and their relatives were expected to attend; and (2) a six-
session seminar that covered some of the same material but that was aimed
at relatives in the community at large, regardless of the patients' involvement at the day hospital. Naturally, the longer format permitted individualized clinical work on problems, with the staff of the day hospital spending
time with each family unit during the second half of each group meeting.
     Curricula and guides for leaders, family interaction exercises, and
handouts were constructed. Questionnaires, administered before and after
the series of meetings, indicated that family members and patients alike
acquired knowledge about mental illness and its treatment and viewed the
sessions as helpful in their coping efforts. The meetings were led by a
psychiatrist who was assisted by other mental health professionals, especially during segments when family units would form subgroups to carry
out exercises or to implement a recommended plan of action. Information
and coping skills were conveyed through lecture–discussion, films, case
studies, and role playing.
     In the 4-month sequence of continuing educational sessions, the
following topics were covered:

1. Reframing of mental illnesses as "problems in living."
2. Determinants of illness behaviors, symptoms and impairments: the
   central nervous system ("the world inside") and the environment
   ("the world outside").
3. Social learning principles: the ABCs of behavior modification
   (learning through imitation and reinforcement).
4. Reinforcing small steps in the desired direction (shaping).

5. The power of social reinforcement: shaping behavior, especially amount and content of conversation.
6. Family contracting: giving and getting needs and rewards through negotiated exchanges.
7. Description of social psychiatric programs at the day hospital: educational workshops, personal effectiveness training.
8. Psychoactive drugs: effects, side effects, and indications.
9. Ways to recognize the early warning signals of relapse.

Maximum use was made of exercises that engaged the interest and active participation of the patients and their relatives; for example, a variation on the "you're getting warmer" children's game was used to demonstrate the effectiveness of reinforcing successive approximations toward a specific behavioral goal. To demonstrate the power of social reinforcement, the group leader differentially responded to positive versus negative comments during the first 5 minutes of an interview with a volunteer who was asked to describe both pleasant and unpleasant features of life in California. During the second 5 minutes of the interview, the contingencies of reinforcement were switched to a focus on negative comments. The audience recorded both types of comments and was able to see graphically the way in which the interviewer's focus of attention affected the content of the conversation.

A six-session "Concerned Families Seminar" was offered to the general public and to relatives of past as well as current patients as a community educational service. The first session was devoted to organizational and introductory matters. After the objectives and content of the seminar were described, the participants introduced themselves and gave short statements about their families. The leaders made note of these concerns and attempted to integrate them into the structure of the seminar.

The next three sessions were lectures covering introductions to mental health and mental illness, and discussions of various modern treatments. The purpose of these sessions was to demystify mental illness and its treatment. Modern psychosocial and somatic treatments were described in terms of effectiveness, as well as costs of money, time, and family involvement. At the end of the fourth session, a film illustrating various elementary principles of behavior entitled *Who Did What to Whom* (see Mager, 1970) was shown and discussed.

The fifth session was devoted to illustrating various treatment methods with case studies. For example, data showing the effects of medication and behavior therapy were presented using a slide projector. The final session began with a film on social skills training, *Actualization through Assertion* (King, Liberman, & Addis, 1975). Following this film, the participants role-played methods for improving communication and personal effectiveness in their families.

PERSONAL EFFECTIVENESS TRAINING
IN A FAMILY GROUP

In 1975, when we were at the Institute of Psychiatry in London, the educational workshop approach was extended. In a pilot study of a comprehensive behavioral approach to the rehabilitation of chronic schizophrenics, a family intervention that employed skills training methods was developed. The focus of this intervention was upon inappropriate communication of feelings (Falloon, Liberman, Lillie, & Vaughn, 1981).

A renewed interest in the communication of feelings toward family members suffering from symptoms of schizophrenia was prevalent at the Institute of Psychiatry at that time, following the completion of a further replication of the EE work of George Brown by Christine Vaughn and Julian Leff (Brown *et al.*, 1972; Vaughn & Leff, 1976). They had found a strikingly similar association between highly critical and overinvolved expression toward a schizophrenic family member at the time of an exacerbation resulting in hospital admission and the subsequent symptomatic course of the illness. Although these data were open to a variety of interpretations, they were presented with a clear emphasis upon the negative contribution of family members. It was our contention that the most effective intervention might involve intensive psychosocial rehabilitation of the patient to enhance his or her interpersonal effectiveness, combined with a family intervention that fostered more appropriate communication of emotions among family members and lowered tension in the family milieu. In keeping with the concept of the detrimental impact of the family, the major thrust of our approach was to separate the patient from the family household effectively, while maintaining supportive contact with the family.

Three single male patients who had clear diagnoses of schizophrenia were chosen for this pilot study. All three had multiple episodes of schizophrenia with lengthy hospital stays, and were living with one parent who had previously exhibited high EE on the Camberwell Family Interview (CFI). The patients were transferred to the Behavior Therapy Unit at the Bethlem Royal Hospital, where they were treated as a small group.

All the parents were currently single, although one had a live-in boyfriend. Two of the parents were overinvolved with at least moderate criticisms; the third had been highly critical without overinvolvement. Throughout the 15-week program, the three families met with their sons for 25 2-hour sessions in a multifamily group. During the first 10 weeks, while the patients were in the hospital, twice-weekly family sessions were conducted; after discharge, weekly sessions were held for 5 weeks.

The family intervention formed a major component of a multiple-baseline design that included 3 hours per day of social skills training for the patients. After 5 weeks' focus on skills relevant to independent community living, the skills training program's focus switched to communication and problem solving within the family. In an effort to avoid an extensive family intervention prior to that point, so that the impact of the social skills training could be discretely and sequentially analyzed, no specific family therapy was conducted during the first 5 weeks of family sessions. Instead, a series of educational seminars closely based upon the Oxnard Workshop program were employed. The major difference was a greater focus on education about schizophrenia and its management. This included discussion about such topics as the characteristic symptoms; the associated impairment and disability; theories of etiology, including biochemical, genetic, environmental stress, and family factors; the role of pharmacotherapy; and psychosocial interventions.

All family members, including the patients, were encouraged to share their experiences of schizophrenia and their fears and difficulties in understanding and coping with it. Parents were explicitly told that it was highly unlikely that they had caused the illness, although it is possible that any environmental stress, including family tension, may help to trigger schizophrenia in the same way that stress is a factor in a wide variety of physical illness. During the last four sessions of the 5-week "baseline" period, behavioral principles were introduced that focused upon operant reinforcement strategies for developing a supportive family milieu. However, no specific attempts were made to alter family interaction and communication patterns during this baseline phase of family involvement.

PERSONAL EFFECTIVENESS TRAINING

At the end of the 5-week baseline period, the targets of the social skills training and the family sessions were shifted to specific family communication deficits. The specific areas that were targeted for intervention in each family had been identified from the pretreatment CFIs, as well as direct observations of family communication and problem-solving behavior during the baseline family sessions. Problems that appeared to contribute to the high criticism and overinvolvement components of the EE index were given high priority. These included unrealistic goals and expectations; generalized criticism; intrusive behavior of parents; a lack of acknowledgment of desired behavior; a failure to ask for change in a constructive manner; and a reluctance to promote independent behavior.

Each 2-hour session was structured to allow a multifamily group format for the 1st hour, followed by an hour of individual family therapy. During the 1st hour, progress in the families was reviewed, including the specific homework tasks assigned at the previous session. This was followed by presentation of the main training theme for the session. Therapists met together before the group and set an agenda for each session. This was based upon ongoing behavioral analysis of each family system. Issues were chosen for the group of three families, and specific related topics were chosen for each family separately. While some structure was imposed by the agenda, considerable flexibility existed to follow themes that developed during the sessions.

All families were trained in effective interpersonal communication such as identifying and giving praise, compliments, criticism, and requests for behavior change. Expression of feelings in a generalized manner was eschewed in favor of emotional expression that specified the behavior that was being praised, criticized, or expected. Training in empathic listening behavior was also provided for families who showed clear deficits in this skill. Family members were encouraged to set specific, realistic goals for themselves and to make independent decisions about their future life plans.

The personal effectiveness format was used throughout these sessions (Liberman, King, DeRisi, & McCann, 1975). This consisted of repeated role rehearsal of typical family interaction, in which family members were provided with constructive feedback and coached through instructions, modeling, and positive reinforcement (praise) to improve their performance. The therapists encouraged other family group members to provide feedback, to suggest and model alternative modes of expression, and to praise small steps toward increased effectiveness. The same approach was employed in the family subgroupings.

While the early family therapy sessions tended to deal with the more general issues of effective communication, the later sessions dealt with specific problem behavior that had been pinpointed as triggering family disputes or tension. The repeated role rehearsal of alternative strategies of dealing with those problems was used to develop coping strategies. The focus on the intervention was patient-oriented and frequently dealt with training the parents in the management of chronically handicapped young adults.

HOMEWORK

In order to expedite transfer of skills learned in the family sessions to the home environment, specific homework tasks were assigned at the end of each session. These tasks had been researched during the session and were designed to deal with crucial areas of conflict for each family. Homework assignments were recorded in pocket books carried by all participants, who were instructed to note the completion of the tasks and the level of competence attained during their performance. In addition to these tasks, which were tailored to each family, a standardized list of 15 common family interactions, such as praising or complimenting another family member or requesting a change in an undesirable family routine, was given to each family member with instructions to carry out as many of these interactions as feasible during the week. While the patients were hospitalized, family contact was limited to weekend visits home, telephone conversations, and time before and after family sessions.

At the beginning of each session, work on homework assignments was reviewed. Family members were praised for *all attempts* to carry out interactive tasks. Both success and failure were closely examined to determine the essential components contributing to the outcome. Where further problems were pinpointed, work continued during the session until a more effective strategy could be found.

EVALUATION OF OUTCOME

The most important question we hoped to answer in this pilot study of behavioral family therapy for schizophrenia was whether the families were able to learn more effective communication skills that would in turn reduce the levels of criticism and overinvolvement in the family interactions. A simple measure of the frequency of completed family interactions that were assigned weekly indicated that at least on these specific areas a change had occurred (see Figure 1). Further confirmation was provided by CFIs con-

FIGURE 1. *Frequency of completed family interaction assignments.*

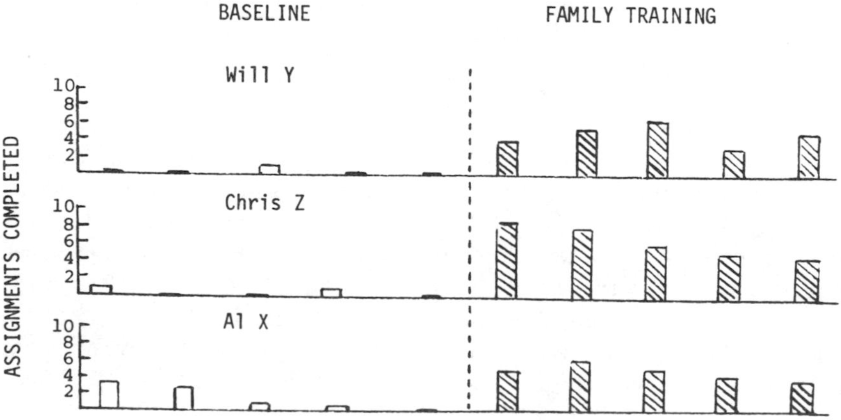

ducted at the end of the treatment period. All three parents showed evidence of reduction in the EE index. One mother was much less overinvolved, while another was less critical. The third parent, an overinvolved and critical father, made fewer criticisms and was more positive toward his son, but was still high on the overinvolvement scale. The patients and families were very enthusiastic about the family therapy and expressed their regret that the program could not continue for a much longer period.

We concluded that the behavioral method was feasible as an adjunct to an intensive inpatient social rehabilitation program, and that it probably led to changes in the communication of praise and criticism in these families. A clear need for education of the families about schizophrenia and its management was noted. The combination of the multifamily group with individual family therapy appeared to work well.

DEVELOPMENT OF A PROBLEM-SOLVING APPROACH

On the basis of the pilot study in London, funds were secured from the National Institute of Mental Health to conduct a controlled study of the approach combining social skills training and family therapy at the Camarillo–UCLA Mental Health Clinical Research Center.

The significance of the EE studies lies in the fact that a vulnerable target group of families can be identified where the family member with schizophrenia is at high risk for a chronic relapsing course. The group at highest risk is that of males with poor premorbid social adjustment who are living with high-EE parents. Various clinical strategies can be employed with this vulnerable group, such as providing them with continued neuroleptic medication and reducing the time spent with high-EE parents. The limitations of these approaches led the staff at the Mental Health Clinical Research Center to conduct a more searching examination of the process by which family factors such as high EE operate upon a vulnerable person to produce breakdowns of interpersonal functioning and symptom exacerbation.

While it is likely that neuroleptic medication substantially reduces the impact of environmental stressors upon a vulnerable individual, it is not clear why many schizophrenics succumb to stressors that others are able to manage. One possibility is that schizophrenic symptoms become manifest when a person is overwhelmed by situational challenges that he or she does not have the interpersonal coping skills to handle. Thus, relapse of schizophrenia may be determined by the balance between life stress and problem-solving behavior. Excessive environmental stress such as excessive criticism from a family member or a major life event, associated with problem-solving behavior that is ineffective to cope with such a stressor, results in a recrudescence of symptoms.

It was assumed that through enhancing the problem-solving capacity of the vulnerable individual and his or her family support system, the prognosis of his or her schizophrenia might be improved. Thus, a comprehensive problem-solving therapy for schizophrenics and their relatives was devised. Our strategy was to strengthen communication and problem solving through direct training of these skills to patients and their families.

The approach adopted in this instance differed from the earlier model in that training in structured problem solving was emphasized to a greater extent. Communication skills became the focus of attention where they provided options for the problem-solving process.

The multifamily (three to four families) approach was again employed in 2-hour weekly sessions over a 9-week period. The groups were conducted in a storefront in a shopping center 25 miles northwest of Los Angeles. During the 1st hour therapists employed an educational workshop structure with lecture–discussions, demonstrations, and instructional handouts. The 2nd hour was spent working separately with the specific problems of each family before the group was reconvened to assign homework tasks.

The initial two sessions were used to educate the families about schizophrenia—its causes, course, and management. Detailed information was presented, and patients and their families were invited to discuss their own experiences and to express their own feelings and concerns. These sessions functioned to relieve some of the guilt, confusion, and helplessness experienced by family members, as well as to enable realistic expectations about treatment outcome and to emphasize the importance of continued maintenance medication. Although the content was similar, these sessions were more structured presentations than the 10 sessions provided in the 5-week baseline period of the London study.

Following these information-giving sessions, the objective then became training communication and problem-solving skills. Each session was devoted to a component of problem solving, with training in the relevant communication skills. The leaders demonstrated effective and ineffective communication skills in brief role plays. This was followed by guided practice with feedback to teach four types of communication:

1. Expressing positive feelings and giving positive feedback.
2. Making requests of others; expressing expectations and setting rules.
3. Using active listening skills to learn the needs and emotions of others.
4. Expressing directly negative emotions and feelings of anger and disapproval.

In addition to these communication skills, parents and patients received training in family problem solving. Patients and their families were taught to do the following:

1. Pinpoint and specify problems in living.
2. Develop several options or alternative responses.
3. Evaluate each option in terms of its possible consequences.
4. Choose option(s) that maximize(s) satisfaction and seem(s) reasonable.
5. Plan how to implement that option (or those options) as a family.
6. Provide mutual support in the implementation.
7. Review the problem after the selected option has been implemented.

These problem-solving steps were repeatedly used to analyze and focus on a wide range of family problems, especially those that were associated with tension, during the second part of each session. The repetitive practice of problem solving, together with repeated practice of the four basic communication skills, was aimed at inculcating durable and general problem-solving strategies.

The relative brevity of this intervention necessitated the more structured educational workshop approach. This was dictated by the constraints on relatives' time that resulted from their having to travel 50 miles or more to sessions. Nevertheless, attendance was excellent.

EVALUATION OF OUTCOME

Our ability to assess the effectiveness of the family intervention was again hampered by its combination with inpatient social skills training for the schizophrenic patients. A total of 14 single males with a clear diagnosis of schizophrenia according to both the Present State Examination (PSE) and the *Diagnostic and Statistical Manual of Mental Disorders*, 3rd edition (DSM-III) and their parents participated in the multiple group therapy. They had been living with high-EE family members for at least 1 out of the 3 months prior to admission to the hospital. Only one parent refused to attend any of the sessions, but cordially received therapist visits to his home on two occasions.

CAMBERWELL FAMILY INTERVIEW RESULTS

All family members were interviewed by an independent research worker before and after the multifamily group sessions. The mean number of critical comments of high-EE parents was reduced by 60% following treatment. A control group of matched high-EE parents who were not involved in the treatment program showed a 16% decrease. The father who failed to attend any sessions, was more critical of his son after treatment, while his wife showed a substantial reduction in criticism and emotional overinvolvement. It was concluded that the family intervention, albeit brief, was probably contributory to a reduction in the expressed emotion status of the parents. Two-thirds of the families moved from high to low on the EE index.

An inventory of 49 common situations that may result in conflict in families with schizophrenic members was developed. Patients and parents rated the frequency of occurrence of these events before and after the family intervention. A significant reduction in conflict was reported after treatment, with a third of the families reporting no serious conflict present on any items after treatment.

During the 9 months after the combined social skills training and family therapy programs, 3 of the 14 patients had relapsed—a 21% relapse rate, compared with 56% among patients who received standard hospital treatment and aftercare who also came from families high on the EE index.

This study offered further support for the effectiveness of behavioral family therapy methods for schizophrenics at high risk for relapse. Reduction in parental EE appeared to be considerably greater in families who completed the intervention program. Both criticism and emotional overinvolvement were reduced, and it is possible that this mediated a reduction in relapses.

However, as with the pilot study, the conclusions about the value of the family therapy approach that can be drawn from this study are limited by the concomitant administration of social skills training. It is possible that changes in the patients' role behavior may have contributed to the reduced amount of criticism they drew, as well as to increased confidence in their independent living skills. Thus, the efficacy of a combined treatment package of behavioral individual and family treatment in producing self-reported changes in the family systems has been established, but the contribution of the family therapy component remains an empirical question.

For the majority of families we treated, the brief multifamily workshop approach was considered highly satisfactory. However, it was difficult to imagine that this intervention could have induced substantial, lasting change in the family interaction patterns. Undoubtedly, the knowledge gained in the educational sessions and the orderly approach to stressful problems may have contributed to a greater understanding about the vulnerability of persons suffering from schizophrenia and to efforts to mobilize family support. The problem-solving procedure appeared somewhat cumbersome, and few families appeared to gain mastery over the multifaceted approach.

The multifamily group format seemed well suited to the behavioral educational approach. Families appeared to derive considerable support from sharing common experiences, suggesting alternate problem solutions, and giving each other praise and encouragement for specific changes. One notable feature was the lack of dropouts from the family sessions and the cohesiveness of the groups. Families frequently commented on the value of the group as a support system. Patients were only slightly less enthusiastic, and even the more chronically disabled appeared to attend closely and to participate in the group surprisingly well.

With the severely impaired patients included in this study, problem solving centered primarily around the patients' adaptational deficits and the parents' coping with the illness; it was concerned less frequently with solely parental issues. A family systems perspective was maintained throughout: For example, the communication training dealt with interpersonal transactions within all family relationships; the structured problem solving focused on family-wide issues; and the index patient was placed in the role of a major problem-solving participant.

In addition to the confounding of individual and family treatment modalities, this study was limited by a lack of observations to validate any reported behavioral changes. Reports of homework assignment performance and problem solving in the home environment suggested that the majority of families did indeed develop more effective communication and problem solving. However, the need for family interaction tests to provide more direct observation of specific changes in family coping behavior was clear.

HOME-BASED FAMILY THERAPY

The educational approaches employed in multifamily groups were used to supplement expensive individual social skills training. The latter sessions were conducted while the patients were out of the home, hospitalized in inpatient units. One major limitation of such an approach is the difficulty of ensuring the transfer of behavior learned in the treatment sessions to the home. While interpersonal skills may be performed in the hospital setting or in a family workshop group, restricted opportunity to practice the same skills at home may result in a major loss of gains once a patient leaves the hospital and returns to daily life at home. However, because the social skills programs strongly emphasized independent living outside of the parental household, this lack of transfer may have been less serious.

But how cost-effective are such intensive hospital-based rehabilitation programs? Examination of the EE data from Britain indicates that half the schizophrenics who return to their homes after an episode of schizophrenia requiring hospital care are well supported by their low-EE families, while, of those who return to high-EE homes, almost half are protected by medication or reduced contact from their "noxious" environment. In these times of economic stringency, the family support system appears increasingly attractive as a resource for the mentally ill. Clearly, substantial support from professional agencies is indicated to bolster the caring capacity of families who are willing to shoulder the burden for their disturbed members. Thus, our next step in developing family approaches for schizophrenia involved a home-based family approach to the rehabilitation of schizophrenia.

Much of the impetus for the upsurge of interest in family treatment for schizophrenia has evolved directly from the compelling British studies of EE. However, an equally compelling series of early studies conducted by the same investigators involved the impact of another type of stressor upon the vulnerable schizophrenic person. These often extrafamilial stressors have been termed "life events." Brown and Birley (1968) suggested that life events were trigger factors that precipitated episodes of schizophrenia. A period of 3 weeks immediately prior to the onset of an episode was defined as the crucial time in the association between occurrence of a life event and the onset of florid symptoms. In designing a family intervention that aims to minimize florid exacerbations of schizophrenia, methods that may enhance the coping resources of the family system to absorb the stress of major life events, such as deaths, changes of job, or physical illness, would be a necessary component. In addition, although the extensive social skills interventions could not be readily adapted for family application, an approach based substantially upon the family may usefully emphasize psychosocial rehabilitation of the index patient through the family system.

It was concluded that a family intervention program that would address the specific needs of a broad population of adult schizophrenics would include the following major components:

1. Education about the nature and management of schizophrenia.
2. Training in effective nonverbal and verbal communication for all family members with apparent deficits. This would include specific emphasis on the appropriate communication of criticism and concern, so that the detrimental consequences of expressed emotion might be reduced.

3. Training in more effective problem-solving behavior to assist family members in the efficient resolution of intra- and extrafamilial stressors.

The emphasis of the approach has been more strongly that of family-centered problem solving than was the case for the methods described earlier in this chapter. Communication training and the educational seminars were included as a means of creating a problem-solving orientation in the household. The intervention was designed to be delivered in homes to facilitate generalization and durability of changes in behavior.

A further major difference from the psychoeducational multiple-family group methods has been the concern to modify the family system and to allow them to make important decisions such as choosing rehabilitation programs and the need for separation. All patients have returned to live at home upon discharge from the hospital, although subsequent problem solving has led to several patients' moving out of their family homes.

However, while there have been philosophical and structural differences in this long-term approach, the major interventions remain remarkably similar. We describe these with an emphasis on the distinctions between this and the earlier methods.

BEHAVIORAL FAMILY THERAPY IN THE HOME

The major rationale for conducting the family intervention in the home concerned the issue of generalization. Skills learned in a clinic setting do not necessarily generalize to the home setting. This is particularly true for patients with schizophrenia and is all too often neglected in community treatment programs. Patients and families are more relaxed in their own homes and are more willing to assimilate new patterns of behavior. Thus, rehearsal of behavior or problem solving becomes more clearly integrated as *real* family interaction. This integration of therapeutic interventions into the family system is crucial to effective changes and appears to be facilitated by conducting the therapy at home. A further useful benefit is the increased participation of members of the household who might resist attendance at a clinic.

FAMILY EDUCATION

Two sessions of family education are employed, with content similar to that of the sessions described earlier. With the individual family group comes greater scope for family discussion about the specific features of schizophrenia, its impact upon each family member, and problems of management. The patient is encouraged to take the role of "expert" and to describe his or her experiences to the family.

A knowledge test given before and after these sessions indicates that substantial change in the level of understanding is attributable to these seminars. Throughout the course of treatment, the therapist may refer back to these seminars. All family members are provided with detailed pamphlets that have been specifically prepared for family education.

COMMUNICATION TRAINING

The two education seminars are presented in a semididactic style with visual aids and written materials. The subsequent family sessions are conducted in a more traditional conjoint family therapy format, although therapists use written materials and chalkboards to prompt family members during sessions. The agenda for the sessions is based upon the deficits that have been pinpointed for each family and its members and is highly variable. Top priority is given to any crises or impending crises, which are problem-solved during the sessions. However, in the absence of such issues, the initial phase of therapy is used to enhance the communication skills of family members, particularly the expression of positive feelings, prompting mutually rewarding behavior and empathic listening. Families that are competent in these areas spend little time on this aspect and move directly on to problem solving. The aim of the early stage of family therapy is to create a warm milieu where family members are able to recognize and reinforce specific positive behavior in one another. In addition, they learn to identify areas of specific behavior they would like others to change, as well as to make appropriate requests for such changes. Finally, they develop the ability to sit down and discuss problems in an empathic, nonjudgmental manner. Expression of strong negative feelings is often avoided at this time, but is presented as an important precursor in the initiation of a problem-solving discussion. The importance of specifying behaviors, making a direct statement of negative feelings, and preparing the way for effective problem solving is stressed.

PROBLEM-SOLVING TRAINING

Once families have developed adequate communication skills, they are then in a position to learn improved problem-solving methods. The ability to specify a problem and to discuss it in detail can only be carried out by families that have competent communication skills. The further steps of problem solving are relatively straightforward, and families require little training to use the approach satisfactorily. They are provided with sheets that outline the steps, with spaces for completion of problem solving. Particular importance is attached to the detailed planning of the problem solution, with all anticipated difficulties discussed fully.

A six-step problem-solving approach, very similar to the method employed in the multifamily workshop, has been employed. Despite the limited educational attainment of the majority of our families, very few have been unable to master this multiple-step approach.

Each family member takes turns at chairing the family problem-solving sessions and recording details of the problem, all suggested solutions, and step-by-step plans to carry out the chosen "best" solution. A folder is kept by each family in which members file all problem-solving records. This folder is kept in an accessible place in each home so that any family member may refer to it at any time. Sometimes problem-solving plans may be displayed on the family notice board or on the refrigerator door to prompt family members of the tasks they have agreed to undertake to assist with the problems.

In addition to the structured problem-solving approach, families are trained in the use of a range of behavioral strategies for dealing with specific problems that arise. These may include contingency contracting for parental discord, token economy programs for enhancing constructive daily activity, social skills training for interpersonal inadequacy, or behavioral management strategies for anxiety and depression. In these instances, *all family members* are usually involved in the execution of the specific strategy.

In contrast to many other recent developments in the family treatment of schizophrenia, this home-based approach is clearly family-centered, and a relatively small proportion of time is spent in dealing with illness-related problems. On the other hand, no attempt is made to formulate schizophrenia as primarily a "family illness." Throughout, schizophrenia is defined as a biologically mediated, stress-related disorder of unknown etiology that is best treated by low doses of neuroleptic drugs combined with psychosocial interventions that serve to reduce stressors in the home as well as extrafamilial sources of stress. Active vocational and social rehabilitation is considered an important component to long-term stress reduction and reduction of morbidity. While intensive rehabilitation may itself be a potential source of stress, these efforts at facilitating change are not sacrificed to minimize the short-term risks of relapse.

ASSESSMENT OF OUTCOME

Behavioral assessment involves a constant reappraisal of treatment goals and subgoals as an integrated component of family therapy. The specific problems targeted throughout therapy are resolved before moving on to the next step. Crises may delay this directive progress, but are, more frequently, useful points for assessing the overall problem-solving capacity of the family system as members gradually acquire a more effective range of coping skills. At times of crises, competent communication and problem-solving skills are essential to developing and carrying out effective strategies to reduce short-term and long-term stress.

The effectiveness of the home-based behavioral family therapy program with schizophrenia is being assessed in a controlled outcome study sponsored by the National Institute of Mental Health (Falloon, Boyd, & McGill, 1982). A total of 40 persons suffering from clearly diagnosed schizophrenia, who are living with their parents in households characterized by major family stressors, have been randomly assigned to receive family therapy or clinic-based individual supportive psychotherapy with an experienced staff psychotherapist. All patients receive optimal neuroleptic therapy that is administered by an independent research psychiatrist, who also evaluates the patients' mental status with standardized rating scales on a monthly basis. Rehabilitation counseling is similarly provided for all patients. The study is designed to compare the outcome of the two treatment approaches 9 months after posthospital stabilization. Treatment is continued for 2 years, and afterward a follow-up assessment is conducted.

At the time of writing this chapter, the data analysis of 9-month outcomes is in progress. A total of 36 patients and their families have completed this assessment (18 in each treatment group). Preliminary findings show a striking impact of the family intervention upon exacerbations of florid schizophrenia: Only one (6%) of the family therapy patients has clinically relapsed, compared with eight (44%) of the individually treated patients. These findings are paralleled by hospital admission data that show minimal utilization of inpatient care by the family therapy patients. The reasons for this superiority are not clear at this time. However, there is evidence that family therapy aided compliance with neuroleptic medication (Strang, Falloon, Moss, Razani, & Boyd, 1981). Compliance with therapy has also been remarkably good with family therapy. Instances where family therapists have been "stood up" have been minimal, while patient attendance for individual psychotherapy has been characterized by missed appointments in a fair proportion of cases.

In addition to the psychiatric assessments described above, we have devised several measures of family behavior. These have included an assessment of family communication and problem solving that has been based upon a modification of the revealed differences approach, where the family attempts to resolve a "hot issue." The Family Consensus Rorschach technique has also been employed. These interaction measures are applied before and 3 months after treatment and at the 2-year follow-up. Coding of communication deviance, EE, and problem-solving effectiveness is being conducted in collaboration with Jeri Doane and Michael Goldstein at UCLA. A preliminary assessment suggested that problem solving was substantially improved after 3 months of family therapy, with less personal criticism, guilt inducement, and intrusiveness. A continued assessment of the coping behavior of the families is made through biweekly telephone assessments of current family stressors. Families who have received family therapy appear to cope more effectively with adverse life events than do the individual treatment families. A cursory examination suggests a stronger link between major life events and symptom exacerbation in the individual cases.

In the follow-up phase (10–24 months), less intensive monthly family sessions are conducted, often in multifamily groups. This allows us to examine the recidivism of patients living with families that have shown less evidence of effective family problem solving, or that have not readily maintained changes. At present, progress appears to be sustained over the entire 2-year period for most families.

CONCLUSIONS

Behavioral family therapy has been employed in the community-based treatment of schizophrenia in a variety of approaches. These have included (1) an educational workshop; (2) communication training in a multifamily group; (3) combined communication and problem-solving training in a multifamily group; and (4) a home-based problem-solving method. Each of these methods has been developed to meet the varied needs of populations of families and has been empirically based. A high proportion of families have expressed satisfaction with their therapy, and objective assessments of change have been favorable. While further refinements of our methods continue, there is a growing body of evidence to support the efficacy of this approach in reducing the morbidity of schizophenia on index patients and their families. However, there is no support for the claim that this approach is superior to any other form of family therapy on any parameter, or that it has any advantages over individual behavioral rehabilitation methods such as social skills training.

From its origin as a relatively simple approach behavioral family therapy has developed into a more elaborate technology demanding extensive therapist training. It is not clear whether increasing sophistication has improved the cost-effectiveness of these methods. To date, the approach has been conducted predominantly under rigorous research conditions. Field trials are currently under way to examine the ease with which the methods are transferred to therapists in community mental health centers, and to determine their efficacy under everyday clinic conditions.

REFERENCES

Brown, G. W., & Birley, J. L. T. Crises and life changes and the onset of schizophrenia. *Journal of Health and Social Behavior*, 1968, *9*, 203–214.

Brown, G. W., Birley, J. L. T., & Wing, J. K. Influence of family life on the course of schizophrenic disorders: A replication. *British Journal of Psychiatry*, 1972, *121*, 241–258.

Creer, C. Social work with patients and their families. In J. K. Wing (Ed.), *Schizophrenia: Towards a new synthesis*. London: Academic Press, 1978.

Falloon, I. R. H., Boyd, J. L. & McGill, C. W. Behavioral family therapy for schizophrenia. In J. P. Curran & P. M. Monti (Eds.), *Social skills training: A practical handbook for assessment and treatment*. New York: Guilford, 1982.

Falloon, I. R. H., Liberman, R. P., Lillie, F. J., & Vaughn, C. E. Family therapy for relapsing schizophrenics and their familes: A pilot study. *Family Process*, 1981, *20*, 211–221.

King, L., Liberman, R. P., & Addis, B. *Actualization through assertion*. Los Angeles: UCLA Neuropsychiatric Institute, Behavioral Sciences Media Center, 1976. (Film)

Liberman, R. P. Behavioral approaches to couple and family therapy. *American Journal of Orthopsychiatry*, 1970, *40*, 106–118.

Liberman, R. P., King, L. W., DeRisi, W. T. & McCann, M. *Personal effectiveness: Guiding people to assert themselves and improve their social skills*. Champaign, Ill.: Research Press, 1975.

Mager, R. F. *Preparing instructional objectives*. Belmont, Calif.: Fearon Publishers, 1962.

Strang, J., Falloon, I. R. H., Moss, H., Razani, S., & Boyd, J. L. Drug treatment and family intervention during the aftercare treatment of schizophrenia. *Psychopharmacology Bulletin*, 1981, *17*, 87–88.

Vaughn, C. E., & Leff, J. P. The influence of family and social factors on the course of schizophrenic disorders: A replication. *British Journal of Psychiatry*, 1976, *129*, 125–137.

Vaughn, C. E., Snyder, K., Liberman, R. P., Falloon, I. R. H., Freeman, W., & Jones, S. Replication of British research on expressed emotion in California. *Schizophrenia Bulletin*, 1982, *8*, 425–426.

III
THE MULTIPLE-FAMILY
APPROACHES

6
MULTIPLE FAMILY THERAPY
IN SCHIZOPHRENIA

William R. McFarlane

INTRODUCTION: THE ORIGINS OF
MULTIPLE FAMILY THERAPY

Relative to other psychosocial therapies that have been used to treat schizophrenia, multiple family therapy (MFT) has had a different and rather curious evolution. Historically, psychoanalysis, group therapy, behavior therapy, and conventional family therapy have all attempted to address the enigma of schizophrenia theoretically; have failed, by and large, clinically; and have moved on to more successful efforts in other syndromes. From hindsight, it seems as if schizophrenia has tended to serve as an arena for epistemological and theoretical advances, while its sufferers have benefited little from the resulting therapies. More recently, clinicians and researchers on the psychosocial side of the field have had to make major revisions of theory to devise more effective treatment approaches. If one uses clinical results as the criteria for judging theories, then Freud's original assumption—that schizophrenia is a neurophysiological disorder —appears to have been closer to the mark. Ironically, the phenothiazines— while more effective than "talking" therapies—were discovered accidentally, not by proceeding from theory to therapy.

During its development 20 years ago, MFT traveled a path more like that of the phenothiazines than that of its fellow psychosocial modalities. MFT was born on inpatient units serving almost exclusively schizophrenic patients, and continues to be so used today. As with drugs, its effectiveness was first noted during an essentially accidental confluence of events. Laqueur discovered the usefulness of the approach while doing insulin coma research at Creedmoor State Hospital in Queens, New York (Laqueur, LaBurt, & Morong, 1964b). Simultaneously, Detre and his colleagues at Yale assembled a multiple-family group (MFG), apparently to solve a

WILLIAM R. MCFARLANE. Department of Psychiatry, College of Physicians and Surgeons of Columbia University, and New York State Psychiatric Institute, New York, New York.

procedural conflict between psychiatric residents and social workers (Detre, Sayer, Norton, & Lewis, 1961). They, too, were pleasantly surprised by positive results, for patients and family members alike. Laqueur at first lacked a theoretical explanation for his observations, while Detre saw the group as part of his "socioadaptive" model. They were seemingly unimpressed with the then nascent family theories of schizophrenia being developed by Jackson, Ackerman, Bowen, Wynne, Lidz, Bateson, and Haley. Instead, throughout the early reports on MFT, the emphasis was on specific clinical effects, especially improvements in patients' symptoms and sociability, and in family morale and communication. MFT clinicians were observing many of the same family interaction phenomena as the theorists were, but they were more interested either in reporting results with schizophrenics or, in Laqueur's case, in developing a theory that encompassed the more complex realities of the MFG as a whole. For reasons that are not clear, the single- and multiple-family lines of family clinical research have continued to be separate, for all practical purposes, until quite recently. With the rise of more pragmatic family therapies for schizophrenia, a confluence is now under way. In the meantime, the use of MFT has grown steadily, especially in aftercare services for chronic patients and in many university-affiliated psychiatric hospitals.

Laqueur's theoretical proposals are worth reviewing, in light of what has been learned more recently about the role of family interaction in schizophrenia. He chose general systems theory as his starting point, with the admirable intent of bringing psychosocial theory closer to that of the basic sciences (Laqueur, 1968). He used the concept of system levels to describe the interrelationship of individual, family, community, and society, mediated by feedback processes. Difficulties derive from dysfunctional feedback loops across subsystem boundaries and from "specific malfunction of [system] component parts" (Laqueur, 1972, p. 401). The schizophrenic patient was seen as deeply affected by his or her family relationships, but these do not, in themselves, "cause" schizophrenia. Laqueur was, in fact, more concerned with the everyday phenomenon of the family's seeming to be able to reverse therapeutic gains made through medication and hospitalization. Implicitly, he seemed to understand family dysfunction an an independent variable in determining course, rather than onset. This view is reflected in one report in which he was able to reduce drug levels for patients in MFT, but not to eliminate drugs altogether (Laqueur & Lebovic, 1968).

For Laqueur, the source of MFT's effectiveness resided in its capacity to sidestep a family's resistance to change by allowing other families to assist in "breaking the code" of each family's idiosyncratic communication style and in promoting new feedback loops as substitutes for existing, dysfunctional ones (Laqueur, 1972). His own experience was that many aspects of the family of the schizophrenic were apt to overwhelm the single-family therapist ((Laqueur, LaBurt, & Morong, 1964a). Especially strong and destructive defenses were mobilized by the family in the single-family context, while the "code" was too often impenetrable. These problems seemed not to occur when other families were present.

Laqueur went on to describe several therapeutic mechanisms in MFGs that exploit their unique social structure to achieve change in family and patient functioning (Laqueur, 1972). The exposure to, and intervention with, each other by the families in MFGs seem to lead to significant structural and communicational change, if the experience is continued for a sufficient time. Many of the means for doing so are indirect, as if families learn to change at a preconscious or nonverbal level just by watching other families' struggles. Further, he emphasized that other families' members have as accurate an eye for problems as therapists do, but can present their observations from the position of being in the same predicament. Such comments are more acceptable, and more effective, than they are if coming from therapists. Thus, direct interventions are also possible in MFT, but come from a different source. Laqueur included other mechanisms, such as interfamily competition, learning by analogy, "amplification and modulation of signals," "focus of excitation," and "tuning in, " all of which may be applicable in working with any disturbed family. The effect of these group operations on positive or negative symptoms of schizophrenia was left implicit: Laqueur assumed that any benefit derived by a family would lead to some symptom reduction in the patient. Though similar to theoretical positions being taken by other family therapists of the time, his claim for this connection was at least partly based on having seen it happen repeatedly in his MFGs.

SCHIZOPHRENIA-SPECIFIC THERAPEUTIC MECHANISMS IN MULTIPLE FAMILY THERAPY

In order to extend an understanding of the basis for the apparent usefulness of MFT in schizophrenia, it seems necessary to relate those family phenomena that are known to be associated with that condition to processes that can be seen in MFGs. It may be hoped that making such connections not only will be intellectually satisfying, but will help the clinician to work more effectively with this population.

As has been more extensively presented in Chapter 14, there seem to be four closely related family factors that have been correlated with schizophrenia, regardless of their role in its etiology. These are enmeshment, or, more narrowly, "expressed emotion" (EE); communication deviance (CD); social isolation; and stigma/burden. In addition, it is assumed here that there is a biological contribution to the etiology and to the course of the illness. Also assumed is the widespread belief that schizophrenia is a syndrome, composed of several "diseases" with heterogeneous forms, courses, causes, and treatments (Wyatt, Cutler, DeLisi, Jeste, Kleinman, Luchins, Potkin, & Weinberger, 1982). Likewise, family factors are likely to be only some of the nonbiological influences in this complex condition. As Scheflen (1981) has suggested, schizophrenia is a multilevel problem, with determinants at the biological, psychological, family, social, and political levels. However, the aspects of concern here are only those that can be influenced through MFT, and that, if changed, would lead to an improved course of illness and a better life for the patient and his or her family.

To summarize, these four factors have been shown to be either influential in determining course (enmeshment, isolation, and stigma/burden) or to covary with schizophrenia (CD). Some of these factors appear to interact with one another. Isolation appears to be associated with high EE (Brown, Birley, & Wing, 1972); high EE seems associated with CD (Doane, West, Goldstein, Rodnick, & Jones, 1981), and isolation may be traced to stigma/burden (Lamb & Oliphant, 1978). It seems possible that isolation and CD tend to coexist. None of these factors appear to be specific to schizophrenia, although the coexistence of EE and CD may be not only specific to but predictive of schizophrenia before the initial episode. Thus, the convergence of all four of these factors within one family is probably to be found only among schizophrenic patients' families, while the anticipated course of a patient whose family had all four factors in high degree would be likely to be poor. In addition, one has to assume, based on these same studies, that families with schizophrenic members are heterogeneous: Some may show all four of these phenomena in extreme degree (and may have other problems, such as marital dysfunction, as well); some, at the other extreme, may show only moderate degrees of one or two.

While the research on which this analysis is based is still in a preliminary stage, it seems clear enough in its implications that any psychosocial treatment reducing or eliminating all of these factors would be likely to have a positive effect on the course of schizophrenia and possibly on some of the predisposing processes in a patient's social environment. Specifically, it would reduce relapse rates below those attainable with drugs alone and would promote higher levels of social functioning than those promoted by other interventions that do not deal with these factors. Beyond helping patients, it could also be hoped to lighten the families' burdens and to address their individual needs as well, if only out of fairness.

Is MFT such a modality? Since reports of outcome in MFGs (reviewed in the concluding section of this chapter) are limited in number and are largely uncontrolled, a definitive answer does not yet exist. Nevertheless, major improvements have been consistently noted in exactly the areas in question—relapse rates, social functioning, and family interaction. What is proposed here is that these observed outcomes are the result of therapeutic mechanisms that (1) specifically affect the four family factors described, (2) are unique to MFT, and (3) derive almost completely from its particular social structure. Thus, with regard to schizophrenia, three aspects of MFT contrast with conventional psychosocial therapies: seeming effectiveness, mechanisms of action, and social structure. It is this convergence that provides one of the principal arguments in favor of MFT. It is not a strong one, to be sure, but, combined with the fact that there has been a steady growth in its use in schizophrenia and that families usually prefer MFT over other approaches (and even over being left out of treatment), one can argue that when used it probably makes a significant contribution to the overall treatment effort.

While there are many processes in a multifamily group that promote growth and symptom reduction in families and patients (Laqueur, 1972; McFarlane, 1982), five are emphasized here: resocialization, stigmatic reversal, modulated disenmeshment, communication normalization, and crisis and medication management. These processes directly address those characteristics that seem central to schizophrenia.

RESOCIALIZATION

Families entering an MFG have one of their problems—family isolation—partially solved simply by continuing to participate. Though the group is an artificial means for regaining contact with others outside the family, it satisfies the requirements for a normal social network: The other family members are not kin and are heterogeneous as to age, sex, personality, ethnicity, and class, yet they share a vital common experience and concern—mental illness in one member of the family. Further, the density of the family's network decreases in that the other families provide many different, more complexly varied, and yet less intense relationships, real and potential. With time and the therapists' encouragement, the group can become an almost "natural" network, whose formal characteristics are identical to those of groups that arise spontaneously. The fact that family members of schizophrenic patients have begun to band together in self-help organizations (Hatfield, 1979; Lamb & Oliphant, 1978) is a testament to the need for, and value of, illness-induced network expansion.

This networking process may be compared favorably to what occurs in single-family therapy. In the therapy itself, no real impact is made on a family's isolation in strictly formal terms. Therapists, both by definition and by training, maintain a social distance, usually have little in common with these families, and occupy a fundamentally complementary social status. They can never really know what families have experienced in their struggles with the illness. Too often, therapists are forced by their theoretical concepts and their institutional contexts into a blaming stance that introduces more distance. Also, no reduction in a *family's* isolation occurs when the patient is in individual or group therapy.

The presence of other families is more than just a means of reducing isolation. The other MFT mechanisms that appear to be especially relevant to schizophrenia all depend on members of other families for their operation. Thus, just as the hypothetical interaction of family factors is circular, so are the therapeutic processes in MFT.

Group therapists are aware of the relief and raised morale that occur when group members share their troubles openly and discover that they are not alone. In MFT this process is crucial and especially powerful. As has been suggested above, families of schizophrenic patients carry much larger burdens and may feel much more stigmatized than they might in other kinds of family difficulty. Thus, when family members are given an opportunity to discuss the experience of living with a schizophrenic patient with others who are in similar straits, there is such a profound sense of relief and acknowledgment that stigma appears to be "reversed." That is, family members appear to experience a kind of pride in being able as a group to begin to master and understand the illness that has until then been a guilt-inducing nightmare. This cannot occur to the same degree or with the same rapidity in any other modality. With time, the group begins explicitly to discuss the issue of family as etiology and the fears, shame, guilt, and resentment that arise when one is implicitly blamed for the catastrophe that schizophrenia still is. Eventually, most groups talk over the sense of loss that plagues many families, especially those in which the patients appeared to have special aptitudes.

Given that many families have experienced varying degrees of rejection and discrimination as a consequence of schizophrenia, the group becomes a source of social acceptance that is sorely needed. Depending on the skill of the leaders, an MFG can achieve an identity that counterbalances the sense of nonacceptance that many families experience, providing the *family* with a more positive identity. In an MFG, one can often trace the reduction in rejection and criticism of a patient shown by family members to prior experiences of being accepted and having their frustrations shared by group members.

MFT can have equally positive effects on family burdens. The subjective aspects are somewhat relieved by the shared realization of what living with a schizophrenic individual is like. The realization that other patients do improve induces a sense of impending relief. By ventilating specific anxieties and receiving support and encouragement, family members experience a remoralization that allows them to carry on. As for objective burdens, group members can trade experiences and advice, develop new coping strategies, arrange to relieve one another, and bring political pressure on the therapists and their institutions to provide sorely needed services. Finally, to the extent that the group induces new family interaction patterns that reduce symptomatology and enhance social functioning, the sense *and* reality of burden are reduced. This phenomenon of reversal of stigma and burden goes a long way toward explaining the enthusiasm and loyalty that families come to feel about an MFG and the high rates of attendance and compliance that have usually been reported.

MODULATED DISENMESHMENT

While the importance of family enmeshment as a key factor in schizophrenia has become increasingly clear, reliable means for helping families to develop appropriate boundaries have been more elusive. The core problem in single-family therapy has been to disentangle family members from one another without inducing such anxiety that the patient relapses or otherwise derails the move toward change. The therapist is constantly faced with Scylla-and-Charybdis-like choices; it seems impossible to support each member adequately while challenging even one of them to change.

The social structure of an MFG provides an intrinsic solution to this problem. Families can develop new, less intense, and more functional relationships in the group while preserving family relationships. With time, these new bonds gradually begin to attenuate enmeshment by partially replacing family ties. The choice between enmeshment and loneliness does not loom before a family as it tends to in single-family work. The rate of disenmeshment can be controlled by the therapists and the family, so that change can proceed at a pace that is not threatening to the family. Yet, if the family continues to attend, change seems to occur inevitably, whenever significant involvement in the group develops. Further, rigidity of enmeshed relationship patterns is difficult to maintain, because group interaction tends to be increasingly complex and unpredictable, usually in positive ways. Family members are often surprised by the different ways in which their intimates behave in the group. The patients, especially, assume more responsible and responsive roles in the group than at home or on the ward, helping parents to be less overprotective.

Beyond the indirect effects of social involvement, specific mechanisms arise in MFT that directly reduce enmeshment. In a well-established group, relatives are quite blunt in their criticism of overprotective, disengaged, or rejecting behavior in other families. Such comments are usually received with acceptance and even appreciation, but only when the source is a fellow sufferer. The pressure brought to bear on some family members is often intense, but someone almost always steps forward to support the targeted individual in ways that are remarkably touching and effective. Thus, the single-family therapist's dilemma is avoided: support and confrontation occur simultaneously.

Another subtype of disenmeshment processes could be termed "cross-parenting." Parents, often involved in dysfunctional, fused relationships with their patient–offspring, will show remarkably sensitive and supportive attention to another patient. This not only benefits the recipient, but becomes the basis for new and more adaptive interaction with the parents' own child. These sequences seem to trigger structural change in *both* families. The receiving patient's relatives see that other kinds of behavior not only are possible, but evoke a very different response in their supposedly intractable offspring. Thus, an MFG allows family members to try more adaptive interaction with members of other families before attempting to use them within their own family.

Disenmeshment also occurs through a process of "indirect restructuring." Family members are remarkably attuned to the structural and interactional dysfunctions in other families. In some instances, they appear to apply these lessons to their own families, *without* having the similarity made explicit. Thus, after a course of active intervention in one family, another family with a similar problem will be noted to have made spontaneous improvements in regard to that issue. The same process can occur overtly, but it seems that family insight is not essential to therapeutic change. What *is* essential, again, is the exposure of troubled families to one another.

COMMUNICATION NORMALIZATION

The capacity to improve family communication has been consistently claimed as one of MFT's principal assets; communication has been a primary focus for most multiple family therapists. However, before one concludes that there is an ideal match between an MFT mechanism and CD, a note of caution is warranted. There are two kinds of communication disorder that may afflict families of schizophrenics—one general and one specific (i.e., CD).

What multiple-family therapists have usually been interested in are general communication problems. In MFT, it is almost always reported that families communicate *more*, especially with the patients, and more *openly*, especially concerning negative affects—guilt, resentment, blame, anxiety, and confusion (Hes & Handler, 1961; Levin, 1966; Lewis & Glasser, 1965; Sculthorpe & Blumenthal, 1965). These changes, largely quantitative in nature, follow directly from the high level of verbal activity in most MFGs. Silences are almost unheard of, and brief when they do occur. The accepting, socially symmetrical nature of the group promotes more open and focused communication than does single-family, group, or individual therapy. Harrow, Astrachan, Becker, Detre, and Schwartz (1967) demonstrated this empirically: More participants made a higher number of comments, therapists spoke less, more problem solutions were offered, more family issues were discussed, and more comments were made about others' interactions than in a conventional patients' group. Interestingly, more casual topics were discussed as well, and there was much less "depression." There is general agreement in the literature that the disinhibition in MFT does induce persisting changes in families' ability to talk more openly.

Some qualitative improvements in communication have been reported as well. Davies, Ellinson, and Young (1966) saw increased *clarity* of communication as their most clearly observable area of success. Paul and Bloom (1970) used MFT to help families disclose secrets and reduce expressed projection, denial and blame of the patients. Curry (1965) emphasized the MFG as the ideal forum for families to examine their habitual patterns of communication and to work toward clearer, less distorted expression. Laqueur, LaBurt, and Morong (1964b) reported that two-thirds of families saw improved communication and enhanced mutual understanding as the major outcome of their participation.

However, though these results occurred in cases of schizophrenia, they do not address directly the specific issue of communication deviance (Singer, Wynne, & Toohey, 1978). This is a constellation of stylistic and formal aspects of family conversation, which, when present, reflect odd, disjointed, or excessively vague interaction. Does MFT affect CD? There is no clear answer in the literature; the question is hardly raised, in fact. It is my impression, clinically, that CD does diminish in an MFG if the family remains in the group for several months. Changes in CD seem to parallel improvements in other aspects of communication and family structure. It often seems as if the group process evokes societal norms for speech and discussion, which then influence the members, through group exposure, to conform to them. This "normalization" process is greatly enhanced by the fact that many families do not "have" CD and tend to set norms that are more linguistically adaptive. Such phenomena are examples of the well-known and powerful influence of groups in enforcing conformity to both group and societal norms for behavior and even the structure of thought (Asch, 1952; Festinger, 1957; Hackman, 1976; Schachter, 1951).

Crises tend to diminish in frequency and severity in those families that continue in long-term MFT. This is partly due to regular contact with the therapists, but with time, group members become remarkably adept at picking up prodromal signs in the patients, intervening with the affected families, and learning basic crisis avoidance and management techniques. Though this capacity takes at least a year to develop, the effort is well worth it. The low relapse rates reported seem to be due partly to the group's ability to intervene in incipient psychoses.

Much the same advantages apply to medication. Families demand, and should get, information about the importance and actions of drugs. With time, they help each other with helping patients to be compliant. The therapists can readily monitor drug levels and side effects. Though maintenance levels can often be lowered, they can be raised acutely as part of crisis intervention tactics. Family members can monitor patients who are best treated without medication.

GOALS OF MULTIPLE FAMILY THERAPY

Before describing typical processes and technical guidelines, the goals of MFT with schizophrenic patients need to be made explicit, since the approach to be suggested here follows directly from them. Simply stated, the general goal is to improve the course of illness beyond that achievable with drug therapy, a course that is partly described by recent studies (Hogarty, Schooler, Ulrich, Mussare, Ferro, & Herron, 1979) placing annual relapse rates of depot-medicated patients at 40%—a poor showing, at best—and suggesting that phenothiazines may exacerbate the deficit syndrome (see Chapter 12 of this volume).

MFT can be seen as having six specific objectives, all following from that general goal. They are grouped with reference to three sequential subgoals.

- Prevention of relapse.
    1. Reduction of isolation.
    2. Reduction of stigma and burden (subjective and objective).
    3. Disenmeshment and reduction of EE.
    4. Reduction of communication dysfunction and CD.
- Improved psychosocial functioning.
    5. Correction of more covert, dependency-inducing interactive patterns, when present.
- Social network expansion.

6. Creation of a semipermanent social network organized around the long-term needs of families with schizophrenic members.

The order is meant to suggest both a hierarchy of priorities and a time sequence. That is, each objective depends on the achievement of those preceding it, while there seems to be a natural tendency for MFGs to proceed in this sequence through time. The order also happens to correspond roughly to the relative difficulty of achievement of the objectives; for example, it is much easier to reduce stigma than to change ingrained interaction patterns. In most groups, resocialization and stigma reduction are almost automatically achieved once the group is assembled, assuming an appropriate selection of families. The other objectives depend heavily on the skills and orientation of the therapists for their realization. In addition, the creation of a social network depends on many factors in the institutional context. It should be noted that an inherent contradiction exists between the process of preventing relapse and enhancing a patient's level of social functioning: The former involves reducing the family stress on the patient, while the latter inevitably involves a degree of increased pressure and risk of relapse.

A SCHEMA OF MULTIPLE-FAMILY GROUP INTERVENTIONS

As an aid to the difficult task of describing processes and techniques in MFT, it is useful to delineate four of the most common types of interventions. These are presented as interactions within the social structure, in which the form and sequence of who talks to whom is of more significance than the verbal content. It is the structure of these interactions that is of crucial importance in achieving particular objectives. Obviously, *what* is said is also important, but this will probably be apparent to most experienced group and family therapists, and, in any case, is described below.

TYPE 1: SELF-TRIANGULATION (FIGURE 1)

Basically, Type 1 interventions involve nothing more than serial individual or family interviewing. Thus, content can include questioning, eliciting

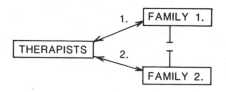

FIGURE 1. *Self-triangulation.*

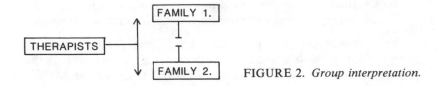

FIGURE 2. *Group interpretation.*

responses or intrafamily interaction, supporting or directly confronting a family or one member, interpreting, clarifying, and so forth. With respect to the group, therapists take a position of self-triangulation, interposing themselves between families or family members. Although the uses of this format are extensive, especially in group formation and regulation of intensity, its overuse is the most common error in the MFT of schizophrenics. It can undermine the most specific and valuable mechanisms of this modality.

TYPE 2: GROUP INTERPRETATION (FIGURE 2)

Essentially, in Type 2 interventions, the therapists take a complementary position to the entire group in order to lay ground rules, share personal reactions, point out commonalities in families or in subgroups, set group themes, and make conventional group interpretations. Group therapists are usually comfortable with this format. Nevertheless, its uses are limited in comparison with those of Types 3 and 4.

TYPE 3: CROSS-FAMILY LINKAGE (FIGURE 3)

Type 3 interventions are based on techniques used in family therapy, supportive group therapy, and community organizing; they are also practiced by talented hosts and hostesses. The therapists use their relationships with family members to promote relationships *across* family boundaries. As in a supportive group, these are not transferential, but real, social bonds, leading to the creation of a task-oriented social network. Usually, the Type 3 technique involves inviting family members to comment about what has been transpiring in another family. This structure is often used

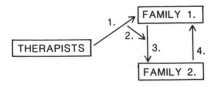

FIGURE 3. *Cross-family linkage.*

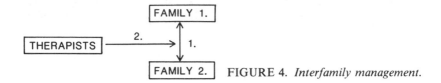

FIGURE 4. *Interfamily management.*

when a question is directed at the therapist: It is simply referred to an appropriate member of another family, or to the group. The art of this tactic is in framing the comment so that it draws two members or families together, in selecting the particular recipients, and in being unobtrusively persistent. Sometimes Type 3 interventions are used to facilitate intrafamily communication and conflict resolution. Many therapists underutilize this technique and thereby short-circuit the potential of their MFGs. It is central to good MFT technique, even though it involves only a narrow range of variations.

TYPE 4: INTERFAMILY MANAGEMENT (FIGURE 4)

Once family members have developed relationships across family boundaries, the therapists use Type 4 interventions to reinforce, to regulate, to expand to others, or sometimes to disconfirm the content of these interactions. The most usual form is congratulating a family member on his or her perspicacity, sensitivity, wisdom, or courage with respect to his or her interventions with another family. On occasion, a leader may take issue with suggestions or observations, either for tactical reasons—to reduce or increase intensity—or because a suggestion, if taken, would produce a poor result. Disagreeing directly is reserved for extreme situations, in that it tends to destroy group integrity if overdone. In its more expanded form (e.g., a comment on the general family issue being addressed), a Type 4 intervention is the most common intervention in an MFG that has achieved a high degree of self-direction; the therapists are largely observers of the group process and make comments from that position. Thus, there is some overlap with Type 2 in an advanced group. The difference is one of intent: Type 2 interventions are most useful in promoting group cohesion; a Type 4 intervention is appropriate as a technique for family problem solving *after* cohesion has been achieved.

VARIETIES OF MULTIPLE-FAMILY GROUPS

Many forms of MFT have been tried over the course of its development. At present, it is possible to delineate four basic types that arise from the combination of two variables: closed versus open membership, and long-term versus short-term course. The typical uses and advantages of each type are reviewed here briefly.

SHORT-TERM OPEN MEMBERSHIP

This is probably the least desirable form for an MFG to take. Simultaneously, it seems to be the most common, in that it lends itself well to the needs of a busy acute care inpatient service in general hospitals and some state hospitals. In this form, the group has a rotating membership. If one subscribes to the view of schizophrenia presented above, it should be clear that little can be accomplished through the multiple-family process, other than a sharing of the acute distress of the psychotic episode itself and a preliminary educational effort. A social network cannot be expected to evolve from this form, so that most of the unique and most powerful mechanisms of MFT will be unlikely to operate. Such groups should be formed only where the alternatives are unattainable. Therapists tend to have all of the difficulties and few of the gratifications that usually go with leading MFGs.

SHORT-TERM CLOSED MEMBERSHIP

Where a long-term group is impractical, this is the better form. Certain degrees of social connectedness can occur; group cohesion reaches a level that allows for some therapeutic intervention; and families can experience enough of the positive value of the modality to make them more open to involvement at a later date. Education can be accomplished in this format and basic applications of family management guidelines, as in Anderson's approach. Again, however, the most far-reaching effects of MFT are unlikely to be realized.

LONG-TERM OPEN MEMBERSHIP

It is sufficient to note that this format is usually adopted by necessity rather than by choice. For reasons of basic group process, with the addition of each new family, the group essentially reverts to the beginning; progress occurs only in the intervals between the integration of new families. With skill, many of the mechanisms of MFT can be utilized if the more experienced families can be induced to take "assistant therapist" roles, easing the new families into the group. This tends to be the format that evolves where the therapists are unable to elicit a group-centered process, usually owing to lack of experience. Clearly, it is the less ideal of the long-term group types.

This is the form that has consistently shown the highest degree of influence on both the process of schizophrenia and the families' involvement in it. The fundamental reason is probably obvious: Much of MFT's effectiveness depends on the formation of a close-knit social network among the families in the group. That takes time, and a minimum degree of consistency of membership, to evolve. This is true for the healthiest of families, and will be even more so for those who are isolated, characterologically shy, and fearful of exposure. Also, since MFT is not curative of schizophrenia, a long-term group seems to fit the chronic course of the illness best. It is my impression that those services that have systematically used this format have also been most successful in realizing MFT's full potential. Organizational arrangements must be made to form this type of group; it is the most difficult to implement in services where there is administrative separation between the inpatient and outpatient services. This is the form recommended here and described in the succeeding pages of this chapter.

PHASE-SPECIFIC TECHNIQUES
IN A LONG-TERM CLOSED GROUP

MFGs that are conducted with a relatively stable membership over long periods of time go through typical phases, much as do all persistent social networks. These are described, and techniques for each phase are suggested.

An effective MFG moves from one extreme (almost totally leader-centered) to the other (group-centered) over a 2- to 3-year course. This process is inherent to this type of group, but it has come to be seen as good technique to exaggerate somewhat these extremes in groups for schizophrenics and their families. This approach tends to place unusual demands on most therapists. For one thing, the requirements of technique vary tremendously over the course of the group. In the beginning, the group is markedly dependent on the therapists, with respect both to process and content. By the last phase, the leaders become almost optional and therefore must be comfortable with an unusually peripheral role. The early phases are very stressful, with conflicting forces, high levels of anxiety, and fast-moving complexity making the format seem almost unworkable for novices. Much later, if they persist, the leaders are able to relax, observe the semiautonomous process in the group, and experience gratification and enjoyment that may surpass that achievable in other modalities. Thus, MFG therapists must possess—or develop—an unusually broad range of therapy styles and techniques, and must be comfortable in both highly active and highly inactive roles. The other requirement is an above average degree of persistence and endurance for those nearly inevitable periods in the beginning when the group seems to be foundering. By contrast, having survived this stage, most therapists report that in their later stages MFGs are the easiest to conduct of all the common therapies. Those who have led them almost universally report that they are the most effective, gratifying, and (paradoxically) untaxing means of treating chronic schizophrenia.

Much can be said about cotherapy in MFT. However, here it is sufficient to note that cotherapy is preferable for all but the most experienced MFG leaders. The difficulties and complexities of the initial phases are usually more than one person can understand or handle. The cotherapists need to have similar views on family dynamics, schizophrenia, and the goals and projected course of the group. They will need a set of signals for alternating their participation in the group, since the best method seems to be a leader–observer division of labor. Ideally, the cotherapists should cultivate an openness that allows for free discussion of group process and intervention tactics. This capacity to be frank will be essential at times of disagreement, because the MFG for schizophrenics will be easily fragmented by covert or unresolved conflict. Often, such conflict derives from the cotherapists' replicating splits in the group or within a particular family.

PHASE I: ASSEMBLING THE GROUP

To organize an MFG for schizophrenic patients, two tasks need to be completed before the first meeting. The first task is to assess and make an empathic alliance with the families. Therapists begin by contacting prospective patients and requesting permission to meet with them and their immediate families. The meetings with the individual families should accomplish the following:

1. *The therapists explore each family's understanding of the illness and its causes, their recent history, precipitating events, and their goals for the patient and treatment.* Some enactment of the family's usual interaction should be created, usually by asking members to discuss among themselves what each of their experiences of the psychosis has been. Any family secrets known to, or shared with, the therapists need to be discussed, with the agreement that they may have to be shared with the group.

2. *The therapists need to estimate each family member's strengths (especially coping skills) and weaknesses (especially vulnerability to criticism and emotional fragility).* The family's stigma and burdens should be assessed, as should their degree of enmeshment and communication disturbance. Family members' attitudes toward groups and their readiness to share their problems need to be assessed.

3. *The therapists need to explain in detail what the goals of the group are, what its usual process is like, and what the leaders' role will be.* Usually, this is a statement that the MFG will help families to understand their ill members' mental illness and to share their experiences and pain with others in the same situation. Further, the therapists can assert that being in the group is a good protection against relapse, because each family will learn new ways of coping. Emphasis can be put on the need for social support when something as serious as mental illness strikes a family. The families' responsibilities are reviewed, especially as regards attending group sessions, saying what they are able in the group, and helping other families as best they can. These sessions may be as few as one, or as many as 10, depending on such factors as the therapists' familiarity with each family, the family members' reluctance to join, the degree of residual psychosis in the patient, or the occurrence of crises during the assessment period. The underlying requirement is that each family develop a solid alliance with the therapists, based on clarity of goals and the therapists' capacities for empathy, warmth, control of the sessions, and so on.

4. *The cotherapists then meet to decide on the composition of their group.* Experience to date suggests the following criteria:

a. *Groups should be homogeneous as to diagnosis and family structure.* Patients, ideally, should all be clearly schizophrenic or schizoaffective, and should be of a roughly comparable degree of ego strength and sociability. Groups should be composed entirely either of couples or of parents with ill offspring and siblings.

b. *Groups should be heterogeneous as to family styles, class, and ethnicity to allow for the greatest variety of values, personalities, and coping styles.* Markedly disturbed families, especially where one of the parents is schizoid, should be grouped, so that there are not extreme disparities of family members' relational abilities. Thus, the general rule is to make groups relatively homogeneous as to both patients' and families' level of functioning, but heterogeneous as to style and social experience.

c. *There is an advantage to grouping by age.* Younger patients with good premorbid social adjustment generally do better with a more interventive, psychotherapeutic approach than do older or more asocial patients. It is difficult to develop a consensus about problem-solving strategies if the strategies themselves must be markedly different for various patients and families.

d. *The best group size appears to be between four and seven families, the smaller size for more highly functional families.*

The second task is to have a few separate group meetings of the patients to be involved in the MFG. The intent is to build a sense of mutual involvement and familiarity among them so that they can better tolerate the initial meetings of the MFG. As may be seen below, the latter can be intense, and the chance to develop a sense of support and comradeship will aid in bolstering patients against being overwhelmed. Pre-MFG meetings will also allow the therapists to ally with the patients, giving them an extra measure of support during the initial sessions.

For most families, the first meeting or two provides an excellent opportunity for lectures and discussion on the phenomenology and management of schizophrenia. The content for these sessions is described in great detail in Chapters 3, 4, and 5 of this volume. Readers are urged to avail themselves of these carefully designed educational programs. What are emphasized here are the process advantages afforded by using one of these formats as the initial intervention in the MFG. By assuming a teacher-like role, the therapists do several things simultaneously. First, they provide a critically important orientation and set of attitudes that creates an overt, shared ideology for the group. This tends to provide a cognitive map for the family members and greatly reduces confusion as to what the illness and the group are all about. Secondly, by putting themselves center stage, the therapists openly take the leadership role, letting the families know that they are taking full responsibility for the group, at least initially. This reduces confusion by clarifying the social structure of the large and seemingly complex MFG, and also reduces anxiety by taking the patients and families out of being the initial focus of the group. Thirdly, the content will act as an elaborate yet reassuring message to the families that the therapists acknowledge their most common underlying need—that they not be blamed for their ill members' psychosis. In this sense, educational activities are powerful joining maneuvers. Finally, by putting themselves at the center of attention, the therapists, through discussion of the content, allow the families to express as much or as little interest in other families as they are comfortable doing, again easing tensions and allowing each family to proceed at its own pace toward social interaction. Clearly, it is preferable for each therapist to perform some part of this function, so that their familiarity to and with the group members is roughly equal. Thus, socialization may begin in the easiest of all formats—the lecture–discussion—while the content emphatically and directly attempts to reduce subjective stigma and burden. This intervention is entirely of Type 1.

PHASE II: BUILDING GROUP COHESION

Greater emphasis will be given to this phase than to the others, because it is the most difficult for most novice MFG therapists and because its successful completion is essential to achieving any substantive therapeutic effect. More than in other phases, technique is vital at this point; as may be seen, it differs from that required for other kinds of groups.

As the heading suggests, the leaders' objective during this stage is to create a comfortable, supportive, goal-directed, and meaningful group climate that prepares for more stressful change-inducing processes later. This does not occur spontaneously. The inherent tendencies are toward chaos and dissolution. More specifically, these include the following: (1) Tension, defensiveness, and confusion on the part of the relatives lead in various families to recalcitrance or agitation and pressured chatter, or to enmeshed, intense blaming. (2) Topics tend to include angry denunciations of the hospital, staff, drugs, and patients for the apparently poor outcome; requests for advice leading to a quick solution; and support for various conventional ideas such as the patients' laziness, lack of will power, desire for retaliation, and so forth. (3) Structurally, the group tends to be grossly imbalanced, with some families dominating the process and others with-drawing, often because they are overwhelmed with the intensity of the group. (4) The group will usually be quite rigidly leader-centered, with the therapists feeling both totally responsible for each family's difficulties and almost overwhelmed by the criticisms and demands of the patients' relatives. This phase is a quintessential example of Bion's "D-group," in which all eyes are on the leaders, waiting for rescue and salvation.

On the positive side, with time there will be some genuine sharing, mostly of the parents' and spouses' reactions to the psychosis. This affords a degree of relief and destigmatization, but, untended, it often veers into depersonalizing blame and/or condescension directed at the patients. Given that their recompensation is fragile at this point (it is assumed that the group is starting early in the recovery phase), too much of this group "high EE" may send at least one patient into a symptomatic regression. At the family level, interaction tends to occur as if the other families are not there; the relatives seem to assume that the format is that of a round-robin, single-family testimonial. Blame, criticism, fragmentation, disorientation, and defensiveness are the rule. At the worst, someone will leave the group; later attendance will be problematic.

It should be clear that spontaneous process at this stage is not therapeutic and that an alternative is required. The key to moving the group through the first sessions with a minimum of these negative processes is to exaggerate leader-centered tendencies in the service of setting a clear direction and set of group norms, avoiding both family and group inter-actions that might derail the task of creating cohesion. As a result, members should feel as if they know one another at their best. The therapists must see the group in the long range and be satisfied by moving slowly, rather than seeing confrontation and catharsis as therapeutic.

In broad outline, the ideal technique begins with a series of Type 1 interventions. As the members appear to become restless with this rather controlled approach, the leaders begin using Type 2 and 3 moves as means of fostering interfamily interaction while still maintaining a moderate degree of control. The group members' dissatisfaction, manifested by directing comments to one another or openly requesting to have more group discussion, is a good indication that the group is sufficiently cohesive and comfortable that a more intensive interfamily process is apt to be therapeutic. In sum, the therapists' purpose at this stage is to reduce social and cognitive ambiguity, by overdirecting if necessary.

This approach is unusually conservative, in the sense that anything that might subvert group cohesion or members' participation is to be avoided, essentially until the spontaneous emergence of tendencies for a more workable therapeutic atmosphere. What is assumed is that the basic human variety in relatives and patients will eventually begin to be expressed in constructive ways that lead inevitably to therapeutic interactions. While this kind of beginning may strike the reader as superficial, the alternatives generally lead to poor results. There is an intriguing contradiction in this technique: Initially exaggerated control of the group by the leaders seems to be necessary for the successful development later of a strongly member-centered, problem-solving social network.

Specifics derived from this general approach will perhaps be apparent to group therapists, but are described here as illustrations of the possibilities. In the first session, after the educational meetings, the leaders again focus the group on themselves by repeating what they have said to the individual families in the pregroup contacts. This should be a somewhat lengthy statement relating the goals of the group to the significant problems experienced by families with schizophrenic members that have been emphasized in the pregroup session(s). The remainder of the meeting is devoted to asking all family members to introduce and describe themselves and their families in as positive a manner as they are able. Anything more than a passing reference to the mental illness in the family is discouraged. The aim is to help families to introduce themselves in as socially conventional a fashion as possible. This can continue into the second session, if necessary.

Following these introductions, all family members, including patients, can be asked to share with the group their perceptions and reactions to the illness. If this proves to be too distressing, a more neutral topic, such as discussions of the educational material or even leisure-time interests, community issues, or work-related concerns, can be the initial focus. Process should be kept to the general discussion format, using Type 1 moves to draw out reactions and Type 2 moves to set the theme and point out commonalities. The leaders should emphasize the things the families share, beyond having mentally ill members. All group members should be drawn out, but only to the extent that they can comfortably tolerate. What is to be avoided is extended focusing on one individual or family and, especially, on intrafamily conflict. The next few sessions should continue to be cordial, social, and relatively superficial.

If intense interactions arise, particularly angry blaming outbursts, the leaders should quickly intervene and reframe criticism either as concern or as the result of frustration over a patient's condition, and quickly move to another topic. A comment that group members need to get to know one another better before such difficult problems can be addressed is usually helpful. As the group progresses, Type 2 interventions that generalize the underlying "concern" or "frustration" can both cut off intense confrontation and exploit the episode as a topic of general discussion. (If this approach appears too superficial, the therapists might remind themselves that they usually do not use discussion of serious family problems as their vehicle for entering a new social milieu.) Throughout, the therapists should emphasize strengths, positive interactions, unique assets of the families, and any changes in the way family members relate to others in their own or another family.

After three to six sessions, a subphase that requires direction and encouragement from the leaders can be observed. Subgroups involving tentative connections across family lines begin to arise, as the result both of a subtle rebellion against the increasingly boring format used to begin the group and of the metacommunication inherent in Type 3 interventions—that cross-family interaction is being sanctioned as a group norm. Interestingly, this process almost always begins with mothers, then involves patients, then fathers, interspersed with an increasing amount of cross-parenting. Gould and DeGroot (1981) have recently documented this sequence empirically in a short-term MFG with a rotating membership. The topic of conversation will inevitably move toward the patient's difficulties. Commiseration is the dominant theme of these emerging subgroups.

This stage calls for the use of Type 2 and 3 interventions. For example, the leaders may ask a specific mother how she reacted to her son's psychosis, then ask another, then ask them to compare notes, and then generalize to other mothers, asking them similar questions. Laqueur (1976) formalized this process by asking all the mothers, for example, to move their chairs into the center of the circle to foster these subgroup formations. The effect on the group, if the process is managed properly, can be powerfully facilitating.

Specific kinds of interactions can be encouraged in the subgrouping process. For instance, arranging that discussions of relatives' reactions to the patients' illness be followed by the patients' describing their own subjective experiences is usually deeply moving, while it begins to break down the barriers between families and between patients and relatives. Such "sequential subgroups" can share disappointments and uncertainties about the future of everyone in the family. The content of subgroup conversations can become too critical and objectifying of the patients, so that the leaders will need to intervene, as before, to convert blame to a more palatable form. The art of it is to do so without interrupting the social joining process that is occurring. This requirement underlines the increasing importance of (often simultaneous) facilitation and limit setting as primary functions of the leaders during this phase. If one's technique is effective, these subgroup discussions have the effect of bringing the group much closer to the status of a "true" group, through the gradual dissolution of both subgroup and, later, family boundaries.

This relaxing of boundaries usually begins during the subgroup phase with the occurrence of cross-parenting interactions, which tend to increase in rough proportion to the emergence of family members as individuals in their own right. In this process, parents in one family take an interest in the patient in another family, usually beginning with exploration of the kind of symptoms or behavior he or she manifested during psychosis. Gradually, however, these contacts take on the quality of real relationships, like other senior-to-junior-adult bonds. They appear to have powerful, healing effects on both parties and are usually quite moving to everyone in the group. The receiving patient will begin to act much more mature and integrated in the group—sometimes immediately—under the influence of such attention. The involved parent, who usually takes a reactive, polarized position with respect to his or her own offspring, begins to show a new-found empathy and respect toward the other family's offspring. As has been frequently described, both sets of new behavior then get transferred into interactions within the respective families. This is an exceedingly complex process: Later, the parent may begin to criticize that patient for being so susceptible to his or her parents' influence, or for failing to see how something he or she is doing is affecting his or her family, or for not complying with medication regimens. Conversely, a patient may quietly but effectively criticize a parent in another family for being overprotective.

During the later sessions of this phase, the leaders should begin to take a less central position. The group becomes transitional between being leader- and group-centered. If the leaders have been successful, the group at this point will be highly cohesive, have a high morale, be relatively intense, and have good attendance. Some of the patients will show gains in responsiveness and social adjustment and will have fewer residual symptoms. Family boundaries, as evidenced in the group, will have diminished significantly. On the other hand, most families will have made relatively few structural or communicational changes. Mostly they will be feeling less burdened, guilty, isolated, and anxious. Given that this phase takes 4 to 6 months to complete, a short-term group will likely resemble this description at its termination.

Technique in this stage, as in the encouragement of superficiality in the initial stage, borders on the paradoxical. That is, by attempting to forestall group process, the leaders will actually tend to promote its development by leaving the initiative to the families themselves. Group members' attempts to move the process to a "higher" level—as in subgroup formation—then become clear and reliable markers for the actual readiness of the group for that and the ensuing stage. This general strategy follows from the all too frequent experience of prematurely pushing MFGs for schizophrenics into intense exploratory intrafamily work and precipitating group dissolution, dropout, regression, or even relapse. Thus, if the leaders can read the process correctly, they can use what have traditionally been regarded as counter-therapeutic group techniques to allow the group to pace itself, with a much larger margin of safety. Sometimes, the "reading" is unnecessary: An overt, independent consensus develops that family problems need to be dealt with by the group. The therapists then follow cautiously along, using the techniques described, while being prepared to resume a more central role if the process gets too intense for a particular family.

PHASE III: DISENMESHMENT AND PROBLEM SOLVING

The demarcation between Phases II and III is often indiscernible. The actual time that precedes this point can vary, depending on the level of health of the families and the skill and determination of the leaders. The emergence of Phase III seems to require the breaking down of family boundaries *and* subgroupings. Cross-parenting processes often signal the approach, if not the arrival, of this phase. Inevitably, members begin to comment on the processes they cannot help observing in other families. Once these observations are verbalized, the group takes on a very different quality. Interaction in the group begins to be increasingly complex, with more and more unpredictability of relationship patterns within the group and, more importantly, within families. Group members' bonds seem to wax and wane, seemingly without reason or pattern. New subgroups arise briefly, then dissolve. In spite of the apparent inscrutability, however, an underlying process is occurring: The group is becoming a kind of task force. To do this, many of the possible relationship and coalition combinations seem to have to be tested out before, or at least during, the group's tackling of intrafamily issues.

It is at this stage that the MFG most closely resembles a therapy group. In groups with young adult schizophrenic patients, the task that begins to emerge and to be often hotly debated is how to help, or force, or trick, the patients into higher levels of social and occupational function. The subtheme, of course, is how parents and relatives may be unintentionally sabotaging recovery and differentiation. The format, previously that of a polite discussion group, now becomes focused on single families or at least single issues, and the mood is increasingly intense and challenging. At a deeper level, the members are drawing on the reserves of support and morale built up during the initial phases in the effort to achieve more satisfying and socially normative family relationships. Thus, Phase III is really group family therapy. Peri passu, individuals begin to emerge from behind family and group role facades, and many new aspects of personality begin to be seen, perhaps most noticeably in the patients.

The leadership role also begins to change, from that of controller to that of facilitator, instigator, interactional model, or even provocateur. The leaders begin this phase by setting a group norm: Glaringly obvious dysfunction in family relationships warrants comment and constructive intervention. Clearly, the first such interventions should be directed to families that either volunteer or are seemingly tolerant and willing. Often, the group itself will take the lead, and the therapists' task then becomes one of facilitating interaction while keeping it on track and at an optimal level of intensity. Throughout, the leaders must modulate intensity and must carefully observe the more fragile of the group's members for signs of being overwhelmed. As time goes by, novice MFG therapists will be surprised at how much intensity schizophrenics can handle in these groups, even though their basic threshold remains about the same.

Another technical problem is to balance a single-family focus against a group-oriented focus. Because some families have a tendency to dominate the group, it is vital to allow each family to request help from the group members. Even while focusing on specific families, there are valuable uses of the discussion format from time to time, both to diffuse affect and to brainstorm on particular common problems, such as job or educational opportunities (to provide a nonfamily activity as part of disenmeshment efforts) or techniques to improve family communication (with some "professional" input from the leaders).

More specifically, technique for this phase has many components. Initially, the leaders must model for the group what kind of family problem is worthy of the group's attention. Examples of enmeshment—speaking for others, interrupting, subtle put-downs and hypercriticism, overprotectiveness, and overreactivity—can be worked with directly by the therapists with Type 1 interventions, framing changes as being helpful in keeping the schizophrenic from being confused. Then, using Type 3 moves, other group members can be asked for their opinions as to how family x might do things differently, or how it handles things. Gradually, the leaders drop back, intervening only to bring in other group members. Subsequently, the leaders can begin sessions by simply asking for a family to present itself, or to follow up with a family that has been the focus previously. Given the rigidity of many enmeshed families, it is to be expected that several interventions by the group will be necessary to effect a structural alteration, so that this phase may continue for an extended period.

In these interactions centering around enmeshment, it is important to make sure that there is someone in the group who is actively supportive of any family member who is being criticized; occasionally, this must be done by one of the leaders, who should then ask if anyone else understands how the member in question might feel or why he or she acts that way. If repeated, this sets up another group norm—that anyone who is asked to account for and/or change dysfunctional behavior by some group members will be supported during the process by others. This combination of confrontation and support is essential for success during this phase. While it is one of the unique properties of MFT, it must be facilitated by the leaders.

Success during this phase is readily apparent. Families will begin to behave differently in the group, with individual family members sitting apart and showing fewer tendencies for being overinvolved, overprotective, and intrusive. The patients will begin to mention interest in looking for work, training opportunities, and sometimes separate living quarters. Family members will begin to volunteer reports of progress in family relations, and group members will begin taking the initiative in making follow-up inquiries of other families. The leaders can encourage this by asking certain group members to inquire, rather than doing so themselves. An issue that often arises at this point is to what extent patients are using the illness to avoid facing difficult life decisions, and to what extent parents are insufficiently or ineffectively challenging them. The process again often begins with cross-parenting interactions, but can be instigated by Type 3 interventions on the part of the therapists. Then they can intervene later to summarize the process and to help given families set gradual goals for their ill members. Actual physical separation should be discouraged until there are other signs of successful differentiation. When (or, for some patients, if) the issue arises, the therapists need to take great care that emancipation is achieved properly.

Many features of the Haley and Madanes approach to "leaving home," summarized in Chapter 9 of this volume, become relevant at this stage, though the leaders should allow the group to carry as much of the weight of work on this issue as is possible. Throughout this phase, the leaders will need to have a model of healthy family functioning in mind, as well as a reserve of family therapy techniques. Both are necessary (1) to judge the usefulness of suggestions by group members, and (2) to intervene with some families directly on occasion, both to effect a sensitive disenmeshment intervention and to model for the group the proper concept and approach. If used discreetly, a paradoxical intervention can be employed, in which the leaders attempt to disqualify group members' efforts to change a certain family's structure by stating that that family needs to avoid change for its own reasons—which should be specified—and that therefore they may resist the group's attempts to help them, possibly for years. This type of maneuver usually has two effects: The group members redouble their efforts, and the family's resistance is greatly weakened as its members struggle to discredit the therapists and join with group members, thus implicitly accepting the proffered criticisms. Clearly, such a move can be made only infrequently to have an effect, and so should be reserved for the most entrenched families at the time of greatest group pressure.

PHASE IV: BUILDING A SOCIAL NETWORK

Again, it is difficult to draw a clear distinction between Phases III and IV, but after 1½ to 3 years the MFG gradually begins to take a different direction, in terms of both process and content. When the families have achieved significantly more appropriate boundaries and relapses have become rare, the group tends to require less and less of the leaders, while the members take a genuine interest in each other as friends or quasi-neighbors. The content of discussions gradually—though haltingly—moves from issues surrounding the patients to marital and personal issues of the nonpatient members. A common theme that emerges is what the parents are going to do with themselves if they need to pay less attention to their schizophrenic offspring. One easy solution is often adopted: to socialize with one another. Thus (unless the group leaders are deluded by conventional strictures against outside contacts), the MFG becomes a social network in which "therapeutic" relationships become "real." It is at this stage that the leaders can begin to turn the process increasingly over to the group members, using primarily Type 4 interventions to encourage the development of social connections. Of course, involvement of relatives with each other is an extension of disenmeshment, and is probably essential to maintaining the gains made in previous phases. Also, it is clear that this is no ordinary friendship network: It is inextricably bound to the clinical service that started it, and will probably always be at least partly oriented toward supporting its schizophrenic participants.

There are certain process features that usually appear. For one, crises —symptomatic and/or family—that were previously handed over to the therapists to handle are now brought to the group. With time, members even help each other to handle problems *outside* the group, only informing the therapists after the fact. Patients and family members begin to come to the group separately, sometimes with other group members. The pre- and post-session periods begin to be as lively as the group itself, if not more so. A degree of humor develops about each family's particular weaknesses, so that teasing becomes an avenue for interfamily intervention. Marital disagreements are openly displayed in the group, or at least reported—a frequent outcome of detriangulation of the patients. Thus, marital problems may become the focus, as may personal issues of individual group members. When single parents predominate, discussion tends toward looking for midlife diversions—returning to school, taking up hobbies, hopes for new relationships, traveling plans, and so on. The group begins to have a definite identity, which is a source of pride and a point of reference for members. Attendance may become more variable, with families apparently feeling free to come and go as they wish.

The real hallmark, as suggested above, is the beginning of spontaneous outside socializing, both by the whole group and by various (usually unpredictable) combinations of group members. Given that many families will have had little social contact before joining the group, this phase is usually deeply appreciated. It is in developing neighbor-like linkages that the sharing in the group becomes concrete: The underlying logic seems to be that people who have been through so much—both in being afflicted with a psychosis and in having as a group overcome many of the ensuing difficulties—and who are possibly facing a lifelong struggle should naturally associate in a more socially normative fashion, like members of any other special interest association. Thus, the MFG can begin to become indistinguishable from a self-help group or a community organization. It is my contention that this outcome will be the highest tribute to the therapists' skills, even though they may become peripheral and may feel deprived of a familiar role. Running through this phase will be intermittent returns to issues of enmeshment and coping strategies, since some families will be much slower in achieving structural and communicational change than others, and because real or threatened symptomatic relapse will tend to send any family temporarily back into old patterns of interaction. The group members need to repeat what was done previously for them, with appropriate assistance from the therapists.

Technical requirements of this phase are, on their surface, simple. The therapists need to turn persistently to the group for leadership, both with respect to continuing to intervene with each other as needed and to working on its conversion to a social network. Thus, Type 3 and 4 techniques will be employed almost exclusively. Intermittent interventions to keep the group on track may be required. Basically, however, the task is more social and emotional: The leaders must endeavor to make themselves as irrelevant as possible. The most common error in this period is for therapists to continue to structure the group around their own role, rather than to foster gradual autonomy. Without this kind of decentralizing effort, the group will tend to stagnate and cycle aimlessly through repetitions of preexisting family dilemmas. Also, the group will begin to seem pointless to many families; dropouts can threaten the existence of the group and its potential.

Most therapists will avoid the obvious mistakes: forbidding outside contact of family members; refusing to make some sessions, especially at holidays, social occasions; refusing to honor requests for separate subgroup meetings (such as parents' meeting alone) or for meetings in members' homes. However, a more subtle error is philosophical—to assume that the group will need the "group therapy" format indefinitely and that it is incapable of achieving a higher level of development. It appears that the proper stance arises out of experience and also out of a commitment to, and understanding of, the power of social networks for mutual support and autonomous coping.

The other source of difficulty at this stage is contextual: Many clinics have no administrative structures with which to support such an amorphous therapy modality. To the extent possible, these problems should be addressed in advance of the group's moving into this phase. One way to handle all of these difficulties is to encourage the group overtly to become allied with one of the national self-help organizations, perhaps even becoming the nucleus of a local branch. Whatever means is chosen, it should be remembered that if the group has survived into this phase, it is a critical part of the families' lives and the patients' long-term treatment package; it should not be terminated, but led to evolve into another form. The time course for this process, at least for most MFGs, will be measured in years rather than months: The average time to reach this point is about 3 years, with wide variations.

THE EFFECTS OF MULTIPLE FAMILY THERAPY

While those who have had some experience in treating schizophrenia with MFT are usually convinced that this approach surpasses other nonbiological methods, the field has a discouraging paucity of outcome data. It is a mystery as to why this state has persisted. One reasonable assumption is that MFT's effectiveness is so obvious to its practitioners that, combined with its economy, it has seemed unnecessary for them to document the results. Another possibility is that since it is both a group and a family therapy, it has never appeared to be novel enough to warrant careful evaluation. One major reason is that Peter Laqueur died before he completed a large outcome study that was in progress. I have recently undertaken a long-term outcome study of different forms of MFT, comparing it to single-family and group therapy, but it will be years before this is completed.

The little data available is worth reviewing, however, in that it is both impressive and consistent. Laqueur (1972), having treated 600 families in

MFT, claimed that hospitalizations of chronic patients were shorter and reduced in frequency, as compared to their own previous course. Lansky (Lansky, Bley, McVey, & Botram, 1978) noted that only one patient of 10 treated with their families of origin relapsed in a long-term group in 2 years. He claimed that all but one patient made significant social and vocational improvements after discharge. He linked the two phenomena: The continuing remission allowed patients to attend to other life issues. His group of married patients also enjoyed a lower relapse rate, but progress in other areas was limited. Levin (1966) reported a complete absence of relapse in a group of 19 psychotic patients, most of them schizophrenic, in a short-term MFG that began treatment shortly after admission to an inpatient service. Berman (1966) organized MFGs in a Veterans Administration hospital, treated psychotic and neurotic patients together, and had no relapses in 12 months, although the number of patients was not specified. Lurie and Ron (1972) reported rehospitalization rates of 19% after 2 years and 12% at 3 years postdischarge. Schaeffer (1969) found that for psychotic patients with two or fewer hospitalizations, MFT significantly improved ward sociability.

As has been mentioned, improvements in intrafamily communication, especially between the schizophrenic and his or her relatives, has been reported as a clinical impression in almost every account of MFGs in the literature (Berman, 1966; Blinder, Colman, Curry, & Kessler, 1965; Curry, 1965; Davies et al., 1966; Detre et al., 1961; Harrow et al., 1967; Hes & Handler, 1961; Lansky et al., 1978; Levin, 1966; Lewis & Glasser, 1965; Sculthorpe & Blumenthal, 1965). This is so consistent a record, and so consistent with my own and others' unreported experience, that it is difficult to discount, especially in light of the importance of family communication in schizophrenia and the tremendous difficulties reported by single-family clinicians in addressing this same problem. Again, clinical impressions are not controlled trials, so a claim of effectiveness is made only with caution.

The other impression shared throughout the literature is that families and patients *like* MFT, in contrast to other modalities. Consistently, families request continuation of short-term groups at their termination or point of discharge. Attendance is rarely a problem, and loyalty and enthusiasm increase throughout the course of the groups. While this effect raises family morale, it also improves compliance, in that the family and other group members become part of the drug and social management process.

Family structural changes, especially reduction of intrusiveness, overprotectiveness, and triangulation, have been noted in several reports (Atwood & Williams, 1978; Berman, 1966; Lansky et al., 1978; Laqueur,

1972; Leff, Kuipers, & Berkowitz, Chapter 7 of this volume; Lewis & Glasser, 1965). In many groups, there has been a tendency for the patients to show remarkable changes in maturity and integration; I have noted this quite consistently as well. The extension of these changes into other areas of functioning has not been documented. To some extent, this effect has been said to derive from their being related to as adults by other patients' relatives in cross-parenting interactions.

Only one report in 20 years has found negative effects. Marx and Ludwig (1969) used an MFG to meet with families that had broken ties with the patients for several years. While the group had all the usual positive effects on the patients, two members (i.e., not previously patients) of the 44 families treated suffered psychotic episodes during the course of the therapy. This appears to reflect the well-documented intensity of MFGs and perhaps the seeming inexperience of the therapists. In spite of this, the authors reported that most of the families became much more allied with the treating staff after the MFG meetings.

CONCLUSION

In recent years, renewed efforts to address the needs of the families of schizophrenic patients have led to the therapies reported in this book. In a way, their underlying assumptions match those held by many multiple-family therapists in the past. One of those assumptions—that the families provide a vital source of therapeutic leverage with patients, if they can be enlisted as allies—has been the core rationale of MFT since its inception. By contrast, previous family interventions, based on the family's culpability for the patient's illness, have assumed that the family must be completely overhauled to "free" the patient. An MFG has generally been seen as possessing both capabilities; it readily enlists family participation and cooperation, reduces feelings of blame, and then provides several avenues for significant alteration in family interaction, all the while providing an opportunity for relatives to share their pain, guilt, and perplexity and to develop a critically needed social support system. At present, two areas seem prominently lacking: (1) rigorous evaluation of outcome, and (2) clinical experimentation with combinations of "psychoeducational" and "structural" versions of MFT with various subgroups of schizophrenic patients. The latter should help in understanding which techniques are appropriate with which kind of patients and families. Until the emergence of data clarifying all these issues, the principal recommendation for MFT is that those who have tried it almost always like it—a statement not often made about other forms of treatment for schizophrenia.

REFERENCES

Asch, S. *Social psychology*. Englewood Cliffs, N.J.: Prentice-Hall, 1952.

Atwood, N., Williams, M. E. D. Group support for the families of the mentally ill. *Schizophrenia Bulletin*, 1978, *4*, 415–425.

Berman, K. K. Multiple-family therapy: Its possibilities in preventing readmission. *Mental Hygiene*, 1966, *50*, 367–370.

Blinder, M. C., Colman, A., Curry, A., & Kessler, D. MFGT: Simultaneous treatment of several families. *American Journal of Psychotherapy*, 1965, *19*, 559–569.

Brown, G. W., Birley, J. L. T., & Wing, J. K. The influence of family life on schizophrenic disorders: A replication. *British Journal of Psychiatry*, 1972, *121*, 241–258.

Curry, A. E. Therapeutic management of multiple family groups. *International Journal of Group Psychotherapy*, 1965, *15*, 90–95.

Davies, I. J., Ellinson, G., & Young, R. Therapy with a group of families in a psychiatric day center. *American Journal of Orthopsychiatry*, 1966, *36*, 134–146.

Detre, T., Sayer, J., Norton, A., & Lewis, H. An experimental approach to the treatment of the acutely ill psychiatric patient in the general hospital. *Connecticut Medicine*, 1961, *25*, 613–619.

Doane, J. A., West, K. L., Goldstein, M. J., Rodnick, E. H., & Jones, J. E. Parental communication deviance and affective style. *Archives of General Psychiatry*, 1981, *88*, 679–685.

Festinger, L. A theory of social comparison processes. *Human Relations*, 1957, *7*, 117–140.

Gould, E., & DeGroot, D. Inter- and intrafamily interaction in multifamily group therapy. *American Journal of Family Therapy*, 1981, *9*, 65–74.

Hackman, J. R. Group influences in individuals. In M. Dunnette (Ed.), *Handbook of industrial and organizational psychology*. Chicago: Rand McNally, 1976.

Harrow, M., Astrachan, B., Becker, R., Detre, T., & Schwartz, A. An investigation into the nature of the patient–family therapy group. *American Journal of Orthopsychiatry*, 1967, *37*, 888–899.

Hatfield, A. B. Help-seeking behavior in families of schizophrenics. *American Journal of Community Psychology*, 1979, *7*, 563–569.

Hes, J., & Handler, S. Multidimensional group therapy. *Archives of General Psychiatry*, 1961, *5*, 92–97.

Hogarty, G. E., Schooler, N. R., Ulrich, R., Mussare, F., Ferro, P., & Herron, E. Fluphenazine and social therapy in the aftercare of schizophrenic patients. *Archives of General Psychiatry*, 1979, *36*, 1283–1294.

Lamb, H. R., & Oliphant, E. Schizophrenia through the eyes of families. *Hospital and Community Psychiatry*, 1978, *29*, 805–806.

Lansky, M. R., Bley, C. R., McVey, G. G., & Botram, B. Multiple family groups as aftercare. *International Journal of Group Psychotherapy*, 1978, *29*, 211–224.

Laqueur, H. P. General systems theory and multiple family therapy. In J. Masserman (Ed.), *Current psychiatric therapies*. New York: Grune & Stratton, 1968.

Laqueur, H. P. Mechanisms of change in multiple family therapy. In C. J. Sager & H. S. Kaplan (Eds.), *Progress in group and family therapy*. New York: Brunner/Mazel, 1972.

Laqueur, H. P. Multiple family therapy. In P. J. Guerin, Jr. (Ed.), *Family therapy: Theory and practice*. New York: Gardner Press, 1976.

Laqueur, H. P., LaBurt, H. A., & Morong, E. Multiple family therapy. In J. Masserman (Ed.), *Current psychiatric therapies* (Vol. 4). New York: Grune & Stratton, 1964.(a)

Laqueur, H. P., LaBurt, H. A., & Morong, E. Multiple family therapy: Further developments. *International Journal of Social Psychiatry*, Congress Issue, 1964, *10*, 69–80.(b)

Laqueur, H. P., & Lebovic, D. Correlation between multiple family therapy, acute crises in a therapeutic community, and drug levels. *Diseases of the Nervous System*, 1968, *29*, 188–192.

Levin, E. C. Therapeutic multiple family groups. *International Journal of Group Psychotherapy*, 1966, *19*, 203–208.

Lewis, J. C., & Glasser, N. Evolution of a treatment approach to families: Group family therapy. *International Journal of Group Psychotherapy*, 1965, *15*, 505–515.

Lurie, A., & Ron, H. Socialization program as part of aftercare planning. *General Psychiatric Association Journal*, 1972, *17*, 157–62.

Marx, A., & Ludwig, A. Resurrection of the family of the chronic schizophrenic. *American Journal of Psychotherapy*, 1969, *23*, 37–52.

McFarlane, W. R. Multiple family therapy in the psychiatric hospital. In H. Harbin (Ed.), *The psychiatric hospital and the family*. Jamaica, N.Y.: Spectrum, 1982.

Paul, N. L., & Bloom, J. D. Multiple family therapy: Secrets and scapegoating in family crisis. *International Journal of Group Psychotherapy*, 1970, *20*, 37–47.

Schachter, S., Deviation, rejection and communication. *Journal of Abnormal and Social Psychology*, 1951, *46*, 190–207.

Schaeffer, D. S. Effects of frequent hospitalizations on behavior of psychotic patients in multiple family therapy. *Journal of Clinical Psychology*, 1969, *25*, 104–105.

Scheflen, A. *Levels of schizophrenia*. New York: Brunner/Mazel, 1981.

Sculthorpe, W., & Blumenthal, I. J. Combined patient–relative group psychotherapy in schizophrenia. *Mental Hygiene*, 1965, *49*, 569–573.

Singer, M. T., Wynne, L. C., & Toohey, M. L. Communication disorders and the families of schizophrenics. In L. C. Wynne, R. L. Cromwell, & S. Matthysse (Eds.), *The nature of schizophrenia*. New York: Wiley, 1978.

Wyatt, R. J., Cutler, N. R., DeLisi, L. E., Jeste, D. V., Kleinman, J. E., Luchins, D. J., Potkin, S. G., & Weinberger, D. R. Biochemical and morphological factors in schizophrenia. In L. Grinspoon (Ed.), *Psychiatry: 1982*. Washington, D.C.: American Psychiatric Press, 1982.

7

INTERVENTION IN FAMILIES OF SCHIZOPHRENICS AND ITS EFFECT ON RELAPSE RATE

Julian P. Leff
Liz Kuipers
Ruth Berkowitz

FAMILY INFLUENCES ON SCHIZOPHRENIA

Family therapy first developed in relation to patients with schizophrenia, the impetus being a number of influential theories concerning the role of the family in producing this illness. These theories were elaborated in the 1950s by Bateson and his colleagues (Bateson, Jackson, Haley, & Weakland, 1956), Lidz (1958), Wynne and his colleagues (Wynne, Ryckoff, Day, & Hirsch, 1958), and Laing (1960). They became exceedingly popular both among professionals and the lay public, partly because they transformed schizophrenia from incomprehensible lunacy to an understandable reaction to family pressures, and partly because the kind of behavior they described in family members was instantly recognizable. The reason these theories had such universal appeal, in fact, undermines them as explanations for the appearance of schizophrenia. If everyone has experienced a "double-bind" situation, it cannot be specific to families containing a schizophrenic member. Another problem with each of these theories is that it purported to be both universal and exclusive. The claim was that each theory totally explained the origin of schizophrenia, from which it follows that only one of the theories could be true. The terms coined by these theorists—"double bind," "marital schism and skew," "pseudomutuality," "scapegoating"— have become part of the language of psychiatry, even though there is no evidence that the behaviors they refer to are characteristic of families of schizophrenic patients (Hirsch & Leff, 1975).

JULIAN P. LEFF, LIZ KUIPERS, and RUTH BERKOWITZ. MRC Social Psychiatry Unit, Institute of Psychiatry, London, England.

A major problem in testing these theories is that they relate to the first appearance of schizophrenia, so that the crucial evidence has to come from preschizophrenic subjects. The only strategy available at the moment is the mounting of long-term follow-up studies of cohorts of subjects at high risk for developing schizophrenia because of their genetic loading. A number of such longitudinal studies are currently in progress but will not come to fruition for many years (Garmezy, 1974).

Since there is no solid evidence that any of the above theories accounts for the origin of schizophrenia, it would seem premature to use them to direct intervention in families of schizophrenic patients. Our own program of intervention stems more from a methodological advance than from any single etiological theory of schizophrenia. Brown and his colleagues (Brown, Bone, Dalison, & Wing, 1966) found that schizophrenic patients discharged from hospitals were less likely to be readmitted if they went to live on their own than if they returned to parents or spouses. Brown suspected that some aspect of the emotional interaction between schizophrenic patients and their relatives was exacerbating their condition. Together with Rutter (Brown & Rutter, 1966), he developed a standardized and reliable technique for assessing the quality of emotions shown when a relative talked about the patient in response to a semistructured questionnaire. The measuring technique they devised is known as "expressed emotion" (EE) and has been subsequently streamlined and modified (Vaughn & Leff, 1976b). The interview now takes about an hour, and the index of EE derived from it is based on the number of critical remarks made by the relative in the course of the interview and on the degree of emotional overinvolvement shown. The rater assesses both the content of the relative's remarks and the way in which they are delivered, taking account of tone, volume, and rate of speech.

A series of studies (Brown, Birley, & Wing, 1972; Brown, Monck, Carstairs, & Wing, 1962; Vaughn & Leff, 1976a) has established a robust association between high EE shown by the relatives and relapse of schizophrenia in the patients during the 9 months following discharge from hospital. A 2-year follow-up of the patients from the last study of the series has shown that this association remains stable over 2 years following discharge (Leff & Vaughn, 1981). A detailed analysis of the data from the studies of Brown et al. (1972) and Vaughn and Leff (1976a) revealed that patients living in high-EE homes could protect themselves to some degree against relapse by taking regular maintenance drugs or by spending little time in the company of the relatives. If both protective measures were employed, the relapse rate dropped even further and became equal to the rate of patients in low-EE homes.

It appeared from this analysis that the relapse rate in schizophrenic patients living in high-EE homes could be substantially reduced by a combination of pharmacological and social treatments. The latter should have two aims: the reduction of social contact between patients and relatives, and the lowering of EE in the relatives. Thus, this body of research work has defined clear aims for the therapist attempting to intervene in the families of schizophrenics, an essential prerequisite for any scientific trial of such treatment (Leff, 1979).

Before describing our current trial of social intervention, it is worth considering the light that the findings on EE throw on the family theories of the etiology of schizophrenia. Firstly, it is important to note that only about half of the schizophrenic patients included in the EE studies were still living with their parents. The remainder had married and were living with their spouses. It was found that spouses were just as critical of patients as were parents, so that this reaction to schizophrenia is quite independent of any genetic link between patients and relatives. Emotional overinvolvement was found in several parents but in no spouses in the published studies. However, in our recent work we have encountered undoubted overinvolvement in a small number of spouses, so that this emotional attitude is also independent of genetics. Furthermore, in a comparison between the relatives of schizophrenic and depressed neurotic patients, it emerged that the level of criticism was the same in both groups (Vaughn & Leff, 1976a). So, once again, the family behavior studied is not specific to schizophrenia. It seems sensible to conclude that we are focusing on a nonspecific form of environmental stress and that the response to this of a subject with a schizophrenic illness is due to a specific inherited vulnerability. Seen from this viewpoint, the etiological family theories probably delineate different varieties of difficult behavior in families, nonspecific in themselves, but acting on the specific genetic vulnerability of particular members.

Another implication from the EE work, of the utmost importance, is that by no means all families containing schizophrenic members show abnormal behavior or attitudes. In the study of Vaughn and Leff (1976a), 43% of families fell into the low-EE category, showing neither excessive criticism nor overinvolvement. In fact, the distribution of EE is markedly skewed toward zero, with 10 (22%) of the 46 relatives scoring nil on both criticism and overinvolvement. It cannot be assumed that the distribution of EE is identical in every culture; indeed, we have preliminary evidence of considerable transcultural variation. However, the lesson to be learned is that any abnormality focused on is not found in every family with a schizophrenic member.

Thus the research on EE contradicts the assumptions of the etiological family theories that the abnormalities detected are specific to families of schizophrenic patients and are common to them all. As we indicate later, this does not necessarily invalidate the observations on which these grandiose theories were constructed.

One final point remains to be explored—namely, the extent to which the EE findings can be extrapolated back in time to before the onset of schizophrenia. This is in fact logically inadmissible, since it cannot be assumed that attitudes detected after the appearance of schizophrenia in a family member necessarily antedated the illness. They might just as easily be a product of dealing with a sick person as an etiological precursor of the disease. However, there are some interesting links with material from other studies. Hirsch and Leff (1975) concluded that the best available evidence relating to family attitudes *before* the onset of schizophrenia came from studies of Child Guidance Clinic records (O'Neal & Robins, 1958; Waring & Ricks, 1965). This work showed that mothers were overprotective of their children long before there was any sign of schizophrenic illness. In addition, the parents of preschizophrenic children showed more conflict and disharmony than did controls. The overprotectiveness of mothers clearly overlaps with the overinvolvement scale of EE, of which it is one component. Parental discord has a less obvious link with EE, but was found in a high proportion of high-EE households where both parents were present. Thus there is some continuity between family factors identified before and after the onset of schizophrenia, which tentatively suggests that high-EE relatives may play a part in the etiology of the condition as well as being implicated in relapse.

A TRIAL OF INTERVENTION

DESIGN

We were impelled to conduct this trial for two reasons, one theoretical and the other practical. Theoretically, the association between high-EE relatives and relapse of schizophrenia can be interpreted in at least two ways: either some feature of the patients' behavior provokes high-EE responses in the relatives and also leads to relapses of the patients' illness, or else high-EE attitudes actually play a causal role in precipitating relapse. To determine the direction of cause and effect, it is necessary to intervene in order to alter high-EE attitudes and observe whether there is a concomitant fall in the relapse rate. From the practical point of view, there would be an obvious clinical advantage to any procedure that could reduce the relapse rate in schizophrenia.

We felt that at this point in time, our knowledge of the effectiveness of maintenance therapy was such that it was unethical to withhold such treatment. The question to be asked is then formulated as follows: Is it possible for social intervention to lower the relapse rate significantly below that achieved by maintenance drugs? In order to demonstrate a significant effect of social treatment over and above that of drug treatment, we have adopted the strategy of singling out the group of patients at highest risk of relapse. These are the patients in high social contact with high-EE relatives. We screen three different hospitals, and when we have identified suitable patients we ask the specialists looking after them to consider prescribing long-acting phenothiazines by injection. In almost every case, the specialists have complied with our request. A few patients, however, are on oral maintenance therapy. The patients are then randomly assigned to our package of social intervention or to routine outpatient care. The viability of the trial clearly depends on these two forms of management remaining distinct in character. Fortunately, the hospitals in which the trial is being conducted are conservative in their treatments, and relatives are rarely involved in the therapeutic process.

Although our trial design is based on the classical double-blind, placebo-controlled trial that is now standard for the assessment of drug treatments, there are many aspects that have to be modified where social therapies are concerned. We have already encountered one problem—namely, that *there is no placebo for a social treatment*, so that a control treatment has to be chosen that is sufficiently different from the treatment under test. In order to be sure that the two kinds of treatment differ substantially, it is necessary to stipulate in considerable detail what care the families in each group receive. This raises the familiar problem of specifying what goes on in a therapeutic session, an obstacle we have not entirely succeeded in overcoming. Fortunately, this disadvantage is partially compensated for by our having two clear aims by which to measure the success of social intervention. If we were to find that social contact or EE or both were reduced significantly more in the experimental than in the control group, this in itself would support the contention that the two kinds of treatment were substantially different.

Another major difference from a drug trial is that not all the patients in the experimental group receive the same treatment. To take an obvious example, it would clearly be inappropriate to provide the same social treatment for patients living in parental and marital homes. In practice, it is necessary to have a package of social treatments that is adapted to the unique needs of each particular family. This raises the problem of standardization, but as stated above, the aims of the experimental treatment are the same for every family and are assessed with a reliable method. Hence, we can judge in each case whether the aims were attained, even though the means may have been very different.

THE PACKAGE OF SOCIAL TREATMENTS

There are certain elements in the package that are applied to every family. One is an education program about schizophrenia. The reason for including this was the finding from a content analysis that the majority of critical comments (70%) related to the negative symptoms of schizophrenia, rather than the florid symptoms, such as delusions and hallucinations (Leff & Vaughn, 1976). In general, relatives did not recognize that behaviors such as lying in bed during the day and failing to help with household chores could be part of the picture of an illness. Instead, they considered them as under the patients' control, and therefore blamed the patients for not behaving more positively. Furthermore, few relatives appeared to understand the nature of schizophrenia or even to grasp some elementary facts about it. Consequently, we have prepared a program of four lectures on the etiology, symptoms, course, and management of schizophrenia, which are read to the relatives during home visits. It was thought likely that relatives would be able to absorb more information in the security of their own homes than in a clinical setting. Following the lectures, which take about 10 minutes each, the relatives are allowed unlimited time to ask any questions they want.

The effectiveness of the educational program is evaluated by means of a Knowledge Interview, a list of 18 questions that is administered before and after the program. The same Knowledge Interviews are given to the control relatives at about the same interval of time, but of course with no intervening attempt to educate them. As yet we have no results from this element of the package, but our initial impression is that the effects are small, though possibly important.

The other element designed to be common to all experimental families is a relatives' group. There were a number of reasons for setting this up, the main one being as follows: We have emphasized above that almost half the relatives living with schizophrenic patients admitted to hospital fall into the low-EE group and are coping very adequately with the problems of daily management of this condition. One might imagine that in contrast to the high-EE relatives, these others are cool, remote, and uninvolved with the patients. Recent work on psychophysiological responses of patients to their relatives suggests that this is far from the case and that low-EE relatives play an active role in helping patients adjust to environmental stress (Sturgeon, Kuipers, Berkowitz, Turpin, & Leff, 1981; Tarrier, Vaughn, Lader, & Leff, 1979). It was therefore considered possible that low-EE relatives could teach the coping skills they had developed to high-EE relatives. A relatives' group was formed, composed of high-EE experimental relatives and of low-EE relatives, all of whom were unaware of their categorization. The group meets once every 2 weeks for an hour and a half, has a maximum of eight members at any one time, and includes two professionals. These are psychologists who are part of the research team (Kuipers and Berkowitz) and who act not so much as therapists but as catalysts to draw out relatives on the problems they face and how they tackle them. Other reasons for setting up the group included the need to counter the sense of isolation felt by many relatives of schizophrenic patients, the possibility that the group would allow relatives to discharge emotions that would otherwise be directed at the patients, and the fact that it was economical of resources.

It is necessary to justify our exclusion of patients from the group, which was done for two main reasons. Firstly, as stated above, we wished to provide a safety valve for high-EE relatives in order to divert their emotions away from the patients. Secondly, the families join the study when the patients are acutely psychotic, and we felt that the patients would be in no state to participate in the kind of processes we wished to encourage; rather, they would act as a distraction from them.

The group is flexible both in regard to membership and attendance. Relatives come when they can, but if they fail to arrive and have given no warning we phone them to enquire about their absence. They are encouraged to attend for the 9 months of the study period, but are free to continue coming thereafter if they wish; a number of relatives have attended the group for over a year. As new patients are inducted into the study, their relatives join the group. When a new member is introduced into the group, the practice is to ask each relative present to give a short account of his or her experience. An attempt is made at all meetings to give each member an opportunity to talk about current problems or just to tell the group how things have been in the past fortnight.

The relatives generally sit in any place they choose, but occasionally the therapists decide beforehand that one of them will sit next to a relative who is having a difficult time, or that two relatives are upsetting each other and should be encouraged to sit apart. Most meetings start with a general question to the whole group about how things have been. The first problem raised becomes the focus of discussion. The therapists try to encourage participation by asking other members if they share the same emotional reaction to the problem. Later on, the group will be asked to provide alternative ways of coping with the problem. The therapists endorse strategies that avoid direct criticism of the patient, or that are likely to lead to greater freedom and independence for both relative and patient.

In addition to this function of peer group pressure on high-EE members to adopt alternative methods of coping with problems, the group also provides a great deal of emotional support to members. This stems largely from each relative's discovery that he or she is not the only person in the world facing the daily problems of living with a schizophrenic patient. They experience considerable relief from guilt, shame, and fear, as well as freedom from their sense of isolation. The group also provides the opportunity for the expression of distressing feelings in a safe atmosphere. Many of the high-EE relatives tend to use the group exclusively for this purpose at first, and they may dominate meetings with an outpouring of emotions. This is a useful start, but has to be curtailed after a while to allow more constructive activities to take place. A characteristic of high-EE relatives is that they talk a great deal and listen very little. After they have settled into the group, the therapists encourage them to talk less, change the subject less often, and listen to other people's problems.

Another high-EE characteristic is the inability to empathize with a patient's experiences and the consequent tendency to invalidate them—for example, to tell the patient that the voices he or she is hearing do not exist. One way of dealing with this difficulty in appreciating the patient's viewpoint is the use of role play. The relative is asked to play the part of the patient, while a therapist or another group member acts as the relative. This can lead to a breakthrough in the relative's understanding of the patient. It is our impression after 4 years' experience that the group has fulfilled the functions originally conceived for it, although we have not built into the design any separate evaluation of its effect on the members. Our experience with the group is presented in more detail elsewhere (Berkowitz, Kuipers, Eberlein-Vries, & Leff, 1981).

The group was not set up to deal with the more dynamic aspects of relatives' relationships with the patients, nor is it an appropriate setting in which to explore marital conflicts in parents. Therefore we have been prepared to supplement the group with home visits to individual families for the purpose of conducting family therapy, marital therapy, or whatever we felt was called for in each case. This exemplifies the flexibility we consider essential in any program of social intervention with families.

The above procedures are focused on reducing levels of EE, but we had the additional aim of attempting to lower social contact between patients and relatives. Indeed, when we first began the study, this was our first priority because we imagined it would be by far the easier of the two tasks. We proved to be wrong in this supposition, as it often emerged that unless the emotional bonds welding patient and relative together are tackled first, neither partner will allow separation to take place. The administrative measures we were prepared to employ to achieve separation are set out in an earlier publication (Leff, 1976). They include placing patients in sheltered accommodations; ensuring their attendance at a day hospital or day center or as day patients on a ward; persuading the relatives to take jobs; and attempting to restructure leisure activities. A major problem in attempting to move a patient from a parental home is that if either parent is emotionally overinvolved, he or she will not allow the patient to leave. Furthermore, the patient also contributes to this bond and is often as emotionally dependent on the relative as the relative is on him or her. So far, we have only been able to move one patient away from his parents, and this has proven to be temporary (see "Family 1," below). Another practical problem is the dearth of sheltered accommodation and the fact that vacancies rarely arise at the time they are needed, which may be a short-lived crucial period. In general, it is easier to discharge patients directly from hospitals to sheltered accommodation than to extract them from home once they have gone back to their parents.

The problems that arise in respect to work are closely related to national unemployment figures. When millions of healthy people are out of work, it is virtually impossible to find a job for someone with a history of psychiatric illness. It is not too difficult to find vacancies at day hospitals or day centers, but many patients experience the work there as boring or demeaning, particularly if they come from the higher social classes. The provision of sheltered work that is not totally repetitive and mindless is dependent on the state of industry, and of course it becomes scarce in a time of economic recession.

Leisure activities also pose problems, partly because of the patients' handicaps and partly due to lack of appropriate facilities. Many schizophrenic patients suffer a loss of interest in sports and hobbies, so that it is difficult to motivate them to make use of their leisure time. There is also the problem of poor social skills, which is compounded by the stigma of the illness, with the result that patients have few if any friends outside the immediate family and so are thrown into more intimate contact with relatives, who may be high in EE. One answer would seem to be social clubs for patients. However, these have the disadvantage that patients only meet other patients there and may well prefer not to be reminded of their recent illness. A solution is to set up clubs that are attended both by patients and by normal people from the community. Obviously the latter have to be specially motivated, but such "mixed" social facilities have been successfully established in a few places.

CLINICAL MATERIAL

In an attempt to convey a clearer idea of the way in which the flexible package of interventions has been applied in practice, our experiences with a number of families in the experimental group are presented here.

FAMILY 1

Colin lived with his mother and stepfather and a younger brother. The mother was a powerful and dominating woman who had thrown her first husband out for excessive drinking when her two sons were very young, and had then brought them up single-handed. She had always perceived Colin as being the more vulnerable of her two children, an attitude that was reinforced when he had a severe attack of pneumonia in early childhood. He had slept in her bed until the age of 15, an extreme manifestation of maternal overinvolvement. The mother had remarried a shopkeeper who was a strict disciplinarian.

Colin's illness began insidiously at the age of 20, and for almost a year neither parent realized that he was psychiatrically ill. His attack of schizophrenia was dominated by negative symptoms. He would lie in bed all morning and let his hair grow long, both of which infuriated his stepfather. When we measured EE levels of the parents, with both of whom Colin was in high social contact, we found that the stepfather was highly critical of Colin, while the mother was both overinvolved and highly critical. She was completely open about her feelings for Colin and said in front of her husband that if she had to choose between the two of them she would have no hesitation in sending her second husband packing, as she had her first.

In this family, we can discern patterns of behavior that fit descriptions given by two of the family theorists referred to above, Lidz and Bateson. The relationships would fit neatly Lidz's formulation of "marital skew," with a dominant mother forming an alliance with her son with sexual overtones, and a peripheral father. In addition, the mother's combination of overinvolvement and criticism can be seen as conforming to most of the criteria for a "double-bind" situation. It is as though she was saying to Colin, "I don't like what you are doing, but I'm not going to let you get away from me." As we stated above, the observations made by the family theorists were not incorrect; only their propensity to make sweeping generalizations from them was. Their descriptions remain useful ways of formulating problems in *some* families.

Our primary strategy for this family was to remove Colin from the home, but we recognized that we would have to deal with the mother's overinvolvement if we were to achieve this aim. We decided that we needed to deal with the poor marital relationship in order to divert the mother's libidinal attachment from her son to her husband. Consequently, we arranged to conduct some conjoint marital sessions in the home, in addition to asking the parents to attend the relatives' group.

We arranged with the clinical team looking after Colin that as soon as he was well enough he would attend the day hospital, a 10 A.M. to 4 P.M. commitment. In addition, we asked them to try to find a place in a hostel for him. Both these strategies were successful, and Colin was discharged from the hospital to a Richmond Fellowship Hostel. He eventually graduated from the day hospital to a paid job, which he has now kept for 2 years. He has continued to receive long-acting injections of fluphenazine.

When we gave the education program to the parents, we noted a dramatic change in the stepfather's attitude. He acknowledged that Colin was suffering from an illness, and lost most of his criticism. However, he showed an alarming tendency to become somewhat overinvolved! Fortunately, he was aware of the danger of this and was able to maintain a certain distance from Colin and to refrain from "thinking for him," as he put it. Both parents attended the group regularly and even requested to carry on beyond the 9-month follow-up. We carried out sessions of marital therapy in their home, using two cotherapists (Kuipers and Leff). We found the mother to be extremely resistant to change, and both of us felt somewhat defeated by her. The stepfather, on the other hand, showed a great deal of flexibility and common sense, and turned out to have much more strength of character than we might have assumed from his peripheral role in the family when first assessed.

We considered that the marital relationship did improve during the conjoint therapy, but unfortunately Colin discharged himself after a few months from the hostel because he felt he did not fit in there, and the mother welcomed him back with open arms. Although he was living at home again, Colin's regular attendance at the day hospital and later at a job reduced social contact with his parents considerably. Furthermore, when we reassessed the parents' EE levels at the 9-month follow-up, we found that both of them made very few critical comments, and surprisingly the mother's rating on overinvolvement had reduced somewhat and was below the crucial level for high EE. Thus we had achieved both our aims of reducing high EE to low EE and cutting down the amount of social contact between patient and relatives. Colin remained well throughout the 9-month follow-up period, and in fact was still symptom-free at a later 2-year follow-up, despite continuing to live with his parents.

FAMILY 2

Marion is a retired schoolteacher living with her husband, a retired computer technician. Marion was retired prematurely because of two episodes of paranoid schizophrenia. The couple lived in a small, well-furnished flat in London and also owned a country cottage that they visited on weekends. They were childless and had few friends, so spent most of their time in each other's company. The husband was a man who rarely showed emotion and whose life was ruled by rationality, an attitude that had fitted him well for his occupation. He found Marion's episodes of irrationality terrifying, and his "instinctual reaction" was one of running away, as he put it. He had no patience with her when she was ill and just wanted to be out of her presence. He was rated as highly critical on the EE assessment.

He agreed to attend the group and did so punctiliously until the 9-month follow-up, when he ceased coming. He never lost control of his emotions in the group and maintained an intellectual attitude toward his wife's problems. We held several conjoint marital sessions in their home in the hope of breaking through to his fear of his own irrational emotions, which we believed to be at the root of his reaction to his wife's madness. However, we had no success in this endeavor.

Our other strategy was to attempt to reduce social contact between them, and in this we were fortunately aided by his previous employers, who offered him another job teaching what he had practiced all his working life. He took this very seriously and started spending long hours daily in a library preparing material for his lectures. We persuaded his wife to take up day classes offered by the local council at very low expense. She began learning German and water-color painting, which took her out of the home two mornings a week and brought her into contact with other people. As a result of these changes in their lives, their social contact with each other was considerably reduced. When we reassessed the husband's EE level at 9 months, he was no longer critical of Marion. We believe that this was not due to any change in his fundamental attitudes toward her madness, but followed from her remaining well and hence rational throughout the 9 months. This we considered to be a probable consequence of their reduced social contact. At a 2-year follow-up, she had had no recurrence of her schizophrenic symptoms.

FAMILY 3

This family was another marital couple, in which the husband, Jack, was the patient. He had experienced four previous episodes of psychosis with variable symptoms and a diagnosis that fluctuated between manic–depressive illness and schizophrenia. The fifth episode, at the age of 50, brought him into the trial and was unequivocally schizophrenic. He had worked very little since his illness began and was currently unemployed. He had married 4 years earlier a woman in her late 40s who had been a senior social worker and who was well aware of the serious nature of Jack's psychiatric condition. She gave up her career when she married. It became evident that she was devoting her whole life to Jack, who had become her sole client. She was extremely overinvolved on the EE assessment, a rarity in a spouse. We have formed the opinion that overinvolvement develops in the context of mothering. Whereas this function is nearly always the prerogative of mothers, it can occasionally be undertaken by fathers or by spouses, as was the case in this instance.

Jack's fifth relapse represented to his wife a gross failure of her function as his professional care giver, and as a consequence she was extremely distressed and overanxious about his psychiatric state. She conveyed this feeling of helplessness and panic to the clinical team looking after Jack, with a deleterious effect on their ability to cope with the couple.

In addition to inducting the wife into the relatives' group, we decided to hold a few sessions of conjoint marital therapy. In the first session we explored her need to be omnipotent and manage his life, and his own feelings of inadequacy that led to his acceptance of her protectiveness. The same theme came up regularly in the group, since it was common to many families, though in most cases they were parental rather than marital. This appeared to have quite a rapid effect on the wife, who made arrangements to resume work again. This first day she returned from work, tired and somewhat apprehensive about Jack's ability to cope on his own. She found that he had done everything efficiently, the house was completely clean, and a meal awaited her. She fell into his arms and wept, able for the first time to give up her pretence at omnipotence and to allow herself to be cared for by him. Their relationship since then has continued on a much more equal basis, and at the follow-up EE assessment her overinvolvement had completely disappeared. Jack had experienced no recurrence of psychotic symptoms.

OUTCOME OF INTERVENTION

We have very recently reached our target of 24 families in the trial, 12 in the experimental and 12 in the control group. The numbers are small, but it has taken us 4 years to collect this many, largely because we are selecting a high-risk group as explained above. The trial still has a year or so to run, so that we are not in a position to give any figures yet. However, now that the majority of follow-up assessments have been completed, we can state that there has been a significant reduction in critical comments in the experimental group, while there has been virtually no change in the control group. All the relatives who were emotionally overinvolved in the experimental group have shifted to low levels of EE, whereas none of the equivalent control relatives have altered in this way. In many of the experimental families there has also been a considerable reduction in social contact between patients and relatives, whereas this has occurred in very few control families. Thus we have been reasonably successful in achieving both the aims of social intervention in the experimental families. What has been the effect on the relapse rate, bearing in mind that all patients have been on regular maintenance drugs, which the majority have received by long-acting injections? In the 12 families in the control group, half the patients have relapsed, a significant difference from the experimental group (exact $p = .041$). If the relapse rate in the control group is compared with that in the experimental families in which we achieved our aims, the difference increases in significance (exact $p = .024$). We must be cautious in placing weight on these figures prematurely, as the number in the trial is small and these proportions could alter substantially by the completion of the follow-ups (see Leff, Kuipers, Berkowitz, Eberlein-Vries, & Sturgeon,

1982). However, the success of our package of social treatments in achieving our avowed aims is undeniable and holds out considerable hope for the development of effective methods of working with the families of schizophrenic patients.

REFERENCES

Bateson, G., Jackson, D. D., Haley, J., & Weakland, J. H. Toward a theory of schizophrenia. *Behavioral Science*, 1956, *1*, 251–264.

Berkowitz, R., Kuipers, L., Eberlein-Vries, R., & Leff, J. Lowering expressed emotion in relatives of schizophrenics. In M. J. Goldstein (Ed.), *New developments in interventions with families of schizophrenics*. London: Jossey-Bass, 1981.

Brown, G. W., Birley, J. L. T., & Wing, J. K. Influence of family life on the course of schizophrenic disorders: A replication. *British Journal of Psychiatry*, 1972, *121*, 241–258.

Brown, G. W., Bone, M., Dalison, B., & Wing, J. K. *Schizophrenia and social care* (Maudsley Monograph No. 17). London: Oxford University Press, 1966.

Brown, G. W., Monck, E. M., Carstairs, G. M., & Wing, J. K. Influence of family life on the course of schizophrenic illness. *British Journal of Preventive and Social Medicine*, 1962, *16*, 55–68.

Brown, G. W., & Rutter, M. The measurement of family activities and relationships: A methodological study. *Human Relations*, 1966, *19*, 241–263.

Garmezy, N. Children at risk: The search for the antecedents of schizophrenia. Part II: Ongoing research programs, issues, and interventions. *Schizophrenia Bulletin*, 1974, *1*, 55–125.

Hirsch, S. R., & Leff, J. P. *Abnormalities in parents of schizophrenics* (Maudsley Monograph No. 22). London: Oxford University Press, 1975.

Laing, R. D. *The divided self: A study of sanity and madness*. Chicago: Quadrangle Books, 1960.

Leff, J. P. Schizophrenia and sensitivity to the family environment. *Schizophrenia Bulletin*, 1976, *2*, 566–574.

Leff, J. P. Developments in family treatment of schizophrenia. *Psychiatric Quarterly*, 1979, *51*, 216–232.

Leff, J. P., Kuipers, L., Berkowitz, R., Eberlein-Vries, R., & Sturgeon, D. A controlled trial of social intervention in the families of schizophrenic patients. *British Journal of Psychiatry*, 1982, *141*, 121–134.

Leff, J. P., & Vaughn, C. Schizophrenia and family life. *Psychology Today*, November 1976, pp. 13–18.

Leff, J. P., & Vaughn, C. The role of maintenance therapy and relatives' expressed emotion in relapse of schizophrenia: A two-year follow-up. *British Journal of Psychiatry*, 1981, *139*, 102–104.

Lidz, T. Schizophrenia and the family. *Psychiatry*, 1958, *21*, 21–27.

O'Neal, P., & Robins, L. N. Childhood patterns predictive of adult schizophrenia: A 30-year follow-up study. *American Journal of Psychiatry*, 1958, *115*, 385–391.

Sturgeon, D., Kuipers, L., Berkowitz, R., Turpin, G., & Leff, J. Psychophysiological responses of schizophrenic patients to high and low expressed emotion relatives. *British Journal of Psychiatry*, 1981, *138*, 40–45.

Tarrier, N., Vaughn, C. E., Lader, M. H., & Leff, J. P. Bodily reactions to people and events in schizophrenics. *Archives of General Psychiatry*, 1979, *36*, 311–315.

Vaughn, C. E., & Leff, J. P. The influence of family and social factors on the course of psychiatric illness: A comparison of schizophrenic and depressed neurotic patients. *British Journal of Psychiatry*, 1976, *129*, 125–137. (a)

Vaughn, C. E., & Leff, J. P. The measurement of expressed emotion in the families of psychiatric patients. *British Journal of Social and Clinical Psychology*, 1976, *15*(2), 157–165. (b)

Waring, M., & Ricks, D. Family patterns of children who became adult schizophrenics. *Journal of Nervous and Mental Disorders*, 1965, *140*, 351–364.

Wynne, L. C., Ryckoff, I., Day, J., & Hirsch, S. Pseudomutuality in the family relations of schizophrenics. *Psychiatry*, 1958, *21*, 205–220.

8
SUPPORTIVE GROUP COUNSELING FOR THE RELATIVES OF SCHIZOPHRENIC PATIENTS

Nancy Atwood

Most mental health programs that serve schizophrenic patients establish contact with relatives during the course of treatment, but the amount of family involvement tends to be small. Typically, the staff schedules diagnostic and predischarge family meetings, and social workers meet intermittently with individual patients and their "significant others." It is fairly unusual to launch goal-directed programs that integrate the relatives of patients into the overall program of treatment and rehabilitation.

When an administration and staff consider taking such a step, they are likely to wonder what form of intervention to select and whether the purposes to be served justify the added amount of time and effort that will be involved. There are various modalities from which to choose: extended therapy and casework with individual relatives; intensive family therapy for individual patients and their relatives; multiple family therapy, which includes several patients and several relatives; and supportive and educational group counseling for relatives.

This chapter focuses upon the latter form of intervention—supportive counseling for relatives—and recommends this modality as preferable to others for staff members to use who are unfamiliar with family treatment, but who wish to expand the range of family-oriented services.

Why particularly supportive group counseling? It is known to be more effective than others? No, it is not; there are no empirical studies that make this type of comparison. Does it have any theoretical advantage over other modalities? No, it does not; there are theoretical justifications for every form of intervention. Why, then, is it recommended? The answer is simple: It is easier to do than the others. Although it has ample clinical justification, the main reason for starting with this form of intervention is pragmatic. It has a high likelihood of appearing helpful, being cost-effective, and giving

NANCY ATWOOD. Trinity Mental Health Center, Framingham, Massachusetts.

professional satisfaction to staff members who have no previous training or experience in family therapy (Atwood & Williams, 1978b).

This intervention is essentially group treatment for family members, rather than family therapy per se. The patients themselves do not belong to the groups. The groups are supportive, rather than insight-oriented, and require the use of techniques that are already familiar to most mental health practitioners. These techniques are associated with the concept of therapeutic support as a means to strengthen preexisting assets of clients and to bolster their adaptive defenses.

PROFESSIONAL ATTITUDES

When clinicians decide to start a new program, they bring an attitudinal set and a cluster of preconceptions to the task at hand. These preconceptions include opinions about the clients whom they serve. Whatever these attitudes may be, they are likely to affect the course of treatment. In every form of intervention, research suggests, the opinions of practitioners towards clients affect the process and outcome of treatment (Lerner & Fiske, 1973; Stoler, 1963). This generalization applies to group intervention with the relatives of schizophrenic patients as well as to other forms of therapy.

The preconceptions of clinicians who organize these groups reflect the influence of society and the professional culture in which practitioners work. Staff members are likely to share the prevailing middle-class, Anglo-American viewpoint that parents are responsible for how their children turn out (Papajohn & Spiegel, 1975) and to be aware of the professional literature indicating that schizophrenia develops in "sick" families. In the absence of first-hand knowledge of actual families, clinicians may assume that the presence of schizophrenia is prima facie evidence that something is massively wrong with a family. This assumption is tantamount to a bias against the family and tends to inhibit clinicians from seeing relatives as they actually are. This attitude communicates itself to families in subtle and not so subtle ways. For example, in one survey of the perceptions that relatives have of the mental health system, many parents "recalled some doctor or social worker who implied or stated unambiguously that it was their fault the patient was ill" (Creer, 1975, p. 4).

Not only may practitioners indiscriminately apply theories of causality; they may also transfer unresolved feelings about their own family members to the relatives of patients (Anderson, 1977). The prospect of dealing with family members stirs up memories of unfinished business in their own lives and contaminates their contacts with families before the relationship has even begun.

Staff members who empathize with patients may infer that families alone are responsible for their patients' problems. In an article on her experiences as a group leader, a clinician describes these feelings. "When I entered the group my preconceived idea was that patients are all good and right, and relatives are all bad and wrong," she recalls. "I was going to find out just what it was that these relatives are doing to the poor patients" (Jersild, 1967, p. 545).

Overidentification with patients, countertransference, and stereotyping all interfere with an accurate understanding of families, inhibit the development of a therapeutic alliance, and undermine the foundation upon which supportive counseling rests. The present model derives from the leaders' belief in the capacity of family members to play a positive role in the lives of schizophrenic patients. An attitude of respect for family members that is consistent with this belief develops through actual contacts with relatives during the course of supportive counseling, through supervision and consultation, and through the clinician's self-scrutiny of biases and countertransference.

SUPPORT GROUPS AND THE
MEDICAL/REHABILITATIVE MODEL

Support groups are a ubiquitous part of the current human services scene. They figure prominently in the process of helping the relatives of various ill and handicapped populations. Their proliferation is reflected in the extensive literature on professionally led groups for the family members of the physically handicapped and mentally retarded (Mandelbaum & Wheeler, 1960; Milman, 1952; Olshansky, 1962; Yates & Lederer, 1961). But the growth of these groups has not been as rapid for the relatives of schizophrenic patients as it has been for the family members of people with clearly identifiable medical illnesses and disabilities.

Psychoanalytic and family systems theory have tended to inhibit professionals from developing this form of intervention for the relatives of schizophrenic patients. Neither body of theory acknowledges that schizophrenia is biologically based, and both emphasize that schizophrenia is causally related to family upbringing and relationships. Because of the belief systems associated with these theories, the tendency of professionals espousing them has been to regard family members as patients for whom either traditional psychotherapy or a family systems model of treatment is appropriate.

The ascription of patienthood to relatives is directly contrary to the assumptions upon which support groups rest. These groups clearly identify the patients as ill—not their relatives—and do not suggest that families are responsible for the etiology of the patients' disorder. According to this perspective, schizophrenia is an illness over whose origins families have had little or no control.

Perceiving schizophrenia in this light suggests both privileges and obligations for families. It absolves them from blame for the past, entitles them to sympathy in the present, and engages them as care givers in improving the patients' prognosis for the future. In a critique of various theories underlying the treatment of psychosis, Siegler and Osmond (1976) write: "Only the medical model can bring families real sympathy and comfort, realistic hope, and a well-known set of rights and duties which will relate them constructively to their ill member, to the practitioner, and to the community" (p. 190).

These duties include learning new ways of interacting with schizophrenic family members. Implicit in the use of the medical model is the expectation that families are willing and able to adopt attitudes and patterns of behavior that contribute to the recovery and rehabilitation of patients. Viewed in this perspective, the medical model is not a static concept, but one that suggests a potential for change.

This emphasis on change may appear paradoxical. On the surface, it seems that allowing relatives to regard their schizophrenic family members as sick encourages dependency and colludes with their tendency to overprotect the patients. But the medical metaphor conveys more than illness. It also implies that sickness is a transitional state and that both the ill persons and the relatives are to do whatever they can to achieve health, or at least to achieve the maximum health that is possible despite the existence of disability (Parsons, 1951).

Counseling that is consistent with this medical/rehabilitative perspective can discourage relatives from becoming overly involved and infantilizing toward their schizophrenic family member, reflecting research that demonstrates that the intrusiveness of relatives puts schizophrenic patients at risk for relapse (Brown, Birley, & Wing, 1972; Vaughn & Leff, 1976). Support groups tend to encourage families to foster as much independent functioning as possible on the part of their schizophrenic members. Good families, these groups suggest, not only support patients and make concessions where appropriate; they also expect improved performance and efforts toward individuation.

This normative aspect of the relatives' role is compatible with the focus of treatment and rehabilitation programs that sponsor group counseling for relatives. While the therapeutic programs for patients equip them with skills for becoming more independent, their relatives' counseling corroborates the value of efforts at constructive separation from their families of origin.

However, true independence rarely occurs, and patients are likely to rely upon their families and the mental health system throughout their lives. The medical/rehabilitative model provides a conceptual base upon which relatives and professionals can build an ongoing alliance. Professionally led support groups are a vehicle for the expression of this partnership.

PRINCIPLES AND METHODS OF
SUPPORTIVE GROUP COUNSELING

Supportive group counseling is particularly suited for engaging relatives in this process of partnership. Several features of this modality are conducive to stimulating and sustaining the participation of family members.

LEGITIMATION OF THE RELATIVES' ROLE AS "SIGNIFICANT OTHERS"

Membership in a relatives' group suggests a continuing, significant relationship between participants and their schizophrenic family members. Since the purpose of the group is to support the supporters, the implication is clear that those convening the group sanction the role of the members as responsible care givers and confirm the value of family unity in dealing with the problems of mental illness. This model both acknowledges the existence of a strong interest on the part of relatives in the lives of their ill family members and at the same time seeks to influence the nature and course of that involvement.

VALIDATION OF THE PROBLEM AS DEFINED BY THE FAMILY

While traditional group therapy is directed at changing various aspects of the members' personalities, support groups are designed to deal with discrete, readily identifiable problems that are often external to the members themselves. In this instance, the problem is mental illness.

This focus validates the relatives' own perceptions and helps them to feel that other people, including the group leader(s), understand the source of their psychological stress. Research suggests that relatives do not accept the implication that groups for the family members of the emotionally disturbed are therapy for themselves. In a study of the reactions of parents to a guidance clinic group to which they belonged, the subjects rejected those questionnaire items implying that they themselves were the focus of therapy (Hausman, 1974). Other studies indicate that continuance in treatment correlates with shared perceptions between clients and professionals about the definition of the problem (Heine & Trosman, 1960; Mayer & Timms, 1970).

SATISFACTION OF THE NEED TO SHARE PROBLEMS WITH OTHERS

When people are under stress, their normal tendency is to seek out others with whom they can share their experiences and reactions, thereby validating their perceptions and gaining mastery over anxiety and uncertainty (Rubin, 1973). One of the tragic by-products of stigmatization is that relatives of the mentally ill are inhibited from making these very natural kinds of connections. Support groups cut through the defensive tendency of relatives to isolate themselves. The groups provide a forum where they can experience the instant rapport that comes from communicating with others suffering from similar problems. This is the "we are not alone" phenomenon—a major source of psychological relief—that figures prominently in every type of mutual help organization (Killilea, 1976).

AFFIRMATION OF THE PROBLEM'S MANAGEABILITY

While all successful psychological treatment instills hope (Frank, 1974), supportive counseling deliberately builds morale by (1) breaking problems down into discrete parts and focusing on specific, manageable aspects; (2) recognizing and capitalizing on emotional and cognitive strengths; (3) accepting and stimulating the use of comparatively healthy defenses that are adaptive for coping; and (4) increasing the amount of knowledge that participants have, including information about resources that are applicable to the solution of the problem.

CONSISTENCY OF SUPPORT

Most, if not all, forms of psychological intervention rely upon support as a means of engaging clients, but in supportive counseling this element predominates throughout. While in formal group therapy much of the learning occurs through emotionally charged interactions among members about "here and now" relationships, this type of exchange occurs rarely in support groups. The supportiveness of this model derives from establishing norms that reduce the likelihood of intragroup conflict and increase the likelihood of developing and maintaining consensus.

Thus, supportive counseling legitimizes the role of relatives as care givers, identifies the purpose of intervention as supporting them in performing this function, and restricts the focus of the meetings to a specific problem area common to all the members. These definitions of role, purpose, and focus reduce the defensiveness of family members, raise their self-esteem, and channel their energies in productive directions. The methods that professionals use in convening and conducting these groups are consistent with these definitions.

CLEAR STATEMENT OF CONTRACT

This intervention aims at suppressing anxiety. From the start, the leader establishes a contract with the group members so that the relatives know why they are there and what they can anticipate from their participation. This contract, with its focus on commonly agreed-upon goals, reduces anxiety-provoking ambiguity.

ESTABLISHING THE GROUP AS TIME-LIMITED AND CLOSED

Establishing the intervention as short-term and the group as closed also reduces ambiguity and enhances the likelihood of commitment.

When counseling is time-limited, problem solving is stimulated and dropout rates are reduced. Studies of groups show that if a group is presented as short-term, prospective members who might otherwise reject services tend to accept them and to focus on the tasks at hand (Weinberger, 1971). Fathers of psychiatric patients, in particular, are less likely to withdraw precipitously if they know a termination date is in sight (Donner & Gamson, 1971).

A closed model fosters group cohesiveness. Although the intervention is not psychotherapy per se, the concept of the "therapeutic envelope" applies. This concept suggests a need for maintaining a stable membership, if possible, and for attending to the specifics of structure. Cohesiveness tends to develop when the members operate on a commitment to the integrity of the group as a group; this commitment is made concrete by an emphasis on norms of attendance, confidentiality, and consistency in the time, place, and duration of meetings. "Close attention to the externals of the envelope, and to the effect of every infringement of this concept" shows the members that the leader "really cares for the group and will protect them" (Day, 1963).

EMPHASIS ON PROMOTING PEER SUPPORT

This intervention is quintessentially a group method. The leaders of supportive groups facilitate the development of rapport among members, so that the members themselves are the primary agents of change (Grunebaum & Solomon, 1980). In a research study on the beneficial factors in groups for the parents of disturbed children, the majority of the parents responding said that the gaining of support from other parents was the chief function of the group (Hausman, 1974). The normative leadership style is enabling: The leader of such a group "always tries to increase the interactions and mutual help among members" (Konopka, 1963, p. 127).

PERMITTING THE EXPRESSION OF AFFECT

Several studies document the stressful effects on families of psychosis and schizophrenic maladjustment (Creer & Wing, 1974; Davis, Dinitz, & Pasamanick, 1974; Hatfield, 1978). The group context gives families a chance to share the pain of their experience. It is essential that the group process provide a safe atmosphere and enough time for the expression of emotions such as grief, anger, and shame. When this opportunity is given, the bonding among members is immediate, and their willingness to move on to cognitive work is increased.

FACILITATIVE STYLE OF LEADERSHIP

While a short-term, problem-oriented focus implies that the leadership style is directive, an emphasis on the development of peer support suggests a more passive technique. The correct approach uses both differentially:

> Activity and passivity are not important in themselves but only in relation to what they are being use for. . . . Sometimes the group learning process calls for a leader to be active . . . to help the group move ahead. At other times, it calls for him to be passive, in the sense that he may not be talking; but even then he is actively involved, listening, observing the course of the discussion and the behavior of the relatives, and letting the group function "on its own" as long as it progresses well and does not need his intervention. (Auerbach, 1968, p. 166)

The leader's activity contributes to interpersonal learning by focusing on what is meaningful for the participants. The leader directs the discussion toward actual situations and the exploration of the circumstances, perceptions, behaviors, and feelings that accompany particular interactions with ill family members. The leader helps the group to examine situations and to understand from them general principles that can be extracted and applied not only to a particular set of circumstances, but to many others that occur within the family setting.

PROVIDING INFORMATION

The group process includes the providing of information about mental illness and its appropriate management. This exchange of information may occur through give-and-take among the members and the leaders, didactic presentations, and discussions of written material. Expanding the members' knowledge implies that the leaders themselves believe that schizophrenia is comprehensible and manageable and that they have confidence in their ability to transmit information that can help relatives to cope. An expanding body of literature suggests what this information might be and how it can be useful to families in interacting appropriately with their schizophrenic members (Anderson, Hogarty, & Reiss, 1980; Arieti, 1979; Bernheim & Lewine, 1979; O'Brien, 1978; Park with Shapiro, 1976).

THE PRACTICE OF SUPPORTIVE GROUP COUNSELING FOR RELATIVES

The discussion thus far has covered the conceptual and methodological bases of supportive group counseling. This section specifies the actual processes that should take place when these principles are put into effect.

PREPARATION FOR THE GROUP

According to Yalom (1970), successful group outcome depends on the leader's effective performance of tasks that precede the first meeting of the group as a whole. The prospective leader of a relatives' group has several tasks to perform.

The first, after discussing the proposed group with fellow staff members, is to talk about the formation of the group with the patients themselves, either at a community meeting or individually. This phase is important because it indicates respect for the privacy and individuality of patients, an attitude that the counseling itself will attempt to inculcate with families. The formation of such a group is potentially threatening to patients. They correctly predict that relatives will reveal personal material about them during the course of their meetings. For this reason, patients should have an opportunity to understand the reasons for forming such a group and why its existence will ultimately benefit them. They should have the chance to ask questions, air their fantasies, and express their reservations. They should also have the option of refusing to allow their relatives to participate, although few are likely to use it. Generally, patients will accept and even welcome their relatives' participation. Those who feel neglected, for example, are pleased that their relatives are willing to take the time and trouble to belong.

Presenting the group to families raises other issues. The invitation to join has to elicit the families' interest without betraying the patients by implying that the group will focus on them as problems. The invitation also has to avoid any veiled criticism of the relatives by hinting that they need corrective psychological counseling. A letter with the following phraseology is designed to attend to the needs both of family members and of patients.

> Dear Mr./Mrs. _____:
>
> . . . Our purpose is to invite you to participate in a discussion group for the relatives of patients [or clients] at [name of mental health program]. We have already talked with the patients about the family group and are taking this opportunity now to introduce it to you.
>
> The group will be composed of the families of patients and will not include the patients themselves.
>
> In this group you will have a chance to share experiences, concerns, and ideas with others who are relatives of people at _____. The meetings will provide information about mental illness in general, about ways of understanding and coping with it, and about the program at _____.
>
> You probably have questions about this group and might like to find out more about it before you decide whether to participate. We'll meet on an individual basis with prospective members during the next few weeks. At this meeting we'll be able to talk in greater depth about the group and about any other concerns that you might have.

The letter serves as an official introduction to the group and should go to the relatives of all patients in a given program. The number of members per group should not exceed 12; therefore, it may be necessary to form more than one group. After the issuing of the original invitation, a process of mutual selection takes place—both on the part of families and on the part of leaders. Some relatives are clearly not interested and cannot be induced to join. Others are more in need of other kinds of interventions. The leaders may try to facilitate cohesiveness by being selective in soliciting membership. Typically, those who consider belonging to the group are likely to regard themselves as having some degree of responsibility for the patients. Relatives who fit this description tend to be parents. If they do not conceive of themselves as at least partially responsible for the patients, they are unlikely to join.

Whatever their relationship to the patients, they will tend to be cautious about joining. Patience and care are necessary in encouraging their participation. For instance, when making follow-up phone calls, the leader should be prepared to respond to the ventilation and resistance of prospective members. In the long run this is time well spent, because it increases the likelihood that the relatives will ultimately decide to participate.

Preliminary interviews in person with prospective members help to form an alliance between the leader and the individual group members, enhance a sense of commitment to the group, and give the relatives an opportunity to discuss material they want the leader to know and might be reluctant to reveal to the group as a whole. These interviews are also an opportunity for contract setting, as follows:

- The purpose of the group is to bring about communication among a group of people sharing a common problem: how to understand and cope with the mental illness of a family member and its effect on the family unit.
- The topics covered at the meetings will be determined by the interests and needs of the relatives themselves. The leader's role will be to help focus and facilitate the discussion and, where appropriate, to provide factual information.
- Only material that the members themselves care to discuss will be brought to the meetings.
- The leader will not report on the progress of any individual patients in the mental health program, although the program in general will be discussed.
- The sessions will be confidential.
- The meetings will be held regularly at a pre-established place and time and will last 1½ hours.
- The group will terminate after a stated number of sessions (8 to 12).
- Regular attendance is expected. Those unable to attend are to give the group or the leader advance notice.

PROCESS OF THE GROUP

The first meeting should include the following: (1) Introductions—the relatives introduce themselves and briefly describe their ill family member's problem; (2) Restatement of contract—the leader (or coleaders) reviews the focus, purpose, and guidelines of the group; (3) Agenda setting—the leader asks the members to suggest topics that they would like to cover at subsequent meetings and guides the members toward reaching consensus on four or five major items that they regard as most important. These topic headings are written down and constitute the subject matter of the meetings that follow. Thus, planning for the structure of the sessions is relatively simple, with the members themselves determining the agenda and the leader responding flexibly to concerns that they themselves raise.

In reality, the content of the meetings is usually predictable. Supportive, time-limited groups for the relatives of the adult mentally ill are remarkably similar in their substantive, affective, and procedural content. Several issues, feelings, and sequences appear to be universal, regardless of the setting of the counseling or the discipline of the leaders. The processes described in this section characterize groups for the parents of adult, chronically handicapped patients at a day treatment program familiar to me. However, similar processes have occurred in numerous other groups conducted by several different leaders at both inpatient and outpatient facilities (Dincin, Selleck, & Streicker, 1978; Frey, Diller, & Hanfling, 1981; Griefen & Lawton, 1980; Grinspoon, Courtney, & Bergen, 1961; Mass & Odaniell, 1968; McLean, Napoleone, Scott, & Beck, 1982; Pildis, 1978; Tarver & Turner, 1974).

Initial sessions are likely to be devoted to the ventilation of frustration, disappointment, and resentment. All of the parents experience a chronic sorrow that their children are not normal. They speak openly of feeling devastated by the illness of their offspring, angry at the failure of various treatments to bring about the longed-for cure, and chagrined by allegations that they might have contributed to the mental illness of their family members. They complain repeatedly about their children's seeming lack of motivation and difficulties in interpersonal relationships. It is a relief, they say, to talk with other people who are not judgmental and who understand what it is like to live with a mentally ill person. They comment that mental illness can occur in families of every description, including "nice" ones like the members of their group.

Gradually, as they commiserate with each other and some of their affective needs are met, they are able to focus on those aspects of their situation that are positive and on those that can be modified. Cognitive components gain significance. They begin to speak more often about their children's strengths, to appreciate the small but sure steps that they are taking towards rehabilitation, and to offer empathic explanations for why their children act as they do. They are interested in learning about any and all community resources that might provide help. Accounts are shared of successfully handling a delicate situation or a difficult encounter. The leader reinforces these coping efforts by highlighting or summarizing suggested approaches for dealing with common problems.

The parents recognize that they tend to be "emotionally involved" with their adult children. They frequently wonder when they should intervene and when they should let their children fend for themselves, regardless of the consequences. They speak of trying to hold themselves back from being too protective, but at the same time they feel responsible for their offspring's inappropriate behavior. Peer support and leader reinforcement follow any evidence that the family members are encouraging constructive individuation between them and their children. Gradually, a norm develops in the group that favors encouraging more autonomous functioning on the part of the adult children and more emotional detachment on the part of parents. Families receive permission from the group to take their own needs into account—to have a social life, to use the public system for financial support, and to get relief for themselves by exploiting all existing mental health resources for their relatives.

Members are likely to report on behavioral change: A mother learns to restrain herself from awakening her son for job interviews and finds that he can set his own alarm clock; parents encourage their children to apply to halfway houses; couples who have not taken vacations in several years make plans to go away during the summer.

As the sessions draw to a close, members speak of having looked forward to the meetings and of valuing the group experience. The final session is likely to be a quasi-social occasion, sometimes held at a member's house. It always includes the sharing of homemade refreshments and warm expressions of empathy and good will.

Experiences of this kind that have so much affective meaning for participants are difficult to evaluate objectively. At present, there are no published, controlled studies of the effectiveness of this intervention with the relatives of adult patients. "Marvelously rewarding" is the way that one professional describes the groups he has led (Dincin, 1975, p. 142). However they are characterized, they undoubtedly have an impact of a significant but as yet unmeasured kind on relatives and on professionals as well.

HOW THE GROUPS FACILITATE CHANGES THAT BENEFIT PATIENTS[1]

Clearly, the groups support the relatives, but how do they help the patients? Group counseling for relatives seem to have attitudinal and behavioral ramifications that are positive for the patients, as well as for the family members (Dincin et al., 1978). Why this is so is suggested by psychodynamic theory (Alexander, 1948; Levy, 1970; Nichols & Zax, 1977) and by the nature of supportive intervention as a therapeutic instrument (Sclby, 1956): (1) The ventilation of negative emotions tends to free psychic energy that might otherwise be channeled into harmful interactions with the patients. (2) Grief work helps to shift the families' emotional investment away from what has been lost to what can be gained through building upon the handicapped persons' remaining assets. (3) Reducing guilt diminishes some of the psychological pressure to overprotect and infantilize. (4) The supportiveness of the group helps to meet the needs of the members for dependency; because the members feel accepted themselves, they are more likely to accept the handicapped persons and to communicate this attitude of acceptance to them. (5) The sense of safety that the family members experience in the group reduces their defensiveness; they tend to become receptive to ideas about what changes they might make in how they think and act.

Thus, support acts as an antidote to destructive tendencies and as a precondition to change. Through the group's "context of social comparison," participants see that other people do not all feel the same way or do things the same way (Grunebaum, 1970; Lieberman, 1975). The members are exposed to a variety of possible attitudes and behaviors and adopt those that are most compatible with their particular personality organizations and circumstances. This process has been called "education by alternatives" (Ablon, 1974; Arnold, Rowe, & Tolbert, 1978).

Learning from one another includes giving and receiving feedback. Often the feedback is positive; occasionally it is not. Family members may be able to accept blunt comments about their behavior from others that they would be likely to resent and consider biased if made by a staff member (Lidz, 1973). The group experience, if properly led, provides both support and stimulation to change, or, to paraphrase, both "pleasure and pressure" (Lowy, 1976, p. 125).

The groups appear to foster a rapport between the family members and the staff that is reflected in how a family as a whole, including the patient, responds to the patient's treatment program. It has been suggested that the formation of a relatives' group is among the factors associated with high levels of patient attendance in a partial hospitalization program (Pildis, 1978). Experience indicates that those who belong to relatives' groups generally have positive attitudes toward the program, tend to encourage their family members to use related mental health resources, and are more likely to call upon the staff for additional help than are those relatives who have little or no contact with the facility. Participation in the group serves as a foundation for an ongoing cooperative relationship between families and staff. Credit for the creation of this type of trust should go only partially to the professional personnel who lead the groups. The true facilitator is the group process itself. The families associate the agency with support, and some of their previous tendencies to isolate themselves are reversed.

FROM GROUP COUNSELING TO SELF-HELP

The group experience may stimulate some of the families to form an autonomous self-help organization (McLean et al., 1982). Professionals should encourage this development (Silverman, 1978). The formation of such a group is a self-perpetuating vehicle for helping relatives to deal with the continuing problems of mental illness and disability.

If relatives form their own organization, the original model of professional intervention described in this chapter is replaced by citizen-based self-help and advocacy. Both types of groups—professionally led counseling and self-help organizations—possess many sources of psychological benefit in common, especially opportunities for emotional support and education. The current growth of a national self-help movement among relatives of the adult mentally ill suggests that these benefits are inherent in the process of sharing burdens that are too heavy to carry alone (Hatfield, 1981).

CONCLUSION

This chapter begins by considering the attitudes of professionals as they begin the process of working with families. It ends by considering the needs of families as they continue their struggle to understand and deal with the mental illness of family members.

Group counseling brings professionals and families together and directs their attention to a mutually agreed-upon goal: what can be done both within the home and outside to increase the likelihood of the recovery and rehabilitation of schizophrenic patients. These groups give families the opportunity to commiserate with one another, to share their knowledge about how to cope, and to develop strategies that promote the independent functioning of their schizophrenic family members.

From this experience relatives gain not so much the advantage of learning from professionals, although they do, but more importantly the benefit of learning from one another—from one another's suffering, setbacks, and strengths. This process among peers of interpersonal support and stimulation to change makes this intervention uniquely useful for the families of schizophrenic patients.

NOTE

[1]Material in this section, coauthored by Martha E. D. Williams, was originally published elsewhere (Atwood & Williams, 1978a).

REFERENCES

Ablon, J. Al-Anon family groups: Impetus for learning and change through the presentation of alternatives. *American Journal of Psychotherapy*, 1974, *26*, 30–45.

Alexander, F. *Fundamentals of psychoanalysis.* New York: Norton, 1948.

Anderson, C. M. Family intervention with severely disturbed inpatients. *Archives of General Psychiatry*, 1977, *34*, 697–702.

Anderson, C. M., Hogarty, G. E., & Reiss, D. J., Family treatment of adult schizophrenic patients: A psycho-educational approach. *Schizophrenia Bulletin*, 1980, *6*, 490–505.

Arieti, S. *Understanding and helping the schizophrenic: A guide for family and friends.* New York: Basic Books, 1979.

Arnold, L. E., Rowe, M., & Tolbert, H. A. Parents' groups. In L. E. Arnold (Ed.), *Helping parents help their children.* New York: Brunner/Mazel, 1978.

Atwood, N., & Williams, M. E. D. Group support for the families of the mentally ill. *Schizophrenia Bulletin*, 1978, *6*, 415–425. (a)

Atwood, N., & Williams, M. E. D. A survey of relatives' groups in day treatment programs. In R. F. Luber, J. M. Maxey, & P. M. Lefkovitz (Eds.), *Proceedings of the Annual Conference on Partial Hospitalization 1977.* Boston: Federation of Partial Hospitalization Study Groups, 1978.(b)

Auerbach, A. B. *Parents learn through discussion: Principles and practices of parent group education.* New York: Wiley, 1968.

Bernheim, K. F., & Lewine, R. R. J. *Schizophrenia: Symptoms, causes, treatments.* New York: Norton, 1979.

Brown, G. W., Birley, J. L. T., & Wing, J. K. Influence of family life on the course of schizophrenic disorders: A replication. *British Journal of Psychiatry*, 1972, *121*, 241–258.

Creer, C. Living with schizophrenia. *Social Work Today*, 1975, *6*, 2–7.

Creer, C., & Wing, J. *Schizophrenia at home* (monograph). London: Institute of Psychiatry, 1974.

Davis, A. E., Dinitz, S., & Pasamanick, B. *Schizophrenics in the new custodial community: Five years after the experiment.* Columbus: Ohio State University Press, 1974.

Day, M. *The therapeutic envelope.* Paper presented at the annual meeting of the American Group Psychotherapy Association, Washington, D.C., January 1963.

Dincin, J. Psychiatric rehabilitation. *Schizophrenia Bulletin*, 1975, *1*, 131–148.

Dincin, J., Selleck, V., & Streicker, S. Restructuring parental attitudes: Working with parents of the adult mentally ill. *Schizophrenia Bulletin*, 1978, *6*, 597–608.

Donner, J., & Gamson, A. Experience with multi-family, time-limited, outpatient groups at a community psychiatry clinic. In H. H. Barten (Ed.), *Brief therapies.* New York: Behavioral Publications, 1971.

Frank, J. D. *Persuasion and healing: A comparative study of psychotherapy.* New York: Schocken Books, 1974.

Frey, L. A., Diller, L., & Hanfling, S. C. Educational group work with parents of hospitalized patients. In *Reflections on social work practice at McLean, 1956–1981* (monograph), Belmont, Mass., April 1981.

Griefen, M. W., & Lawton, R. K. Parents' groups at partial hospital. In J. T. Maxey, R. F. Luber, & P. M. Lefkovitz (Eds.), *Proceedings of the Annual Conference on Partial Hospitalization 1979.* Boston: American Association for Partial Hospitalization, 1980.

Grinspoon, L., Courtney, P. H., & Bergen, H. M. The usefulness of a structured parents' group in rehabilitation. In M. Greenblatt, D. J. Levinson, & G. L. Klerman (Eds.), *Mental patients in transition.* Springfield, Ill.: Charles C Thomas, 1961.

Grunebaum, H. The family. In H. Grunebaum (Ed.), *The practice of community mental health.* Boston: Little, Brown, 1970.

Grunebaum, H., & Solomon, L. Toward a peer theory of group psychotherapy: I. On the developmental significance of peers and play. *International Journal of Group Psychotherapy*, 1980, *30*, 33–49.

Hatfield, A. B. Psychological costs of schizophrenia to the family. *Social Work*, 1978, *23*, 355–359.

Hatfield, A. B. Self-help groups for families of the mentally ill. *Social Work*, 1981, *26*, 408–413.

Hausman, M. Parents' groups: How group members perceive curative factors. *Smith College Studies in Social Work*, 1974, *44*, 179–198.

Heine, R. W., & Trosman, H. Initial expectations of the doctor–patient interaction as a factor in continuance in psychotherapy. *Psychiatry*, 1960, *23*, 275–278.

Jersild, E. A. Group therapy for patients' spouses. *American Journal of Nursing.* 1967, *67*, 544–549.

Killilea, M. Mutual help organizations: Interpretations in the literature. In G. Caplan & M. Killilea (Eds.), *Support systems and mutual help: Multidisciplinary explorations.* New York: Grune & Stratton, 1976.

Konopka, G. *Social group work: A helping process.* Englewood Cliffs, N.J.: Prentice-Hall, 1963.

Lerner, B., & Fiske, D. W. Client attributes and the eye of the beholder. *Journal of Consulting and Clinical Psychology*, 1973, *40*, 272–277.

Levy, D. M. The concept of maternal overprotection. In E. J. Anthony & T. Benedek (Eds.), *Parenthood: Its psychology and psychopathology.* Boston: Little, Brown, 1970.

Lidz, T. *The origin and treatment of schizophrenic disorders*. New York: Basic Books, 1973.

Lieberman, M. A. Groups for personal change: New and not-so-new forms. In D. X. Freedman & J. E. Dyrud (Eds.), S. Arieti (Ed.-in-Chief), *American handbook of psychiatry* (2nd ed.). New York: Basic Books, 1975.

Lowy, L. Goal formulation in social work with groups. In S. Bernstein (Ed.), *Further explorations in group work*. Boston: Charles River Books, 1976.

Mandelbaum, A., & Wheeler, M. E. The meaning of a defective child to parents. *Social Casework*, 1960, *41*, 360–367.

Mass, P., & Odaniell, J. Group casework with relatives of adult schizophrenic patients. In F. J. Turner (Ed.), *Differential diagnosis and treatment in social work*. New York: Free Press, 1968.

Mayer, J. E., & Timms, N. *The client speaks: Working-class impressions of casework*. London: Routledge & Kegan Paul, 1970.

McLean, C. S., Napoleone, K., Scott, J., & Beck, J. C. Group treatment for parents of the adult mentally ill. *Hospital and Community Psychiatry*, 1982, *33*, 564–568.

Milman, D. H. Group therapy with parents: An approach to the rehabilitation of physically disabled children. *Journal of Pediatrics*, 1952, *41*, 113–116.

Nichols, M. P., & Zax, M. *Catharsis in psychotherapy*. New York: Gardner Press, 1977.

O'Brien, P. *The disordered mind: What we know about schizophrenia*. Englewood Cliffs, N.J.: Prentice-Hall, 1978.

Olshansky, S. Chronic sorrow: A response to having a mentally defective child. *Social Casework*, 1962, *43*, 190–193.

Papajohn, J., & Spiegel, J. *Transactions in families*. San Francisco: Jossey-Bass, 1975.

Park, C. C., with Shapiro, L. N. *You are not alone: Understanding and dealing with mental illness*. Boston: Little, Brown, 1976.

Parsons, T. *The social system*. Glencoe, Ill.: Free Press, 1951.

Pildis, M. A multifamily group in a day hospital setting. In R. F. Luber, J. M. Maxey, & P. M. Lefkovitz (Eds.), *Proceedings of the Annual Conference on Partial Hospitalization 1977*. Boston: Federation of Partial Hospitalization Study Groups, 1978.

Rubin, Z. *Liking and loving: An invitation to social psychology*. New York: Holt, Rinehart & Winston, 1973.

Selby, L. G. Supportive treatment: The development of a concept and a helping method. *Social Service Review*, 1956, *30*, 400–414.

Siegler, M., & Osmond, H. *Models of madness, models of medicine*. New York: Harper & Row, 1976.

Silverman, P. R. *Mutual help groups: A guide for mental health workers* (monograph). Rockville, Md.: National Institute of Mental Health, 1978.

Stoler, N. Client likability: A variable in the study of psychotherapy. *Journal of Consulting Psychology*, 1963, *27*, 175–178.

Tarver, J., & Turner, A. J. Teaching behavior modification to patients' families. *American Journal of Nursing*, 1974, *74*, 282–283.

Vaughn, C. E., & Leff, J. P. The influence of family and social factors on the course of psychiatric illness. *British Journal of Psychiatry*, 1976, *129*, 125–137.

Weinberger, G. Brief therapy with children and their parents. In H. H. Barten (Ed.), *Brief therapies*. New York: Behavioral Publications, 1971.

Yalom, I. D. *The theory and practice of group psychotherapy*. New York: Basic Books, 1970.

Yates, M. L., & Lederer, R. Small, short-term group meetings with parents of children with mongolism. *American Journal of Mental Deficiency*, 1961, *65*, 467–472.

IV
THE INTENSIVE
FAMILY THERAPIES

9
STRATEGIC THERAPY OF SCHIZOPHRENIA

Cloé Madanes

This chapter presents a method of therapy to prevent the hospitalization of young people diagnosed as schizophrenic. Although the main theme is the therapeutic strategy, the chapter starts with a digression into a controversial area: the diagnosis of schizophrenia. At a time when diagnostic categories are changing, particularly in the area of schizophrenia (see the *Diagnostic and Statistical Manual of Mental Disorders*, 3rd edition—DSM-III), it is necessary to address the issue of classification before addressing the subject of therapeutic change. The first section of the chapter clarifies the characteristics of the population of schizophrenic patients, their families, and their social context. The second part presents a strategy for the prevention of institutionalization. This strategy deals with shifts of power within the family and between the family and the mental health profession. Before presenting this strategy, the social issues involving the diagnosis of schizophrenia must be clarified.

DIAGNOSIS

A revolution has recently begun to take place in the mental health field. It is similar to the human freedom movement that some time ago freed homosexuals from the bondage of mental illness after having succeeded in liberating women from the limitations of diagnostic categories such as nymphomania. These limitations imposed by the well-meaning helpful professions were not only a curtailment of freedom in an ideological sense, but sometimes led to unfortunate inquisitory techniques such as electroshock therapy, aversive therapy, and chemical dulling of the brain. (In those days dialysis had not been perfected; therefore it was not attempted with homosexuals.) Nymphomania slowly faded away as women became

CLOÉ MADANES. Family Therapy Institute of Washington, D.C., Chevy Chase, Maryland, and Department of Psychiatry, University of Maryland, Baltimore, Maryland.

more assertive about their rights. Homosexuality was eliminated as a source of concern for the mental health field by one sweeping blow at a historical meeting in San Francisco. On July 1, 1980, two major diagnoses disappeared from the field as DSM-III became officially adopted. Neurosis is no longer a source of concern—to the great relief of many of us— and acute schizophrenia has disappeared, to the confusion of second-year residents who were trained otherwise in the first year. Neurotics and acute schizophrenics have now been liberated. However, the schizophreniforms who do not recover after 6 months and a day automatically become chronic and incurable. What a difference a day makes!

Is there hope that chronic schizophrenia may disappear from view, as have nymphomania, homosexuality, acute schizophrenia, and neurosis? This seems far from possible at present, yet there are certain social indicators that something is in the air.

Diagnosis is the area in which there are signs of change. It used to be that classifications of schizophrenics into subtypes only took into account the characteristics of the patients themselves. Recently, the families of schizophrenics have been included in the diagnosis and prognosis, broadening the perspective in a way that for the first time takes into account the social context of schizophrenics. Today this perspective has been broadened even further to include, in the diagnostic subtypes, not only schizophrenics and their families but also mental health professionals. This has occurred because of two historic trends: the movement to discharge patients from mental hospitals, and the reports on irreversible neurological damage as a result of antipsychotic medication (Chouinard, Annable, Ross-Chouinard, & Nestoros, 1979; Granacher, 1981).

These two events constitute dimensions along which the professionals in the mental health field can be classified. At one extreme are those working in state hospitals under the mandate to discharge, and at the other extreme are those working in private hospitals under the mandate to fill the beds. On a second dimension, that having to do with medication, at one extreme there are those mental health professionals who think it is better to be psychotic than brain-damaged, and at the other extreme are those who feel it is better to accept brain damage than to be psychotic.

TYPE I: PARANOID AND POOR-PROGNOSIS SCHIZOPHRENIA

These patients have delusions that their families or the staff of the hospital are trying to influence them, to harm them, or to take advantage of them. During hospitalization, such patients are usually heavily medicated to alleviate symptoms so that a therapeutic relationship can be established. The parents or spouses are involved and dedicated while the patients are in the hospital, but become anxious and agitated soon after discharge, blaming their condition on the patients. They usually request further hospitalization and medication. The prognosis varies from very poor to moderately poor, depending on the subtypes of mental health professionals involved in the case. The prognosis is worse if such a patient is under the care of a professional who, even though holding humane views in areas such as racial issues, sexual discrimination, and capital punishment, does not question the ethics of diagnosing incurable schizophrenia (based on failure to recover after 6 months and a day) and condemning a young person to stay with this label for perhaps 40 or 50 years. It may be hoped that the field will become more liberal and the time limit will be extended to as long as 7 months before the state of incurability is diagnosed. The prognosis is also bad if the patient is in a private hospital under the care of a professional who medicates heavily in the belief that psychosis is worse than brain damage (Chouinard *et al.*, 1979). The prognosis is best if the patient is in a state hospital, where he or she will probably be discharged quickly without a proper follow-up and will probably discontinue his or her own medication, perhaps also changing careers after discharge.

Certain ameliorating family circumstances influence prognosis:

1. The prognosis is better if there is no financial benefit from the illness of the patient and so issues of trusts, inheritances, or disability payments are absent.
2. It is a positive indicator if the spouse or the parents of the patient are not ill, out of work, retired, under stress, or themselves fallen under the care of mental health professionals and so in a diagnostic category.
3. The prognosis is ameliorated by the presence of a trouble-making sibling who distracts the family members from their other concerns.
4. The prognosis is also improved if the spouse or parents have not been taught that the patient is incurable and must remain on medication for life, with the relatives' only alternative being adjustment to this unfortunate condition. When professionals compare the patient's condition with chronic ailments such as diabetes, the prognosis is poor.
5. A positive prognostic indicator is the presence of a kindly parent while the other parent is rejecting, or when both parents are overtly rejecting (rather than both parents being alternately extremely kind and surprisingly cruel, as is often the case).

When most of these ameliorating circumstances are present, there are dramatic periods of spontaneous remission.

TYPE II: SCHIZOPHRENIA, SIMPLE TYPE

These patients are characterized by extreme laziness and refusal to go to work. Family members usually exhibit boredom, irritation, and the strong belief that others should support the patients, since the patients are incurable and unable to change. In these cases antipsychotic drugs do not usually improve the therapeutic relationship, and so the patients are often saved from brain damage. They are given antidepressants or lithium instead, particularly if the apathy is confused with depression, and so patients are only damaged in minor ways. The prognosis is poor when patients are in private hospitals, where they remain for long periods of time since they are docile and compliant (as long as they are not expected to go to work). The prognosis slightly improves when patients are in state hospitals, where they will be likely to be discharged no matter how compliant they are, since the demand for beds is great and funds are scarce.

TYPE III: SCHIZOPHRENIA WITH CONFOUNDING SYMPTOMATOLOGY

This is a special group where the prognosis is moderately good, even in cases that were originally diagnosed as paranoid or simple-type and later developed confounding symptomatology. Apart from schizophrenic symptoms, these patients may have a variety of other conditions, such as grand mal seizures, mental retardation, deaf-muteness, and so forth. These cases are often mistakenly considered hopeless, but not because of madness. The patients do not adjust well to the hospital situation; they do not respond well to antipsychotic drugs; and halfway houses decline them. Frequently the families must take responsibility for such patients, a good prognostic sign. This group includes those schizophrenics who are also drug abusers and so have a better prognosis because the drug abuse sheds doubts on the diagnosis of schizophrenia. It has been suspected that patients purposefully develop this confounding symptomatology to take advantage of the confusion of families and professionals and so improve their situation.

This classification of schizophrenia into three types is useful in understanding the sources of power over a patient in each particular case, as well as the power of a patient over others, so that a strategy for change can be planned.

THERAPY[1]

An adolescent or young adult often is diagnosed as schizophrenic when he indulges in disturbing behavior, such as aggressive or self-destructive acts, bizarre communication, or extreme apathy. Family and community often respond by admitting such a youth into a psychiatric hospital. Eventually everyone calms down and the young person comes out of the hospital. If he causes trouble again and is rehospitalized, the career of a mental patient has begun. The goal of the therapist is to prevent this cycle of hospitalization and rehospitalization.

Behavior that precipitates hospitalization can be thought of as the expression of internal conflicts in the youth, as the result of the wrong chemistry, or as the result of an unfortunate combination of genes. However, if one asks what the consequences of these behaviors for the youth and for the family are, a different perspective emerges. The disruptive acts and the resulting hospitalizations keep a youth and his parents involved with each other in a special way. The young person is a constant source of concern for the parents, and the parents are the only significant relationship that the youth has, except for relationships with professional helpers. The disturbing acts, the repeated failures, and the trouble the young person causes become the main themes in the parents' lives. No matter what the other personal problems of a parent (such as social, financial, health-related, or marital difficulties) are, they will be set aside as less important in contrast to the tragedy of the youth's life. Parents will neglect their own difficulties and overcome their own deficiencies, holding themselves together in order to help the youth. In this sense, the young person's disturbing behavior is helpful to the parents. This helpfulness, however, is unfortunate in that it merely distracts the parents from their problems and in this way prevents them from finding solutions.

The disturbing behavior of the youth may take the form of passive threats of going crazy, harming himself, or doing physical violence against the parents. Whatever the nature of the disturbing behavior, the parents of the youth become too incapacitated to help him because they are afraid of causing him harm or afraid that he will harm them. If the youth behaves normally, he loses the power that the threats of extreme behavior give him over the parents. The youth is incompetent, defective, and dependent on the parents for protection, food, shelter, and money, and the parents are in a superior position, providing for and taking care of him; yet simultaneously the parents are dominated by the youth because of his helplessness, threats, or dangerous behavior. In this sense, two incongruous hierarchies are simultaneously being defined in these families.

It is possible that the youth's disruptive behavior originally had a helpful function for the parents. However, the consequence of this helpfulness is an increase in the youth's power over the parents. When the parents try to restore their position in the hierarchy by resorting to agents of social control (the police or the mental hospital), the youth is institutionalized and consequently behaves more helplessly and with less control. Paradoxically, this gives the youth more power over the parents, because they must focus more on him or her in their attempts to provide help. Yet this helpfulness of the parents defines the youth as even more helpless (or out of control) and contributes to the power that can be derived from such helplessness. In this way, a system of interaction can be established that perpetuates itself over time, particularly if there is the stigma of schizophrenia attached to the situation of the youth and if society (through social agencies) contributes to maintaining it. Whether the youth's behavior originally had a protective function, whether it was meant to prevent a separation between the parents, or whether it was only related to a bid for power is quite irrelevant. The issue is that to solve the problem, the hierarchy must be restored to one in which the youth does not dominate the parents through helplessness and abuse.

The therapist's problem is how to get the young person to give up the disturbed behavior that is the basis of his power. This cannot be done directly by the therapist. The youth's power is over the parents, and it is the parents who must take it away from him.

The therapy of these difficult cases can be thought of in stages. In the first stage, the therapist lays down the agenda: to prevent further hospitalization and to return the youth to a normal life involved in work or school. The parents are asked to make decisions about the youth and to take charge of his life (Haley, 1980). In the second stage, the parents react to the therapist's requests by attempting to avoid taking power over the youth, and the therapist must respond with counteracting maneuvers to keep the parents in charge. In the third stage, there usually is a crisis in which the youth escalates his disturbing behavior. There may be suicide threats, and hospitalization may be considered. The therapist must offer alternatives to hospitalization and support the family through the crisis. In the fourth stage, the youth develops normal activities and gradually disengages from the therapist and from the parents. These four stages are discussed in what follows.

THE FIRST STAGE

Before a first interview, the therapist must arrange to be in charge of the case so that this fact can be stated clearly to the family. This includes being in charge of medication, discharge, and rehospitalization. If the therapist is not a physician, he or she must arrange for a physician to back him or her up in these decisions. If the therapy starts before release from the hospital, the discharge should be contingent upon the plans that the parents make for the youth. This gives power to both the therapist and the parents, since the young person's release from the hospital is then dependent on them.

The parents must state what their expectations are for the youth when he comes out of the hospital, in terms of where he will be living and what he will be doing. It is best if the youth comes home to his parents so it is possible to reorganize the hierarchy in a way that will ultimately enable the youth to leave his parents successfully. The family should be told that at this time the young person needs the parents' guidance and support.

The parents must talk to each other and reach agreement on expectations and rules for the young person. These include issues of work or school, behavior in and out of the home, scheduling of activities, chores, use of drugs or alcohol, and indulgence in violence. The rules must be as specific and practical as possible. The parents must also set consequences in case their rules are disobeyed. Depending upon the severity of the problem, the consequences can vary from mild to extreme. Coming in late may entail the loss of an allowance, but use of drugs may necessitate house arrest. The young person should not be allowed to intervene while the parents are setting rules and consequences.

After parents have agreed on rules and consequences, they must communicate them to the youth, even though he has been present during the discussion. It is best if parents can obtain some commitment from him that he will obey the rules. The young person will usually object and demand more independence. The therapist must then state that the youth's irresponsible or disturbing behavior had led to his hospitalization and that the parents must give him the guidance that he needs until he shows that he behaves like a responsible person.

If a youth's problem is apathy, the parents must set rules that will ensure activity and prescribe consequences if these rules are not followed. Often deadlines must be set for certain types of activities, such as finding a job, and there must be consequences if these deadlines are not met. Only after the youth has begun to be active will he abandon the apathy.

If in the past, a youth has indulged in violence, bizarre behavior, or drug or alcohol use, a recurrence must be anticipated and plans for future difficulties must be made. These acts must be defined as misbehavior and not mental illness, so that they are in the realm of expertise of parents and not of professionals. Severe consequences should be planned ahead of time to discourage the youth from behaving in extreme ways. The parents must agree on a plan to handle the next episode of extreme behavior if it occurs. It is best to encourage the parents to use their own resources to control the youth, even if this involves restraining him or her physically and requesting the help of relatives or neighbors. The therapist should make clear to the parents that hospitalization should not be part of their plan.

The young person should only be discharged from the hospital when the therapist is satisfied that there are clear rules about how he is to behave at home, consequences if he does not obey these rules, and plans for what he is to do with regard to school or work.

THE SECOND STAGE

Over the next weeks, the therapist should review with parents whether the rules have been followed, and if not, whether the consequences were applied. New rules and consequences must be set up. The therapist must struggle to maintain the parents in a superior position as the young person puts them to the test. In this stage, not only the youth but also the parents respond against the therapist's attempts to correct the hierarchy.

Parents typically avoid defining the family hierarchy as one in which they have power over their offspring. They do so because the youth is more powerful than they are; because society has intervened to take power away from them; because they are afraid to do the wrong thing and harm the youth; because they are afraid they are to blame and wish to do no more harm; because they are afraid to lose their child; or simply because they do not want to make the effort of taking responsibility emotionally and materially for their child. Parents can decline authority over the youth in various ways, and the therapist must respond with various counteracting maneuvers to keep the parents in charge.

GIVING AUTHORITY TO EXPERTS

Parents might invoke the authority of experts by saying, for example, that the therapist or the chief of the ward should make the decisions concerning the disturbed young persons. The therapist must transfer the power back to the parents by relabeling the young person's problems so that they are in the area of expertise of parents rather than of medical or psychiatric experts. Even the most bizarre behavior can be redefined as discourteous communication, in that others cannot understand it or in that it upsets others. Then the youth can be asked to communicate more clearly and politely. Apathetic behavior can be reformulated as laziness so that the parents can be moved to demand regular activity. If a youth is on medication, the therapist must state that he or she will reduce the medication and discontinue it altogether as soon as possible. As long as the young person is on medication, he or she is a mental patient under the care of a psychiatrist, instead of a misbehaving son or daughter whose behavior must be changed by the parents. A similar issue often comes up with the question of whether the youth should be on disability benefits. If the therapist accepts this idea, he or she is defining the youth as a mental patient incapable of making a living like a normal person.

Parents often give authority to experts by expressing ignorance of what should be done. The therapist should persuade them that they must tackle the difficult task of giving clear guidance to their confused son or daughter so that the youth's confusion about his or her own life will be

cleared. It would be a mistake to believe that the parents are actually igno-
rant. Their expressions of ignorance serve the purpose of arranging for
others to take charge.

The therapist should not set rules and consequences for the youth, but
should require instead that parents do so. Since the therapist wants a hierarchy with the parents in a superior position, he or she cannot put them
down in front of the offspring by taking over a parental position. Only if the
therapist feels strongly that the parents' decisions about the young person
are seriously wrong should he or she undermine their authority by suggesting
an alternative, and then this should be done with the parents alone, not in the
presence of the youth.

GIVING AUTHORITY TO A PROBLEM YOUTH

Sometimes parents will offer the authority to the problem youth, turning
to him for decisions and advice. The therapist must emphasize that it is
necessary for the parents to provide the guidance, and that only when the
youth is behaving properly will he be in charge himself. In the meantime, the young person will live in a predictable world, knowing what his
obligations and privileges are.

At the beginning of therapy, chances are that every time the parents
begin to talk to each other, the young person will call their attention
to himself or herself by behaving in bizarre or disruptive ways. This
disturbing behavior will interrupt the possibility of an alliance between
the parents that would give them power over their offspring. The therapist
must quiet the youth or ask the parents to do so, so that they can proceed
to talk to each other and reach agreements.

When a family with a severely disturbed youth comes to therapy, there
is a split between the parents. This split might be the result and not the
cause of the pain, bickering, accusations, and guilt that inevitably accompany this kind of problem. The disturbing behavior of the youth
perpetuates this problem, and, although it often prevents a separation and
divorce since the parents must stay together to take care of their defective
offspring, it also prevents the parents from coming together in joy and
good feeling. It may be that the youth behaves disruptively both when the
parents are too far apart (i.e., if they threaten to separate or divorce) or too
close together (when there is agreement between them), because in both
cases the young person loses power over the parents.

Sometimes the parents will give authority to the problem youth
by threatening to expel him from the family home as the only consequence for the youth's misbehavior that is available to the parents. In this
way, the parents threaten to renounce their position in the hierarchy as
parents who are responsible and in charge of their offspring. This threat

must be blocked. The therapist must emphasize that this separation from the parents must happen when the youth is behaving competently and when the parents know and approve of where and how he is going to live. Expulsion is a threat that is rarely carried out; in any case, the chances are good that soon parents and youth will be involved with each other again and the cycle will be repeated.

Sometimes parents want to expel the youth from home, put him in jail, hospitalize him, or enforce other extreme consequences. In these situations, it is important for the therapist to distinguish between firmness and rejection. The parents should be encouraged to be firm but kind. Rejection of the youth should be discouraged, because it escalates the confrontation between parents and youth and increases a malevolent use of power rather than the benevolent guidance that the therapist seeks for parents to accomplish.

Sometimes a young person makes a strong bid for power by threatening suicide. In this case, there are two possibilities for the therapist: (1) to hospitalize the youth, which means that the therapy will have to start all over again when the young person is discharged; or (2) to put the parents in charge of the youth and help them organize to prevent suicide. This is a difficult decision to make and should depend on the seriousness of the suicide threat; on whether there have been previous attempts; on an evaluation of the parents' investment in keeping their offspring alive; and on their ability to work together to prevent the suicide. If the therapist decides against hospitalization, he or she should carefully help the parents organize to prevent the suicide. They should institute a 24-hour watch, and the parents should take turns watching him so that the youth is never alone. This usually tests the limits of the parents' patience and helps them to take a more firm position in demanding normal behavior from the youth.

DEFINING THEMSELVES AS INADEQUATE

If a parent behaves in disruptive ways—for example, crying, screaming, or threatening violence in a session—it is better for the therapist to deal with this behavior without the young person in the room. The therapist should emphasize all that the parent has done in the past, should stress the parent's kindness and dedication, and should ask little of the parent—for example, one more week of patience until there is a plan for what the young person will do with his life.

DISQUALIFYING THE OTHER PARENT

Sometimes one parent will define the other parent as incompetent and disqualified from taking charge of the offspring. There are a series of tactics that the therapist can use to counteract this maneuver, which prevents the parents from allying to take charge of the youth. He or she can say that this is a new situation where they will be working with the therapist who will help them to get together and jointly take charge of their offspring; whatever has happened in the past is irrelevant. The therapist can also reformulate the disqualified parent's behavior so that weakness becomes sensitivity; harshness or brutality becomes desperate attempts to provide clear guidance to a disoriented youth; or depression and emotional instability become dedicated concern. Once the incompetence has been reformulated, it can be discarded.

DISQUALIFYING THE YOUTH

Parents may disqualify a youth from the possibility of changing in positive ways by describing him as inadequate or defective. This can be achieved by reminding the young person and the therapist of how confused, disoriented, or disruptive the youth has been. The reminder often occurs at times when the therapist is struggling to encourage self-sufficiency in the young person or when the youth is planning to take the first steps toward a new life. Sometimes the disqualification comes from benevolent siblings or relatives who want to remind the therapist of the severity of the problem the youth is struggling with or who wish to protect the youth from disappointments derived from high expectations.

The disqualifications can sometimes be phrased as positive comments: for example, "He has been so much better this last month. He did not even get lost in the street." The therapist must be alert and quick to perceive these devastating remarks so that he or she can immediately block them, while keeping in mind that this maneuver by parents and relatives does not have the purpose of simply undermining the youth. Rather, it is an excuse to avoid taking responsibility for helping the young person. The therapist must act quickly as soon as a statement from a relative begins to take the form of this kind of disqualification. He or she must interrupt and bring back the conversation to the issue at hand, which is to focus on a plan for the youth's future and not on the misfortunes of the past.

Sometimes these disqualifications are phrased not as comments on past events but as observations on the young person's current behavior in the interview. Negative remarks and dire predictions may be made on the basis of the way the youth is sitting, his attire, the facial expression, tone of voice, or silence. The therapist must insist that such comments by parents be phrased as positive suggestions for change rather than as mere criticisms. The therapist must remember at all times that a good part of his or her job is to protect the young person from personality attacks, unfortunate reminders of past failures, and dire predictions. If these are blocked, the youth will have a chance to improve, and parents and relatives will have the satisfaction of helping him.

Putting the therapist down is another way that parents can avoid being in charge of their family, since they need not follow the directives of a therapist they do not respect. A youth's parents may suggest that the therapist is incompetent and does not know what he or she is doing, quoting the opinion of other professionals whose position differs. The therapist can reply by suggesting that the parents try his or her approach for a limited period of time—for example, for 3 months. In this way they will understand the modality of therapy, and after the 3 months they can decide whether to continue or not. Also, after 3 months the young person might be on his or her feet, and the therapy might no longer be necessary.

THE THIRD STAGE

Changes in other relationships in the family can be expected to occur when there have been changes in the hierarchical relationship between parents and child. Sometimes a sibling will make an alliance with the disturbed youth to support him against the parents and to reinstate an organization in which the parents are not in a superior position. Often a grandparent, a divorced parent, or another relative will ally with the youth, and there will be the danger that two incongruous hierarchies will again be defined in the family. In fact, the more disturbed the young person is at the beginning of therapy, the greater the possibility is that as soon as the hierarchical organization of the nuclear family begins to become congruent, the therapist will discover involvements with extended kin that define a hierarchy incongruent with one in which the parents are in a superior position. The therapist must block these coalitions and shift the relative(s) from allying with the disturbed youth to supporting the parents in their efforts to guide him or her. In order to do this, it is often necessary to have the relative(s) present at one or more sessions.

It is usually at this stage that important issues concerning money become explicit. If the family is poor, there is the issue of disability. If the young person begins to live normally, the youth and the family run the risk of losing disability payments that sometimes help support several family members. It is best for the therapist to insist that the youth can make an honest living like normal people and to refuse to collaborate in arranging for disability payments. If the family is in a good financial position, often there are quarrels centering around inheritances, with implications that the mentally ill family member will have easier access to funds. Sometimes trusts have been explicitly established to pay out funds to the disturbed youth if he is under psychiatric care. The therapist must discover and block these possibilities, or the promise of a financially secure future may be more attractive to the youth and to the family than the focus on work and school offered by the therapist.

As the parents take charge, the young person may escalate his disturbing behavior to the point of becoming extremely bizarre or threatening. Often, there is a crisis; parents then usually consider hospitalization. This would be an error, since it goes against the efforts to put the parents in charge of the problem by giving authority to the hospital staff. In addition, it goes against the goal of the therapy, which is to keep the young person out of the hospital. The therapist can suggest alternative consequences to the youths' extreme behavior, such as restrictions on money or food, or confinement at home. It can be suggested that the parents call the police if there are threats of violence. If hospitalization occurs, the therapy must start all over again, following the same steps that were carried out previously.

It is important at this point, if hospitalization becomes necessary for a youth, for the therapist to remember that the young person can be discharged after a few days and therapy resumed where it left off. Some families never quite seem to get through this third stage; every year there is a crisis and a hospitalization. The therapist should not become discouraged and should keep in mind that hospitalization is preferable to the risk of neurological damage produced by medication, since one is reversible and the other is not. Also, the therapist should remember, even when economic trends lead to budget cuts and the mandate to discharge patients, that hospitals are meant to take care of people undergoing physical or emotional crises.

THE FOURTH STAGE

As soon as the youth becomes regularly involved in a normal way of life centered around work or school, the therapist can begin to meet with him individually to plan tasks related to activities and social relations. There should also be meetings with the youth and his parents to plan for possible eventualities and for ultimate goals, such as the young person's social and financial independence from the parents. As various goals are met, the sessions are reduced in frequency until the therapy is discontinued.

SPECIAL CIRCUMSTANCES

The emphasis of this chapter has been on families consisting of two parents and a disturbed youth. However, a variety of family structures and circumstances is possible. For example, there may be a single parent, or the young person may be married and the young spouse must then be considered in the therapy. Also, questions of organicity may complicate and confuse the goals of the therapy. I address these issues briefly here.

In cases in which there is a single parent, it is best to try to include in the therapy a significant adult relative who is involved with the young person as a parental surrogate. This person can be a grandmother, an aunt, the mother's boyfriend, or another relative; however, he or she should be the most significant parental person in the youth's life, apart from the parent. The therapy will proceed in the same way. If there is no relative to involve in the therapy, the treatment plan will still be the same, but the therapist will have to use himself or herself more in the discussion with the single parent and will have to encourage and support the parent in making the decisions that are necessary during the course of therapy.

A word of caution is necessary about those cases in which the disturbed young person is married. It is a mistake to put the spouse in charge in the manner that has been described here for the parents of the youth. For parents to have extreme control of their children is appropriate in Western culture during certain developmental stages. When things go wrong, it is appropriate to go back to those stages and to put parents in charge again until the youth accomplishes more mature behavior. It is not appropriate in Western culture, however, for one spouse to have extreme control of the other spouse. To arrange this leads to an inappropriate hierarchy that may result in violent or suicidal behavior. Also, the spouse who goes into a mental hospital is often making a desperate attempt to escape an unfortunate marriage. To come out of the hospital under the control of the other spouse is not an appropriate solution. It is better for the disturbed spouse to come home to his or her parents or to some other kind of living arrangement first, and then slowly to move back together with the spouse or to decide to separate from the spouse. These steps should be carefully planned during the course of therapy.

Schizophrenia may or may not have an organic basis. The question, however, is irrelevant to therapy. Even if there were evidence for an organic or genetic base, the therapist would still have to organize as normal as possible a life for the schizophrenic young person, keeping him out of the mental hospital and using medications only sparingly and with caution. In fact, this approach to therapy has been used in cases that were clearly organic, such as with mentally retarded individuals, victims of tardive dyskinesia, epileptics, and young people with irreversible neurological damage from PCP ("angel dust") use.

SUMMARY OF THE THERAPEUTIC STRATEGY

When a youth diagnosed as schizophrenic is coming out of a mental hospital, the therapist is typically presented with a situation where there is an incongruity in the family hierarchy. The young person is a helpless patient, with the parents taking care and providing for him. At the same time, the youth has superior power over the parents, threatening them with his behavior, and holding them together by providing them with crises that distract them from their problems but also prevent them from resolving their difficulties. If the youth abandons this behavior, he loses this power over the parents.

The therapist's goal is to get the young person to abandon the disturbed behavior that is the basis of this power, which means that the parents must be able to gain control over the youth. The parents must set expectations and rules for the youth and must establish consequences if these are not followed. The therapist must influence the parents to establish rules and consequences that are stringent enough to build up their power vis-à-vis the youth. When the young person loses power over the parents, he will begin to behave normally. At this point, the therapist must help the parents to deal with their own difficulties without involving the youth. This task will be made easier because of the experience of expecting appropriate behavior and negotiating agreements with each other that the parents have acquired while going through the process of setting rules and enforcing consequences for the young person.

To summarize the therapeutic process: The therapist arranges a situation in which the young person comes home from the mental hospital to be guided and cared for by parents who are strict but kind. The hierarchy is corrected not only in terms of authority but also in terms of affect, with the parents not only making appropriate demands but also showing appropriate caring for the young person. If the therapist is able to hold parents and youth in this situation for a period of time, then, if there is a conflict, if the youth decides to leave, or if the youth is expelled from the home, he will be able to separate successfully because he will leave the memory and the experience of a family situation that was hierarchically correct and emotionally appropriate.

A clarification of how *not* to understand this approach is in order. This is not a theory about how youths should leave home. It is not suggested that in order to leave home successfully, without ending in a mental hospital, a young person must have good experiences and good memories of his parents. Many young people separate successfully from parents who have abused them, have mistreated them, or have been totally irresponsible. I am not saying that it is necessary to be raised in a correct hierarchy by caring parents to avoid mental illness. What I am saying is that once there has been a hospitalization, the way to prevent the cycle of hospitalization and rehospitalization is to return the youth to a family situation where the parents are responsible and caring and the young person is obedient and respectful. Then, after this experience, the parents and the youth can separate successfully, and the young person can become independent and pursue his own life.

Psychiatric and psychological classifications and predictions have often reflected cultural values rather than scientific truth. psychosis is sometimes only a temporary phase and reverses spontaneously, while irreversible neurological damage produced by medication does not (Bleuler, 1978).[2] The method of therapy presented here is based on a respectful, humane view of mental patients and their families. It is based on the ethical position that as long as a patient is alive, he or she should not be thought of as chronic, hopeless, or incurable. It is based on a careful distinction between proper patient care and economic trends such as "empty the hospitals" or "fill the beds." It is based on an awareness of the tenuous distinction between therapeutic practice and social control: If a therapist is not to be merely an agent of social control, chemical restraints, electroshocks, and hospitalization should be used with extreme caution. It is based on respect for human freedom and the idea that it is better to allow a person to remain organically intact, without side effects from medication, even if it is at the cost of occasional hospitalizations. The cost of medications versus the cost of hospitalization should not be a consideration for the therapist. The approach is based on the conservative position that measures of social control should only be used in cases of danger to oneself or others and on the idea that experiences such as auditory or visual hallucinations and disturbed communication are not dangerous and can be tolerated. Human beings have often harmed one another for benevolent reasons, and one should take a cautious, skeptical view of extreme measures to influence others in helpful ways. The outcome of the approach has no research data to support it. It derives from clinical experience of success and failure with difficult patients and their families and from the logical consequences of a humane view of mental illness.

NOTES

[1]This section of the chapter has been published in slightly different form in C. Madanes, *Strategic Family Therapy* (San Francisco: Jossey-Bass, 1981), and in C. Madanes, "The Prevention of Rehospitalization of Adolescents and Young Adults," *Family Process*, 1980, *19*, 179–191. Reprinted by permission of Jossey-Bass, Inc., and Family Process, Inc.
[2]Manfred Bleuler (1978) followed his own personal cohort of 208 schizophrenics at his clinic for up to 36 years. He observes, "On an average, after 5 years' duration, psychosis does not progress any further. It tends rather to improve" (p. 633). "At least 25% of all schizophrenics recover entirely and remain recovered for good" (p. 634).

REFERENCES

Bleuler, M. The long-term course of schizophrenic psychosis. In L. Wynne, R. L. Cromwell, & S. Matthysse (Eds.), *The nature of schizophrenia*. New York: Wiley, 1978.

Chouinard, G., Annable, L., Ross-Chouinard, A., & Nestoros, J. N. Factors related to tardive dyskinesia. *American Journal of Psychiatry,* 1979, *136,* 79–83. (See also *Psychiatric Annals,* 1980, *10,* 1, passim.)

Diagnostic and statistical manual of mental disorders (3rd ed.). Washington, D.C.: American Psychiatric Association, 1980.

Granacher, R. P. Differential diagnoses of tardive dyskinesia: An overview. *American Journal of Psychiatry*, 1981, *138*, 1228–1297.

Haley, J. *Leaving home*. New York: McGraw-Hill, 1980.

Madanes, C. *Strategic family therapy*. San Francisco: Jossey-Bass, 1981.

Madanes, C. The prevention of rehospitalization of adolescents and young adults. *Family Process*, 1980, *19*, 179–191.

10
SYSTEMIC FAMILY THERAPY IN SCHIZOPHRENIA

William R. McFarlane

Systemic family therapy, an approach developed at the Milan Center for the Study of the Family by Mara Selvini-Palazzoli, Gianfranco Cecchin, Giuliana Prata, and Luigi Boscolo (1978), has gained considerable popularity in America since its introduction here in the mid-1970s. With this growth of interest has come a general consensus that this method is effective for severe psychopathology, unusually disturbed families, and especially cases where other therapies have failed. Inevitably, the question has arisen as to whether schizophrenia should be included as an indication. While one of the contentions of this discussion is that there is no reliable answer on that issue at present (the Milan team has yet to publish even one case description of an adult schizophrenic, let alone controlled evaluations), the present chapter takes the view that many features of their technique, with respect to schizophrenia, lend themselves well to dealing with selected families and with critical aspects of the therapy context.

What follows, then, is a short history of the use of paradox in psychotherapy; a description of the Milan team's theory and technique; the modifications that seem to be necessary for using this approach with adult schizophrenics; and a case study. Paradoxical family therapy in schizophrenia is presently an experimental treatment, so that these views are to be taken as work in progress. This approach does not fully rank with the others in this volume, particularly regarding reliability. Further, what is described here is only an orientation and a minor alteration of technique; this is not even a fully developed therapy, in comparison to the others described within these pages. Nevertheless, there are promising possibilities in the systemic method that seem to warrant continued, though more rigorous, trials with it.

WILLIAM R. MCFARLANE. Department of Psychiatry, College of Physicians and Surgeons of Columbia University, and New York State Psychiatric Institute, New York, New York.

PARADOXICAL TECHNIQUES WITH THE INDIVIDUAL:
A SHORT REVIEW

The use of paradoxical methods in psychotherapy has a long, if obscure, history. They have arisen, like most of the new therapies for schizophrenia, from pragmatism and serendipity rather than from theory, which has always been (and still is) in the position of trying to account for these methods' dramatic results. Nowhere is the theory–technique contradiction more glaring than in Freud's work (1919/1955) with phobias, where the present history seems to begin. He insisted that, for a successful analysis, the patient had to put himself or herself in the feared situation repeatedly and intentionally, in order to "bring into analysis the material indispensable for a convincing resolution of the phobia" (pp. 165–166). He noted, however, that the symptom would often resolve, without insight, after this forced reenactment—something he could not explain and so tended to ignore. The example has all the basic elements of paradoxical methods—reframing the symptom (it is good to have it, to "deepen" the analysis); requiring its intentional, even scheduled, repetition; and taking control of the symptom by the therapist—all in the context of a double bind (if a patient has the symptom, it will promote the therapy; if the patient does not, he or she will be resisting, but getting well).

From there, one can trace paradoxical themes to Dunlap's work (1930) with "negative practice" in the 1920s, then to Frankl's (1967) "paradoxical intention" and to Stampfl and Levis's (1967) "implosion technique" (flooding the patient with anxiety by recreating feared conditions). Milton Erickson, combining elements of hypnotic technique and paradox, became justifiably revered for the sheer artistry, elegance, and uncanny precision of his interventions, which Jay Haley (1967, 1973) explicated and elaborated. The latter suggested that the basis for the effects of paradoxical prescription is the patient's getting a new view of himself or herself and the communicative value of the symptom, while it erodes the patient's complementary struggle with the therapist. Thus, though seeming to disqualify his or her own power, the therapist actually gains a higher level of control over the relationship and the symptom. Many of Erickson's techniques exaggerated the symptom to the point of its becoming not only absurd but intolerably bothersome: The combination usually led patients to drop it, as if they were just tired of the whole business. His oft-cited case of an enuretic couple, who were instructed to urinate intentionally and ritualistically on the bed *together*, *before* they went to sleep, is a good example. Another component in this case should be noted: Erickson's prescriptions subliminally made available a more adaptive alternative to symptoms—the couple's learning to have fun in bed, instead of fearing "accidents." Cloé Madanes (1981) has added a clever new variation on the theme with her techniques of pretending to have a symptom or pretending to help another family member through having it. I return to these themes—the shifting of the therapeutic context and of the meaning of the family's interaction—later.

Paradoxical treatment has had less use in schizophrenia than in other syndromes. John Rosen's (1953) carefully timed prescriptions of psychosis are well known. The usual effect was observed: The healthier part of the patient was activated and fought off the incipient psychotic regression. While Rosen had poor long-term results, his work illustrated the fact that schizophrenics are still human, with many personal resources, and can be recruited in the struggle to suppress their illness. Likewise, Don Jackson (1963), one of the preeminent founders of family therapy, reported reversing a paranoid patient's suspiciousness and delusions by first joining, then outstripping, the patient in his delusional vigilance. The patient insisted that Jackson's office was bugged, so Jackson insisted that they both dismantle the office until they found the microphones. The patient gradually concluded that Jackson was more insane than he and asked that they stop, dropping his delusion in the process. One recent study illustrates the complexity of both paradoxical and psychotic phenomena: Post and Goodwin (1973) have shown that cerebrospinal amine metabolite levels can be elevated by asking remitted manic patients to "act manic." They seem to be able to do a good job of it, even at the biochemical level.[1]

THE MILAN METHOD

Over the past decade, the Milan team has been experimenting with several family therapy techniques, many of them paradoxical. They have focused on anorexia nervosa, autism, and childhood psychosis, from which work they have been identified as paradoxical therapists of schizophrenia. This is at least partly a faulty impression, but it has been reinforced by their identifying a common pathogenic interaction—reciprocal self-disqualification —as "schizophrenic transaction" (Selvini-Palazzoli et al., 1978). Since it is observable in other syndromes, it is by definition not specific or unique to schizophrenia. This is not to disqualify their observations—only to emphasize that their approach focuses not on diagnostic entities, but on family characteristics and processes, which are relatively independent of diagnosis.

I examine the Milan theory more closely here. The Milan associates' frames of reference are the Batesonian school of communication theory and general systems theory. They see the family as a typical social system, obeying cybernetic principles, particularly those of positive and negative feedback. Negative feedback processes are exaggerated in severely disturbed families, leading them to be rigid, unchanging, and brittle systems that,

when they do shift to positive feedback, tend only to go into crisis and
deteriorate, not to grow, evolve, and differentiate, as do healthier families.
In spite of their use of an impersonal cybernetic model, the team members
translate it into profoundly human, existential, and dramatic terms; their
cases read like operatic libretti. They have great respect for, and an exquisite
understanding of, the unique relational and adaptive system that a disturbed
family develops over time. They assume that the patient member is remaining symptomatic as a radical solution to an especially complex and seemingly irresolvable family dilemma, in which the stakes, regardless of the
eventual outcome, are unusually high. The patient remains bound out of
loyalty to the entire family; he or she seems as reciprocally committed to
the present status as everyone else.

In schizophrenia, the patient remains insane to prevent the emergence
of catastrophic extended family conflict, which would lead to much wider
and more serious disruption than the existing disability of one member. As
for "schizophrenic transaction," that is simply "autodisqualification," in
which every family member not only disqualifies the others' statements, but
his or her own as well, so that no commitment to or definition of any
relationship emerges. (The similarity with Wynne's concept of pseudomutuality should be noted.) The Milan associates do not go so far as to say
that the family drives the patient crazy—a "linear-causal" concept and
therefore useless. Rather, these processes, by being analogical, nonverbal,
and out of awareness, progressively and democratically entrap *every* member of the family. Thus, the real problem is not the symptoms or even the
family's suffering, but the fact that all exits, all possibilities for change, are
blocked, especially those leading to growth, disenmeshment, and movement
to the next stage of the family's life cycle. Nevertheless, the team members,
like most of their paradox-prone predecessors, assume and believe deeply
that capacities for growth are inherent in every person and every family.

While the Milan theory owes much to Bateson, Jackson, Watzlawick,
and Haley, the Milan solution to these dilemmas is a radical departure.
Assuming that change in rigid family systems must occur as a disjunctive,
quantum-like process, the team members proceed to drive the families into
crises that suddenly break the existing homeostatic stalemate.

This is accomplished by consistently describing, in exquisite detail, the
sacrifices and adaptations that each member of a family is making to
preserve the psychological integrity of the other members and the relational
balance of the whole family. This technique is called the "positive connotation." Great care is taken to present these statements as genuine praise and
appreciation, avoiding all traces of criticism or sarcasm. The Milan associates see criticism and even suggestions for change by the therapist as
"disqualification, negation" of a family. In one case, "words had to be
chosen which were not to imply any judgment on the part of the therapist

. . . accepting the system of the here and now as the only explanation of itself"; "the slightest hint of self-conceit or, worse, of arrogance" is to be avoided (Selvini-Palazzoli, 1976, p. 4).

> We had to say clearly that we were well aware of the difficulties of the task and far from denying the possibility of failure. However, our sympathetic tone, far from charging the couple with obstinacy and stubbornness, was intended to hint that their unhappiness was so deep as to be, perhaps, beyond our therapeutic skill (thus avoiding the danger of being accusers and punishers). (Selvini-Palazzoli, 1976, pp. 4-5)

In short, while it may seem to some to be cynicism, the motivation behind the positive connotation is a deeply empathic effort to join the family, especially the parents, and to validate *their* motivation, values, judgment, and perceptions of the situation.

This validation leads to the Milan team's most distinctive contribution: the paradoxical prescription for the family system. In schematic form, this involves a suggestion that a patient and all other family members continue their present symptoms and interactional behavior (which are again described in great detail), as protective measures to avoid more serious consequences, such as divorce, overt intergenerational conflict, extended-family fragmentation, or the departure of a key member (often the patient or a sibling). These prescriptions follow so logically from the positive connotation that they are sometimes omitted, allowing the family to infer them, thereby avoiding alienating a new or very sensitive family with their seeming outrageousness. In fact, recently, the team (actually two teams, after an internal split in 1979) has increasingly relied on a stance of neutrality, "circular questioning," and perceptive systemic description of the family's quandary as their intervention, with the therapy context providing the requisite degree of implied paradox (Selvini-Palazzoli, Boscolo, Cecchin, & Prata, 1980).[2]

The logistics of their approach are equally unusual. They meet with families for a limited number of sessions, usually 12, spaced widely in time, up to a month apart. One or two team members act as interviewers, while the others observe through a one-way screen. Tremendous attention is paid to the details of each family's interaction in regard to the presenting symptom and to details of the immediate family history. The positive connotation, with or without a paradoxical prescription or ritual, is delivered at the very end of the session, with no allowance for further discussion. The intervention is carefully worded, usually by the other team members. At ensuing sessions, new data, often including the emergence of previously unmentioned but influential family members, is brought out in response to the preceding session's intervention. The team typically warns against any progress that has been made in the interval by framing it as risky, or as emerging family disloyalty. The therapists exhibit a remarkably steadfast neutrality; the format remains fixed, discussion by the family of interventions is proscribed, and the team takes no responsibility for medication, crises, hospitalizations, or other services. The only overt positions they take are that the present family equilibrium is of value to everyone and that change is to be avoided, or, at most, should only be allowed to occur in very small steps.

A THEORETICAL ADAPTATION FOR SCHIZOPHRENIA

The Milan team's approach seems important to schizophrenia not because it is either a rigorously applied or tested treatment for that condition, but because it appears to be a highly effective method of reducing severe family enmeshment in which there is a strong investment in the continued dysfunction of the patient. This kind of family system is probably a minority in schizophrenia, but one that is a source of very difficult cases for which other modalities are usually insufficient. These are *dysfunction-maintaining* families, not those that drive the patient crazy. This pattern is a family variable that, on occasion, crosses paths with schizophrenia to produce an unusually catastrophic outcome. It can be seen as the social underpinning of secondary gain. What follows is an attempt to explain the effects of positive reframing or connotation and, to a lesser extent, paradoxical prescription in the family therapy of schizophrenia.

FAMILY PHENOMENA

As has been suggested by many of those who have used paradoxical family techniques (Papp, 1980; Stanton, 1981), they should be reserved for families in which "linear" (directly helpful, supportive, and/or structural) interventions have failed. These families may have several responses to such therapies, but three that are recognizable and relatively predictive of a likely response to systemic intervention are isolated here. It should be noted that these are therapy responses, not necessarily coexistent with other intrafamily factors (high "expressed emotion," communication deviance, double binding, etc.). For mnemonic purposes, this constellation is termed the "three-D complex."

Defiance
"Defiance" here is a behavioral response in which members of a family, especially one with a chronic patient, present themselves as if daring the therapist to succeed. Often, this is because they have seen so many previous

therapies fail that the process begins to seem like a game to them, with the present object not cure, or even arrest of the downward course of the illness, but only preservation of their self-esteem and dignity. So the family patiently listens to the latest formulations and suggestions, discounts them (often with open contempt), and then completely ignores them. Help of any sort is rejected, sometimes even medication and/or hospitalization.

Determination

"Determination" here is an attitudinal factor. The family members, having witnessed and/or been the object of so much therapeutic confusion and apparent incompetence, have reached their *own* conclusions about what is wrong, why the patient is ill, what the prognosis is, and what *really* helps him or her—usually their careful attention and sacrificial ministrations. Given all that, they counter most new information with a volley of rejoinders, all to the effect that they are determined that the patient will and should stay the way he or she is (i.e., only partially recompensated). The same responses are given to the patient's attempts to change, to redefine the situation, or even to disagree, at least within the therapy context.

Deterioration

"Deterioration" relates to the patient. Too often, the patient simply collapses in the midst of the attempts to provide direct aid, primarily because he or she is in the middle of *two* triangular struggles, one within the family system and another in the therapy system. The therapist, faced with a seemingly uncooperative and/or severely disturbed family *and* a relapse, often retreats in confusion.

The Three Ds as Aspects of a Homeostatic System

In order to understand these responses, it seems necessary to see them as examples of one side of the dynamic equilibrium that is inherent in any living, enduring system. Biological and social systems have fundamental tendencies, coexisting and competing, to change (either to grow and differentiate or to shrink and disintegrate) and to maintain a steady state. Other terms have been used—"deviance amplification" versus "deviance reduction" (Hoffman, 1971) or "morphogenesis" versus "morphostasis" (Wertheim, 1973) or simply "change" versus "homeostasis." The three Ds are forms of homeostasis, efforts by the family to avert change.

A purely homeostatic living system is actually deviant and dysfunctional, from the above perspective, since it is not changing and adapting to new external inputs and internal differentiating forces (given that all environments are constantly changing). One has to assume, then, that if homeostasis is the predominant tendency in a family system, it is not just "unhealthy." That state is being maintained through extra effort on the part of some or all of its members. Wynne (1980) has recently pointed out that the impression has been created in the family therapy field that homeostasis is a passive process—that families only change through forces from the outside, such as the heroic efforts of family therapists; it is only growth that is active. This portrayal ignores the fundamental reality that all life processes—homeostasis included—are intrinsically active. The alternative to life is death, not social stability. This idea was inherent in the original concept of homeostasis as put forth by Walter Cannon. He was duly impressed by the self-regulating processes in the body, but was not deluded by their being passive. Since they use energy and maintain a high level of information and organization, they are "negentropic." In simpler terms, a family giving the therapist a hard time by attempting to avoid change is working just as hard as the therapist is. (In such cases, it is the *therapy* system that becomes homeostatic.) In addition to disqualifying the therapist, the family is actively squelching its own inherent tendencies to differentiate—to allow deviance amplification and positive feedback to take over and produce a new family organization.

THE THERAPY SYSTEM

Before examining the effects of systemic therapy on the three-D complex, it is necessary to take a closer look at the therapy system itself, composed of the chronic schizophrenic, his or her family, and the psychiatric institution and/or therapist. It is proposed that, in many cases, the three Ds result directly from the fact that *the family is being double-bound by the therapy system*. This concept is discussed here by describing four contextual injunctions separately. (The reader not familiar with the double-bind theory is referred to Bateson, Jackson, Haley, & Weakland, 1956.)

1. *Primary injunction.* This is relatively straightforward. When the family meets with a therapist, the overarching contextual imperative is that therapy will and should help the family and the patient, but that it must do so by changing some aspect of its organization, particularly the way someone is behaving, thinking, feeling, or perceiving. Almost everyone now carries this rudimentary cultural concept of psychiatric treatment and psychotherapy. As Selvini-Palazzoli and others have pointed out, suggesting a change is tantamount to blame and criticism, or can easily be construed as such.

2. *Secondary injunction.* This is where the trouble lies. The previous experience of the family within the treatment system has usually created another, directly contradictory, contextual imperative—that change should be avoided. Different families have expressed or implied many variations on this theme. A few are presented here:

It was change—usually attempts by the patient to achieve an autonomous status as a young adult—that caused this catastrophe in the first place, and that have caused many of the subsequent breakdowns.

The psychotic episodes themselves are more horrible and demoralizing than anything we had imagined could have happened to *us*, so who knows what will happen if we try to change even the smallest aspect of our present fragile equilibrium? Let us accept this present status, as bad as it is, and be happy, as insurance against even more unimaginable problems.

If we change and the patient improves, that means we *did* cause his or her problem in the first place. If we cooperate, we confirm the contextual accusation. Anyway, who could possibly believe that we could do *that* (create schizophrenia in our child)? It defies all reason.

Why do anything any differently than we are? It is only *our* help that keeps the patient even *this* well.

Just to add another layer of contradiction, many therapists deny to the family that they think the family caused the patient's illness, while actually believing that it did and acting in accordance with that belief.

3. *Tertiary injunction*. This takes the form of a contextual *and* cultural imperative, that of not openly questioning the authority of professionals. While decreasing in generality in the culture at large, this assertion still seems particularly true in schizophrenia. Since the relatives usually believe that the problem is neurological or medical, they tend to grant authority to psychiatrists and, by extension, to the rest of the institutional context. This condition satisfies the requirement for an injunction against commenting on the contradiction (between the first and second injunctions). Further, it is difficult to comment on an unstated accusation, especially if it is overtly denied.

4. *Quaternary injunction*. The schizophrenic and his or her family cannot leave the field of the other injunctions, since the field is the institutional therapy context. Schizophrenia and psychiatry are inextricably bound by history, culture, and the legal system. American psychiatry was exclusively concerned with care for the mentally ill at its inception and still has that as its fundamental mandate. The converse is also true: There is nowhere else for the schizophrenic to go but into the psychiatric context, in one form or another. As a result, the schizophrenic, his or her family, and the local treatment system are in relationship, whether or not they are in regular contact. The permanence of this relationship approaches that of family ties. One example is telling, though many could be cited: *Espiritistas* (Hispanic faith healers) in New York City will readily accept cases of anorexia nervosa, hysterical conversion, phobia, marital disorder, childhood neuroses—in fact, almost any other condition—but almost always

refer schizophrenics to psychiatrists, who are their direct competitors. Thus, once a person becomes schizophrenic, he or she is in the field of the other injunctions, quasi-permanently.

To the extent that the treatment system is double-binding the family, one would expect to find several processes occurring within it, including the three Ds. First, double-bound systems are rigidly and homeostatically paralyzed. Incipient change only induces the cancellation of change. Thus, therapeutic effort within such a context is unlikely to produce change, if only because the family is forced into a position of continually defending itself. Secondly, there will be widespread, reciprocal, and hostile disqualification of most communications, so that no one is heard, let alone acknowledged, on any side of the patient–family–therapist triangle. Thirdly, all commitment to the relationship will be avoided, denied, and/or disconfirmed. That is, no joining will occur between family and therapist; there will be no therapeutic alliance. Fourthly, irrationality will gradually occupy a greater proportion of the communication in the system, so that less and less will be understood by therapist *and* family, particularly in regard to the issue of blame and responsibility and the derivative issue of what should be done. Fifthly, the patient, or someone else, may become overtly irrational or even psychotic under the influence of the accumulating confusion and covert hostility. Thus, in an extreme version of the above scenario, the family would appear *defiant* in behavior and *determined* in attitude—in an effort to disconfirm the therapist and to avoid commitment to the accusatory context—and the patient would *deteriorate*. Even if only partially "true," this analysis suggests that it would be nearly impossible to ascertain reliably what part of the three-D response derives from the family's inherent tendencies and what part is simply iatrogenic—a product of therapeutic insensitivity, institutional contradiction, and ideological confusion.

THE APPLICATION OF SYSTEMIC THERAPY
IN SCHIZOPHRENIA

If one accepts the concept that the "difficult," three-D family is not only actively suppressing its own internal growth-inducing tendencies but is being driven to do so by a double-binding therapy system, then an obvious solution seems to present itself. It amounts to little more than the old adage, "If you can't beat them, join them."

Consider the effects on the kind of situation described above if a therapist consistently, genuinely, and empathetically stated to the family that (in schematic form) "I accept, understand, and truly respect your diligent efforts to maintain this fragile arrangement; furthermore, it is likely that, for the time being, it is the only alternative that helps everyone to feel good about what they are doing and that helps the patient. You should not change. I will meet with you to help you maintain it or, at most, to help you decide what very small changes you think that you might make that will also allow everyone to remain loyal to one another and the family as a whole." Of course, this is a positive connotation and an implied paradox. The overt paradoxical prescription is discussed later.

What seems to happen and what explains the often dramatic therapeutic responses that follow this kind of comment is as follows. Basically, the therapist takes the responsibility of eliminating the secondary injunction—first, by making it overt; second, by directly confirming the family's bias against change; and third, by contradicting all its implied disqualifications and accusations. If well done, the effects can be for the therapist (1) to assume responsibility for the active homeostatic effort; (2) to validate, at a very fundamental level, the family's identity, values, and motivation; (3) to make the members feel safe and allow them to relax; and (4) to make unnecessary their active, change-avoidance maneuvers—all by reducing the pressure to change. The "metaparadox" is this: by joining, validating, and bolstering the family's efforts to keep things static, the therapist provokes change by freeing or unleashing the members' own capacities for growth. It allows for the emergence of the family's unique resources and solutions. The energy that has been expended on maintaining the previous adaptation may be freed for seeking a newer and more open family adaptation. Change, as it occurs, can be seen and experienced by the family as self-initiated (and should be so described by the therapist).

Other advantages are apparent. For one, there is less chance that the therapist will be expelled by the family. For another, the dialectic of change and stability is made overt, a topic for concern and discussion. If properly done, the outcome of this stance will be an unbound therapy system under the control of the therapist, and a reliable, working alliance of the therapist with the whole family. The stage may be set for several possible developments—including syntonic endeavors by the family toward healthier or more adaptive functioning. Further, it may be possible to make tentative and tactful suggestions (along the lines of the linear approaches) as to some of the "small changes" that could be made.

It may be apparent that the emotional and kinesic style of the therapist is critical to the success of this type of intervention. The positive connotation can neither be viewed nor used as a connivance. The therapist must have gathered enough information to appreciate the reality of the family's dilemma and the adaptive motivation and value of what may seem to be severely dysfunctional behavior. This aspect of the Milan team's work has been relatively ignored, at some risk to those who see their methods as simply tactics. They are not. One has to have learned enough to believe what one is saying and to seem to be doing so to family members.

As for paradoxical prescription per se, I propose, as have Fisher, Anderson, and Jones (1981), that this is a more powerful level of intervention to be reserved for those families that do not respond to positive reframings. A useful rule of thumb is for the therapist to escalate the "depth" of the connotation until a mild but favorable response is achieved. The therapist then stays at that level, using variations of the theme ("Go slow," or "This change may cost the family some degree of closeness or harmony"), with occasional and judicious suggestions of linear alternatives, until an impasse occurs. If none develops and progress continues, however slowly, prescriptions of symptoms and the homeostatic aspects of the family system are not used. They are kept in the therapist's kit bag as impasse-transcending interventions, especially when a struggle with the therapist seems to be brewing. Thus, to a large extent, the prescription is seen as a dramatic technique for inducing change when the therapy stalls and for avoiding confrontation; its shock value is of some use in letting the family know how far the therapist is willing to go to steer away from the suggestion of change.

One form of the prescription seems especially useful for schizophrenic patients. It could be called the "short-circuit maneuver." In outline, it is this: If the symptom is embedded in a circular sequence of interactions within a particular context, and if all the participants seem to be deeply involved in the process, the therapist prescribes that the sequence be repeated, often on a schedule, in the same context, *without* the symptom or while the patient *pretends* to have the symptom. This is usually accepted by most families, whereas prescribing psychotic symptoms by themselves may either seem too outrageous for some to tolerate or even too dangerous if taken literally. The effect is often symptom reduction, bemused cessation of the reinforcing interaction, and/or its conversion to a more functional form without the symptom.

While an entire book could be filled with variations on the prescribed paradox (see Weeks & L'Abate, 1982), the above should suffice, given the speculative and experimental nature of this kind of work at present. It should be clear that the emphasis here is on positive connotation/reframing as the more useful, safer, and more generally applicable aspect of systemic therapy for schizophrenia, with paradoxical prescriptions reserved as tools to break through more serious resistance. It remains to be seen whether, for families of schizophrenics, these interventions are means of inducing second-order change, as suggested by Watzlawick, Weakland, and Fisch (1974) or, less glamorously, means of reversing iatrogenic contextual forces that cause families simply to *appear* resistant to some treatments. Perhaps these methods do both things concurrently, and, if so, they are that much more parsimonious.

A CASE OF INTRACTABLE HEADACHE

The case described here attempts to illustrate the use of systemic techniques in a remarkably chronic case of headache, with accompanying schizoid, psychotic, and psychosomatic features, and a long history of multiple treatment failures. In addition, the family met the criteria of defiance, determination, and deterioration. It is arguable whether the patient was definitely schizophrenic, but the combination of severe, intractable psychopathology and rigid family enmeshment made it a more difficult problem for treatment than many more clear-cut cases of schizophrenia.

Sylvia, age 45, and her parents, with whom she had always lived, were referred to a systemic therapy team with the chief complaint of incapacitating, nonmigrainous headaches of 22 years' duration. (The intake worker, an experienced and usually unflappable therapist, asked to be relieved of the case after having to go home with a splitting headache after each family assessment session.) In addition, the patient had had many episodes of unilateral and bilateral paralysis and blindness. For years, she spent her entire day in endless compulsive cleaning rituals; she had fixed persecutory delusions that she was being watched through the curtains and that there were machines in the basement that controlled her actions and gave her headaches. On occasion, she heard men talking about her in the apartment above and through the heating pipes. Her affect was bland and her thinking tangential. In spite of the many symptoms suggestive of schizophrenia, she could carry on a passably coherent conversation and was far from being completely deteriorated, given her age and lack of treatment. The final, though far from satisfactory, diagnosis was severe borderline personality disorder.

The headaches had begun when she was in her early 20s, shortly after she had been forced by her father to break off a relationship with a man she had met while working as an elevator operator in a large department store. The immediate precipitant had been an incident in which a male stranger, after whistling at her from a passing car, drove into a utility pole and required removal by ambulance. The headache had commenced immediately, forcing her to quit her job a few weeks later. From that date forward, she had stayed home, dropped her friends, and never worked or attempted to develop a romantic attachment again. She had had several neurological workups, the most recent in a world-renowned pain center, all with negative results. Medication (including phenothiazines), biofeedback, and psychotherapy had been tried repeatedly, without effect. For brief periods, her symptoms had remitted spontaneously, but had always returned. A recent remission had followed a comment made by her mother, while she and the patient were sitting in their car as it was being washed with a hose by the father, that "the gate needs to be closed."

The family structure was all too clear. The father, especially since his forced retirement 5 years previously, was completely preoccupied with his daughter and her many symptoms. He spoke for her when seeing doctors, reciting her medical history in endless detail. He and Sylvia bickered constantly, he trying to make her stop cleaning or open the window shades, she complaining of his messiness and refusal to believe and cooperate with her delusions. She awoke frequently in the middle of the night, screaming out in pain, whereupon he arose, went to her bedroom, and rubbed her back, lulling her to sleep. He had a pronounced thought disorder, often to the point of looseness of association, for which she criticized him. He saw himself as providing for his family's every need, regardless of the sacrifice required. He had no friends; besides his disturbed daughter, his only hobby was tinkering with their aged auto.

The mother, who had been, by her own account, "a real fighter" in her younger days, had bowed out of the struggle at home by turning over, with appreciation, the household chores and cooking completely to Sylvia. She had achieved thereby a retirement for herself, which she used daily to visit her many neighborhood friends. It became apparent that much of her earlier fighting had been with her husband. The parents' relationship had improved after Sylvia's compulsive rituals and delusional ravings had given her mother an excuse to find interests outside the family. As a result, the parents appeared to get along tolerably: They spent some time together, out of the house, because Sylvia forced them to leave in order to complete her cleaning. They sometimes used these opportunities to visit Sylvia's sisters, who were happily married and living at a good distance from the nuclear threesome. The mother and the patient, by all appearances, thoroughly detested each other and were openly competitive over the household responsibilities and the father's attention. Sylvia always won any direct contest between herself and her mother or father, either through sheer will power or through one of her symptoms. In effect, she controlled the family. Neither parent dared to force an issue with her; if appearing to lose in a confrontation, she would eventually resort to physical violence.

Since both parents were in their 70s and seemed to have capitulated long ago to their daughter, structural and strategic interventions—relying on the parents to set limits on her behavior—seemed out of the question, if only because they refused even to consider such suggestions. Given that, the members of the team, most of them experienced family therapists, agreed that this was the most rigidly dysfunctional family they had seen; they decided to use a consistently systemic approach, limiting the therapy to 12 biweekly sessions and following guidelines being used by the Milan team at that time (Selvini-Palazzoli *et al.*, 1978). What follows is an account of the major observations, family responses, and team interventions in each session. The clinic's chief social worker and I volunteered to serve as therapists.

SESSION 1

The first session was consumed in a long, painfully critical, and condescending recounting by the father of Sylvia's medical history, the story of her last romance, and the endless list of symptoms and family troubles. In the process, he disqualified all of her attempted corrections of the story. The mother deferred totally to the father, stating, "It's what he says, just like that." After consulting with the rest of the team, the therapists suggested that Sylvia continue her headaches for another 2 weeks, since they might be important in some uncertain way to the whole family and the team might understand them better by then.

SESSION 2

Sylvia had had no headaches in the intervening period. More family history was taken. The team cautioned her against giving up her headaches so quickly. To be safe, it was agreed that she would "take pains" to have two headaches in each of the next 2 weeks, to avoid causing too much change in the family.

SESSION 3

Sylvia had had no headaches and had refused to develop headaches as prescribed. She looked better, was less distracted, and was more friendly to everyone. The father's nocturnal attentions to Sylvia emerged and were explored in detail. He was instructed to wake Sylvia at 3 A.M. and rub her back, whether or not she had a headache or was screaming. "If necessary," she was to pretend to have a headache and scream. The mother was also to arise and join them, but only to observe in order to report to the therapists. Words of caution about premature loss of her symptoms were repeated, warning that the parents might begin "fighting" again if Sylvia remained well.

SESSION 4

The mother came dressed much more stylishly than she had been previously and announced that she was dieting. The father looked brighter and was less disorganized in his thinking. Without being forced by Sylvia, the parents had gone shopping together and for some long drives. The father had awoken only twice to follow the prescription. Sylvia had had no headaches.

The team suggested that the mother and father should not yet give up sacrificing their lives for their daughter and abandon their strivings for the joys of retirement and the calm of the golden years. The therapists expressed their sympathy for the mother, adding that the parents had no safe alternative but to turn their home over to their daughter and accept her abuse. Sylvia was asked to resume her symptoms to prevent the parents from creating a new relationship that would exclude her.

SESSION 5

Sylvia's headaches had returned, but the parents seemed much less involved in her difficulties. Instead, they had continued to go out and enjoy themselves. The relationship of the three of them to the two sisters was discussed. The team members expressed their deep respect to Sylvia for volunteering to renew her sacrifice to prevent her parents from any possibility of arguing and to save her sisters from having any responsibility for her parents.

SESSION 6

The basic themes continued. The parents had continued their outside interests; they talked mostly with each other in the session. As they did so, Sylvia buried her head in her hands with a severe headache. Her fears of their leaving her emerged. She was convinced that if they died or moved without her, she would "go crazy." The team reiterated the message of the previous session. She was told that it appeared that she had to continue her pain a little longer until she became convinced that it was safe to give it up.

SESSION 7

On the morning of the appointment, Sylvia became paralyzed from the waist down. The parents canceled the seventh session. The team sent her a letter, to be read to her at bedside by her parents, stating that they understood that she wanted to avoid change and that her paralysis was necessary to keep the family together. She was to remain in bed until her parents appeared to be less interested in getting along without her. The parents were to do whatever she asked.

SESSION 8

The paralysis had ceased, and the family returned for the eighth session, which was taken up with a careful exploration of this new symptom and the interaction around it. The pattern was essentially the same as that surrounding the headaches, except that now the parents seemed increasingly impatient with Sylvia in general and her ever-changing symptoms in particular. The team shared their deep appreciation of the fact that Sylvia would give up her health to keep the family together, and that the parents continued to be willing to set aside their own enjoyment to look after their ill daughter.

SESSION 9

On the day of the ninth session, Sylvia again became paralyzed, but also was blind in the left eye. The parents came to the session anyway, where they received another letter from the team, this one to be read to her by the father again at her bedside. It was quite long and was more explicit than the other interventions had been. In effect, it said that the team "saw" that she could "perceive" that another life might be possible for her and her parents, that they might be more separate and all enjoy life a great deal more, but that she should be steadfast in her refusal to change in that direction. They appreciated how deeply she felt about avoiding any possible harm to her parents' relationship and about losing them, even if the latter were to occur through her becoming more independent. She was advised to remain blind and paralyzed to make sure that no one in the family gave in to their temptations to create a better life.

SUCCEEDING EVENTS

The therapy was then interrupted by Sylvia's making a suicide gesture and being hospitalized. I (and, to a lesser degree, the entire team) was most distressed by this development, since it was unquestionably an effect of the therapy. No one was sure whether this represented another treatment failure for Sylvia, or a confirmation of the unfolding hypothesis. (One team member noted that her being in the hospital was the first time she had slept outside the home in 23 years.)

The answer became clear on her return to the clinic, 10 days after her inpatient admission. Within a week she had no headaches, obsessions, compulsions, hysterical conversions, delusions, or hallucinations. She was admitted to a day program, where she quickly became the star patient. She was cheerful and generous with the other patients and was elected president of the patient government. She in no way appeared to be schizophrenic. By the end of her stay, she had, on her own initiative, found a volunteer job at another hospital; had made a friend in the local laundromat; and had become much less anxious and tyrannical at home. She went away on a few short weekend trips with her friend and visited her sisters by herself. She even began flirting with one of the male volunteers.

She remained well, living what for her was a remarkably functional life, with minimal supportive contact for another 2 years. She terminated therapy in a good way, with the agreement of the cotherapists. Four years after her admission to the clinic she suffered a brief relapse and was hospitalized for 2 weeks, after her good mental health (and a new Republican administration) led her to be removed from the Social Security disability rolls. The parents and the patient handled this setback well, without getting overly reinvolved. At the time of this writing, they are trying to get her reinstated on disability.

DISCUSSION

This case illustrates both the strengths of systemic family therapy and its limitations in the schizophrenia-spectrum disorders. What seems to have been accomplished here was a change in the fundamental interaction patterns in the family and thereby the elimination of their reinforcing effects on Sylvia's many deficits. It seems clear that her underlying deficits remained, leaving her vulnerable to influences from outside the family—in this case, national political and economic trends. This view departs from that of the Milan group, who appear to see the outcome of therapy in either-or terms, even in schizophrenia. On the basis of this and several other similar cases, that position seems overambitious and may carry within it the seeds of later disillusionment and rejection of the method; whereas if one attempts to use these *family* techniques to deal with *family* processes, rather than all the possible influences on a case—especially the biological and societal—one stands a better chance of achieving a lasting result. Of course, it is readily admitted that the Milan team would have handled the case much more elegantly, but that would not have entirely solved the more basic problem.

The case of Sylvia also demonstrates that these techniques must be used with a full awareness of both their formidable power and the risk that always seems to go with "invasive" techniques. This reality has not been sufficiently emphasized, in my view. This approach usually achieves results through *creating* a major crisis in the life of a family; one must be prepared for the possible outcomes in any such crisis. For certain, these techniques should be reserved for truly intractable cases with major psychopathology— those where the benefits more directly justify the risk. Further, this method requires a thorough understanding of the family as system, in addition to considerable experience with other family therapy techniques. It is not for beginners.

As a partial qualification of the above precautions, it should be noted that the team treating Sylvia later agreed that using paradoxical prescriptions so early in her case may have added a proportion of unnecessary risk. It was this case, in fact, that led us to adopt the rule of thumb described previously (positive connotation before paradoxical prescription). Since the adoption of this guideline, it has seemed possible to regulate the rate of change more easily and so to avoid serious complications more readily. In other words, "going slow" is occasionally good advice for families *and* therapists.

CONCLUSION

What seems to be needed at this stage in the evolution of paradoxical approaches is a number of carefully controlled experimental trials with them. That they are effective in many cases now seems beyond question, but whether their effects persist or whether some types of problems and families are more amenable than others is unknown—yet vital—information. Perhaps this need is nowhere more evident than in schizophrenia. For instance, Kopeikin, Marshall, and Goldstein (see Chapter 3) have found that family resistance, even if noted for only a few sessions at the very beginning of crisis-oriented family therapy, predicts a poor outcome. Is it possible that a judicious use of positive connotation at that point might reduce those relatives' negativity sufficiently to allow other aspects of that approach to be more effective?

These kinds of questions seem to multiply as therapists acquire more experience with the method. They point up another need. That is, a more adequate theoretical model to explain the action of these techniques might make the task of integrating them with other approaches simpler. Thus, if a model for use in schizophrenia could be devised that included an assumption of multiple levels of causal influence, it might be possible to use these techniques more selectively and specifically, along with other interventions, to maximize the long-term outcome. Family therapy, no matter how powerful, seems unlikely to eliminate the possibility of subsequent relapse in schizophrenics completely. This suggests that continued supportive work with individuals and families and some minimal use of medication may have to follow systemic therapy, especially to deal with later life stresses. Thus, this modality may become a breaker of logjams in family development, rather than a cure for schizophrenia.

With these provisos, it seems likely that paradoxical techniques will play an increasing role in the treatment of especially serious cases of schizophrenia. At the very least, they should prove useful as a means of creating a clearer and more functional therapy context. From the family's point of view, this might be a sufficient relief by itself to recommend the approach.

ACKNOWLEDGMENTS

I wish to acknowledge explicitly the assistance of Lyman C. Wynne for some of the initial inspiration and the final review of this chapter.

NOTES

[1] The reader interested in a more detailed history is referred to Raskin and Klein's excellent review (1976).
[2] Selvini-Palazzoli's latest innovation—a direct instruction to a patient's parents that they simply leave the house mysteriously for progressive amounts of time—seems equally effective but is, in my opinion, a powerful "structural" maneuver that shares little with the team's previous work.

REFERENCES

Bateson, G., Jackson, D. D., Haley, J., & Weakland, J. Towards a theory of schizophrenia. *Behavioral Science*, 1956, *1*, 251–264.

Dunlap, K. Repetition in the breaking of habits. *Scientific Monthly*, 1930, *30*, 66–70.

Fisher, L., Anderson, A., & Jones, J. E. Types of paradoxical intervention and indications/contraindications for use in clinical practice. *Family Process*, 1981, *20*, 25–37.

Frankl, V. E. *Psychotherapy and existentialism: Selected papers on logotherapy*. New York: Washington Square Press, 1967.

Freud, S. [Lines of advance in psychoanalytic therapy.] In J. Strachey (Ed. and trans.), *Standard edition of the complete psychological works of Sigmund Freud* (Vol. 17). London: Hogarth Press, 1955. (Originally published, 1919.)

Haley, J. Commentary on the writings of Milton H. Erickson. In J. Haley (Ed.), *Advanced techniques of hypnosis and therapy: Selected papers of Milton H. Erickson, M.D.* New York: Grune & Stratton, 1967.

Haley, J. *Uncommon therapy: The psychiatric techniques of Milton H. Erickson, M.D.* New York: Norton, 1973.

Hoffman, L. Deviation-amplifying processes in natural groups. In J. Haley (Ed.), *Changing families*. New York: Grune & Stratton, 1971.

Jackson, D. D. A suggestion for the technical handling of paranoid patients. *Psychiatry*, 1963, *26*, 306–307.

Madanes, C. *Strategic family therapy*. San Francisco: Jossey-Bass, 1981.

Papp, P. The Greek chorus and other techniques of family therapy. *Family Process*, 1980, *19*, 45–58.

Post, R. M., & Goodwin, F. K. Psychomotor activity and cerebrospinal fluid amine metabolites in affective illness. *American Journal of Psychiatry*, 1973, *130*, 67–72.

Raskin, D. E., & Klein, Z. E. Losing a symptom through keeping it. *Archives of General Psychiatry*, 1976, *33*, 548–555.

Rosen, J. *Direct psychoanalysis.* New York: Grune & Stratton, 1953.

Selvini-Palazzoli, M. *Recent developments in our treatment of families with anorectic patients.* Unpublished manuscript, 1976.

Selvini-Palazzoli, M., Boscolo, L., Cecchin, G., & Prata, G. Hypothesizing–circularity–neutrality: Three guidelines for the conductor of the session. *Family Process,* 1980, *19,* 3–12.

Selvini-Palazzoli, M., Cecchin, G., Prata, G., & Boscolo, L. *Paradox and counterparadox.* New York: Jason Aronson, 1978.

Stampfl, T. G., & Levis, D. J. Essentials of implosive therapy: A learning-theory-based psychodynamic behavioral therapy. *Journal of Abnormal Psychology,* 1967, *72,* 496–503.

Stanton, M. D. Marital therapy from a structural/strategic viewpoint. In G. P. Sholevar (Ed.), *Marriage is a family affair: A textbook of marriage and marital therapy.* Jamaica, N.Y.: SP Medical & Scientific Books, 1981.

Watzlawick, P., Weakland, J., & Fisch, R. *Change: Principles of problem formation and problem resolution.* New York: Norton, 1974.

Weeks, G. R., & L'Abate, L. *Paradoxical psychotherapy.* New York: Brunner/Mazel, 1982.

Wertheim, E. Family unit therapy and the science and typology of family systems. *Family Process,* 1973, *12,* 361–376.

Wynne, L. C. Paradoxical interventions: Leverage for therapeutic change in individual and family systems. In J. Strauss, M. Bowers, T. Downey, S. Fleck, S. Jackson, & I. Levine (Eds.), *Psychotherapy of schizophrenia.* New York: Plenum, 1980.

V
FORCES FROM OUTSIDE
THE FAMILY: TIME, BRAIN,
AND SOCIETY

11

A PHASE-ORIENTED APPROACH TO TREATMENT WITH SCHIZOPHRENICS AND THEIR FAMILIES

Lyman C. Wynne

My orientation to treatment of schizophrenia begins with a series of propositions that are, or should be, viewed as truisms: This disorder typically involves a multiplicity of dysfunctions—in cognition and communication, in affect and attachment, in initiative and goal-directedness, and in social and occupational skills. Further, these dysfunctions unfold to make a bewildering patchwork over time, with a highly uneven pattern of severity and with counterbalancing assets and healthy functions. Finally, the reciprocal transactions between the diagnosed schizophrenic and other persons are crucial in evaluation and treatment; the family, the treatment teams, and the social network of the community all are demonstrably relevant.

It should be noted that one can begin from an alternative starting point—most notably, the family unit—and work with the schizophrenic symptoms and other problems within the matrix of family relatedness. However, schizophrenic symptoms, especially in the florid phase, have a highly demanding quality for both family and community that focuses the initial attention in treatment on the identified patient. This understandable fact calls for special treatment strategies that I consider in this chapter.

The complexity of schizophrenic processes has direct implications for comprehensive treatment while at the same time making piecemeal efforts commonplace and, in many settings, difficult to avoid. What I describe here is a model for more or less optimal treatment with special attention to the family's participation. However, this is not what I anticipate can usually be achieved in present-day treatment settings.

LYMAN C. WYNNE. Department of Psychiatry, University of Rochester Medical Center, Rochester, New York.

A MULTIFACETED APPROACH

Writing as a family therapist, I believe it is important for me to state explicitly that family therapy as ordinarily understood may be a crucial component of treatment, but that, *alone*, it is never an adequate or sufficient approach to schizophrenic problems. Indeed, *therapy* of any kind is only part of the approach that is needed. Actually, much of what family therapists do, or should do, includes activities other than those traditionally encompassed in the term "therapy."

Too often, this term seems to refer only to scheduled office appointments. That notion is far too constricted. A comprehensive approach needs either to include, or to link to other activities (including administrative and case management activities), educational activities, vocational rehabilitation, and building of social skills. Unfortunately, most mental health professionals, especially psychiatrists trained to give medication for a symptom diagnosis, lack knowledge about the nature and scope of the dysfunctions and the resources in schizophrenics and their families. They are poorly qualified to coordinate and plan a comprehensive treatment approach. Much more thought and effort is needed to explore how psychiatrists and their professional colleagues can work more effectively with one another and with support systems in hospital and community, including the families themselves.

A PROBLEM-ORIENTED APPROACH

Symptom diagnoses, such as those provided by Axes I and II of the *Diagnostic and Statistical Manual of Mental Disorders*, 3rd edition (DSM-III), are clearly inadequate for treatment planning, even for pharmacotherapy (Lewis & Usdin, 1982). Data of many other kinds are essential to map out a minimally sensible treatment strategy. A far more appropriate starting point for treatment than a symptom diagnosis is the formulation of the problem. Such a formulation will include both symptoms and contextual circumstances and will emphasize how these difficulties are perceived and by whom, what the consequences have been thus far for all of the persons affected, and what these persons believe can and should be done. Increasing evidence—for example, from Longabaugh (1979)—has compared outcomes when treating "problems" versus treating "diagnoses." Outcomes, assessed multidimensionally, are superior when the treatment goals have been directed to problems or clinical situations, rather than to symptom disorders.

A PHASE-ORIENTED APPROACH

In partial contrast to some of the personality disorders and chronic "neuroses," the schizophrenic disorders are associated with presenting problems that change drastically over time, and in the early phases, over short periods of time. Thus, a problem-oriented approach requires repeated, substantial modifications of treatment plans. I object strenuously to the common practice in treatment of schizophrenics that is largely limited over many years to reviewing prescriptions of a fixed dosage of neuroleptic medication. Nevertheless, tardive dyskinesia resulting after such thoughtless pharmacotherapy does not justify blanket and equally thoughtless opposition to all medication. The efficacy of neuroleptics for schizophrenics is clearly established, though the most suitable circumstances and phases of treatment for discontinuation and for combination with other methods is not well explored. Similarly, family therapy, individual psychotherapy, or other approaches each can be utilized at several different phases of treatment, but not in the same form nor in *all* phases. To recommend and to evaluate relentless continuation of *any* treatment method for schizophrenia is a way to discredit it unfairly, or at least to muddle the understanding of its most relevant and effective application.

The phase-oriented approach is framed in terms of the unfolding of a series of presenting problems. The goal is to treat the problem that is most salient at any given point. Evaluation of outcome is then concerned with the degree of resolution of each major problem, phase by phase. Nearly always, each problem requires a modified treatment approach and a changing cast of participants.

In my opinion, one of the major hazards to successful treatment and to outcome research with schizophrenia comes about when therapists and researchers fail to assess changing issues at different phases of treatment and, hence, do not obtain or sustain a consensus with the patient or family about treatment goals. Unclearly defined goals and discrepant perspectives engender suspicion and estrangement among patient, family, and the so-called helping services, which then are accurately seen as not very helpful. If therapists and researchers assess results within phases of treatment, not taking one procedure from the beginning to the end, they may avoid discounting methods that may be very successful in one phrase but are totally ineffective or worsen the situation in another phase. (Individual psychotherapy is a probable case in point.) Unless therapists take a phase-oriented, problem-oriented approach, they confuse and weaken their treatment efforts.

Let me emphasize that it is more crucial to be phase-oriented in the treatment of schizophrenics than it is in the treatment of other psychiatric problems. If a presenting problem is a narrowly defined phobia, such as fear of flying, this may be treated with a focused behavioral approach because treatment of other issues often is not necessary, even though a dynamic therapist can *find* other problems. But in the difficulties presented by schizophrenics and their families, there always are serious *multiple* issues that need to be sorted into phases and with manageable priorities.

FIRST-CRISIS CONTACT

A key aspect of the first phase of treatment that is neglected in many settings is the integration of the family into the treatment process at the time of first contact, often with a crisis visit to an emergency department. In most settings, staff members trained in family crisis interviewing are not located, administratively or geographically, so that they can participate in the first contact with schizophrenics and their families. The early experience of Langsley and Kaplan (1968) and the more recent observations of Adam, Bouckoms, and Scarr (1980) and Perlmutter (in press) suggest that contact with families during the first-phase, emergency contacts with patients, when the family members are usually left outside in the waiting room, is especially timely and beneficial for later collaboration.

The scope of this problem can be indicated by a recent study by Perlmutter in the psychiatric emergency service of Strong Memorial Hospital, which serves an entire community, representing all socioeconomic and racial groups (in press). He reviewed data from 1000 consecutive emergency patients. For 700 of these patients, the central problem was clearly family-related or the patient was accompanied to the Emergency Department by a family member. These data were based upon reports by non-family-oriented intake workers who merely recorded what the patients themselves regarded as the problem for which they were coming. Most of these patients were either psychotic or suicidal. Unfortunately, even in this setting where there is an unusually strong interest in family approaches, only a small fraction of the patients were treated with a family approach at that phase. The traditional neglect of families in emergency services is therapeutically unfortunate, because this is a moment when family members usually are very eager and willing to work with the staff. If the staff fails to consult and support the family at that point, the family understandably is likely to speculate that the staff regards them as blameworthy, uninformed, or an obnoxious nuisance, or all three. I have been dismayed at how often there is no note in many emergency department records of whether the relatives were there at all, or whether anyone talked with them. Even in otherwise well-run hospitals, relatives routinely are neglected from the beginning. It is hardly surprising that they feel shut out and nonparticipant in the whole process, even though they usually are the ones who have initiated the request for help.

If a therapist has already made contact with a family at the moment of entry, there is very little problem in involving the family at a future time. If there has been no contact within 24 to 72 hours, the therapist may have an uphill battle later, sometimes because the family feels ostracized and sometimes because the family undergoes an internal emotional reorganization, which R. D. Scott calls "closure" (1976). In a high percentage of families, there is closure along a boundary between the patient and the part of the family that has turned the patient over to the institution. A boundary also forms between the treatment institution, which has now incorporated the patient, and the family. If there is relief from the tension and fatigue preceding hospitalization, together with continuing or heightened guilt, mystification, and confusion, it is understandable that the family may want to close off and try to set aside the problem. This may be done temporarily by perceiving the problem as now in the hands of the staff, with a breach between family and patient. On the other hand, I believe that families, far more often than not, want to move on to an improved set of relationships with the patients and do not wish to end the relationships even when they may be intensely critical of the patients. The criticism usually reflects a wish for change, not for permanent disruption of the relationship, at least after fatigue and frustration have subsided. If the professional can maintain an attitude of positive, interested, undemanding, noninterpretive availability toward a family at this time, the way can be paved for later collaboration.

In other instances, during the first days after admission, the family members may be seen, but in a manner that is not helpful to them and, in fact, conveys the message that the staff members primarily want the family off their collective back. For example, a family member may want to come in but is told, "No, we can't permit it at this time. We'll call you later." Or the contact may be a phone call by or a brief visit with a staff member who presents a unilaterally derived discharge plan, or engages in perfunctory history taking. None of these staff responses recognizes the legitimate needs of the family.

After the crisis of onset, a period of 1 to 2 weeks of acutely florid psychosis commonly follows, during which inpatient care with neuroleptic medication typically occurs. During the acute psychosis, most therapists believe that conjoint family meetings with the patient present are contraindicated (Mosher & Gunderson, 1979). Such meetings are viewed as stimulating an already overstimulated patient. While this possibility is indeed a valid consideration with some patients initially, I believe that maintaining a degree of continuity in the direct patient–family relationship is usually valuable. Conjoint meetings may be brief at first, then more extensive as discharge planning begins. The details depend upon the nature of the symptoms, the state of the family relationships, and the staff member's experience and ability to set limits. However, conjoint family meetings should not be automatically avoided during the acute phase. On the other hand, a fixed schedule of hour-long family therapy meetings with everyone present is sheer folly during the acute phase.

The interviewer should be willing to terminate the interview when useful contact is over, or to divide the family into subgroups. The family members have been living together, often for weeks or years, until the moment the patient came into the hospital. A staff decision that they should not meet in the same room even for brief periods is arbitrary and demeaning of the family and patient. This is the point at which the clinician can formulate more fully what the nature of the problem is, how the family sees it, and how they structure themselves around the problem. By going ahead with the whole family together and also meeting with subsystems, a picture of the alignments and splits in the family can start to emerge (Wynne, 1961). The support patterns within the family will need to be nurtured and may not be apparent without direct observation.

In most settings, psychiatrists move immediately during the acute phase to the prescription of high-dosage neuroleptics. Indeed, there has emerged a reflex tendency to give large doses of medication before assessment has been made, often even before the patient has arrived on the inpatient floor. The eventual primary therapist then cannot figure out except by second-hand report what the early symptoms were, much less how they fit into the problem as a whole. I feel that it is a disservice to patients to prevent the primary therapist from seeing the problem fully. With an adequate nursing staff and support system, a minimum of 3 days to a week of assessment is invaluable for informed treatment planning. There are exceptions when the time must be shorter if the inpatient service cannot handle difficult behavior. But once acute psychotics are in a setting that is supportive, is not emotionally charged, and sets limits clearly and sensibly, it is surprising (to those who started working in the medication era) that fewer acute psychotics need medication than is now assumed. The work that Carpenter did at the National Institute of Mental Health in setting up a treatment unit without medication (so that he could obtain a baseline for later medication studies) illustrated that an initial medication-free period for such long periods as a month may improve later outcome in certain schizophrenics (Carpenter, McGlashan, & Strauss, 1977). This also has been my experience in other settings. This sort of alternative, flexible approach needs to be tried out whenever possible, but is contraindicated when staff are frightened, poorly trained, and poorly motivated to deal behaviorally with psychotic patients.

SUBACUTE PHASE

During both the acute phase and the subacute phase that follows as florid symptoms subside, therapists have an interesting and complex problem in achieving a dynamic balance between overload and underload of stimuli. During psychotic decompensation, I assume that schizophrenics typically have been flooded with stimuli, contributing to the personal disorganization and fragmentation of experience. A treatment program with structure, and sometimes with medication, can tone down the overstimulation fairly quickly to a point at which the patient becomes tenuously stabilized. At this point, a therapist is apt to worry whether the patient is going to decompensate again, and may take strenuous measures to forestall this from happening. It seems to me that because of the popularity of the overstimulation–understimulation hypothesis (Wynne, Cromwell, & Matthysse, 1978), which *in general* I subscribe to, there has been perhaps an overconcern about maintaining this balance. The patient is viewed as being on a tightrope from which he or she may fall at any moment. The tendency then is to become extremely managerial and concerned that the patient is starting to have a "*slight* decompensation," a bit of sleeplessness, or *one* loose association. Instantly, more medication or more stringent controls are implemented.

I submit that therapists should look upon this as a problem of systems equilibrium in which there is a balance between the need for stability and the need for change and instability. Instability, as is well known from crisis theory, can proceed in the direction either of chaotic decompensation or of reorganization on a changed and sometimes improved basis. It is not a romantic notion that many schizophrenics *do* have definite resources and assets to fall back upon, both in their own personalities and in their families and social settings. Even in the subacute phase, therapists need not be so frightened of psychotic decompensation that they overtreat, and they can overtreat both with medication and with psychosocial interventions. I would like to encourage those who have the courage to engage directly with elements of the psychotic experience not to rush in to stamp it all out before knowing what is involved. By overtreating, therapists block the opportunity for anyone—patients, families, themselves, and other hospital staff members—to observe and participate in more effective ways of functioning as minor symptoms and small degrees of stress are experienced.

The family's experience of the illness unfolds alongside that of the patient, but in a somewhat different form. There is a stage of being confused, angry, and perplexed, and of feeling guilty and blamed—all the concerns that escalate when progress is lacking or spasmodic. There is a human tendency that, if anything goes wrong, to blame oneself, someone else, or something else. If anything goes wrong, one wonders, "Might I have done something differently?" Even with physical illnesses where there is no possible reason for blaming oneself, one still says, "Maybe I should have had a medical examination sooner," or "If I'd only gotten a different surgeon," or something of the sort. Blame is a natural and inevitable human response, but helping agencies do augment it. Therapists should not indulge, however, in the self-flagellation of thinking that health professionals are the only source of blame that families experience. It does not help to have the helpers blame themselves.

SUBCHRONIC PHASE

If a collaborative relationship with the family has been established from the beginning, the issue of blame is attenuated. But this difficulty refocuses as time passes. After the florid symptoms are gone, deficit symptoms usually remain: lack of initiative and direction, apathy, unwillingness to cooperate with conventional expectations, and so on. To the family, the patient may look "normal" except that he or she is "lazy," "stubborn," or otherwise uncooperative. On the other hand, the patient may be regarded as suffering from drug effects (a possibility that is, of course, all too difficult to evaluate). Most families have understandable difficulty in viewing such perplexing symptoms as having continuity with the preceding psychosis.

After a relapse and readmission, the chronic nature of the disorder becomes more definitely apparent to everyone. Alternative diagnoses can no longer be readily sought and entertained. The possibility begins to be more seriously considered that expectations for the life pattern of the patient and family must be enduringly altered. At a point when the illness is no longer perceived as an acute episode, the need that families experience for further assistance undergoes a shift. Interest in and receptivity for information about schizophrenia as a named disorder emerges. Indeed, if such information is *not* available in detail at this time, members of most families become angry, despairing, and highly critical—sometimes of the patients, more often of one another, and nearly always of the (non)helping psychiatrist and other mental health professionals.

The most effective approach is quite contrary to the traditional secretive, withholding attitude of physicians toward patients and families about most disorders, psychiatric or otherwise. The method that I have increasingly used over the last several years is strikingly similar to the psychoeducational approach described by Anderson, Hogarty, and Reiss (1980). I think this approach is crucial for the families of most schizophrenics as the patients progress from being subacute to subchronic or chronic. My delight with the effectiveness of this approach reflects my view that this is one of the most refreshing new and needed developments in work with the families of schizophrenics in recent years.

The benefits often have many reverberations. Let me give one example: the parents of a daughter who had had four prior hospitalizations during the preceding five years and was currently rehospitalized. This couple was invited to join a half-day meeting of what we at the University of Rochester call an "educational workshop" for several families together. It is not called "therapy"; the parents do not have a disorder for which they are seeking treatment. Rather, we provide an informational, cognitively structured opportunity to discuss the problem that is labeled "schizophrenia." In this instance, this couple somewhat reluctantly accepted the invitation to come. While I outlined a plan for the meeting, they were negativistic about the venture, announcing their doubts that this could be of any use to them. Within an hour, as they started to hear both from me and from some of the other families, they grew visibly enthusiastic and actively participatory.

Two days after the workshop, the father called me to say that the workshop had been the most important experience that they had had in all the years since their daughter had been ill. He wanted to come in with his wife and tell me about what it had meant to them. It turned out that the workshop had stimulated them to cancel a previously scheduled appointment with a divorce attorney for that very day. After the workshop, it had dawned on them, without any therapeutic discussion specifically oriented to them, that the problems they had been fighting about were legitimate concerns: They had been quarreling for years about the nature of their daughter's problems and about who was to blame. They now had decided they should work together with their daughter, and they requested family therapy, which they had previously completely resisted. Progress for both the parents and the daughter has been remarkably improved and sustained for the past 2 years. Most cases are not so dramatic, of course, but the primary point is surprisingly applicable: Families *can* be helped with an educational approach, which is valuable in its own right and also builds a perspective that facilitates their participation and support in other aspects of a treatment program.

SOCIAL NETWORKS

Educational workshops, together with the family support groups and multiple family therapy that often follow, are apparently effective in part because each participant family starts to learn that their despair and frustration are expectable and shared by other families. Meeting other families often cuts through the painful estrangement that families have undergone as they have become caught up in coping with this catastrophe. Other ways of rebuilding networks, both with extended family members and nonfamily individuals, also are valuable as the illness becomes protracted and chronic. In order to assess the presenting problem comprehensively, it is also helpful to the therapist to have input from the family network beyond the closest key relatives.

In the process of identifying relevant social networks, the clinician should *not* define the family as the patient—a misguided slogan of some family therapists of the past. Both the nuclear family and the social support network are better viewed as resources and allies. Such an approach does not needlessly generate blame and can facilitate discussion of the issues of blame and responsibility that families often bring with them, or later develop fears about, especially when the illness takes mystifying turns. A useful approach to the family is this: "We need you, and we cannot work effectively without you. Your knowledge and ideas will be valuable about this complicated situation, and we are available to share our knowledge and suggestions with you."

DEVELOPMENTAL PHASES OF THE FAMILY

It is beyond the scope of this chapter to elaborate on other, more well-established components of treatment of chronic schizophrenia. However, another aspect of a phase-oriented approach to treatment calls for assessment of the developmental phase of the family, along the lines described by Carter and McGoldrick (1980) and Haley (1980). Often families are in a developmental impasse when psychiatric dysfunction, including schizophrenia, emerges (this clinical observation is relevant therapeutically, regardless of any possible implications for "causality"). As Haley has emphasized, the family impasse about the adolescent or young adult's leaving home is frequently associated with schizophrenic symptomatology (1980). In other instances, the developmental impasse may involve being caught between confusing pulls from a family of origin and a new marital relationship. Recognition by the therapist of these dilemmas will help to identify who needs to be included in the treatment process. As treatment proceeds, developmental changes may require refocusing of the problem over surprisingly short time periods.

In addition, basic features of the social context need to be given weight in assessing the potentiality for change. For example, in a rural Black Mississippi family that has moved to Rochester, or an unemployed auto worker's family that has moved from Detroit to Houston, the family as a whole and each individual in it will go through several phases of developmental reorganization in order to acclimate themselves to the new setting.

Therapists often neglect to attend in detail to these sources of extrinsic disadvantage, as John Wing calls them (1978). They may affect both choice of treatment and outcome. Too often, in the office, therapists hear very little about problems that may seriously mystify and demoralize families and patients, who cannot identify specifically just what it is that is making life so chaotic. One very common example is the confusion engendered when trying to wend one's way through the bureaucracy of a strange social agency. The handicap is by no means limited to the symptomatic patient. If the parents are eligible for welfare or health care benefits, they usually need to be uncommonly intelligent and persistent to discover how to get the needed funds, especially in an unfamiliar setting. One has to be persevering in order to wait around for many hours, only to be told that, for instance, the mother's birth certificate is required before assistance can begin.

These are some of the issues that start to be important as a hospitalized patient begins to move back into the home or to some other site in the community. This kind of problem heightens as the florid symptoms of schizophrenia diminish and the residual, deficit symptoms predominate.

A SYSTEMS ORIENTATION TO TREATMENT

For me, these multiply interwoven, developmentally patterned processes are comprehensible only if I place them all, from symptoms to social setting, in a systems-oriented context. My colleague, George L. Engel, has insisted that a properly conceived medical model, which he calls "biopsychosocial," applies to such situations (1980; see Figure 1).

Biomedical technology has focused on the lower (organ and tissue) part of a systems hierarchy, usually discounting the person, and certainly ignoring anything broader than the person. Engel feels that this technology is a perversion of the best medical traditions and of what good physicians, including psychiatrists, should be doing. It is a mistake for anyone to forget that these are *open* systems, related to one another, so that changes at any one of these levels will have an impact on another. If one affects the nervous system with phenothiazines, the person will be affected, as well as all of the other systems, in sequence and in due course.

The relevance of the systems hierarchy for treatment is this: At which system level is it most strategic to intervene? Where is the most salient presenting problem about which people will feel something useful is happening, and where will the therapist gain the leverage through generating hopefulness as quickly as possible, preferably in the first meeting? In small

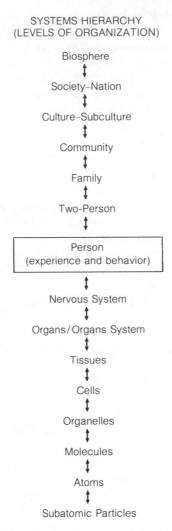

FIGURE 1. (*From Engel, 1980.*)

steps that are identifiable, the therapist needs to think continuously about where in the hierarchy of systems is the most strategic constellation of persons with whom he or she should work initially. This may not begin with the presenting psychotic patient. There may be something that the family needs to work out that will provide them with a sense of possible change and engagement and that will facilitate change for the patient at a later point.

The systems approach has fallen into three kinds of misuse in practice:

first, looking at only one system level and ignoring everything else; second, getting overwhelmed by the linkages between systems, drifting from one to another, and not zeroing in on a given problem where leverage can be gained; and, third, neglecting to work with one system level at one phase of treatment and with another level at another phase. A realistic factor is that few therapists are equipped with knowledge or experience to work at all of the relevant levels. Clearly, all therapists and clinicians need to have a healthy sense of their own limitations, combined with knowledge of appropriate colleagues and other resources to whom they can turn.

A FOUR-PART PERSPECTIVE

Another way to formulate this treatment approach is in terms of a four-part perspective. Strupp and Hadley (1977) have proposed a "tripartite approach" to treatment evaluation. They suggested that three perspectives are needed in order to determine whether goals of treatment have been achieved: first, the *patient's* perception of his or her well-being; second, *society's* view of useful and valued change; third, the *mental health professional's* view. Each perspective may be quite different in terms of what is regarded as a successful outcome. I would like to add a fourth perspective. "Society" is far too broad a middle category. I would specify the *family*, or the immediate primary group of the social network, as having a distinct perspective, and put "society" as a separate "perspective" in terms of its expectations about working, not breaking the law, not assaulting people in the street, not being a drain upon the community unnecessarily, and so forth. The mental health professional's point of view is highly variable. There are many psychiatrists who want to treat the "disorder." DSM-III specifically states that this is a classification not of persons but of disorders *within* persons. It is, of course, not at all a classification of families. Much of some mental health professionals' treatment is oriented toward relieving only the symptoms. When therapists talk only about florid symptoms and the prevention of relapse, they are taking a "subperson" viewpoint. If they look at the total functioning of the person, then they have another frame of reference, and beyond that, they move to the perspective of the family. Therapists do, as mental health professionals, have some options.

My point of view is that for minimally responsible treatment planning, therapists have to discover and work as well as possible from the perspective of the identified patient as a person *and* as a symptom bearer, and also from the perspective of the immediate primary group of the family, while also being knowledgeable about the perspective of society. The family's perspective is a *shared* view, but the views of *each* individual member also need to be given explicit attention.

In some family work, I fear that therapists do not listen enough to discrepancies in viewpoints of the identified patient and other family members. Such discrepancies can provide leverage for defining the presenting problem adequately. The initial problem may be that there is *not* a consensus about what is the problem. These, then, are some of the options when the mental health professional attempts to delineate a comprehensive but focused and therapeutically useful perspective for schizophrenics.

A POSTSCRIPT

In the area of research on treatment, I make only one brief suggestion. A major research problem that has been grossly neglected is the way in which to study clinical services across phases of treatment. Researchers have not kept pace with the present clinical trend to define treatment plans in terms of problems and phases. Many non-research-oriented psychiatric institutions are now using a problem-oriented approach to treatment. The time is overdue for a reorganization of research on treatment of schizophrenics so that it becomes congruent with current treatment concepts and practices. Defining outcomes within each phase of treatment will be a crucial step in making these investigations relevant to comprehensive clinical care over time.

REFERENCES

Adam, K. S., Bouckoms, A., & Scarr, G. Attempted suicide in Christchurch: A controlled study. *Australian and New Zealand Journal of Psychiatry*, 1980, *14*, 305–314.

Anderson, C. M., Hogarty, G. E., & Reiss, D. J. Family treatment of adult schizophrenic patients: A psycho-educational approach. *Schizophrenia Bulletin,* 1980, *6,* 490–505.

Carpenter, W. T., McGlashan, T. H., & Strauss, J. S. The treatment of acute schizophrenia without drugs: An investigation of some current assumptions. *American Journal of Psychiatry*, 1977, *134*, 14–20.

Carter, E. A., & McGoldrick, M. (Eds.). *The family life cycle: A framework for family therapy*. New York: Gardner Press, 1980.

Engel, G. L. The clinical application of the biopsychosocial model. *American Journal of Psychiatry*, 1980, *137*, 535–544.

Haley, J. *Leaving home: The therapy of disturbed young people*. New York: McGraw-Hill, 1980.

Langsley, D. G., & Kaplan, D. M. (Eds.). *The treatment of families in crisis*. New York: Grune & Stratton, 1968.

Lewis, J. M., & Usdin, G. (Eds.). *Treatment planning in psychiatry*. Washington, D.C.: American Psychiatric Association, 1982.

Longabaugh, R. Problems versus diagnosis as predictions of treatment. *Problem-Oriented Systems and Treatment*, 1979, *2*, 1–2.

Mosher, L. R., & Gunderson, J. G. Group, family, milieu, and community support systems treatment for schizophrenia. In L. Bellak (Ed.), *Disorders of the schizophrenic syndrome*. New York: Basic Books, 1979.

Perlmutter, R. A. Family visits to a psychiatric emergency service. *Hospital and Community Psychiatry*, in press.

Scott, R. D. "Closure" in family relationships and the first official diagnosis. In J. Jørstad & E. Ugelstad (Eds.), *Schizophrenia 75*. Oslo: Universtitetsforlaget, 1976.

Strupp, H. H., & Hadley, S. W. A tripartite model of mental health and therapeutic outcomes: With special reference to negative effects in psychotherapy. *American Psychologist*, 1977, *32*, 187–196.

Wing, J. K. Social influences on the course of schizophrenia. In L. C. Wynne, R. L. Cromwell, & S. Matthyssc (Eds.), *The nature of schizophrenia: New approaches to research and treatment*. New York: Wiley, 1978.

Wynne, L. C. The study of intrafamilial alignments and splits in exploratory family therapy. In N. Ackerman, F. L. Beatman, & S. N. Sherman (Eds.), *Exploring the base for family therapy*. New York: Family Service Association of America, 1961.

Wynne, L. C., Cromwell, R. L., & Matthysse, S. (Eds.). *The nature of schizophrenia: New approaches to research and treatment*. New York: Wilcy, 1978.

12

THE COORDINATION OF FAMILY THERAPY WITH OTHER TREATMENT MODALITIES FOR SCHIZOPHRENIA

Douglas W. Heinrichs
William T. Carpenter, Jr.

INTRODUCTION

It is no surprise that the ideas people have about the role of family therapy in the treatment of schizophrenia influence the ways in which they attempt to coordinate it with other treatment modalities. Generally, there are two basic perspectives: the etiology-oriented and the outcome-oriented.

The etiological perspective is the most traditional in the family field, approaching the treatment of schizophrenia with a specific model of family therapy based on a concise, often highly complex theory of the family's pivotal role in the origin of the illness. It has tended to apply theory and therapy uniformly to schizophrenic patients and their families, acting as if schizophrenia were a homogeneous illness. This is a serious problem, as there is persuasive evidence that schizophrenia represents a heterogeneous collection of illnesses, presumably with different etiologies, while the etiological theories underlying the traditional family approaches remain speculative and essentially unproven. Furthermore, it is far from self-evident that knowing the etiology of schizophrenia would define its optimal treatment in any simple way. Our final criticism of the traditional etiological perspective is that it tends to relegate other treatment modalities to a secondary status, usually viewing them as sources of symptomatic relief until the "definitive" family treatment takes effect. This discourages creative collaboration with clinicians from approaches that are not family-oriented.

DOUGLAS W. HEINRICHS and WILLIAM T. CARPENTER, JR. Maryland Psychiatric Research Center and Department of Psychiatry, University of Maryland, Baltimore, Maryland.

The second approach mentioned is the outcome-oriented approach. Because the etiology of schizophrenia is unknown and probably varied, it is critical to integrate treatment modalities by relying on the empirical standard of what treatment or combination of treatments produces the best course and outcome of the illness. By acknowledging that schizophrenia probably represents several diseases with different etiologies, and by not granting *a priori* preference to any treatment modality, the empirical approach encourages collaboration between clinicians of varying orientations and expertise. It also recognizes the importance of controlled outcome studies. We find this approach more true to our current understanding of the illness, yet more attention by far has been paid to etiology-oriented approaches. This results in part from the fact that these approaches are usually imbedded in interesting and intellectually satisfying theories. Such models are more easily written about and acquire scholarly prestige. Furthermore, even when of limited utility in selecting efficacious treatment, such approaches can be valuable in answering other questions, just as intensive psychoanalytic work with chronic schizophrenics has contributed extensively to an understanding of the subjective experience of schizophrenics in their struggles to establish relationships, although it has not been demonstrated to be a highly efficacious treatment.

Even if therapists and clinicians resolve to use an outcome-oriented perspective in selecting treatments, it is not apparent how to proceed. Without a precise formula, what guiding principles can aid a clinician in choosing between and/or combining modalities with a given patient? This is even more of a problem since each treatment modality tends to be understood in a distinct frame of reference. For example, clinicians are told that neuroleptic drugs help the schizophrenic by blocking dopamine at the postsynaptic membrane. They are also told that a particular form of family therapy helps the schizophrenic patient by rectifying a pathogenic pattern of interaction among family members. But since clinicians can neither explain family therapy in terms of dopamine transmission nor explain neuroleptic drug effect in terms of pathological interpersonal systems, they have no common ground for assessing which approach is optimal for a given patient or whether different approaches should be employed separately or in combination. The same considerations apply when comparing two forms of psychotherapy and even when comparing different approaches to family interventions.

CLINICAL MODEL

We have stated elsewhere (Carpenter & Heinrichs, 1980) that models can be developed through which varying treatment modalities, with their respective theories, can be simultaneously considered and compared. These models have as their primary constructs intervening variables that are closer to the actual clinical data than are the various theories upon which each treatment is based.

One useful model is the "inverted U" relationship between arousal and level of functioning (see Figure 1). This relationship is applicable to a wide range of situations and indicates that functioning is optimal with intermediate levels of arousal, while functioning deteriorates at very high or very low levels of arousal. A common example of this relationship is taking an examination. Most individuals have learned that excessive levels of anxiety (excessive arousal) interfere with their functioning but, if they lack the fine edge that moderate anxiety provides and are too apathetic (insufficient arousal), their performance, again, is less than optimal.

Although oversimplified, we have found it useful to discuss schizophrenia and its treatments in terms of this model. Concepts of arousal have been important in psychophysiological explorations of schizophrenia for many years. More recently, arousal has been integrated into sophisticated models as it relates to attention and information processing (Spohn & Patterson, 1979). Unfortunately, arousal has proven to be neither a simple nor a unitary dimension. The various indexes of physiological arousal correlate poorly with one another, and their relationship to manifest psychopathology is ambiguous. Furthermore, physiological arousal cannot always be accurately inferred from behavioral observation. A socially withdrawn, underactive schizophrenic patient may have high blood pressure, rapid pulse, increased galvanic skin responsivity, or increased cortisol secretion. Even though the term "arousal" is common parlance, it has been used technically to refer to activity levels in the autonomic nervous system, usually as measured in some end-organ response. It is premature to develop a therapeutic paradigm based directly on physiological arousal, but a clinically relevant heuristic model can nevertheless be constructed on the basis of observable affect and behavior. Clinicians need to replace "arousal" with a term that is less specific, but not confusing. The term should facilitate conceptualizing at the biological, psychological, and social levels of human function (including interaction between and among levels). Confusion will be reduced if the term is not taken to imply a discrete area of scientific enquiry. Words like "excitation," "stimulation," or "degree of alertness" would perhaps suffice, but we use the term "activation" rather than "arousal" to elucidate this clinical concept here. Even though current knowledge does not permit the clinician to use psychophysiological arousal as a practical guide to treatment decisions with the schizophrenic, we have found the behaviorally based concept of "activation" useful in suggesting choices between treatments and optimal combinations of therapeutic modalities for a given patient at a specific point in his or her illness. Acute psychosis can be seen as the manifestation of impaired performance due to excessive activation in schizophrenic patients. Conceptual disorganization,

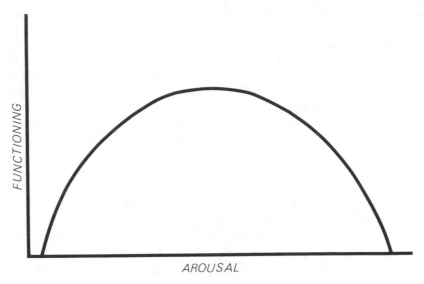

FIGURE 1. *The "inverted U" relationship between arousal and functioning.*

hallucinations, delusions, and affective chaos characterize this state. The proposed relationship between activation and these productive or positive symptoms is shown in Figure 2. Two curves are shown because, although the pattern is the same, the quantitative relationship between activation and symptoms will vary among persons. The horizontal dotted line represents the threshold at which symptoms can be clinically detected.

There is yet another set of symptoms that typically afflict the schizophrenic person. These negative or deficit symptoms include apathy, social withdrawal, anhedonia, constriction of the ideational field, reduced energy level, impaired motivation, and dampening of the emotions. This deficit syndrome can be conceptualized as an expression of dysfunction resulting from inadequate activation. Figure 3 shows the proposed relationship between activation and deficit or negative symptoms. Again, two sample curves are shown. Descriptions of the schizophrenic illness such as those of Kraepelin (1919/1971) see the deficit syndrome as the core of the disease. Furthermore, although chronic psychotic states certainly exist, it is the deficit syndrome that is most likely to be enduring and to result in chronic impairment for a schizophrenic patient. While clinicians have been relatively successful in developing treatment interventions that control florid psychosis, they have been conspicuously unsuccessful in finding remedies for the deficit state. Given all of this, it is unfortunate that in recent years priority has been given to preventing or controlling psychosis, while the

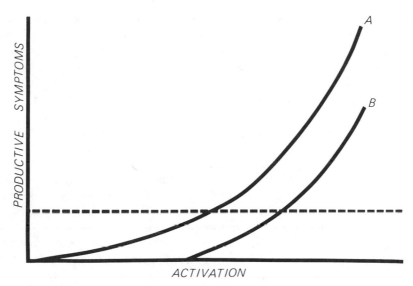

FIGURE 2. *The relationship between activation and productive symptoms.*

FIGURE 3. *The relationship between activation and deficit symptoms.*

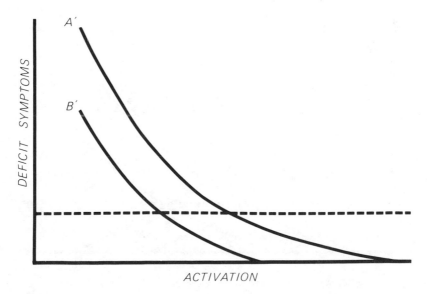

deficit syndrome has been relatively ignored. It may be in part due to the fact that chronic states of quiet dysfunction are less disruptive to society and to clinicians than are acute bouts of psychotic chaos. It is also less frustrating and less assailable to focus attention on an aspect of the illness where there is something very definable and effective to offer as treatment.

When both positive and negative symptoms are considered, the relationship to activation is reflected in the interaction of both curves (see Figure 4). Theoretically, the best location for a patient would be the intersection of the curves, since movement away from this point would result in rapid intensification of either positive or negative symptoms. For Patient B, the intersection is below the threshold so that relatively asymptomatic states can be achieved. For Patient A, the intersection is above the threshold so that a minimal mixture of positive and negative symptoms may be the best possible result. If both positive and negative symptoms can be seen as impairing a patient's functioning, then activation can be plotted against functioning simply by inverting the curves (see Figure 5). If one is interested in the level of functioning in spite of both types of symptoms, this can be simplified as appears in Figure 6. Here there is the familiar "inverted U" relationship, with dysfunction at the lower levels of activation primarily due to negative symptoms and at higher levels primarily due to positive symptoms.

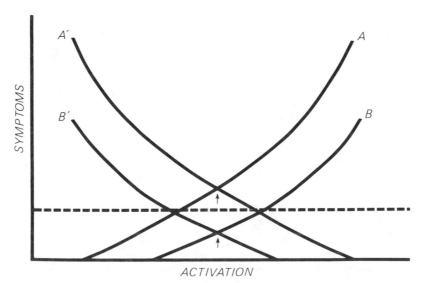

FIGURE 4. *The relationship between activation and symptoms.*

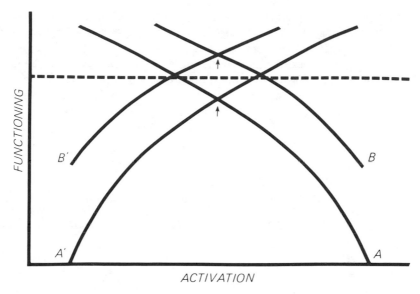

FIGURE 5. *The relationship between activation and functioning.*

FIGURE 6. *The interrelationship of activation, functioning, and symptoms.*

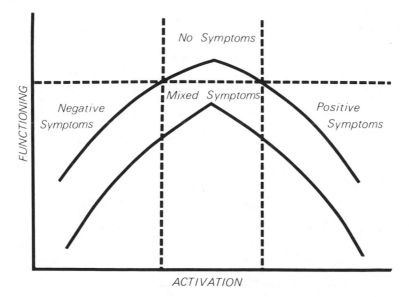

It is possible to characterize a range of life circumstances and treatment interventions in terms of whether they act to increase or decrease
activation for the schizophrenic patient (see Figure 7). Factors such as
interpersonal stress, social stimulation, and expectations for performance
all act to increase activation, whether they are part of a formal therapeutic
effort or simply present in nonspecific ways in the patient's environment.
Effective defense mechanisms and coping strategies of the patient help him
or her to reduce the level of activation. Within this framework, antipsychotic medication can be viewed as decreasing the patient's activation.

FIGURE 7. *The effect of various treatments on activation.*

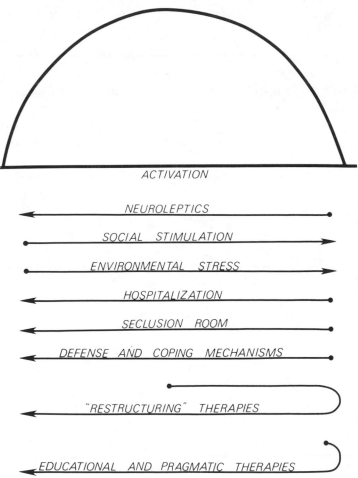

When considering the impact on activation, a clinician can dichotomize the various psychotherapies, whether administered in an individual, group, or family context. Those therapies that intend to bring about a fundamental restructuring of the patient's personality or family interaction usually strive thereby to reduce stress and thus activation. Most of these approaches do acknowledge an initial period in which painful and distressing issues and conflicts are highlighted and evoked. These therapies will have a biphasic impact on activation: Initially, they will intensify activation as stressful material is accentuated, while later there will be a significant reduction in activation as successful restructuring occurs. The other sort of psychotherapeutic intervention includes those that are fundamentally educational or are of a practical, "problem-solving" orientation. Here the assumption is that specific information or concrete solutions to troubling factors in the patient's or family's life will minimize stress and lead to a quick reduction in activation. Any initial increase in activation associated with stating problems explicitly is intended to be very short-lived.

In simplifying the model to this degree, of course, certain limitations and imperfections are introduced. There are certainly qualitative differences among interventions beyond their effect on activation. Nevertheless, it provides a common framework in terms of which the mode of action of the various treatment modalities can be understood, apart from the diverse theoretical mechanisms offered by the proponents of each treatment. As a result, it is possible to derive a number of guidelines for choosing between and optimally combining therapies to fit the needs of a given patient. We consider five of these.

1. *Since a given treatment or environmental factor is likely to have different impacts on positive and on negative symptom complexes, a fully empirical appraisal of the efficacy of a treatment or the effect of an environmental factor must assess changes in both psychotic and deficit syndromes* (Carpenter, 1980). This is true for controlled clinical trials on large groups of patients, as well as for the individualized evaluation of a treatment's effect on a given patient. Yet this is seldom done (Carpenter, Heinrichs, & Hanlon, 1981). Most studies of neuroleptics in aftercare focus on positive symptomatology. Similarly, the work on "expressed emotion" (EE) has relied on psychotic relapse as the primary outcome variable (Brown, Birley, & Wing, 1972; Brown, Monck, Carstairs, & Wing, 1962; Vaughn & Leff, 1976). Yet could it be that patients in low-EE families have a lower relapse rate because their families accept quiet dysfunction without complaint or prodding? Before therapists decide that low EE is a desirable attribute of families and proceed to design programs intended to induce it, a careful consideration of its relationship to deficit symptoms is warranted.

2. *Treatments vary in the specificity of their effect.* Some treatments can be expected to have the effect predicted by the model on the vast

majority of schizophrenic patients. For example, most, though not all, patients show some evidence of dearousal when given neuroleptic drugs. Likewise, since almost every family has some gaps in its understanding of a patient's illness and is likely to labor under some misconceptions, psycho-educational approaches with patients and their families should serve to reduce some unnecessary frustrations and conflict in the majority of cases. Conversely, other treatments are intended to act by addressing very specific factors in patients or their environment. Thus, a technique of family intervention designed to alter a certain pathogenic pattern of interaction and/or communication in families can only be expected to have its predicted effect on those cases possessing that pathological pattern. In all other cases, no systematic effect of the intervention can be expected. It is reasonable, thus, to expect proponents of such treatments either to demonstrate that the pathogenic pattern in question is found in a large majority of schizophrenic families (and such efforts have not generally been successful—see Goldstein & Rodnick, 1975; Jacob, 1975; and Liem, 1980), or to provide criteria for identifying that subgroup of cases possessing the pattern and thus appropriate for the treatment. Otherwise, at the very least, a great deal of effort is expended on providing a treatment to persons for whom it is inappropriate. At worst it can do definite harm by unnecessarily exposing patients and families to any side effects inherent to the treatment, as well as provoking stress and frustration in family members by attacking non-existent conflicts and pathological patterns that for theoretical reasons are assumed to be present. In short, then, with limited knowledge of a given patient and his or her family, only the effects of the more low-specificity treatments can be predicted. A more detailed assessment of the individual case is required before the likely impact of a high-specificity treatment can be estimated.

It follows that an educational approach is a sensible starting point in work with families. Having low specificity, it is likely to be of value in a high percentage of cases and can be applied initially without extensive knowledge of the idiosyncrasies of a patient and his or her family. Furthermore, seeing the family's behavior in the educational setting—particularly if the patient is included in the process—is an ideal forum for recognizing any extant pathogenic interaction patterns, distortions of family members' views of one another, communicational limitations, and peculiarities in the family's stance toward the outside world. Such detailed knowledge subsequently allows an individualized and critical application of interventions with greater specificity—family-based or otherwise. For instance, family members with an unhealthy need to keep the patient dependent might resist or distort positive aspects of the prognostic picture or any practical suggestions to encourage individuation presented to them as part of an educational experience. Similarly, family members for whom scapegoating the patient serves an important function may resist or distort noncritical, neutral interpretations of the patient's behavior offered to them. Or the family with severe communicational impairment may fail to grasp and retain verbally communicated information reliably and accurately. This may subsequently lead the therapist to prefer family interventions less dependent on verbally transmitted information (e.g., environmental manipulations, behavioral techniques).

3. *The choice of treatments depends on the location of the patient on the activation–functioning curve.* For the floridly psychotic patient, and thus one conceptualized as dysfunctional via hyperactivation, the clinician should consider the range of interventions that have in common a deactivating effect. Neuroleptic medication is a prime example. Hospitalization, with the attending separation of the patient from the stimulation and stresses of his or her usual environment, is also a force in the same direction. A more extreme maneuver to reduce stimulation is the use of a seclusion room. Less intensive than hospitalization are environmental manipulations to relieve stress temporarily and reduce expectations and responsibilities for the patient while the patient remains in his or her usual environment. This usually is most effective when the family is included in planning and implementing such maneuvers.

Conversely, the patient with little or no active psychosis but pronounced deficit symptoms is conceptualized as dysfunctional due to inadequate activation, and treatment strategies with an activating effect should be considered. Under some circumstances, significantly decreasing or even stopping neuroleptics may be indicated. This is a complex and controversial issue, about which we have some additional comments later. Other interventions to be considered included socialization groups, activity programs, job training, graded increases in expectations for the patient to work and socialize, and planning for independent living. Concrete social casework interventions may expand the options available to the patient to increase his or her functioning. Exploratory psychotherapy can sometimes resolve intrapsychic conflicts that have inhibited the patient's functioning and sustained defensive social withdrawal. Again, the family's informed collaboration in implementing these strategies is invaluable.

It is essential to remember that a patient's position on the activation performance curve shifts dramatically over time. Therefore, treatments that are ideal at one point may be ineffectual or even harmful at another. The need to decrease neuroleptic dose following resolution of a psychotic episode is a clear example. Or hospitalization, with its beneficial effects on acute psychosis, can become a powerful promoter of deficit functioning when its thoughtless continuation leads to institutionalism. The clinician is required to remain alert to changes in the patient's condition that justify a reappraisal of treatment needs. Because of the dramatic nature of psychosis, clinicians seldom miss significant shifts in this direction, although the recognition may not always be as prompt as it could be. We suspect, however, that, clinicians are all much more likely to miss the gradual, but frightfully entrenched, moves into the range of deficit symptoms that so often characterize the progressive course of chronic schizophrenia.

If this constant reassessment of shifting therapeutic needs is challenging and at times confusing for mental health professionals, how frustrating and perplexing must it be for family members? Family members generally come to therapists confused and distressed, looking for clear answers and un-ambiguous treatment recommendations. Instead, in response to the shifting vicissitudes of the patient's condition, the therapeutic stance must vary, at times seemingly contradicting a previous position. We have found it extremely important in working with the families of our patients to provide an understandable rationale for such temporal variation in treatment strategy. This has usually taken the form of presenting, at varying levels of sophistication and completeness, the model of the "inverted U" relationship. With appropriate adjustments for different intellectual and educational levels, most families readily achieve a sufficient understanding to serve as a basis for meaningful collaboration with therapists and patients in planning and implementing therapeutic strategies. One of the advantages of a model based on intervening variables such as the "inverted U" is that it is relatively easy to free it of theoretical jargon so as to use it as a basis of shared understanding with patients and their families.

4. *Treatment modalities interact in an additive way that can be predicted from the model.* This is nicely demonstrated in the work on EE by Vaughn and Leff (1976). High EE can be viewed as increased interpersonal stress and hence as activating. As would be expected, it has been related to increased rate of psychotic relapse. Reduced amount of face-to-face contact with high-EE relatives would thus be a quantitative reduction in inter-personal stress and perhaps, less specifically, a general reduction in social stimulation. This would be seen as deactivating and thus as reducing the rate of psychotic relapses, which it did in the British work. Neuroleptic drugs also reduced relapse rate, which again would be predicted by the model. Furthermore, when both deactivating conditions were present, their effect was additive, with a resultant maximal reduction in relapse rate.

It follows that when a patient is at an extreme location on either end of the activation–performance curve, the clinician can consider combining those modalities that act in the desired direction so as to maximize therapeutic potency. It is equally true that when the balance is delicate, or when dramatic changes in one factor are anticipated, off-setting modalities may be employed as a buffer against excessive shifts in activation. For instance, it has been argued that in the early phases of exploratory psychotherapy with schizophrenics, when the stage of increased activation can be anticipated, it is critical to continue or initiate neuroleptic drugs to counter the increased risk of psychosis (Gunderson, 1979). The same reasoning applies to certain "restructuring" forms of family therapy.

5. *Apart from this additive interaction, treatment modalities can interact in a facilitative manner.* This refers to the fact that some treatment interventions serve to provide the necessary groundwork to allow another treatment either to be successfully implemented or to have its desired effect. For example, Goldstein, Rodnick, Evans, May, and Steinberg (1978) found that in some cases neuroleptic medication was needed for their six-session family therapy to have certain effects. Likewise, for some patients, a positive psychotherapeutic relationship is needed before the patients are receptive to using neuroleptic drugs.

ILLUSTRATIONS

We briefly present our own experience with family interventions here to illustrate a family-oriented strategy developed as a component of a larger treatment program with special attention to its interactive effect on other modalities. This yields especially cogent examples, because the primary research interest was not originally family therapy at all, but, rather, another modality—strategies of neuroleptic drug use. The family therapy was designed with considerations of both its additive and facilitative interaction with the experimental drug strategy.

A meaningful discussion requires a digression about the approach to medication being used. Briefly, our interest was to explore alternatives to continuous neuroleptic use in aftercare. This was largely prompted by the growing concern about tardive dyskinesia, but also by the possibility that neuroleptic use in the remitted, nonpsychotic patient may significantly contribute to deficit symptomatology. The phenomenon of patients' brightening when taken off drugs is well known. This would, of course, fit the activation–performance model. Our thought was that it might be desirable to discontinue medication in a remitted schizophrenic. The compelling argument against doing that, of course, is that the increased relapse rate would be an unacceptable price to pay. It has been clearly demonstrated, probably most convincingly by Hogarty, Goldberg, Schooler, Ulrich, and The Collaborative Study Group (1974), that continuous neuroleptics strikingly reduce the relapse rate as compared to a placebo. However, another alternative suggested itself: If patients in stable remission were taken off drugs, would it be possible to reinstitute medication quickly at the first evidence of an impending relapse, and thereby abort the episode with little or no disruption of the patient's life or functioning? Work on stages of decompensation such as that by Docherty, van Kannen, Siris, and Marder

(1978) suggests that recognizable changes precede the florid psychosis. A study by Herz and Melville (1980) indicated that the majority of schizophrenic patients (70%) were able retrospectively to report recognizable changes during a prepsychotic prodromal stage, most lasting days to weeks. In addition, there is other evidence (Gardos & Cole, 1976) that it is easier to manage a relapse due to drug discontinuation simply by reinstituting drugs than it is to control relapses that occur on medication. Thus, our strategy of "targeted" drug use seemed at least theoretically possible. The feasibility of the approach, then, hinges essentially on whether the strategy can in fact be implemented promptly before an impending decompensation becomes full-blown and disruptive.

This makes two requirements of the patient—that he or she be able to recognize early signs of impending decompensation, and that he or she be disposed to cooperate promptly with treatment at such times. Although we have put considerable effort into cultivating these capacities in our patients, it is often the case that the family is better able to accomplish both tasks than the patient is. Herz and Melville (1980), for instance, found that, while 70% of patients were able to identify a prodromal phase, 93% of the families were able to do so. Furthermore, family members are not handicapped by those distortions in judgment and the loss of insight that sometimes accompany prodromal experiences for patients. Consequently, we have developed a strategy of family intervention designed to maximize the family's capacity to facilitate the successful use of targeted neuroleptic treatment.

Upon entering our program, usually immediately following discharge from a hospital, a patient is assigned to a therapist/case manager who will work with the patient for the next 2 years. The treatment experience begins with six sessions with the family members (or important household members), including the patient. The format for this is the psychoeducational approach described by Goldstein et al. (1978), with its four goals: knowing that a psychosis has occurred, identifying stressors, anticipating future stressors, and planning practical steps to reduce stressors or their impact. Our major modification has been in respect to the first goal, where we have expanded beyond acknowledgment of psychosis to a basic discussion of schizophrenia in general and a detailed exploration of the patient's illness in particular, including special emphasis on the early phase of onset or exacerbation of psychosis. We reserve didactic material until specific gaps in knowledge or areas of misinformation become apparent, or until questions are asked. Instead, we begin by encouraging both the patient and the family to discuss the unfolding of the illness as experienced from each of their perspectives. We were surprised early in our work to find how unprecedented such a discussion was in the vast majority of cases. Families who had time and again experienced angry, threatening, hostile behavior from patients did not realize that at such times the patient felt fearful, endangered, and confused. Conversely, patients who angrily complained that their parents always called the police to have them taken to the hospital frequently failed to realize that this was not essentially a punitive act, but a response to the intense anxiety and fear that their threatening behavior evoked.

This process of mutual sharing of the experience of the illness inevitably leads to questions by patient and family about schizophrenia in general and the patient's illness in particular—concerns about etiology, the role of genetic transmission, the impact of early familial influences, the prognosis, the meaning of various symptoms, and the role of different treatments. The requested information is given to the family at an appropriate level of sophistication. In addition, family members are encouraged to discuss their fantasies and opinions about these matters. Needless to say, guilt, shame, and futility are common themes. We have been particularly disturbed at the frequency with which families report feeling either explicitly or implicitly blamed and held responsible for the illness of schizophrenics by mental health workers. This is usually accompanied by the sense of being rejected and excluded from the treatment experience, including being deprived of basic information. We have come to realize that much of the resistance to family participation that we had regarded as reflecting disinterest, despair, or pathology intrinsic to the family, was in fact the family's fear that we, too, would attack them as either malicious or incompetent. When such issues arise, we generally find it useful to state our position explicitly: There is no evidence to justify an assumption that their treatment of the patient currently or in the past caused the illness, but the challenge of living with and helping the schizophrenic person is difficult and confusing in spite of good intentions, and thus we can be helpful as a source of information and support.

Another inevitable area of confusion concerns deficit symptomatology. It is relatively easy for families to realize that hallucinations, delusions, and other productive symptoms are sick behavior, but, once the psychosis is resolved, how does a family member regard the patient who does not want to talk with old friends, fails to do assigned household chores, never gets around to applying for a job, or sits up all night only to sleep all day? Families struggle to understand such behavior—whether to regard it as a manifestation of illness, with which the patient is plagued, or laziness, over which the patient has voluntary control. This familial concern with deficit symptoms is reflected in the content of critical comments in studies of EE, where the most frequent complaints related to enduring nonpsychotic behavior of patients (Vaughn, 1977). The extent to which many patients also struggle with these issues is striking: At times they are depressed by a deadening process that seems beyond their control; at other times they feel guilty for failing to function at levels expected by families and themselves. This is no simple matter, even for us as treaters. As soon as we go beyond pat answers and take such questions seriously, we are embroiled in some of the thorniest of philosophical issues regarding free will, determinism, and the theory of action. At the practical level, however, we can discuss how some deficit symptoms are an expectable component of the illness in most cases; how some measures designed to activate the patient may help to prevent or reduce them; how, if such efforts are applied excessively or at improper times, there is a risk of precipitating psychosis; how, conversely, some treatments that control psychosis may exacerbate deficit symptoms; and how interventions with the patient can be assessed in terms of their effect both on psychosis and deficit functioning. In short, we apply the activation–performance curve and its corollaries. This model allows a clear discussion of our rationale for targeted drug treatment and the critical importance of early detection and intervention if relapses are to be aborted. Toward this end, we review with each family and patient the prodromal phase of past psychotic episodes in order to develop a list of warning signs to be watched for by the patient, family, and therapist. We stress the importance of contacting us immediately should such signs occur. For this purpose, a psychiatrist and nurse known to the patient are always on call and available to the patient and family. The prodromal pattern varies among patients, but tends to be the same for a given patient from episode to episode. Frequent components include sleep disorder, difficulty in thinking, perceptual and conceptual distortion, dysphoria, fleeting hallucinations and delusions, and referential thinking. The following are examples from our clinic:

1. A young woman reports feeling "spaced out" and perplexed. Her parents note withdrawal from family members, sleeping all day, and staying up all night. Her therapist notes poor engagement during sessions, vagueness in her speech, and occasional instances of formal thought disorder.
2. A middle-aged housewife reports being tired all day and complains of numerous vague aches and pains. Her husband notes progressive deterioration in her housework. The therapist notes poor grooming in dress, some thought blocking, and poverty in the content and amount of speech.
3. A young, single man reports increased feelings of jealousy and anger toward his older sister. His parents report frequent calls from the patient complaining of myriad vague physical complaints. The therapist notes the patient to be increasingly irritable, angry, and obsessed with conflicts with his family.

4. A young woman finds herself standing around doing nothing and giggling excessively. Her family observes the same thing. The therapist detects ideas of reference and notes a deterioration in the patient's grooming.
5. A young man reports difficulty in sleeping. His parents note irritability and withdrawal. The therapist reports irritability and mild haughtiness.
6. A young woman reports anxiety, pains in her extremities, vomiting, anorexia, insomnia, and the concern that during a previous hospitalization her food had been poisoned. Her husband reports that she at times stares off into space and does not sleep well. The therapist has found the patient frequently to be febrile at these times.
7. A middle-aged woman complains of tinnitus.
8. A young man reports difficulty in thinking, bouts of depression, and referential ideas. His mother reports that he keeps the light on in his room all night and that he is getting into fights with his brother. The therapist notes that the patient has some thought blocking and poverty in the amount of speech, and that he is chain-smoking cigarettes.

In cases like these, the triad of patient, family, and therapist learns to recognize the prodromal symptoms that signal an impending psychotic relapse, to correlate their observations with one another, and then to intervene with antipsychotic drugs and psychosocial support, so that the psychosis can be aborted without hospitalization or major disruption of the lives of the patient and family.

In addition to its specific value in facilitating the targeted drug strategy, we have found this initial series of family sessions very useful as a source of information about the patient and the family that can guide discussion about subsequent treatment strategies. As noted earlier, pathological features of a family can be revealed by the resistances to and distortions of information provided to its members. Direct observation of the interaction between the patient and his or her family is very revealing, not only of family characteristics, but of qualities of the patient as well. Often such qualities could only have been assessed after extensive time and effort from individual contact with the patient. The degree and nature of deficit symptoms and social withdrawal is an example of such a quality; the extent to which denial and distortion interfere with the patient's perception of his or her interpersonal environment is another. This latter issue has been relatively neglected in recent family research: For instance, assessments of EE in the classic studies have been based on the direct interaction of the investigator with the key relative. Presumably, the impact of EE on relapse rate is mediated through an effect on the patient. Thus, the extent to which patients perceive their relatives to be hostile and critical toward them may well be more important than an outside observer's assessment may be. Therapists are all familiar with patients who possess remarkable capacities to deny negative affect that the therapists feel to be present, as well as others who are painfully sensitive to the slightest suggestion of anything less than enthusiastic approval; yet this variable has been essentially unexplored.

The assessment of the strengths and limitations of both the patient and the family help in the selection of a strategy to deal with problems of family interaction when they are found to be present. We do not automatically assume that the family problems are best treated with family intervention. The following are two brief examples from our experience of alternative approaches to problematic family interactions.

CASE EXAMPLE 1

Mark was a 32-year-old single man living with his parents. He had a long and stormy history of schizophrenia with many episodes of psychosis, interspersed with occasional brief periods of good functioning. Mark's father was a bright but neurotically tormented man gripped by obsessions and inhibitions in spite of many years of psychoanalysis. Mark's mother appeared weary, detached, and embittered. Both parents felt hopeless about Mark's chances of recovery and resentful that needing to care for him would always plague their lives. They acted as if they were being intentionally punished. It gradually emerged that the father, in fact, was riddled with guilt and self-doubt; he suspected that his wife had been cold and rejecting toward Mark as an infant and that he had failed to intervene, due to his unwillingness to confront his wife and the demands of graduate school that distanced him from home life. He entertained the fantasy that Mark's illness was a punishment for this. Every time Mark did begin to show improvement—both in reduced symptoms and in increased functioning—his parents responded as if it were just a cruel torment designed to raise their hopes and then to plunge them into deeper despair when Mark's condition deteriorated. This pattern was especially apparent when Mark got a job. As a result, at such times, the parents actually became more critical and hostile toward Mark. He would become increasingly defensive and insecure, finally developing paranoid delusions, and usually would be hospitalized in a panicky and agitated state.

All of this became apparent during the psychoeducational sessions. When the pattern was pointed out to the family, they were able to recognize their self-fulfilling prophecy and were motivated to deal with it. As a result, the therapist decided to see the family together. Concrete instances of the pattern and its consequences were explored, and alternative responses by the parents were developed. The therapist encouraged both the parents and Mark to discuss their anxieties and doubts about Mark's progress, rather than to stir up one another's expectations of failure. The therapist had regular individual sessions with Mark as well as the family sessions. As a result, Mark has successfully held a job for an unprecedented 12 months.

CASE EXAMPLE 2

Harry was a single man 26 years old, living with his two cousins in a home owned by his mother. He had had multiple hospitalizations since the age of 19. Although his mother lived in another house nearby, she was very involved in Harry's life—controlling his money and attempting to dictate his activities. She was an extremely difficult and overbearing woman. She had a remarkably severe inability to hear even simple communications without distortions or confusion. She was adamant and intolerant in her opinions. Harry reported a monotonously consistent pattern leading up to each of his recent hospitalizations: His mother would try to make decisions for him; he would resist and an intense argument would ensue; his fury at his mother would intensify until he became threatening and agitated; at this point his mother would call the police, and he would be involuntarily hospitalized. Attempts by the therapist to discuss this pattern with the family made it quickly apparent that there was little hope of successfully solving the problem through family sessions. The therapist worked with Harry alone. As a result, the patient came to see the role he played in enacting the pattern. Since certain financial realities made it impractical to leave the house owned by his mother, he learned to limit his interactions with her to necessary business dealings. He developed strategies for avoiding unnecessary arguments. At times, disagreements about practical matters were unavoidable. In such circumstances, the therapist made himself available as a mediator between Harry and his mother. This may seem to be an unhealthy encouragement of regression and dependency in the patient; however, the therapist's experience with Harry's mother in the initial sessions made it clear how utterly maddening it was for anyone to deal with her. Thus to expect Harry to do it alone was unrealistic. As a result, Harry has done quite well for close to a year and a half without rehospitalization.

CONCLUSION

In summary, we have argued that outcome-oriented assessment should replace speculative theories of etiology, however elegant, in selecting treatment approaches. We have proposed a heuristic model based on intervening variables (i.e., activation and functioning) as a framework for guiding decisions about selecting and combining treatment modalities, including family approaches for a given patient at a given phase of his or her illness. We have argued for the utility of an early, nonspecific family approach that is primarily psychoeducational in nature. We have illustrated the role of such an approach in facilitating a strategy of targeted neuroleptic use, as well as in providing the necessary information about patient and family to plan subsequent, more specific treatment interventions.

REFERENCES

Brown, G. W., Birley, J. L., & Wing, J. K. The influence of family life on the course of schizophrenic disorders: A replication. *British Journal of Psychiatry*, 1972, *121*, 241–258.

Brown, G. W., Monck, E. M., Carstairs, G. M., & Wing, J. K. The influence of family life on the course of schizophrenic illness. *British Journal of Preventative Social Medicine*, 1962, *16*, 55–68.

Carpenter, W. T. Clinical research methods applicable to the study of treatment effects in chronic schizophrenic patients. In C. Baxter & T. Melnechuk (Eds.), *Perspectives in schizophrenia research.* New York: Raven Press, 1980.

Carpenter, W. T., & Heinrichs, D. W. The role for psychodynamic psychiatry in the treatment of schizophrenic patients. In J. Strauss, M. Bowers, T. W. Downey, S. Fleck, S. Jackson, & I. Levine (Eds.), *The psychotherapy of schizophrenia.* New York: Plenum, 1980.

Carpenter, W. T., Heinrichs, D. W., & Hanlon, T. E. Methodologic standards for treatment outcome research in schizophrenia. *American Journal of Psychiatry*, 1981, *138*, 465–471.

Docherty, J. P., van Kannen, D. P., Siris, S. G., & Marder, S. R. Stages of schizophrenic psychosis. *American Journal of Psychiatry*, 1978, *135*, 420–426.

Gardos, G., & Cole, J. Maintenance antipsychotic therapy: Is the cure worse than the disease? *American Journal of Psychiatry*, 1976, *133*, 32–36.

Goldstein, M. J., & Rodnick, E. H. The family's contribution to the etiology of schizophrenia: Current status. *Schizophrenia Bulletin*, 1975, *1*(14), 48–63.

Goldstein, M., Rodnick, E. H., Evans, J. R., May, P. R. A., & Steinberg, M. R. Drug and family therapy in the aftercare of acute schizophrenics. *Archives of General Psychiatry*, 1978, *35*, 1169–1177.

Gunderson, J. G. Individual psychotherapy. In L. Bellak (Ed.), *Disorders of the schizophrenic syndrome.* New York: Basic Books, 1979.

Herz, M., & Melville, C. Relapse in schizophrenia. *American Journal of Psychiatry*, 1980, *137*, 801–805.

Hogarty, G. E., Goldberg, S. C., Schooler, N. R., Ulrich, R. F., & The Collaborative Study Group. Drug and sociotherapy in the aftercare of schizophrenic patients: II. Two-year relapse rates. *Archives of General Psychiatry*, 1974, *31*, 603–608.

Jacob, T. Family interaction in disturbed and normal families: A methodological and substantive review. *Psychological Bulletin*, 1975, *82*, 33–65.

Kraepelin, E. *Dementia praecox and paraphrenia.* Huntington, N.Y.: Robert E. Krieger, 1971. (Originally published, 1919.)

Liem, J. H. Family studies of schizophrenia: An update and commentary. *Schizophrenia Bulletin*, 1980, *6*, 82–108.

Spohn, H. E., & Patterson, T. Recent studies of psychophysiology in schizophrenia. *Schizophrenia Bulletin*, 1979, *5*, 581–611.
Vaughn, C. E. Patterns of interactions in families of schizophrenics. In H. Catschnig (Ed.), *Schizophrenia: The other side*. Vienna: Urban & Schwarzenberg, 1977.
Vaughn, C. E., & Leff, J. P. The influence of family and social factors on the course of psychiatric patients. *British Journal of Psychiatry*, 1976, *129*, 125–137.

13
FAMILY THERAPY OF THE SCHIZOPHRENIC POOR

Steven J. Goldstein
Lawrence Dyche

INTRODUCTION

The past few years have witnessed a blossoming of family therapy approaches and techniques that offer the potential for significant progress in the treatment of schizophrenia. This chapter presents an approach to making this potential more available to that portion of the population who are experiencing poverty together with schizophrenia and who have been traditionally underserved by the mental health professions.

Our concern for this group of patients has developed from 11 years of working together in two day hospitals. For the past 6 years we have worked in the South Bronx area of New York City as the director and supervising social worker, respectively, of an acute day hospital. The population, primarily Black and Hispanic, is among the poorest in the city. Much of the housing is crumbling and abandoned, adolescent pregnancy is of epidemic proportions, and most of the population lives in fear of violence. The prevalence rate of schizophrenia is known to be excessive in the lowest social class (e.g., Mishler & Scotch, 1963) and is reflected in the press of psychotic patients for services.

Here are examples of some typical patients that come to our clinic:

A 29-year-old Black male, one of five children, had been locked up in a state hospital for 11 years with the diagnosis of chronic undifferentiated schizophrenia. He had received no visits during his incarceration. A victim of deinstitutionalization, missing most of his teeth, barely socialized, chronically hallucinating, terrified of the "real world," he was summarily released to his family. As the neighborhood facility, our hospital became responsible for his treatment.

STEVEN J. GOLDSTEIN and LAWRENCE DYCHE. Morrisania Neighborhood Family Care Center, Mental Health Services, Bronx, New York.

An 18-year-old Puerto Rican girl came to our clinic speaking incoherently. She was one of seven children, five of whom were mentally retarded, with an alcoholic father and a desperate, lost mother who could easily pass for a bag lady.

An 18-year-old Black waif was brought in by a local minister who had housed this child in an all-male seminary for a few days. She had no immediately apparent residence, no source of income or food; to put it bluntly, no one seemed to want her. She had an interesting set of delusions and fit well the *Diagnostic and Statistical Manual of Mental Disorders*, 3rd edition (DSM-III) criteria for schizophrenia.

A 25-year-old, massive Black Puerto Rican man, street-wise, a superb athlete, came rushing into our clinic, terrorizing even the security staff and demanding treatment. He seemed propelled by grandiose delusions. Upon calling his mother, with whom he had been occasionally living, we learned that she felt too frightened of her son even to come in to the clinic.

All of these cases were approached with a systems formulation, using family intervention strategies. However, each case required theoretical and technical considerations not usually necessary in other settings.

PHILOSOPHIES, THEORIES, AND TECHNIQUES

The diversity and complexity of the families we treat has forced us to explore a variety of theories and techniques. A view of schizophrenia is described here that attempts to provide a workable focus to integrate theory and practice. We hope that the resulting approach to treatment, while pragmatic, is complete enough to help clinicians succeed (against the odds) in the treatment of the schizophrenic poor, coming, as such patients often do, from underorganized families living in the chaos of the inner city.

Our work has been influenced by several family approaches. Primary among them is the structural approach of Salvador Minuchin. The action-oriented techniques so skillfully developed by Minuchin and his colleagues are often well suited to the immediacy of experience of poor families (Minuchin, 1974; Minuchin & Fishman, 1981; Minuchin, Montalvo, Guerney, Rosman, & Shumer, 1967). Other sources for our approach include Jay Haley and Cloé Madanes (Haley, 1980; Madanes, 1980), who have developed a powerful method for breaking up the chaotic family dance that supports nonfunctioning in young adults. Their focus is primarily on strengthening the parental subsystem as a means to help the identified patient function normally.

We have explored the use of the systemic approach of the Milan and Ackerman groups, and found the techniques useful for those families appropriate for the "neutrality" central to that modality (Selvini-Palazzoli, Cecchin, Boscolo, & Prata, 1980).

Recently some convincing research has been presented to support the effectiveness of a psychoeducational approach (Anderson, Hogarty, & Reiss, 1980; Goldstein, Rodnick, Evans, May, & Steinberg, 1978; Leff, 1979). Central to that approach is an attempt to educate the family in the biochemical view of schizophrenia as a means of calming family tendencies toward critical and intrusive interactions.

However, Ludwig Wittgenstein once made an observation about philosophy that applies well to family therapy of the schizophrenic poor. "Philosophy unties knots in our thinking; hence, its results must be simple; but philosophizing has to be as complicated as the knots it unties." From the vantage point of a public clinic in the South Bronx, most family therapy approaches are not "complicated" enough to untie the knots confronting therapists working in the urban ghetto as we know it. These methods do not deal with issues such as how to manage acute states without hospitalization, what to do about family members who refuse to participate, how to handle survival issues brought on by poverty, what to do about the profound effects of racism, and how to generate a sense of success and competence while avoiding repetitions of previous failures.

THE NEED FOR AN ECOLOGICAL FRAMEWORK

The main issues for the clinician working with the complexities of the urban ghetto, the underorganized family, and the confusion of psychosis are that failure is promoted at every level and that the prerequisites for survival often stand in the way of even the newer family intervention strategies. The problem of schizophrenia seems locked into all these layers of context. This might be best illustrated by a vignette familiar to anyone who has worked in an inner-city emergency room.

A disheveled Black man in his early 20s paces furiously around a small examining room hurling a staccato of confused epithets at the security guard at the door and others within. An older Black woman sits just inside the doorway in her coat and scarf. Motionless, she holds her purse in her lap and stares impassively as the young man moves back and forth past her.

In situations like this, several levels of analysis are relevant, all with different implications for treatment. Perhaps this young man's behavior is

the result of intense confusion and frustration as his neurochemistry trans-
forms his world into a waking nightmare. From that perspective, he needs
medications and a regulated environment. But the behavior may also
concern his intense involvement with a depressed, isolated mother who
cannot accept his growing up. This calls for family intervention. And,
furthermore, this vignette might also reflect the rage of a Black man with
no chance for work who is taunted by a welfare system that calls him lazy.
Any intervention that does not provide him a new opportunity could
hardly be called a success. Any treatment model that excludes one level
cannot be consistently useful and will probably be unable to generate
multilevel change.

A workable theory for us has been found in the ecological approach as
set forth in the writings of Auerswald, Minuchin, and Aponte (Aponte,
1976a, 1976b; Auerswald, 1968; Minuchin et al., 1967). This model attempts
to take a complex, holistic view of a problem that involves several layers of
context beyond that of the family. With reference to children, Aponte's
(1976a) concept of "context replication" shows how dynamics in the home
can be repeated in the school. Similarly, for working with the schizophrenic
poor, we have sought to identify a dysfunctional process that is repeated at
several systemic levels toward which to direct our strategies.

The process on which we have chosen to focus is the *deficit in organization* at several levels of the ecosystem, as both the determinant and
the result of schizophrenia. By this, we mean (1) deficits in the ability
of the patient to organize; (2) underorganization in the family; and (3) disorganization in the network and community. The individual cannot organize stimuli; the family cannot organize to allow its individual members
to grow; and the community cannot organize a context to allow families
the resources they need to thrive. Furthermore, a disorganized context
confuses a person who has trouble organizing stimuli. Likewise, a psychotic
member easily disorganizes an underorganized family's fragile structure.
Aponte (1976b) writes persuasively about how lack of support for families
of the poor at the community and societal levels saps their ability to create
flexible, differentiated boundaries. This view implies a circular process in
which poverty and schizophrenia amplify disorganization at every level.

The model we have developed attempts to provide the therapist with a
clear, straightforward guide to organizing his or her efforts toward organizing the family. At the same time, we believe that its underlying basis is
comprehensive and "complicated" enough to incorporate contributions of
diverse thinkers and to wrestle with the difficult family knot of concurrent
schizophrenia and poverty. We think of our treatment in three distinct
phases, each having at its center a single task to guide the therapist's efforts:
The first phase is directed toward getting someone in charge; the second

phase involves working to change family patterns that are no longer adaptive; and the third phase focuses on supporting the patient in making decisions about his or her life.

THE WORKING CONTEXT

If a therapeutic model is a recipe of sorts, we also acknowledge the importance of a good kitchen. Therapists must themselves have a working context that is highly nurturant and clearly organized. Our notion of a nurturant setting emphasizes ongoing live and videotaped supervision in small support groups for the entire staff, as well as a parallel group for the supervisors working with live supervision material. Organizationally, we attempt to keep our staff hierarchies flexible as well as clear. A carefully organized program makes available daily activities that act as stepping-stones to more demanding activities such as work. The patient attends the day hospital on a daily basis, participating in a variety of groups that are graduated in the degree of demands.

Crisis intervention is part of our organizing concept as well as an important technique. Much of the work in the initial phase of our model goes into helping a family resolve major life crises and dilemmas. Thus, staff members should have daily work schedules that allow them periodically to devote all their energy to single cases at the expense of other responsibilities. They need to have mobility to go to the problem when necessary, whether this means a home visit or a trip to a social service agency. Both advocacy and medication are considered essential ingredients to our work; staff members must become knowledgeable about both.

Some characteristics of therapists are particularly suited to this model. We seek a staff that is mature and energetic, that is balanced in clinical expertise and life experience, that regards both the wisdom of the street as highly valuable and theoretical knowledge as essential. Thus a therapist familiar with the community, comfortable with local colloquialisms, down to earth, and relatively optimistic usually finds this work rewarding. We have attempted in each phase of treatment to leave ample space between the lines for the therapist's own style.

BEGINNING PHASE

The essence of the initial phase in our model involves helping a family contain unmanageable behavior by putting a competent person in charge. Conformity to behavioral expectations generally increases with organization. Since aberrant behavior in schizophrenia relates to a person's difficulty with integrating information, it is particularly influenced by the clarity of his or her social surroundings, especially the family or social network. This leads us to work with the people comprising the patient's context to increase the definition and effectiveness of their family roles. We actively bring the resources of the mental health profession and of community institutions to bear on supporting this endeavor. In effect, interventions as diverse as prescribing medication, advocating for a client at welfare, and helping a mother stand up to her adolescent son can each be moves to help a family organize itself.

The structural model that Haley (1980) has described is similar to the one we propose for this phase, but his clientele is markedly different. Haley is apparently able to initiate treatment by calling the family in and talking to the parents about how to set rules and enforce them. In work with families of the schizophrenic poor, the task is usually more complex. The therapist must first locate the family, assemble them, and convince them that he or she has something to offer. Both reaching the family and establishing credibility are major preliminary tasks.

GAINING ACCESS TO FAMILIES

Quite often in our community, the person with symptoms comes in alone and claims to have no family or none that would attend a session. While we know this is sometimes so, we never take the claim at face value. Our effectiveness in involving families in our work is based largely on our own determination and a conviction that it can be done. With the awareness that many poor families avoid us because they expect to be treated as welfare recipients, we assume the burden of proving otherwise. Creative, persistent outreach, on the assumption that most individuals maintain some family or social network, helps us to unearth collaterals with surprising regularity. Since we have learned that working with a family executive who can be in charge of the patient during an acute episode increases our success rate dramatically, we have developed a broad range of skills in reaching out to poor families.

For instance, the involvement of fathers is a special challenge in our setting. In general, the posture required for being in therapy seems less comfortable for a man than for a woman and, we suspect, least so for a minority man. Despite their importance in their families, Black men are defined as outsiders by the dominant culture. Unemployed fathers are extruded from their families by the welfare system. The men in our community who do hold jobs tend to have longer hours and less flexibility for time off than the middle-class worker has. The tendency to define less available fathers as irresponsible must be rigorously avoided. An orientation that presumes paternal concern has brought us considerable success in enlisting the father in our work. At the times we fail to bring him into session, we continue to acknowledge his position with an empty chair, and we attempt to post him on the session with a phone call or a letter.

Often a patient's mother will rely heavily on her mother. A grandmother's quiet presence is easily overlooked, but may be crucial in resolving a child's problems. We watch closely for her influence, because a dysfunctional system of this sort is quite resistant to change when the entire configuration is not addressed.

It is occasionally necessary to be flexible and begin treatment with less than the entire family participating. But since family work is such a powerful tool for change, we yield to family resistance begrudgingly and only after careful consideration. We expect the person seeking help to join us in advocating family sessions, and we are reluctant to treat symptoms without some family participation.

In the real absence of family, we search for members of the social network: friends, neighbors, an occasional roommate. Often the most valuable resource in the inner city is the church; we actively involve local ministers in our work. In some instances, a social agency has been used as the executive. One client in her early 40s had been hospitalized on 49 different occasions for bizarre, disruptive behavior. It was not until a criminal court became involved that she took her treatment between breaks seriously. In conjunction with a legal aid lawyer, we helped her negotiate a strict probation agreement. She is currently in treatment, is working, and has been symptom-free for over a year.

ESTABLISHING CREDIBILITY

A therapist must not assume that treatment will seem relevant to a family. Recently a pretty, youngish 18-year-old girl was brought to our Walk-In Clinic by her mother. She was quietly hallucinating. We learned that she had been staying home since dropping out of school 3 years before. It was quickly established that the girl's diagnosis was schizophrenia; the clinician assumed that she would improve with medication and that she would resume functioning with family intervention. However, he also learned that this frazzled mother had five retarded children, no lights, and an alcoholic husband who beat her. It seemed understandable that her daughter's schizophrenia was given low priority in this woman's life. The therapist had to get the lights turned on, help a retarded brother return to school, and give a great deal of supportive attention to this mother's needs before he had the credibility for even simple structural moves. Standard family interventions would have almost certainly led to failure and the diagnosis of an "unmotivated family" or "an impossible mother."

Skill as an advocate is crucial in working with poor families. For many, the social service bureaucracies provide their income, shelter, food, and medical and child care. These agencies are often capricious and punitive, and they require of recipients an exhausting collection of papers and documents, giving rise to the adage, "Being on welfare is a full-time job." A solid grasp of this reality is essential to a therapist's credibility; the ability to intervene helpfully is perceived as being as important as clinical skill by patients' families.

Since poverty and schizophrenia sustain each other, the therapist must give paramount concern to helping the family build a stable economic base. He or she must be knowledgeable in advocacy but able to evaluate the clinical implications of its use. We often defer treatment of symptoms while a genuine economic crisis is being managed. Haley (1980) suggests that public assistance is a deterrent to functioning, because free money saps motivation. However, we have found with our clientele that welfare may be an essential stage on the road *to* functioning.

ESSENTIAL FAMILY MEMBERS

Since assembling the family is a particularly complex task in our setting, it is valuable to have a set of priorities for doing so. The executive subsystem of the family is even more important to successful treatment than the patient is. This subsystem consists of the person or persons who have the authority in the family or who need to assume responsibility for the patient during the acute phase. In the case of a young person living at home, this would be the parent or parents. It might also need to include a particularly influential friend or relative, such as a grandparent or godparent. The executive for an adult patient might be a spouse or other relative, perhaps even a concerned neighbor. We have had occasion to involve one of the older children in a household as the temporary executive for a psychotic mother. While this poses problems for the generational organization in a family, at times it is the only alternative to complete family breakup.

An important variation in executive systems is the one spanning several states or even countries. Families that we see are often separated by migration from the South or from Puerto Rico, and a disturbed member may be regularly moved from one household to another, preventing the continuity essential to effective treatment. We have found that successful work can proceed only after we have secured the support and cooperation of absent executives.

In addition to the executives and the symptomatic family member, we try to include peer supports for each. With an adolescent patient this might be a sibling; for a single parent, a relative or friend. This kind of membership for the sessions can facilitate the middle phase of treatment, in which we work to loosen parent–child enmeshments by helping parents and children expand relationships in their own generations.

THE STRUCTURAL INTERVENTION

At the point where the family group is assembled and the therapist has the members' confidence, the work of getting someone in charge can begin. As the family's sense of helplessness and anger emerges, the therapist can begin by asking the members questions such as "What is your job in this situation?" and "How can you get him to listen to you?" The therapist will be systematically eliciting the operating rules in the household and the arrangement for setting and enforcing them.

Inevitably, family expectations are confused by the psychotic symptoms of the ill member. The family executive often handles the patient's diminished functioning by avoiding the taking of responsibility. The appropriate family leader and subleaders must be identified, and family rules appropriate to the situation at hand must be affirmed. If someone is in an acute psychotic state, the therapist can support the need to take over some of that person's decision-making power temporarily, for the person's own safety and that of the household.

Each step in this phase is directed to the goal of supporting the family executive's authority and effectiveness. Enactments can be structured in the session to show the executive how to make effective rules and enforce them, and how to correct the most common leadership errors of passivity on the one hand and critical overreactivity on the other. The executive can be shown that he or she has access to community authority to support his or her authority in the household. For instance, we often direct parents to lock out a threatening adolescent or call the police. The place of medication as a support to the family can be established at this time.

Teaching a family executive to increase the structure of the symptomatic member's home environment without totally overwhelming him or her is greatly simplified by the availability of a day treatment program. The work during the acute phase of schizophrenia usually involves the family's organizing to insure the patient's program attendance. As an initial task, it has a high probability of success; it tends to decrease enmeshment; and it gives the exhausted patient some space from the equally exhausted family. Also, since it allows the use of medication and milieu therapy, it usually brings about a prompt symptom improvement for which the family can take some credit. We ask the executive to involve the family in doing whatever is necessary to get the patient to the program, or at least out the front door in the morning.

For a therapist new to this work, these kinds of interventions with a severely underorganized family can feel confusing and may seem to contradict the democratic tenets of traditional family therapy. However, the leaders in a chaotic family feel impotent, and every positive change must be framed to support their efforts. For instance, when an adolescent makes it to the program for the first time, the therapist gives the credit to the mother. Other interventions might involve such taboos as ignoring the patient in his or her presence, talking about the patient to other family members, or not immediately challenging the family's label of incompetence. The therapist must work with the executive's own modes of discipline, even when they seem harsh and intrusive. In return for clearer family role definition, the therapist temporarily promotes one member's overfunctioning and neglects the patient's sense of incompetence. We make these moves with our eyes open and see them as a necessary tradeoff in gaining a foothold in severely underorganized families. They establish a base for the work in phases to come.

MIDDLE PHASE

The initial phase of treatment is an effort to create a stable living situation, to handle survival issues, and to create a therapeutic unit with someone in charge of the family. In the middle phase, we look beyond survival to help families expand their adaptational options. We challenge them to take risks and to press for something better. We attempt to start a process in which we join a family in assessing its needs, enhancing its strengths, and confronting its dilemma.

Adaptation to poverty often comes at the expense of family organization. Family involvement may be intensified as a protection from the dangers of the street or may be minimized in response to a fragmenting, chaotic environment. But such patterns may pose constraints on a family's growth and may increase a member's vulnerability to psychotic episodes, as well as pose particularly difficult problems in the management of a psychotic episode.

Setting appropriate goals in the light of our families' unique adaptations sometimes seems to us the most complex task confronting family therapists: that is, how to build enough intensity for change without stimulating more disorganization, and how to encourage taking risks without implying false promises.

Our initial decisions in choosing treatment directions are based on our assessment of a family's ability to change, on the members' accessibility, and especially on the success in the first phase of treatment and the potential the patient shows in the day hospital program. The appropriate directions in treatment emerge less from a static assessment than from an evolutionary process in which the therapist challenges the family to consider the effectiveness of its adaptational patterns and then presents specific alternatives.

Early in the treatment process, we have found that psychiatric history wrongly tempts us toward a pathology orientation. However, after the therapist and family have succeeded at some of the initial tasks, history can often add useful information and help guide the therapist. For example, we focused initially on helping a mother gain control of her son's rigid religious delusions by helping her set appropriate rules to enable her son to attend the day hospital, and by supporting her need for welfare. Medication was prescribed. As we entered the middle phase of treatment, we began challenging the enmeshed dyad via a series of enactments. The history established that the repeated psychotic episodes of the son served to confirm the mother in her need for intense involvement in every aspect of her son's life. Appropriate strategies were then developed by the therapist to permit the mother to allow her son some independence in appropriate areas.

STRESSING COMPETENCE

A guiding principle for all our work is to stress competence. We seek to nurture existing strengths and relationships instead of emphasizing pathology. When we directly challenge an adaptational pattern, we first insure a series of small successes. If a single mother is intrusively involved with her adolescent daughter, we begin by supporting her efforts to control the girl's rebellious psychotic behavior. We do not focus on her deficits or over-involvement, and we wait for her success before bringing potential critics (e.g., grandmother, ex-husband) into the session. Only after the mother can successfully manage her daughter's behavior do we explore mother–daughter overinvolvement, primarily by encouraging network expansion for the mother. Another example occurs when a mother has a psychotic episode. We work to support her competence to keep her children, though this may bring us into conflict with foster care agencies or well-meaning in-laws. If a spouse is experiencing schizophrenia, we give the couple realistic information about the illness and work to support the relationship.

In seeking to support competence, the therapist must also steer clear of certain pitfalls. Discrediting absent fathers, focusing on a mother's deficits, and lauding middle-class values (e.g., promoting school over work) must be carefully avoided. The therapist must not be casually accepting of obstacles to success in treatment such as canceled sessions, frequent lateness, neglect of tasks, or drug use. The family will take the therapy seriously only if they see that the therapist does. If a therapist is at an impasse and can no longer find competence in a family, the solution can be to expand the system by including a supervisor, a cotherapist, or another family member.

Poverty often exaggerates adaptational patterns. These may remind the therapist of extreme situations in nature, such as plant life on high mountains near the timber line. Some trees have been felled by wind, lightning, or time; some trees huddle together for protection; and some trees stand isolated, curious in shape, scarred by climate, appealing only as scientific or photographic oddities. So it seems with those afflicted with poverty and schizophrenia. Some seem beaten, left with little or no hope; some are deeply entwined in a family dance so involved that survival seems to depend on it; and some stand alone, alienated, isolated, eccentric, and fragile. Such unique adaptations can be effective at one point but have negative consequences during other phases of the life cycle.

Enmeshment

Most family therapists have treated deeply entwined families, since these families seem to attend treatment more consistently than disengaged families do. Enmeshment, lack of generational boundaries, double-bind communications, triangulation, and so forth, are familiar concepts to family therapists.

Enmeshment involves a family turning in upon itself, isolating itself from its social surroundings. Relinquishing these patterns involves moving outward to something beyond the family. But poverty by definition means decreased options, and socialization is often inhibited by neighborhood violence, so intense family overinvolvement becomes more and more likely.

We have been impressed with the variety of viable techniques for intervening in enmeshment. However, therapists should not use them without considering actual situations. Simply to push people apart can be destructive. The therapist must take responsibility for finding viable options for the family members. For example, to pressure a 20-year-old man to work and leave home when he has little education, no marketable skills, and problems with goal-directedness is unrealistic.

We usually opt for a series of interventions that prepare for eventual parent–child separation. First we opt for a strategy that decreases family isolation. We might involve a community resource such as the church, or we might encourage participation in a multiple-family group or a mothers' group. As the work to decrease family isolation proceeds, we might help arrange for a training program for any member of the family ready to learn a new skill. Finally, we might build on early successes by supporting the patient's age-appropriate independence via a move to a local supervised residence.

One of the cases admitted recently was as follows:

The family consisted of a single mother with two schizophrenic children—a 19-year-old daughter who spent more than a year in her room, probably as a result of paranoid delusions, and a 20-year-old son with extensive antisocial destructive behavior related to paranoid and grandiose delusions. The daughter was referred to the day hospital, and the son was briefly hospitalized on an inpatient service.

In early sessions the therapist supported the mother in making generational boundaries, reasonable rules, and consequences for dysfunctional behavior. When the daughter refused to attend the day hospital, her television privileges were suspended and the mother was encouraged to lock her daughter out of the apartment during the day. Appropriate medication was prescribed to both children, and when they refused to cooperate, the mother gave approval for fluphenazine injections. Medicaid, welfare, and Supplemental Security Income (SSI) problems were handled by the family, with the support of the therapist. As mother began to succeed, the father (who was a migrant worker, divorced from his wife for many years) was invited to some sessions to support her when the son's behavior became too aggressive. When the son was found smoking marijuana, the father agreed to watch him during the day for the few weeks that the father was living in the city.

As the family chaos decreased and psychotic behavior diminished, interventions focused on enmeshment. A series of enactments were choreographed to encourage the children to talk for themselves in an age-appropriate manner. A series of individual sessions with the mother supported her desire to socialize and particularly to date a male friend. As the children tested the new order with provocative behavior, the therapist humored the family, reminded the mother of the agreed-upon consequences for broken rules, and wondered aloud if she could survive without something to worry about. Later sessions were mainly devoted to work with the mother. The children were referred to a training program, and the mother was helped to find a new job.

Although this mother and her children were highly involved, the demands for survival allowed them little practice in helping to meet one another's emotional needs. It is now possible for them to participate together in some mutually satisfying activities, such as visits to relatives.

Disengaged Family Styles

While we are indebted to a variety of theorists for useful ways of intervening in enmeshed families, the fact is that we see a large number of seemingly disengaged families.

While schizophrenia is a burden for all families, the availability of resources, stability, and larger networks shields the middle and upper classes from some of the pressures prevalent in the inner city. Ultimately, the result of schizophrenia for many of our patients is alienation from their families. State hospitals and single-room-occupancy (SRO) hotels are populated with people in this situation, and it seems imperative to conceptualize family strategies for them. Effective work requires a series of interventions to help the patient become part of a family, to stimulate nurturant contacts, and to increase networks. There is no use working on "leaving home" when so many of our patients have no sense of where "home" is.

We usually confront underinvolvement in two forms: (1) the family alienated from the patient and/or the mental health system; and (2) the family that is nonexistent, for all practical purposes.

For the family in which the members refuse to come in or to support the patient's treatment, it is vital that clinicians be supported in reaching out—usually a time-consuming process. In this situation, the middle phase of treatment involves an elaboration of joining efforts begun in the first phase; it is hoped that these efforts create a nurturant social structure for the *family*, as well as the patient. Home visits may be necessary. Lengthy "sessions" on the phone are often a useful strategy. For families disposed to verbal interventions, a carefully worded letter can be a force for change. It may be necessary to stop treatment of the patient temporarily as a way of pressing for family participation. We prefer having demonstrated our ability to be of help before using such a strategy, but sometimes a family's lack of involvement in treatment needs to be challenged early in treatment if the clinician is to make a difference.

When family members do come in, we usually find them expecting blame and feeling enormous impotence. A useful strategy is to find some simple ways in which the family can be helpful and in which mutual satisfaction can occur. Michael Goldstein's brief psychoeducational method (Goldstein *et al.*, 1978) is a sensible way to help these families grasp the seriousness of the psychosis, to relieve some of the stigma, and to present some practical solutions.

As an example of our work with underinvolvement, our clinic has been involved with the family of a 35-year-old Black man for the past 6 years. Prior to coming to our clinic, the patient had been hospitalized in the state hospital system for 11 consecutive years. We considered his transition to the community an acute problem appropriate for our day hospital program.

Initially the family refused to come in and refused to allow a home visit; the patient's mother repeatedly told the therapist that she was overwhelmed with her five children, three of whom had experienced psychotic episodes. We decided to allow the patient to continue in the day hospital without family sessions as an inducement to the family to remain connected to the therapist. Finally, with the agreement of the mother, one of the patient's sisters attended family sessions. This sister remained a steady ally throughout the first year of treatment. As a strategy for increasing the patient's network, the patient and his sister joined a multiple-family group. During the succeeding 5 years numerous crises were handled by phone interventions between the therapist and the mother or the therapist and the sister. The patient lived with both his sister and his mother. He has worked performing errands for a sheltered workshop program for the past 4 years.

Another strategy available with many of our isolated female clients is to solidify their role as mothers when circumstances allow. Play therapy involving a mother and her child, parental education, a mothers' group, and enactments allowing the patient to succeed in the mothering role are all strategies that counter disengagement. So often children of our patients are placed in foster homes or become the responsibility of other family members. We usually strive to keep our mothers involved with their children on some level, even though therapists in the public sector may be required by law to decide whether a schizophrenic mother is "capable" of mothering.

A second form of disengagement, and an even more difficult treatment challenge, is the nonexistent family—the situation of the person truly isolated from any network. In such circumstances, structure and nurturance must be created by an energetic therapist. A quasi-family must be found or built from the ground up. An example of a recent case involved a woman in her 20s with a particularly persistent set of paranoid delusions. Her family, living in another state, had virtually disowned her. She was wily enough to survive in the streets for months at a time; however, her relationships were transient, and she had been regularly readmitted to our program, usually after another stay in the state hospital. A particularly persistent therapist got her into a local residence for psychiatric patients, despite her protestations. The therapist moved quickly to hold a series of "family" sessions with the house parent, the patient, and a peer she chose for support. Questions of limit setting were handled in a common-sense fashion, and the woman's most difficult behaviors were effectively handled. A treatment that was failing for almost a year dramatically changed, once this woman became secure in a clearly organized and supportive social environment. She is now successfully involved in a training program and attending aftercare sessions.

THIRD PHASE

In the final phase of our work, we shift to an arrangement that allows for attenuated and long-term involvement. We do this simply because we observe that acute states recur, that they are increasingly debilitating, that teaching a family to manage them effectively requires time and availability, and that the limited resources in the community potentiate disorganization.

The timing and form of this maintenance phase derive as much from the economics of the public sector as from clinical considerations. We begin this phase at the point when the client is completing the day program (this averages 6 months for our clients) and has been able to make plans for a daily routine that does not define him or her solely as a patient. Most clients from our day program opt to pursue work, vocational training, or schooling.

As soon as seems reasonable after discharge, we end regular family sessions and leave the door open for sessions at a later date if either the family or the therapist feels they are needed. Ongoing treatment from this point is done primarily with the former day hospital client, either individually or in a group of former clients. We work to hold treatment contacts weekly in a form that suits the economics of our service. The backbone of our aftercare program is the "Keep-in-Touch Club," an evening socialization group held weekly; several other ongoing groups have been developed recently, including a psychoeducational multiple-family group. These are supplemented by individual sessions for therapy and medication evaluation at intervals that are manageable for the clinicians. Frequent contacts help to support the interpersonal involvement that schizophrenia erodes, to interrupt social withdrawal before it arises. The simple awareness that these contacts occur can help a family moderate its tendency to fix anxiously on any erratic behavior of the patient.

The central task in this phase of treatment is the development of a therapeutic context within which our clients can make thoughtful choices about their treatment and about their lives. The therapist must have a grasp of a client's social context and must understand the meaning of treatment recommendations in light of the client's life situation, not simply the state of his or her illness. The therapist's posture in this phase makes a substantial shift from the somewhat authoritarian directiveness of the initial phase. The medium in the third phase is dialogue, and the emphasis is not simply on symptom control but on the larger issue of quality of life experience. A therapist's honest efforts to understand the meaning of a client's struggle with schizophrenia and poverty is among his or her most compelling therapeutic tools.

While the steps for minimizing recurrence in schizophrenia are rather simple, they are frequently ignored, particularly by the schizophrenic poor. Two of the most significant choices a client makes that affect his or her vulnerability to recurrence in schizophrenia pertain to the use of medication and to daily activities. The value of psychotropic medication in containing subacute symptoms and preventing acute episodes is well established, but the tendency of clients is to stop using medication after the acute symptoms diminish. While this might be explained by simple denial or discomfort with side effects, the stigma that clients feel is attached to medication is another factor they often bring to our attention. Time and again, a client will respond as if medication were itself the illness. It seems that negative feelings about accepting schizophrenia as a chronic illness become funneled into the ritual of taking pills. We have come to appreciate the value of group therapy as a modality for securing compliance with medication and handling issues of stigma. Peer support seems to make treatment easier to follow.

The very effectiveness of medication in preventing symptoms can produce an unexpected effect. Though painful and humiliating, the intensity of psychotic experience can provide diversion from a life of poverty and a history of repeated failure. Freedom from symptoms means a change in lifestyle; becoming "responsible" can require a new identity. Clients need support in facing the challenge and frustrations that improved functioning can pose.

Another factor that complicates the choice of long-term medication for the schizophrenic poor is its inevitable comparison to drug addiction. Parents raising children in poverty have wisely cultivated strong negative attitudes toward any mood- or mind-related drug. Because avoidance of drug addiction is essential to survival in the inner city, this is a strong and rigidly held precept. Education of the family takes on additional importance in this light, but the individual's use of medicine after the need is no longer in evidence may only be accepted very slowly by those in his or her network.

Daily activity poses a second set of important choices for our clients. The ways in which a person spends his or her waking hours has a major influence on his or her identity and sense of competence, as well as his or her disposition to schizophrenic recurrence. It is an issue in which questions of treatment and those of quality of life seem to converge.

The properties of daily activity that seem to provide the best protection from acute psychotic disorganization are structure, predictability, and some insulation from family contact. Work, job training, school, and volunteer activities are all choices that can offer a sense of achievement. They discourage the withdrawal that usually precedes a relapse into psychosis, and so our aftercare programs tend to promote their choosing some activity. However, the meaning and availability of these choices are substantially different, depending on whether a client comes from white, middle-class, or poor/minority circumstances. A therapist in our setting soon becomes aware that for the schizophrenic poor, work and school are scarce commodities and must compete with other available types of daily activity. Women often become involved in family roles of sharing the care of a large number of children with their mothers, despite the fact that this particular lifestyle can amplify enmeshment where the tendency exists. Street life is often the most available source of stimulation, status, and financial reward for a man, although it is stressful, unstructured and highly unpredictable. When we encourage our clients toward work, job training, or school, it must be with an understanding of these realities. The advantages of emotional stability and longer-term economic gain will have meaning only if a client is presented with an understanding of the full range of choices. The therapist must always begin by asking clients what will help them make sense of their own lives. He must not promote his or her own life choices, but neither should he accept clients' resignation or apathy.

SUMMARY

The problem of schizophrenia in the poverty of the inner city is particularly resistant to traditional interventions. It must be understood in its relationship to several levels of context, including the biological, the familial, and the societal. This chapter presents a view of schizophrenia in poverty that focuses on the deficits in effective organization at these various levels, which sustain the symptoms of the illness.

A three-phase model is presented for the treatment of the schizophrenic poor and their families. The first phase examines the special issues of joining with poor families and presents some structural techniques for reducing symptoms by improving family organization. In the second phase, families are challenged to expand their adaptational patterns, with particular attention to forms of family organization that tend toward overinvolvement or underinvolvement. The treatment of the completely isolated individual is also considered. In the third phase, the focus is on using long-term contact to help individuals with schizophrenia make helpful decisions about their treatment and their lives.

REFERENCES

Anderson, C. M., Hogarty, G. E., & Reiss, D. J. Family treatment of adult schizophrenic patients: A psychoeducational approach. *Schizophrenia Bulletin*, 1980, *6*, 490–505.
Aponte, H. The family–school interview: An eco-structural approach. *Family Process*, 1976, *15*, 303–311. (a)
Aponte, H. Underorganization in the poor family. In P. Guerin (Ed.), *Family therapy: Theory and practice*. New York: Gardner Press, 1976. (b)
Auerswald, E. H. Interdisciplinary versus ecological approach. *Family Process*, 1968, 205–215.
Goldstein, M. J., Rodnick, E. H., Evans, J. R., May, P. R. A., & Steinberg, M. R. Drug and family therapy in the aftercare of acute schizophrenics. *Archives of General Psychiatry*, 1978, *35*, 1169–1177.
Haley, J. *Leaving home*. New York: McGraw-Hill, 1980.

Leff, J. P. Developments in family treatment of schizophrenia. *Psychiatric Quarterly*, 1979, *51*(3), 216–232.

Madanes, C. The prevention of rehospitalization of adolescents and young adults. *Family Process*, 1980, *19*, 179–191.

Minuchin, S. *Families and family therapy*. Cambridge, Mass.: Harvard University Press, 1974.

Minuchin, S., & Fishman, C. *Techniques of family therapy*. New York: Basic Books, 1981.

Minuchin, S., Montalvo, B., Guerney, B., Rosman, B., & Shumer, F. *Families of the slums*. New York: Basic Books, 1967.

Mishler, E. G., & Scotch, N. A. Sociocultural factors in the epidemiology of schizophrenia. *Psychiatry*, 1963, *26*, 315–351.

Selvini-Palazzoli, M., Cecchin, G., Boscolo, L., & Prata, G. Hypothesizing–circularity–neutrality: Three guidelines for the conductor of the session. *Family Process*, 1980, *19*, 3–12.

VI
TOWARD A SYNTHESIS

14

FAMILY RESEARCH IN SCHIZOPHRENIA: A REVIEW AND INTEGRATION FOR CLINICIANS

William R. McFarlane
C. Christian Beels

While the dominant theme throughout this volume has been family therapy, many clinicians may be curious about the status of recent basic research on family processes in schizophrenia. As has been noted in the Introduction, the idea that unique family processes cause schizophrenia has been all but discarded by most thoughtful figures in the field. However, family research has focused on many issues besides that of etiology. A number of other questions, most of them of greater clinical significance, have recently been addressed in a systematic way, using more rigorous research methodology. Some of these questions include the following:

- The effects on families of having schizophrenic members.
- The effects on patients of family responses to the illness.
- The degree of difference between families of schizophrenics.
- The specificity to schizophrenia of factors such as "expressed emotion" (EE) and "communication deviance" (CD).
- The relative importance of these factors to the clinical status of the patient.

This chapter presents a brief and highly selected survey of the more reliable research findings on these issues. These data have been important in the design of many of the therapies described herein. We have also included a proposed model for describing interactions among family variables. It may be hoped that such a model will guide the clinician in his or her thinking about the family therapy of schizophrenia.

WILLIAM R. MCFARLANE and C. CHRISTIAN BEELS. Department of Psychiatry, College of Physicians and Surgeons of Columbia University, and New York State Psychiatric Institute, New York, New York.

KEY FAMILY CHARACTERISTICS

The following discussion leaves largely untouched the question of a family etiology for the disorder, a topic that has been reviewed by Liem (1980) and Wynne (1981) and that a recent report by Doane, West, Goldstein, Rodnick, and Jones (1981) seems to clarify somewhat. The following assumes the validity of the large volume of research pointing to a major biological contribution to, if not an etiology for, schizophrenia, as well as the validity of studies suggesting that it is a syndrome with heterogeneous forms, presentations, course, causes, and treatments (Wyatt, Cutler, DeLisi, Jeste, Kleinman, Luchins, Potkin, & Weinberger, 1982). We assume, further, that it is a multidetermined phenomenon with contributing factors at the biological, psychological, and social levels of analysis, as described by Scheflen (1981).

A small number of studies, most of them recent, shed light on the queston of whether there are any family characteristics that are specific to schizophrenia. At present, it appears that at least four (probably interrelated) family processes can be *correlated* with chronic schizophrenia, but none of them appear to be *unique* or *specific* to the condition. The four factors we describe here seem to be influential in the course of a given case, while it remains to be demonstrated whether any are preexisting determinants of the onset. We outline these factors in order of their increasing specificity to schizophrenia.

FAMILY ENMESHMENT

A discussion of the importance of enmeshment in families of schizophrenics begins with the concept of EE. In an original study (Brown, Monck, Carstairs, & Wing, 1962), then in a replication (Brown, Birley, & Wing, 1972), and more recently in the work of Vaughn and Leff (1976), a constellation of family interactional and emotional phenomena has been consistently linked with the schizophrenic patient's tendency to relapse, apparent need for medication, and vulnerability to "life events." The primary components of high EE are criticism and overinvolvement (overprotectiveness, excessive attention, and prolonged face-to-face contact) (see Leff, Berkowitz, & Kuipers, Chapter 7 of this volume). The source of the parent's tendencies for overinvolved, critical behavior toward the patient is not yet identified, although disappointment, displacement, loneliness, and marital discord have been proposed. Anderson, in Chapter 4 of this volume, has posited a more circular, yet simple, explanation: The high-EE parents are those with high expectations, whose criticism and overinvolvement can be understood as dogged, poorly informed attempts to make their patient/offspring well, with alternating periods of frustration and resentment arising out of their obvious failure to succeed. It is crucial to note that the high-EE construct is utterly *non*specific to schizophrenia. Depressed patients seem even more sensitive to the effects of these kinds of interactions than are schizophrenics (Leff & Vaughn, 1980).

The expansion of the EE concept to that of enmeshment requires explanation. Minuchin (1974), refining earlier ideas such as Bowen's "undifferentiated ego mass," Bateson's "double-bind" hypothesis (the inability to leave the interactive field), and Boszormenyi-Nagy's "family loyalty," has proposed "enmeshment" as a central, comprehensive, and common characteristic of dysfunctional families. It shares with EE an emphasis on overcloseness, poorly defined intrafamily boundaries, and high emotional reactivity and intensity. Communication problems are implied in both concepts, as are inadequate problem solving and conflict resolution. While the overlap is not complete, clinical experience strongly suggests that the two constructs describe a common set of characteristics in many severely disturbed families. Vaughn and Leff (1981) have recently refined the concept of EE by specifying four associated behavioral characteristics: (1) intrusiveness, (2) anger and/or acute distress and anxiety, (3) overt blame of the patient, and (4) marked intolerance of symptoms and long-term impairment. This elaboration brings the two concepts very close indeed.

We have chosen to see EE and enmeshment as similar in an attempt to bring the British work and the American family therapy field into closer alignment, and also to suggest that some techniques for creating disenmeshment are similar to those for reducing EE. Enmeshment, as a concept, is more systemic (everyone in the family is affected by it), and it is less blaming (everyone is *equally* entrapped in the process; therefore no one is necessarily at fault). Enmeshment and EE are the opposite of that other equally dangerous state of families of schizophrenics: "disattention" or "disengagement," in Minuchin's terms, which, Wing (1978) has noted, leads to the negative symptoms of patient withdrawal and apathy.

FAMILY ISOLATION

The common observation that many families with schizophrenic members seem more socially isolated has been partially confirmed by studies of social networks. Brown and his colleagues (1972) noted that 20% of the families in their study were both extremely isolated and high on the EE rating. Another 50% were moderately isolated and showed consistently higher EE than did the 30% who seemed to have low levels of isolation. Of course, family isolation in this way correlated strongly with relapse rate and need for medication. Hammer (1963–1964) had noted earlier that those patients whose friends and family members were known to one another tended to keep those relationships intact after hospitalizations, compared with those without such "dense" (i.e., interconnected) networks. Tolsdorf (1976) found that schizophrenics at first admission had smaller, more family-based, and more "asymmetrical" (giving less than what is received) networks than medical patients. This tendency has been noted in several studies by Pattison, Llamas, and Hurd (1979), who have defined a "psychotic-level" network strongly associated with acute and chronic schizophrenia— that is, a network about half the normal size, composed predominately of immediate family members who in turn appear more involved with the patient and each other than with nonrelated friends or neighbors, although this apparent family isolation was not measured directly. Garrison (1978), studying Puerto Rican women in New York City, found an inverse relationship between degree of psychopathology and the size (and type) of network of the patient; in the schizophrenics' families, the relatives seemed almost as isolated and withdrawn as the patients were. A related finding is that the constriction of networks noted at or just prior to the first episode is much magnified by that episode itself and by the burdens imposed by the subsequent course. There is evidence that *being* schizophrenic induces network contraction and condensation for the patient and, to a lesser extent, for the family (Lipton, Cohen, Fischer, & Katz, 1981). For family members, this probably results from their own preoccupation with the patient and a certain degree of withdrawal from and by friends and more distant relatives.

It seems, then, that families with schizophrenic members are often isolated, but at present such a conclusion is tempered by at least three qualifications: (1) direct data on the socializing of family members are quite limited; (2) not all families are isolated; and (3) some isolation certainly is a *result* of the onset of schizophrenia and cannot be considered an independent contributor. Family isolation probably worsens course as a result of association with higher degrees of EE or enmeshment. It should be noted that family isolation is not specific to schizophrenia, but of all the syndromes studied, schizophrenia is associated with the most extreme degrees of isolation that have been found.

Isolation of the family assumes significance when one considers the functions of a social network. Hammer (1981) has emphasized social and instrumental support, access to others, mediation of information, the placing of demands, and the imposition of constraints, all of which are essential in dealing with a chronic mental disability. Dean and Lin, in their review (1977), concluded that lack of social support markedly increases vulnerability to ordinary stressors in both medical and psychiatric illness. This reflects the common clinical observation that events primarily affecting a patient's relative may be precipitants to a relapse, because that relative turns to the patient for support, rather than to more intact but less available members of the network.

It is important to remember that the family is not simply a noxious influence, as many clinicians have been led to believe. Steinberg and Durell (1968) found that *separation from* the family, for both military recruits and college students, was the most frequent precipitant of the initial episode in very large samples. Thus, the family emerges as a major source of protective support *and* stressful interaction; the family's social support may be one of the differentiating variables, the lack of it making everyone, especially the schizophrenic, more vulnerable to stress.

The social network of the family may have characteristics that have positive or negative effects on the course of illness, probably through effects on the family's ability to cope, as well as on EE. Social support also includes contributions from the culture at large, especially its expectations of the roles of work, of sickness, and so on. These effects are suggested by several lines of investigation. The best evidence that support affects course comes from cross-cultural studies (Waxler, 1979) showing that, for example, although the lifetime risk of schizophrenia is about the same the world over, its course is more benign in developing nonindustrialized cultures with a village social structure. An American example is Midelfort's work in a traditional Lutheran farming community in Wisconsin (see Chapter 1). He achieved high social function and a very low rate of rehospitalization in a group of schizophrenics treated with a nonspecific form of family therapy. The combination of a supportive family approach, available social and occupational roles (supported by farm life and family structure), exceptional continuity of care (provided by the low mobility of both the community and the clinic staff), and a congruent religious ideology seems to make an important difference. There are some contexts, then, where social support for the family is built into the local culture. Where it is not available, the treatment context may have to provide that support.

FAMILY COMMUNICATION DEVIANCE

A large body of research evidence has accumulated suggesting that many families, even in the absence of their schizophrenic members, tend to communicate in ways that are more fragmented or amorphous than do families without ill members (Liem, 1980; Singer, Wynne, & Toohey, 1978). More specifically, many parents of schizophrenics tend to communicate with each other using odd, ambiguous, or idiosyncratic language, allowing the focus of conversation to drift tangentially, with the introduction of illogical thoughts. That is, their conversational style has a formal structure reminiscent of schizophrenic thinking and speech, but to a much less obvious or pathological degree. This family characteristic is more specific to schizophrenia than those described previously, but commonly occurs in the nonpsychotic schizophrenia-spectrum disorders (Hirsch & Leff, 1975). The possibility that this phenomenon is a subclinical expression of an underlying heritable disorder has yet to be investigated.

For those primarily concerned with clinical practice, the complex issue of the etiological significance of CD may seem less important than whether it affects course or is modifiable. As has been repeatedly indicated, the answer to the etiology question depends on long-term, longitudinal, prospective studies and the careful separation of many possible confounding variables, all major and difficult undertakings. However, one prospective study has shown that this characteristic can be found in most families that subsequently have schizophrenic members, 5 years or more before onset. The combination of CD *and* the presence of a poor "affective style" (which the authors equate with high EE) predicts quite accurately for schizophrenic psychosis, again 5 years in advance (Doane *et al.*, 1981). (These are preliminary results in a large and ongoing study, and could be invalidated by the outcome of other cases yet to reach the 5-year interval; they should be interpreted cautiously.) There are no data that elucidate the relationship of CD to overall course. As to its modifiability, only the unreported clinical experience of many multiple-family therapists and that of Falloon and Liberman (see Chapter 5 of this volume) suggest that one can improve or normalize CD.

Other aspects of family communication beyond CD are relevant. It is almost a given that families with any sort of psychiatric problem have some sort of communication difficulty: blaming; double meaning and double binding (Sluzki & Veron, 1971); speaking for others; failing to listen; distorting meaning; interrupting; and so on. Families with schizophrenic members are no exception, so these more general communication problems may be superimposed on the more specific CD. Further, if one accepts that double-binding interactions can create distorted, even irrational, communication, then many "therapeutic" situations can be seen as pathogenic: For instance, covert blame of the family by professionals is often combined with overt attempts to help them, while the contradiction is denied (Appleton, 1974). Finally, Hammer, Makiesky-Barrow, and Gutwirth (1978) have suggested that social isolation may contribute to communication dysfunction.

FAMILY STIGMA AND BURDEN

Rabkin (1974) reviewed the literature on the stigma of mental illness and concluded that only slight progress had been made in reducing the degree of revulsion and contempt the public feels toward the mentally ill. In view of the public rejection of patients, it is remarkable that most families do not report *feeling* stigmatized by the emergence of schizophrenia in one of their members (Freeman & Simmons, 1961). On the other hand, many family members attempt to conceal the presence of the illness from friends and more distant relatives and, in many cases, drop friends following the initial episode (Yarrow, Clausen, & Robbins, 1955). Lamb and Oliphant (1978) reported that many parents found it difficult to talk to other parents about their children's achievements—simply because the contrast was too painful—and gradually saw less of them. While the data are in some conflict, the conclusion can reasonably be drawn that a patient's family members do not automatically *feel* stigmatized but often *behave* as if they do, and that friends and relatives do tend to avoid them as if they are stigmatized. Kreisman and Joy (1974) have pointed out that the discrepancy between subjective reports and objective reality may be partly explained by the length of the illness (relatives of first-break patients may feel worse and withdraw more than those of chronic patients) and by the tendency of most people to underreport negative affects. The common assumption that families play a role in causing schizophrenia is probably a significant contributor to the stigma that family members receive and feel. From these studies, it seems possible to assume that every family will at some time be dealing with some aspect of stigmatization.

A related aspect of the family's situation is the burden imposed by having a schizophrenic relative. Here, again, it is useful to differentiate subjective and objective components. The difficulties patients pose for their families are multiple (Grad & Sainsbury, 1963; Herz, Endicott, & Spitzer, 1976; Hoenig & Hamilton, 1969; Myers & Bean, 1968). In general, however, most objectively burdened families complain little about their problems to researchers. Very few translate their complaints into outright rejection and abandonment. The most common elements include economic drain, sleep disruption, interferences with daily routine, tension from fear of unpredictable behavior and from difficulties in communication, and strained family relationships. Parents, especially, appear to resent having become captives of the situation. In poorer families, the tendencies for rejection are more pronounced, apparently because they feel more stigmatized and their burden is more intolerable, given their limited resources (Kelman, 1964).

The meaning of the illness may constitute a source of subjective burden. Many families react with a sense of defeat, as if the entire family has undergone a major change in its worth as a result of the illness, accompanied by feelings of guilt, inadequacy, and anger. Disappointment and even depression follow the realization that the potential of the patient is no longer what the family had hoped. The subtly blaming treatment that relatives too often receive in psychiatric hospitals and clinics rarely alleviates any of these feelings. The lack of education and guidance from professionals contributes to the family's sense of confusion and helplessness (see Hatfield, Chapter 2 of this volume).

Thus, a picture emerges that families may *be* burdened and stigmatized, and may *feel* so as well, in combinations that may be complex and idiosyncratic. These problems produce strains that are relatively specific to schizophrenia, though they are clearly and primarily consequences, not causes. When present, it is likely that they predispose the patient to a degree of increased risk of relapse and incomplete recovery.

INTERACTIONS OF FAMILY FACTORS
ASSOCIATED WITH SCHIZOPHRENIA

Given that the research on the factors reviewed is in many cases still under way, it is too early to demonstrate any conclusive relationships among them. What is needed is multivariate study of the family to see if there are indeed regular patterns of correlation. In the meantime, we are proposing here a heuristic model that, at least, is consistent with what is known and seems to follow from clinical experience and simple logic (see Figure 1).

To begin with, the reader may recall that there are data showing that high EE and family isolation coexist (Brown *et al.*, 1972), as do EE and CD (Doane *et al.*, 1981). There is suggestive evidence that stigma and burden tend to go with social isolation of the family. Two correlation pairs (CD–EE, EE–isolation) tend to be associated with a poorer outcome for the patient. Although it has been suggested that CD is more severe in socially isolated families, there seems to be no direct data on the question. We are left with syllogizing: If CD correlates with EE, and EE with isolation, then CD probably correlates with isolation.

The interactions proposed here are almost entirely positive feedback processes, in which a change in one factor will tend to induce change in the others, all in the direction of poorer functioning. Clearly, at some point an equilibrium would have to be reached, whether through a crisis and hospitalization or through stabilizing adjustments in the family, such as the patient's withdrawing from contact.

The interaction between isolation and enmeshment can be seen as a manifestation of a single systems characteristic: a relatively impermeable

FIGURE 1. *Interactions of key family phenomena in schizophrenia.*

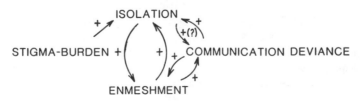

family boundary. In everyday terms, this implies that if one is preoccupied with intrafamily problems—especially a mentally ill child—one may tend to see less of the rest of one's network. Conversely, others will tend to see less of those who seem to be more involved with each other and offer less by way of social exchange (Beels, 1981). It is a circular or, over time, a "helical" process.

The same kind of circularity describes the interaction of enmeshment and CD. For instance, family members must be able to communicate clearly and to maintain a focus of attention in order to disentangle an enmeshed relationship. Conversely, enmeshment, which almost always includes interruptions of dyadic conversations, will tend to exacerbate any coexisting communication difficulties. The interaction of both factors will result in incomplete, anxious, tangential, and confusing transactions.

With respect to isolation and CD, one would expect that the latter tends to be exacerbated when family members have less exposure to the rest of the (presumably) less deviant communicational world. Conversely, CD itself is probably a stimulus for the avoidance of and by the more peripheral members of a high-CD family. It is our impression that communication patterns outside the family may be less comprehensible to some families of schizophrenics and, as a result, anxiety- and withdrawal-provoking. Anthropology provides several examples of the deviation of language and other aspects of culture in subgroups that have remained semi-isolated for a period of time.

Finally, stigma and burden, while having many effects, seem from the data primarily to lead to isolation, at least in some families. This is only stating the obvious: Most people who are simultaneously feeling ashamed, defensive, rejected, and overwhelmed will be somewhat socially withdrawn, as well as socially avoided.

As present, an account of the relationship of each of these factors to a presumed constitutional vulnerability (i.e., an illness, narrowly defined) is quite complex and at some points speculative. Taken one by one, the following points emerge:

1. Enmeshment (EE) is a coincidental factor, completely *nonspecific*, yet has a powerful *effect on* course of illness.
2. Isolation may predate the initial episode, thus perhaps *contributing* in a minor way to the onset of the illness, while it is clearly *exacerbated by* the social processes that follow from it.
3. CD, in the presence of enmeshment, may be a *contributing factor to* onset, while it has been speculated that it is at least partially an *effect of* an underlying heritable disorder.
4. Stigma and burden have to be considered an *effect* of the patient's illness, yet *highly specific* to it.

None of these factors appear to be uniquely specific to schizophrenia, yet the convergence of all four in one family would be likely to occur in association with schizophrenia. Note that the converse is not true, from research to date: Schizophrenia will not *necessarily* be associated with any one factor, or even with all four together.

OTHER KEY DIMENSIONS:
THE PATIENT AND THE TREATMENT SYSTEM

There are a few nonfamily factors and considerations that, while not as well researched as the factors just described, should be included in any design for a family treatment.

CONSTITUTION AND COURSE

We look first at the schizophrenic patient, as an individual with a disorder. Family treatment is bound to be different, depending on whether one is dealing with a first episode of psychosis that will not recur (not truly schizophrenia, according to the *Diagnostic and Statistical Manual of Mental Disorders*, 3rd edition—DSM-III); a schizoaffective or atypical affective disorder with good interval functioning; or a slowly deteriorating and dementing course with minimal social function. If for no other reason, these considerations need to be made explicit, because the family needs to know as much as the professionals do (or how little that is) if they are to be fully involved in planning and carrying out the treatment. The various therapies described in this volume are based on somewhat divergent views about the issue of constitution and how it affects family therapy.

RESISTANCE–COMPLIANCE AND IDEOLOGY

An idea that appears frequently in the family therapy literature—"family resistance"—refers to the quality of the relationship between the family and the treatment organization. From the beginning of the family therapy movement, much has been written about the ability of families to outwit and defeat therapeutic efforts. This concept of resistance is beginning to be seen, like all definitions of relationship, as having two sides, especially with respect to schizophrenia. That is, the treatment organization and its ideology may contribute as much as the family does to the phenomenon of resistance.

In the welter of arguments about the treatment of schizophrenia, we discern two opposing ideologies, which have been called the "medical model" and the "communications model." They are not mutually exclusive, and most thoughtful practitioners acknowledge and use aspects of both. Treatment programs, however, are often dominated by one or the other, simply because some kinds of treatment are most easily carried out with one or the other in mind. Roughly, the medical model sees schizophrenia as a collection of psychiatric syndromes occurring in constitutionally vulnerable people. It regards diagnosis as important, and medication and hospitalization as helpful in the acute phase. The communications model lumps schizophrenia together with many other severe problems of youth, such as addiction or anorexia; calls them all problems of differentiation within the family system; and avoids diagnosis, medication, and hospitalization as all tending to victimize and/or institutionalize the patient in the sick role.

As is perhaps evident to the reader of preceding chapters, family therapies based on the medical model seem to assume that, given adequate sympathy and support, the family will comply with a good program. Their agendas are rather "linear" and behavioral. Communications strategies, on the other hand, are designed to overcome resistance on someone's part, either the patient's (as in strategic family therapy) or the whole family's (as in systemic family therapy). We suggest that it is important to distinguish resistance, which comes from the family's defensiveness, from iatrogenic uncooperativeness, which comes from the therapy system's inept induction of guilt and resentment. A truly resistant family, to us, is one that has rejected a well-designed program based on the medical model. Such resistance may be an indication for a strategic or systemic approach. However, it should be noted that the ideology of these intensive approaches may, in some cases, *provoke* resistance in more cooperative families.

Finally, though there is no systematic evidence for the next point, a hypothesis we frequently have heard advanced by clinicians is that there is a connection between diagnosis and compliance. That is, the families that offer the most therapeutic difficulty tend to be those in which the patients are less "truly" schizophrenic, having severe borderline or other character disorders. This trend, if true, would be consistent with the success that family therapies based on the medical model report with well-diagnosed chronic cases. It is also consistent with the tendency of therapists working within the communications model to lump their successful "schizophrenic" cases with their successful cases of addiction, delinquency, and anorexia.

These factors and dimensions are complexly interrelated with reference to family therapy. In the following chapter, we have used them as indications for the various approaches to family intervention in schizophrenia. As for the factors themselves, their relationship to each other and to schizophrenia as presented here is only beginning to become clear. The rest of the story may well emerge over the next decade. In the meantime, one can readily appreciate that the correlation of any one factor or dimension to schizophrenia says very little about the direction of causality, or even whether the concept of causation is relevant. Caution remains the best policy in this area. The fact that schizophrenia, on the basis of existing research data, will not be necessarily associated with any family factor (or even constellation of factors) seems to us to require the abandonment of the term and concept of the "schizophrenic family," since it has usually implied that an identifiable type of family will be uniquely and ubiquitously associated with schizophrenia. Our multivariate model, while more complex, seems a more accurate reflection of the situation. The trade between simplicity and accuracy may well be the price that must be paid to achieve a reliable advance in our understanding of the schizophrenic process.

REFERENCES

Appleton, W. S. Mistreatment of patients' families by psychiatrists. *American Journal of Psychiatry*, 1974, *131*, 655–657.

Beels, C. C. Social support and schizophrenia. *Schizophrenia Bulletin*, 1981, *7*, 58–72.

Brown, G. W., Birley, J. L. T., & Wing, J. K. Influence of family life on the course of schizophrenic disorders: A replication. *British Journal of Psychiatry*, 1972, *121*, 241–258.

Brown, G. W., Monck, E. M., Carstairs, G. M., & Wing, J. K. Influence of family life on the course of schizophrenic illness. *British Journal of Psychiatry*, 1962, *16*, 55–68.

Dean, A., & Lin, N. The stress-buffering role of social support. *Journal of Nervous and Mental Disease*, 1977, *165*, 403–416.

Doane, J. A., West, K. L., Goldstein, M. J., Rodnick, E. H., & Jones, J. E. Parental communication deviance and affective style. *Archives of General Psychiatry*, 1981, *38*, 679–685.

Freeman, H., & Simmons, O. Feelings of stigma among relatives of former mental patients. *Social Problems*, 1961, *8*, 312–321.

Garrison, V. Support systems of schizophrenic and nonschizophrenic Puerto Rican women in New York City. *Schizophrenia Bulletin*, 1978, *4*, 561–596.

Grad, J., & Sainsbury, P. Mental illness and the family. *Lancet*, 1963, *1*, 533–547.

Hammer, M. Influence of small social networks as factors on mental hospital admission. *Human Organization*, 1963–1964, *22*, 243–251.

Hammer, M. Social supports, social networks, and schizophrenia. *Schizophrenia Bulletin*, 1981, *7*, 45–57.

Hammer, M., Makiesky-Barrow, S., & Gutwirth, L. Social networks and schizophrenia. *Schizophrenia Bulletin*, 1978, *4*, 522–545.

Herz, M. I., Endicott, J., & Spitzer, R. L. Brief versus standard hospitalization: The families. *American Journal of Psychiatry*, 1976, *133*, 795–801.

Hirsch, S. R., & Leff, J. P. *Abnormalities in parents of schizophrenics*. London: Oxford University Press, 1975.

Hoenig, J., & Hamilton, M. *The desegregation of the mentally ill*. London: Routledge & Kegan Paul, 1969.

Kelman, H. The effect of a brain-damaged child on the family. In H. G. Birch (Ed.), *Brain damage in children*. Baltimore: Williams & Wilkins, 1964.

Kreisman, D. E., & Joy, V. D. Family response to the mental illness of a relative: A review of the literature. *Schizophrenia Bulletin*, 1974, *10*, 35–57.

Lamb, H. R., & Oliphant, E. Schizophrenia through the eyes of families. *Hospital and Community Psychiatry*, 1978, *29*, 803–806.

Leff, J., & Vaughn, C. E. The interaction of life events and relatives' expressed emotion in schizophrenia and depressive neurosis. *British Journal of Psychiatry*, 1980, *136*, 146–153.

Liem, J. H. Family studies of schizophrenia: An update and commentary. *Schizophrenia Bulletin*, 1980, *6*, 429–455.

Lipton, F. R., Cohen, C. I., Fischer, E., & Katz, S. E. Schizophrenia: A network crisis. *Schizophrenia Bulletin*, 1981, *7*, 144–151.

Minuchin, S. *Families and family therapy.* Cambridge, Mass.: Harvard University Press, 1974.

Myers, J., & Bean, L. *A decade later: A follow-up of social class and mental illness.* New York: Wiley, 1968.

Pattison, E. M., Llamas, R., & Hurd, G. Social network mediation of anxiety. *Psychiatric Annals*, 1979, *9*, 56–67.

Rabkin, J. Public attitudes toward mental illness: A review of the literature. *Schizophrenia Bulletin*, 1974, *10*, 9–33.

Scheflen, A. *Levels of schizophrenia.* New York: Brunner/Mazel, 1981.

Singer, M. T., Wynne, L. C., & Toohey, M. L. Communication disorders and the families of schizophrenics. In L. C. Wynne, R. L. Cromwell, & S. Matthysse (Eds.), *The nature of schizophrenia.* New York: Wiley, 1978.

Sluzki, C., & Veron, F. The double bind as a universal pathogenic situation. *Family Process*, 1971, *10*, 397–407.

Steinberg, H. R., & Durell, J. A. A stressful social situation as a precipitant of schizophrenic symptoms. *British Journal of Psychiatry*, 1968, *114*, 1097–1105.

Tolsdorf, C. C. Social networks, support, and coping: An explanatory study. *Family Process*, 1976, *15*, 407–417.

Vaughn, C. E., & Leff, J. P. The influence of family and social factors on the course of psychiatric illness: A comparison of schizophrenic and depressed patients. *British Journal of Psychiatry*, 1976, *129*, 125–137.

Vaughn, C. E., & Leff, J. P. Patterns of emotional response in relatives of schizophrenic patients. *Schizophrenia Bulletin*, 1981, *7*, 43–44.

Waxler, N. Is outcome better for schizophrenics in nonindustrialized societies? *Journal of Nervous and Mental Disease*, 1979, *167*, 144–158.

Wing, J. K. Social influences on the course of schizophrenia. In L. C. Wynne, R. L. Cromwell, & S. Matthysse (Eds.), *The nature of schizophrenia.* New York: Wiley, 1978.

Wyatt, R. J., Cutler, N. R., DeLisi, L. E., Jeste, D. V., Kleinman, J. E., Luchins, D. J., Potkin, S. G., & Weinberger, D. R. Biochemical and morphological factors in schizophrenia. In L. Grinspoon (Ed.), *Psychiatry: 1982.* Washington, D.C.: American Psychiatric Press, 1982.

Wynne, L. C. Current concepts about schizophrenics and family relationships. *Journal of Nervous and Mental Disease*, 1981, *169*, 82–89.

Yarrow, M., Clausen, J., & Robbins, P. The social meaning of mental illness. *Journal of Social Issues*, 1955, *11*, 33–48.

15

A DECISION-TREE MODEL FOR INTEGRATING FAMILY THERAPIES FOR SCHIZOPHRENIA

William R. McFarlane
C. Christian Beels

In sharp contrast to the somewhat dismal status of family therapy for schizophrenia only 5 years ago, it seems to us that a small but exciting revolution is presently under way. The approaches described in the preceding pages make families of schizophrenic patients the working allies of mental health professionals at the very time that more families are becoming inevitably involved in the long-term care of their ill members. The new therapies recognize that it is the social unit of patient–family–staff that first confronts the schizophrenia syndrome. The hope is that if that unit can meet the crisis with a common philosophy, language, and set of expectations—and, most importantly, a strong organization—then the later course of life of the patient and family will be significantly improved. If families and professionals truly coordinate their respective contributions, patients may be better able to go on to take advantage of institutional supports, such as the special work and living arrangements being offered by progressive care systems.

Such an alliance would, by itself, be a significant change—a welcome contrast to the rejection, blame, and mystification that have been the usual result of staff–family contact in the past. The additional possibility that, with respect to the patient, these approaches may greatly reduce the frequency of relapse beyond the effects of drug therapy and may improve social functioning makes them seem significant indeed.

In addition to being improvements in the treatment of schizophrenia, these approaches represent a major conceptual development in the field of family therapy. They illustrate a point that is being made about the family therapy of other chronic illnesses: Something must be added to the therapy

WILLIAM R. MCFARLANE and C. CHRISTIAN BEELS. Department of Psychiatry, College of Physicians and Surgeons of Columbia University, and New York State Psychiatric Institute, New York, New York.

325

that specifically addresses what is going on between the illness and the family, in both causal "directions." In the case of a disorganizing and confusing problem such as schizophrenia, organizing and educational features need to be added to the family therapy. Especially with reference to schizophrenia, special attention needs to be given to how the therapist's ideology regarding the illness may affect the way in which he or she attempts to join with the family in a common therapeutic enterprise. These considerations appear to be true of mental retardation, the addictions, deafness, affective disorders, and possibly psychosomatic conditions. They may eventually apply in cancer and heart disease as well. These organizing, educational, and ideological aspects of a family therapy can create a *context* in which family therapy may be acceptable as well as useful, and in which resistance to it is minimized. We return at the end of this chapter to the place of this dimension—resistance–compliance—in the scheme of treatment that can be derived from the approaches in this book.

The present chapter is primarily a summary and so concludes the volume. It contains two sections: a set of general principles for family intervention suggested by recent family resarch and by the new therapies; and a decision-tree model for combining these approaches, with some possible indications. It comes at the end because we feel that summaries and speculative models are of less significance than practical, tested treatment strategies. Here, last—while perhaps useful—is least.

GENERAL PRINCIPLES

With the arrival of these new therapy approaches, the reader is faced with a question: Given that there are significant differences between these modalities, how does one choose one over another for a given patient or a given phase of the treatment process? One answer, clearly the more rigorous, would be to wait for large-sample evaluation studies to show which is the preferable alternative. Instead, we are proposing here an interim strategy. That is, there appear to be ways to combine these therapies into a useful and comprehensive package, with indications and sequences for their application. What is presented here is a strictly hypothetical model that follows logically from the results, target populations, and degree of therapeutic power and risk of each therapy. This is not to be taken as a tested macrotherapy, but only as a schema that, given the present data, seems persuasive and worthy of clinical trials and research. It is hoped that this approach satisfies Wynne's recommendations for phase-specific interventions, and that it does only slight damage to the intentions and findings of the respective contributors.

Before describing our decision-tree model, it seems advisable to make explicit the assumptions we used in constructing it. These derive from (1) the four research dimensions (enmeshment, communication deviance or CD, stigma/burden, and isolation) outlined in the previous chapter; (2) the major commonalities running through the new therapies; and (3) our limited experience in using them both singly and in combination. We present these assumptions in the form of general principles for family intervention in schizophrenia.

1. For patients living in close proximity to their families, family intervention is necessary, although not sufficient, to reduce overall morbidity beyond that achievable with drugs, because
   a. after the patients, families are the most affected *by* this illness;
   b. they have the most powerful effect *on* the patients, either for better or for worse;
   c. available medications have serious, limiting side effects and seem to do nothing toward raising the patients' level of social functioning (and in some cases may lower it somewhat).
2. Treatment design for family work should reflect circular, multi-leveled models of causality to have an even chance of success. The crude formula we have used is punctuated thus: Illness affects family affects illness, ad infinitum, preceding and following onset.
3. Families, like schizophrenia, are heterogeneous along many axes, especially with respect to their relative degrees of primary versus secondary dysfunction, the four dimensions mentioned above, strengths and coping skills, attitudes toward their predicament, and homeostatic dependence on the patients' disability.
4. Heterogeneity of family characteristics clearly requires a variety of family approaches, the choice of which depends on, among other things, certain of those characteristics, the phase of the illness and of a family's life cycle and specific patient factors.
5. Family intervention will not cure schizophrenia, which we conceive of as a constitutional vulnerability, so that family work must be accompanied by careful diagnosis and drug management, social skills training, occupational rehabilitation, alternative housing, and employment programs.
6. Common to the treatment approaches described in this volume are the following core components of family work:
   a. An empathic, validating, nonblaming, task-oriented alliance with a patient's parents, spouse, or other key relatives; that is, a therapeutic partnership (this is probably the sine qua non—the reader may note its primacy in every therapy described herein).

b. Family assessment of the following:
   - enmeshment, CD, and structural anomalies
   - the social network and its potential for support
   - sense of stigma and burden
   - previously demonstrated strengths and coping abilities
   - family history, both developmental and genetic
   - premorbid functioning of the patient
   - precipitating life events
   - degree of investment in the illness
c. Straightforward education about schizophrenia—the symptoms, subjective experience, usual course, role and action of medication and psychosocial treatments, basic neurochemical aspects, as well as what is still not known.
d. Creation of a clear and congruent family hierarchical organization—putting the parents in charge of the patient during recovery, helping them set limits on destructive and/or extremely bizarre behavior, and thereby creating a calm, predictable, and less enmeshed social context (helping the patient, in turn, to organize himself or herself cognitively and behaviorally).
e. Regular contact with other affected families, whether in the form of multiple family therapy (MFT) (our first recommendation), parents' groups, educational sessions, informal associations, or more formal self-help groups.
f. Adjusting the family's emotional intensity and proximity to the patient to an optimal level, especially with respect to criticism.
g. Training in the seemingly reliable techniques now available for
   - learning to recognize prodromal signs and symptoms
   - managing crises and medication
   - handling paranoia and delusions
   - optimizing social activity of patient and family
   - anticipating effects of major life stresses
   - effective communication
   - using professional help
7. There are apparent risk–benefit factors for each therapy, suggesting that there are likely to be indications, as well, that justify the associated risks.

While the first six points follow rather directly from the therapies themselves, the seventh does not and requires explanation. Thus far, risks and indications have not been addressed by the architects of these various approaches, because their work is still in an early stage of development and evaluation. Be that as it may, we believe, based on considerations of their methods and some clinical experience with the therapies, that the more powerful strategic and systemic approaches, for example, carry risks of family dropout, alienation, and outright deterioration of the patient, if only in the short term. Conversely, the more "benign" approaches (psycho-education, long-term MFT, parents' groups) seem to have risks of inducing unnecessary degrees of apathy and other deficit symptomatology. These negative effects must be weighed against the immediate need and antici-pated benefit to each patient and family. At present, it does not seem possible to assert that any of these therapies are risk-free, let alone panaceas, for all patients and all families.

If relative risks and benefits suggest indications, then we propose that absence of therapeutic response, or "resistance," to the benign therapies is the primary indication for the more powerful intensive interventions. That is, families that require the continued or periodic psychosis of the patients to maintain stability—those in which the illness is truly a family homeo-stat—will not use and will even be threatened by information, direct support, and guidance about straightforward coping methods. They will manifest *defiance* (to the therapists and/or the content of suggestions), *determina-tion* (to maintain their previous interaction patterns and their definition of the patients' role in the families) and *deterioration* (in clinical status). We have termed this the "three-D complex" (see Chapter 10). This subgroup shares these characteristics with families of borderline, psychosomatic, and addicted patients; is not unique to schizophrenia; and is often found to engage in double binding and other pathogenic interactions. As is explained more fully below, this appears to be the group of families that will do best with the systemic approach. However, we are primarily emphasizing that this subgroup can only be conclusively identified by initially offering them therapy that intervenes on the "illness affects family" side of the causal circle. In this respect, the benign therapies are either therapeutic *or* they become diagnostic. Also, it is assumed that risks of dropout or clinical deterioration are more serious, at least early in the recovery process, than are those of deficit symptoms. Thus, the psychoeducational and multiple-family group (MFG) approaches might be offered to all families initially, while the strategic and systemic therapies would be held in reserve for failures in those less intensive modalities.

The different therapies appear to us to have other indications, particu-larly a patient's diagnosis, length of previous illness and premorbid social adjustment, and the family's genetic background (presence of schizophrenia in first- or second-degree relatives). In addition, we are proposing that the type of patient with which a particular therapy has been shown to be effective be used as an indication. For example, since Anderson's program seems successful with somewhat older and more chronic patients whose families are high in "expressed emotion" (EE), that kind of patient should probably receive that therapy. Likewise, Madanes's therapy seems ideal for the type of patient with whom it seems to do well—younger, seemingly better-prognosis patients whose families have abdicated control. In so doing, we have assumed that each of these therapies has an internal consistency that fits well the type of family that meets its criteria for inclusion.

A DECISION-TREE MODEL

Figure 1 depicts our decision-tree approach. The schema is somewhat complex—not because it is more elegant that way, but rather because this is as far as our present knowledge of these intervention strategies allows us to go in making even speculative choices among them. The following description is arranged by phases, from the top of the diagram to the bottom.

FIGURE 1. *A decision-tree model for selecting family interventions.*

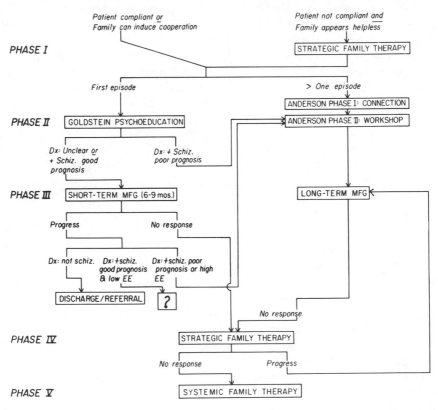

Phase I involves an assessment of a family's ability successfully to encourage the patient to participate in treatment, especially maintenance medication. We assume here that noncompliance is usually symptomatic of an inadequately organized, self-disqualifying social network. In such a situation, work with the relatives along the lines of the strategic approach (see Chapter 9) will probably be necessary before beginning any other intervention. When sufficient control and consistency have been achieved, the family is referred to Phase II. Those families in which the patient is initially cooperative, even if only with the family's pressure, would begin therapy at Phase II.

In Phase II, the principal indication is the number of previous episodes, while clarity of diagnosis and prognosis are secondary criteria. All first-episode patients are offered the Goldstein approach, as it is described in Chapter 3. All multiple-episode patients are treated using the "Connection" and "Survival Skills Workshop" aspects of the Anderson program, again as described in Chapter 4.

It is often difficult to make a definitive diagnosis of schizophrenia at the time of the first episode. The Goldstein approach is ideal for this reason, since it is nonspecific, applying equally well to most forms of acute psychosis. Conversely, giving the patient and family full information about schizophrenia, as in the Anderson workshop, only seems justifiable if that is, in fact, what the patient has.

At the completion of the brief psychoeducation sessions, lasting about 6 weeks, two alternatives are possible for first-episode patients. If the diagnosis has become schizophrenia, especially if the patient is of the poor-prognosis type (with an asocial premorbid personality, a withdrawn and apathetic presentation, slow onset, soft neurological signs, and a genetically loaded family), it seems preferable to proceed directly to the Anderson package. This seems justified by the emerging evidence that many of these patients are probably slightly brain-damaged, with CAT-scan abnormalities, and may be much more vulnerable to stress and high EE than good-prognosis patients may be (Wyatt, 1981). Thus, they would be at some risk in the more intense, change-oriented, short-term MFG described below, while the low-pressure Anderson approach appears to be highly relevant to their needs. Also, it seems important to orient the parents of these patients as early as is ethical to the real prognosis and their crucial role in long-term care.

For good-prognosis patients and those with a persistently unclear diagnosis, an intensive short-term MFG is indicated. The arguments are the converse of the above. Many of these patients may have no biological deficit (schizophreniform and atypical psychoses, for example); family intervention of this type may help to initiate a nonrelapsing lifetime course.

PHASE III

Phase III is the follow-up component of the model. During this phase, the basic lessons of the psychoeducational work are individualized and applied, in one of two MFG formats. These therapies are amalgams of several of the new approaches.

The "short-term MFG" is conceived of as small (three to five families), relatively focused and intense, with strong emphasis on problem solving, improving communication, and correcting family hierarchical incongruities and disorganization. This constitutes a multifamily variation and extension of Falloon and Liberman's and Goldstein's approaches (see Chapters 5 and 3, respectively). It is conducted in a time-limited, closed-membership, and relatively leader-centered manner. This type of group would continue for approximately 6 to 9 months.

The "long-term MFG" is a multifamily version of Anderson's Phase III (see Chapter 4), Leff et al.'s relatives' groups (see Chapter 7), and many aspects of Falloon and Liberman's follow-up phase (see Chapter 5). This is a slightly larger (four to seven families), closed (with replacements for dropouts), low-key, and more group-centered MFG, continuing indefinitely, along the lines of the approach presented in Chapter 6. Major emphases include reduction of EE and enmeshment, work on basic communication skills, and gradual resumption of responsibility by the patient; the group is also seen as a social network in which relationships between families are fostered. After 2 to 3 years, this group should strongly resemble, if not actually become, an autonomous self-help group.

As may be evident from the diagram, the MFGs would constitute the backbone of an aftercare service's family program. By substituting these groups for the single-family forms of the corresponding therapies, we have assumed that their *content* can be effectively communicated to families in this format, and that the added *process* benefits of bringing families together in these efforts are worth the slightly greater complexity. This is hardly a radical departure, since Leff et al.'s, Anderson's, and Falloon and Liberman's therapies include multiple-family intervention.

The short-term MFG is for first-break patients, either those with a good prognosis or an unclear diagnosis. The long-term MFG is for all those who complete the Anderson workshop. At the end of the short-term group, there are two alternatives, if a full clinical response is achieved:

1. If a diagnosis of schizophrenia with poor prognosis (which here includes family enmeshment/high EE) is made during the course of the group, the family is referred to a workshop and then on to a long-term MFG.
2. If the final diagnosis is clearly not schizophrenia, and the patient is doing well, the family is either discharged or referred for other services, while the patient might be offered whatever aftercare seemed indicated.

Thus, these MFGs are the final treatment modality for those families that respond to Phases I–III and whose schizophrenic members are in remission and showing continued improvement in psychosocial functioning.

There are two areas of uncertainty in Phase III where there is no information on which to base reliable suggestions. One is the preferable treatment for good-prognosis patients whose families were, or have become in the MFG, disenmeshed/low-EE. It may be that some of these patients will be able to leave home to a semistructured residence or independent living and be referred for close psychiatric follow-up, perhaps with occasional family sessions. The other question concerns families of patients diagnosed as schizophreniform or atypical psychoses. Those who request continued assistance, are unusually isolated, or have shown definite but incomplete, improvement might be referred to a specially designed long-term MFG without the workshop. These questions illustrate the speculative nature of our model; they are among several decision points where new data will probably alter the final choices and/or where clinical judgment and consultation with the family should prevail over hypotheses.

PHASE IV

Phase IV is strategic family therapy in its complete form. The indications are simply elaborations of those for Phase I. Families are referred for this approach when, for them, the MFG intervention has failed to achieve results. For example, strategic therapy seems preferable if the patient suffers an unprovoked relapse (i.e., one not brought on by life events), especially after refusing medication because the family remains unable to control his or her behavior and/or noncompliance. Concurrent drug abuse, delinquency, violence, and self-destructive behavior might be other indications, especially in younger patients who were good premorbids. In other words, this seems the preferable alternative when a family does not seem to have learned enough in the less directive MFG format to prevent relapse and/or severe misbehavior on the part of the patient. This does *not* imply that they are invested in treatment failure. Rather, a strategic approach for this type of family is another—more powerful, yet strictly linear—method of accomplishing the goals of Phases II and III. If the family responds to this intervention and the patient improves, they are referred back to the most appropriate MFG, or perhaps discharged.

PHASE V

This part of the model—systemic family therapy—is reserved for those families who fail in all other treatment formats. They will be likely to manifest three-D responses throughout the earlier interventions, and to fail to reorganize with the help of the directive approaches. It is for them that the systemic approach, with its neutrality and refusal to struggle, seems essential. A careful assessment of risks needs to be made before beginning; previous attempts at suicide are probably a contraindication for this method. Success here indicates a return to Phase III. This recommendation is by far the most speculative, since it is based largely on theory and our experience and does not follow the indications of the originators. At the moment, there is no suggestion for Phase V failures.

It remains to be noted that the scheme proposed here depends heavily upon making a reliable diagnosis, a somewhat insubstantial foundation. Diagnostic criteria have changed recently and are likely to be revised again as subtypes of schizophrenia become more clearly recognizable. As diagnostic methods change, so would indications for the various family therapies.

CONCLUSION

Using this model in an aftercare clinic would require many changes in administration and procedure. We are aware that as a model it raises more questions than it answers. By way of conclusion, we only consider some of the changes that might be required in training and in attitude.

The reader may already have become worried about the size and scope of an organization offering all these different approaches. Those readers familiar with problems of professional training may well have noted that each of these phases requires a special kind of training. Most of the staff will be occupied with Phases II and III (since most of the families are expected to benefit from these phases of treatment alone). Fortunately, the skills of these phases—conducting educational programs and MFGs—are, in our experience, imported or taught with relative ease. Phase IV, and especially Phase V, require not only well-developed family therapy skills, but also some personal characteristics that are not widely distributed. It is likely that these higher-powered therapies would have to be performed by a specially trained team of the clinic's most experienced clinicians. That part of the scheme may not be realistic everywhere. Furthermore, the problem of continuity of care created by shifting therapists or teams would have to be compensated for by a very strong attachment between the family and the total institutional program; hence, again, the importance of the orientation and alliance phases (I and II).

We turn finally to the problem of attitude. As Anderson and others have observed throughout this book, and as Hatfield (see Chapter 2) has emphasized from the point of view of family members themselves, the most important ingredient of the new approaches to the families of schizophrenics is the change in the professional attitude from one of blame to one of support. Blaming the family for the problem was really a curiously un-systemic view for the early systems thinkers to adopt; it ignored the other parts of the system. As Scheflen has recently written, these include synapse, brain, social network, institutions, and the culture as a whole. The early systems thinkers stopped short in their analysis of the total environment, which includes the biological level. In therapists' frustration with the difficulties of treating this illness, and their wish for an encouraging and therefore simplistic explanation, it is easy to forget that generations of earlier psychiatrists have come up with unitary theories of schizophrenia, rarely to the benefit of the patients who were treated accordingly. The multilevel, heterogeneity-based hypotheses now being tested seem to reflect that humbling lesson of history. We think it will be especially fitting if these pragmatic therapies, with their emphasis on measurable results, actually contribute to theory building in the future. Perhaps psychiatry has taken the first turn in a new cycle in which therapy suggests theory suggests improved therapy.

REFERENCE

Wyatt, R. J. Personal communication, 1981.

AFTERWORD

Family therapy of schizophrenia is part of a larger enterprise, the social management of the illness outside the long-term hospital. That kind of management has been introduced, especially since the 1950s, as a way of avoiding the "social breakdown syndrome" (Gruenberg, 1974), the depletion of the patient's meager social skills, which was seen as the result of years spent in the chronic hospital. Social management in the community, then, was seen as a program which, apart from its financial and civil-libertarian appeal, would have the clinical advantage of maintaining social skills. The assumption was that such skills, in order not to be lost, should be exercised and practiced, no matter how feebly or in what strange community circumstances. Some evidence for this assumption has lately come from the community support literature (Braun, Kochansky, Shapiro, Greenberg, Gudeman, Johnson, & Shore, 1981).

Another hopeful note has come from a series of European long-term studies of the course of schizophrenia in middle and old age (Ciompi, 1980; Huber, Gross, Schüttler, & Linz, 1980). These suggest that there is a late recovery or improvement in many cases of schizophrenia. It is not at all clear whether such good outcomes are the result of earlier management, however; indeed, many occur after very long periods of hospitalization. Nihilists will expect from these studies that all the effort going into community programs will not affect the end state, whereas enthusiasts for community treatment will infer that our efforts there should be intensified because now we have some evidence that some schizophrenics have a future to look forward to in which the social skills they have preserved might be valuable to them. Which of these views is correct will depend on evaluation of what environmental experiences predispose to what outcomes in later life.

At the point, some time in his or her youth, when the diagnosis is made, the schizophrenic patient, his or her family, and the therapist are faced with a number of choices. My purpose in this essay is to set some of these choices, which may be fateful for family burdens and patient careers, in a larger context. In doing so, I hope to interest epidemiologically minded

337

social scientists and administrators in some of the questions which, it seems to me, this book should raise.

Family therapy is a choice among several in a branching series:

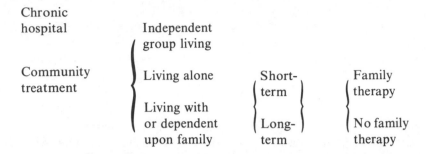

and, finally, to the different programs described in this book.

Unfortunately, there are two vital senses in which these are not real choices: (1) The different possibilities are not freely available, but are constrained by money, location, and policy, and (2) the policy and money constraints that limit the choices are not based on a knowledge of the consequences of those choices, since we know very little about what path leads to a desirable final outcome. I am suggesting here some of the questions that might be asked in the course of discovering that path, or paths.

There are two ways of asking these questions: epidemiological field studies and random-assignment treatment experiments. In studying an illness that lasts for so many years, it is very hard to control the treatments received over the entire course—so experimental studies are best for answering short-term questions. Most of the experimental studies described in this book are doing well to follow their cases for 5 years, and by that time the experimental and control groups may be undergoing quite mixed experiences of more importance than the original treatment. Long-term, preferably prospective, natural-history field studies of large numbers of cases for periods of 20 to 40 years are what we need to generate good experimental hypotheses, and to reveal the ultimate power of treatment interventions on lifelong conditions. The European studies mentioned above are good models. Their subjects number from 500 to 1000 and more, enough to encompass the complexity of the many different courses under study. Reading them, however, it is clear that there are some important questions that were not asked, and indeed could not have been asked, about a cohort of patients who lived most of their lives in the first half of the century. For such a sample today we are able to ask, and want to know: Did the quality of their social environment, their treatment, the efforts to keep them out of the hospital, or the support given the family, make any difference?

I have chosen to organize the questions around a distinction that comes out of the book: the difference between medical and nonmedical programs. Many other ways or organizing questions are possible; what I want to do here is to make the point that the debate between the medical and nonmedical advocates is not (as it sometimes seems) an ethical argument about medical responsibility versus systems theory. It is rather a choice with research and treatment implications of some complexity. As I will show, there are several kinds of medical models of treatment besides the exemplary programs of Julian Leff, Carol Anderson, Michael Goldstein, Ian Falloon, and Robert Liberman described here, with their emphasis on careful pharmacology and family education. There are also nonmedical approaches other than those of Whitaker, Madanes, and McFarlane, with their communication-system strategies. I will be looking for dimensions of medical and nonmedical programs which are of interest in long-term follow-up.

Some of the medical approaches described here are exemplary in their possession of the six scientific virtues referred to in the Foreword (diagnoses, specific description, large samples, outcome criteria, long-term follow-up, replicability). The nonmedical approaches, on the other hand, are still in the case-report stage. We might conclude that for well-selected and diagnosed cases the medical approaches have a demonstrated short-term (2- to 5-year) effectiveness. How would they hold up as services delivered in regular (nonexperimental) programs, whose effectiveness is measured over longer periods of time?

1. In the medical approaches, medication is used liberally, and is found in fact to enhance the results of family therapy in the acute phase (see Kopeikin, Marshall, & Goldstein, Chapter 3). Others (Heinrichs & Carpenter, Chapter 12; Herz & Melville, 1980) have pointed out, however, that one of the aims of long-term family and environmental treatment is to decrease the need for medication. We need a study of the various social therapies to see which ones do in fact decrease dependence on neuroleptics. It is possible that a prejudice against medication has different effects from a prejudice in favor of it. The ideal, of course, is discriminating use of medication, as in Carpenter's (1982) studies, but this may be difficult to achieve in the real world.

2. Another problem with medical management in the real world is that for most schizophrenic patients it is embedded in the bureaucracy of the public-care delivery system, with its questionable efficiencies and economies of scale. We have traded the state hospitals for the insensitivities and ineffectiveness of outpatient management dictated by insurance and other reimbursement policies, and by the draconian strictures of state mental health departments. Some of the most effective environments for schizophrenics are not reimbursible because they are farms and other special communities, rather than hospitals and clinics. Parents' groups,

multifamily groups, home visits, and educational sessions—all essential parts of the good medical programs described here—are very hard to establish in aftercare systems as they are now organized. It remains to be seen whether the medical establishment is capable of the medical programs proposed. Does any other kind of organization do better? It is time we examined the claims of alternative treatment organizations such as the orthomolecular therapies, the mental patients' liberation groups, and others which provide educational and ideological support to patients and families. Some of their literature suggests that they are effective with selected patients. The only way of checking that claim is with long-term follow-up. We may find, for example, that orthomolecular therapy is an elaborate placebo treatment that operates by unifying family, patient, and therapist in a blame-free treatment regimen. That would explain its apparent success in some cases when supplied by its own organization, and its failure when tested by independent investigators. If the hypothesis has merit, the course of orthomolecular patients should be similar to that of others in programs which are high in ideology and morale, and which attempt to avoid phenothiazines (e.g., Soteria House; Mosher & Menn, 1978).

3. Compulsive overmedication and bureaucracy are, of course, *not* part of the model medical programs described here by Anderson, Falloon, Liberman. Goldstein, and Leff. The question to be asked about these programs was put succinctly by Scheflen (1981): In perfecting medical programs to deal with acute schizophrenic episodes and their sequelae, have we created a social system that promotes chronic schizophrenia—a medical subculture in which it is difficult for the patient to escape his or her identity as a person with chronic impairment? Estroff (1981), an anthropologist, analyzed the social-system aspects of another model treatment program (the Madison, Wisconsin, PACT program for chronic patients; see Stein, Test, & Marx, 1975). She pointed out that dedicated medical management is also medical control, in the subtle sense that it educates family and patient to expect a certain course of illness and limitation of function. Is this also the case for the programs of Anderson and others? That is certainly what Madanes implies in her chapter. The answer, if there is one, will only come from following for very long periods the careers of carefully matched patients from each type of treatment. We need to know, for example, what happens to young patients after they "leave home" at the end of Madanes's treatment. From the treatment's point of view they are set free to make their way among the culture's opportunities for marginal careers. Which ones do they find and how are they supported? Do some of them enter medical treatment programs in other places?

4. Consider the interview with Midelfort. His medical model is very different from the others, embedded as it is in a rural homogeneous culture with strong folk traditions. Midelfort points out the importance of the

patient's membership in a supportive religious group, congruent with the beliefs of family and surrounding culture. This reminds us that finding an acceptable definition of one's self and of one's impairment, which can be shared with the family and the larger culture, is a problem faced by all schizophrenic patients. Such a definition of self may be better achieved by some nonmedical models than by the locally available medical one. Examples include the careers of religious or other monastics, or, as Garrison (1978) has shown, in Hispanic culture, the career of the apprentice spiritist in development.

On the other hand, the addict, alcoholic, and homeless careers are types of nonmedical marginal sociability in our culture which are not associated with a good course of schizophrenia. No doubt this is due in part to the nutritional and other environmental hazards which they present, in addition to social ostracism. We might think of these as the heavy price the person pays for a special social position which is all our culture allows to people who cannot compete and will not be patients.

5. In summary, what I am suggesting is an analysis of the several ways in which schizophrenia is (or is not) accepted in the culture of the small group. One way of acceptance may be as a medical illness about which the group is expert and organized because it is part of a treatment organization. This analysis would lead to a classification of groups—families and others—related to good and bad courses of the illness.

The analysis would include classification of the varieties of social support, about which I have written elsewhere (Beels, 1981). It should also include the nature of behavior sequences which the group expects of the patient. This may be one of the keys to the better course of schizophrenia which is observed in the developing as opposed to the industrial nations (Waxler, 1979). Scheflen pointed out that work sequences required in industrial cultures—operating machinery or clerical work, or even isolated housekeeping and child care—require a kind of initiative and independence which are difficult for schizophrenic patients to maintain. Agricultural village society, on the other hand, where child care, housekeeping, and farm work take place in a supportive group, provides social and physical cues to correct work sequences, plus a certain tolerance for error and delay.

Clearly, the hypotheses and the methods of study are available. The current tide of "young chronic" patients flooding our services represents an opportunity which should not be missed. We now have a generation of patients growing up without the chronic hospital. Some are doing well: in medical family programs like those described in this book; in nonmedical ones such as Soteria House (which keeps the family at a friendly distance); in sheltered environments far from the family such as Spring Lake Ranch in Vermont. Some, as most of the "young chronic" literature points out, are doing very badly indeed, and they and their families are suffering enormously as a result. What accounts for the differences between these careers? If we get to work on this problem and pursue it patiently over the years, we may have something to recommend next time the money comes around.

C. Christian Beels

REFERENCES

Beels, C. C. Social support and schizophrenia. *Schizophrenia Bulletin*, 1981, *7*, 68–72.

Braun, P., Kochansky, G., Shapiro, R., Greenberg, S., Gudeman, J., Johnson, S., & Shore, M. Overview: Deinstitutionalization of psychiatric patients, a critical review of outcome studies. *American Journal of Psychiatry*, 1981, *138*, 736–749.

Carpenter, W. Presentation at New York State Psychiatric Institute, September 24, 1982; forthcoming in *Schizophrenia Bulletin*.

Ciompi, L. Catamnestic long-term study on the course of life and aging of schizophrenics. *Schizophrenia Bulletin*, 1980, *6*, 606–618.

Estroff, S. *Making it crazy: An ethnography of psychiatric clients in an American community.* Berkeley: University of California Press, 1981.

Gruenberg, E. M. The social breakdown syndrome and its prevention. In S. Arieti (Ed.), *American handbook of psychiatry* (Vol. II, 2nd ed.). New York: Basic Books, 1974.

Garrison V. Support systems of schizophrenic and nonschizophrenic Puerto Rican migrant women in New York City. *Schizophrenia Bulletin*, 1978, *4*, 561–596.

Herz, M., & Melville, C. Relapse in schizophrenia. *American Journal of Psychiatry*, 1980, *137*, 801–805.

Huber, G., Gross, G., Schüttler, R., & Linz, M. Longitudinal studies of schizophrenic patients. *Schizophrenia Bulletin*, 1980, *6*, 592–606.

Mosher, L., & Menn, A. Community residential treatment for schizophrenia: Two-year follow-up. *Hospital and Community Psychiatry*, 1978, *29*, 715–723.

Scheflen, A. *Levels of schizophrenia.* New York: Brunner/Mazel. 1981.

Stein, L., Test, M., & Marx, A. Alternatives to the hospital, a controlled study. *American Journal of Psychiatry*, 1975, *132*, 517–522.

Waxler, N. Is outcome for schizophrenia better in non-industrial societies? *Journal of Nervous and Mental Diseases*, 1979, *167*, 144–158.

AUTHOR INDEX

SUBJECT INDEX

Activation
  and arousal, 269
  and deficit symptoms, 270–273
  effects of treatment on, 274, 275
  and neuroleptic medication, 11, 119, 126,
    134, 135, 253, 255, 256
Actualization through Assertion (King *et al.*),
    121
Adaptation as theoretical framework, 56, 57
*Advocacy for Persons with Chronic Mental
    Illness*, 61
Age and family perceptions of therapy, 46–48
Alliances, and therapy, 10, 102, 113, 157, 182,
    191, 217, 237
Altruism, 110
American Family Therapy Association
    (AFTA), 18
American Lutheran Church, 19
American Psychological Association, 62
Analogy, learning by, 143
Anhedonia, 270
Antidepressant drugs, 212
Antipsychotic drugs, 212
Anxiety, 49, 51–53, 57, 100–102, 113, 114, 283
  and behavioral treatment, 119, 134
  and communication, 149
  in crisis-oriented therapy, 83, 86
  family understanding of, 108
  flooding with, 228
  and interpersonal contact, 194
  in long-term closed group, 155, 158, 162
  and support groups, 194, 195
APA Monitor, 62
Apathy, 215, 270
Arousal
  and activation, 269
  and functioning, 269, 270
Assessment (*see* Diagnosis)
Autism, 60
Autodisqualification, 230

Batesonian theory, 229
Behavioral family therapy program, 135
Behavioral treatment, 117–136, 141
  and anxiety, 119, 134
  and communication training, 133
  conclusions on, 136

and depression, 119, 134
  educational workshop for, 120–122
  and generalization, 132
  and guilt, 119
  home-based therapy, 130–136
    communication training, 133, 136
    education in, 132, 133
    outcome assessment, 134–136
    problem-solving training, 133–136
  personal effectiveness training, 122–126
    homework for, 124, 125
    outcome evaluation, 125, 126
  problem-solving approach, 126–130,
    132–136
    Family Conflict Inventory, 129
    homework, 130
    outcome evaluation, 128, 129
    relapse ratings, 129, 130
Benzotropine mesylate, 81
Bethlem Royal Hospital, Behavior Therapy
    Unit at, 122
Biofeedback, 239
Biomedical technology, 261
Blaming, 316
Borderline personality disorder, 239
Boundaries
  family, 107, 111, 162
    and poverty, 292
    and social network, 166
  interpersonal, 107, 110, 111
Brain damage, 211, 212
Brief Psychiatric Rating Scale (BPRS), 83, 84,
    86, 89, 90
Burnout of family, 42, 119

Camarillo–UCLA Mental Health Clinical
    Research Center, 126
Camberwell Family Interview (CFI), 122, 125,
    126, 128, 129
Capital punishment, 211
CAT scan, 331
Causality, 321
  interactive, 7
  linear, 7
Change
  family bias against, 237